Recovering the Commons

Recovering the Commons

Democracy, Place, and Global Justice

HERBERT REID
AND BETSY TAYLOR

UNIVERSITY OF ILLINOIS PRESS
Urbana, Chicago, and Springfield

© 2010 by the Board of Trustees
of the University of Illinois
All rights reserved
Manufactured in the United States of America
1 2 3 4 5 C P 6 5 4 3 2
♾ This book is printed on acid-free paper.

Library of Congress Cataloging-in-Publication Data
Reid, Herbert G.
Recovering the commons : democracy, place, and global justice /
Herbert Reid and Betsy Taylor.
p. cm.
Includes bibliographical references and index.
ISBN 978-0-252-03495-4 (cloth : alk. paper)
ISBN 978-0-252-07681-7 (pbk. : alk. paper)
1. Democracy. 2. Internationalism. 3. Justice.
I. Taylor, Betsy. II. Title.
JC423.R332   2009
321.8—dc22   2009027103

Dedicated to Turner Bend
in the Arkansas Ozarks,
to Landour in India's Himalaya,
and to the many other places
that have given us life
and world to care for . . .

Without clay, without embodiment, there is no humanity, not only nowhere to be, in the sense of landscape, but no one to be there.

—Marjorie Grene

Our era is destined to judge itself not from on high, which is mean and bitter, but in a certain sense from below.

—Maurice Merleau-Ponty

Disillusionment with the world knows nothing of the sacrament of coexistence. It can find no place for the sacramental act. It can conjure out of itself no philosophy of action, for its ultimate implication is inaction.

—Henry Bugbee

Contents

Acknowledgments xi

Introduction 1

1. Space-Times of the Nation-State and the Effacement of the Body~Place~Commons 19
2. Reclaiming the Democratic Republic: Historical Retrieval and Political Reconstruction 51
3. De-toggling "Consumer Republic" Dreamworlds 79
4. Regenerating Public Culture: Ecological Ontology for Democratic Publics 108
5. Merleau-Ponty and the Flesh of the Political 132
6. Participatory Reason and Democratic Professionalism 155
7. Translocal Politics, Ecological Hermeneutics, Democratic Struggles 185
8. Learning from the Global Justice Movement 215

Notes 237

Bibliography 247

Index 279

Acknowledgments

This book arose from conversations. It has been sparked by the extraordinary reflections and activism of grassroots activists and organizations with whom we have worked over the past decades. It will take several more books to speak adequately about the ideas and actions of these justice innovators. We name here but a few of the grassroots leaders who have inspired us—Aloma Burke, Joan Robinett, Teri Blanton, Daymon Morgan, Lynne Faltraco, Andy Jones—and salute the many others doing the crucial work of care for communities and earth. Our friends with Kentuckians for the Commonwealth, the Ohio Valley Environmental Coalition, and Coal River Mountain Watch have organized numerous conferences and events providing information, insights, and inspiration. Wendell Berry's work has been an invaluable reminder of a commonwealth alternative to Big Coal in Kentucky and elsewhere.

Mary Hufford has been a crucial friend and interlocutor. In her work as a public folklorist, Mary exemplifies the grace, brilliance, and groundedness of what we call participatory reason. We are especially thankful for the insights, generosity, and encouragement of Glenn Perusek over many years. Wolfgang Natter is a valued collaborator on several projects and enabled us to present some of these ideas—including at the 2006 International Social Theory Consortium in Roanoke and a forum at Virginia Tech organized by the Alliance for Social, Political, Ethical, and Cultural Thought, which he directs. At the University of Kentucky, we have enjoyed the intellectual companionship of Dwight Billings, Christopher Rice, and Ernie Yanarella. Ananta Kumar Giri and Sanjoy Hazarika have been important windows on the world from India and elsewhere, and so has Ana Isla from Canada and Peru. We are indebted to Jack Herranen for his reports from Bolivia and East Tennessee.

Herbert Reid takes this opportunity to remember two marvelous friends who passed away in 2002 and 2003—Erling W. Eng and Adolph Reed Sr. He is also indebted, in a variety of ways, to Randal Ihara, Tim Luke, David Rouse, Hwa Yol Jung, John O'Neill, and Steve Fisher, among others. Film artists Anne Lewis and Herb Smith have been consistent sources of insight and inspiration. Betsy Taylor thanks Dana Nelson, Kathleen Stewart, and Christopher Davis for the conversations over the years that have catalyzed many insights about many things—including the connections between democracy, talk, and friendship. Taylor developed key ideas in this book during the 2005–2006 year when she was Visiting Scholar at the Anthropology Department of Johns Hopkins University. She thanks Veena Das and others in the department for the hospitality, lively ideas, and quiet office during that year.

We were fortunate in being able to explore these ideas in various forums. We note the helpful debates of the conference "Culture Matters: Understanding Development from the Perspectives of Margins," in October 2006, organized by the Deshkal Society and wonderfully hosted in the peaceful Sanskriti Kendra outside New Delhi. Betsy Taylor also thanks the Asian Development Research Institute for all the rich conversations connected with sessions they organized in February 2006 in Ranchi, Jharkhand, and Patna, Bihar, and points in between.

We give hearty thanks to our superb editor, Laurie Matheson, who has made it a pleasure to pull these complex conversations into a publication.

Some parts of individual chapters have been drawn from previous publications, with extensive rewriting and revision. We thank these publishers for permission to draw concepts from these earlier writings:

Reid, Herbert G. (2001). "The Resurgence of the Market Machine-God and the Obsolescence of Liberal Democracy: On Academic Capitalism as Unsustainable Professionalism." *Rethinking Marxism* 13(1): 27–44.

Reid, Herbert G., and Betsy Taylor (2000). "Embodying Ecological Citizenship: Rethinking the Politics of Grass-Roots Globalization in the United States." *Alternatives: Social Transformation and Humane Governance* 25(4): 439–66.

Reid, Herbert G., and Betsy Taylor (2003). "John Dewey's Aesthetic Ecology of Public Intelligence and the Grounding of Civic Environmentalism." *Ethics and the Environment* 8(1; special issue on "Art, Nature and Social Critique"): 74–92.

Taylor, Betsy, and Herbert G. Reid (2000). "Recovering Place-Based Knowledge and Cosmogenic Agency in Struggles for a Sustainable World." *Indian Folklife* 1(3) (October): 10–11.

Recovering the Commons

Introduction

Googling for Moonscapes

Looking for allies, some community activists in New Guinea turned to cyberspace. But, what word to use to find people like themselves? *Moonscape* was the word they chose. This extraterrestrial word googled out for them a surreal geography of other communities, bound together in global cyberspace by common expulsion from earthly life forms and landscapes—places-of-non-place that four of them were able to visit on a recent global tour of the unearthed. This is how Grace Koa, Poin Caspar, Wina Kayonga, and Patrick Pate came to visit Larry Gibson on Kayford Mountain in West Virginia (Fout, 2003).

Once the lowest mountain along its bend of the then deeply forested Coal River, Kayford Mountain now towers above "moonscapes" that have spread to the visible horizon and beyond in one decade. Dinned out in the national mediascapes by the latest confession from Paris Hilton (or whatever), the explosions bringing down the mountains of central Appalachia are heard by few Americans. This is the largest earthmoving project in human history—as coal companies turn from mining to what even they call *mountaintop removal*, exploding more firepower, every week, than the bomb that leveled Hiroshima. Kayford Mountain continues to exist only because Larry Gibson refused to sell fifty acres of his family land. And so Kayford Mountain rises as a fragile green mesa above the bizarre postbiotic, post-industrial landscape hundreds of feet below and falling. By staying put, Larry has created a landform of stark aesthetic power. Kayford Mountain has become a global pilgrimage site, gathering to itself tales, feelings, and pathways of a distinctively twenty-first-century sort.[1]

This book is about the kinds of pathways that met and parted on Kayford Mountain that day, and the kinds of conversations provoked by such crossroads. We believe that if there is hope for our species, it is in the hard thinking taking place at crossroads like this. We don't know much about the talk that day, since we only read about it in a half-page article in the newsletter of one of the always outgunned but tenacious Appalachian grassroots groups at the frontlines of the (as yet) chronically losing battle against mountaintop removal.[2] But we can picture it only too clearly. We have made that sad journey up Kayford Mountain in various seasons with many people—activists, scholars, and students from the surrounding region as well as Nigeria, South Africa, India, Peru, and elsewhere. All over the world, at crossroads like this, something is afoot—a courageous, creative, and elusive rethinking of politics, economics, and culture. Nobody seems to know what to call this. It travels largely beneath the radar of mainstream media and academe. David Orr aptly calls it the "movement for the habitability of earth" (Orr, 2004). The Zapatistas call it the "movement of movements" (Mertes, 2004). We mostly call it the *global justice movement* and wish we knew of a better term.[3]

One way to think about this movement is that it is a great diversity of spontaneous, mostly local refusals of neoliberal globalization—a myriad of small-scale push-backs against the transmutation of everything into infinite, displaced transactability in global markets. Many of these struggles arise against assaults on particular places, bodily well-being, and local commons—in fights against strip-mining, toxins, collapse of local economies and ecologies, food insecurity, privatization of water, displacement, corporate colonization of children's play, worker exploitation, predatory or corrupt flows of capital, and so on. But, this movement of movements is not simply a collation of localisms, and, it gets unity from more than what it is against. We believe that a positive political project of great significance, and potentially global scale, could be emerging in this heterogeneous movement-with-no-name. There are efforts to build multiscalar alliances between these diverse struggles. Experimentation in translocal organizational structure to scale up justice struggles has included formally incorporated voluntary associations, networks refusing formal leadership structures, alliances sheltered and aided by established social movement organizations (including labor and religious organizations), reclaimed pre-state governance structures (such as in Andean reclaiming of indigenous political structures for resistance movements) as well as attempts to reclaim nation-state governance. At the global level, the

World Social Forum (and its spin-off regional forums) plays an important role by providing regular spaces for transnational networking and sharing of ideas, inspiration, and experience—although its ability to affect politics directly is limited.

These efforts to build multiscalar alliances raise daunting strategic and normative questions. Much of the burgeoning scholarly literature on the global justice movement has focused on questions of organizational structure. Are emerging organizational structures democratically representative—internally and of the people and land they claim to serve? Are they strong enough to grapple with the sources of injustice? These are important questions, but not our focus. This book attempts to clarify *the basis for solidarity*. We believe that if there is more clarity about this, there will be less anxiety and confusion about what collective structures, goals, and strategies are appropriate—opening up auspices for collective action *and* heterogeneity. Intellectuals can be particularly helpful in this clarification because they are part of the problem insofar as they are embedded in professional institutions or ideologies that have served to disembody, displace, and privatize public debate about the desirability of "moonscapes."

Social Theory on the Frontlines of Solidarity

We have written this book because we think critical social theory can be in stronger conversation with these emerging politics—theory has much to learn from, and to give to, conversations such as take place on Kayford. This is a social theoretic text for a social theoretic audience. But its key ideas have arisen from the global justice movement, from pondering on the run with activists in pitched or covert battle with princely, smooth-talking, and violent powers. We attempt, as it were, to hold critical social theory up against the needs, ideas, and organizational practices of the global justice movement. We try to put social theory into the register of emergent politics, to ask—in the context of *these* struggling global and local alliances, in *these* battles for livability of place and livelihood, at *these* limits to global climate—what intellectual projects are most important?

We almost always feel more hope driving *toward* campus than away. This is strange, because most of our engaged scholarship has been with grassroots social and environmental justice struggles in difficult, or worse, situations—in Appalachia, India, and elsewhere. Why, in the relative comforts of academic campuses, does it so often feel as if political hope is scarce and collective will is stricken? Well, we'll get to that by the end of the book. But why the stubborn upwelling of hope in tragic circumstances of social and environmental justice struggle? Something happens that is hard to name when people get together at places like Kayford Mountain. There is a kind of solidarity that, paradoxically, finds common identity and collective action *through* particularistic and locally grounded struggles, local and embodied knowledges, and place-based political participation. We argue that this is not simply a seizure of existing or official powers (although one hopes that can follow). Rather, it is a generative process of *em*powerment, of finding a new pivot of social being that renders individual being more capacious, strong, apt for solidarity, and able to make do over the long run. We argue that these nondualistic relationships—between universal and particulars, thought and body, transcendent identity and immanent poetics, self and other, ideal plan and strategic action—unsettle reigning political and intellectual verities in ways that critical social theory is not adequately helping to conceptualize.

One way to understand these emergent, fragile solidarities is that they are a *rescaling and reclaiming of temporal and spatial being*. On one hand, this is the negative and necessary project of throwing off the space-times of *developmentalism*—the false dreams of modernity based on a vitalistic notion of irreversible "progress" growing inevitably from the linear, lockstep march of technological and scientific improvement, market efficiencies, universalizing human reason, bureaucratic rationalization of government, and, the "any day now" of consumerist promises of sure-fire happiness if we just stay hitched to that gizmo-evolution train.

On the other hand, there is the positive project of building an alternative vision of the good life. This is, we argue, a rescaling and reclaiming of social being that pivots on the very complex temporalities and spatialities of *re-inhabitation*—rebuilding infrastructures of embodied being, in particular places, in sedimented and emergent dependencies within ecological matrices and *given* limits of the nonhuman surround and placed histories. Body~place~commons is the name we are giving to these chronotopic infrastructures—a theoretical notion developed to try to describe the pivot of social and ecological being that the global justice movement struggles to reclaim as durable portals of democracy.[4]

What Is Social Theory For?

We have written this book because we think critical social theory can help itself, and help the global justice movement, by working shoulder to shoulder on these projects. Social theory has already done much on the negative project, but more, much more, needs to be done on the positive project. Toward that sort of positive politics, we propose the notion of body~place~commons—subjectivity as intersubjectivity arising in embodied practices in concrete places within heterogeneous temporalities of the ecological commons. *To be a creature—human or nonhuman—is to be hinged between one's own embodiment and the particularity of places that accrue the grounds for life from unruly and ruly cycles of interdependence, mortality, and natality of the ecological commons.* Our being is not "in" us, like something poured in a bag of skin, nor is it "outside" our skin in signs, economies, machines, or powers. The stuff of our being arises as dynamic infrastructures of forms of life that we share with nonhuman creatures—generative matrices of co-constitution among particular bodies within the chaotic piling up of particular conditions of ecological relations within particular places.

Certain political and economic conclusions derive directly, we believe, from this nondualistic, generative and dynamic stuff of being. John Ruskin distinguished between wealth and illth as that which increases or decreases well-being for individuals and collectivities. He says, "To be 'valuable'... is to 'avail towards life.' A truly valuable or availing thing is that which leads to life with its whole strength" (Ruskin, 1985, 69). Illth is not simply poverty and distress, but production and accumulation that causes "various devastation and trouble around . . . in all directions" (73). Or, what current economic jargon labels *externalities*. Almost any statistical measures of illth and wealth suggest planetary trajectories at almost unimaginable scales of injustice and danger. These are not problems of "poverty" and "environmental externalities" that can be cleaned up through remediation, regulation, and redistribution—as if they were in tidy packages sitting, ready to hoist, next to handy work tables with just the right toolkits. Our concern is that institutionalized inattention to body~place~commons is *integral* to systemic synergisms of increasing inequality, insecurity, violence, displacement, and suffering (ecological, political economic, cultural). The crucial word in Ruskin's definition of wealth is *for*. Wealth understood as well-being *for* particular beings recenters questions of value within the embodied, emplaced, given particularities of existing beings within enabling or disabling matrices. This is thinking from *within* body~place~commons. It is development-from-within. Development understood etymologically—as *de* (un) *vel* (veil)—the unfolding of becoming out of the *given* infrastructures of being. In many ways, modernity has been a long war against this kind of thinking.

We have just lived through several centuries of structured inattention to body~place~commons—a circuitry hardwired with logics of modernity that are infrastructural to now globally dominant political, economic, and knowledge institutions. For now, let us call this circuitry *mind (space) matter*. Mind (space) matter constructs subjectivity and world as ontological products of epistemological tasks. The damage from Descartes' "I think, therefore I am" has not been undone by the postmodern "It writes, therefore 'I' (seem to) be." Both are in flight from the given. This book argues that both create their authority (intellectual, political, ethical) by disvaluing the givenness, particularity, and durable proportionalities of the enabling conditions of life. Foundational to mind (space) matter is the distance it constructs, and constantly must reconstruct, between itself and embodiment, place, and the commons—and their co-generativity. Modernity tends to cast itself in opposition—reducing such unruly, creaturely interdependencies to the merely given, the always prior matrix from which modernity rises up triumphant, shining in newness. For all its celebration of sensual flux as ludic radicality, postmodernity continues this nervous flight from the given, in curiously elaborate and timid new ways.

To understand social being as the nexus of body~place~commons is to mark both the simplicity of the stuff of social being and its radical, unimaginable strangeness. The simplicity of the notion of body~place~commons comes from the fact that it is happening all around us. We know it in the mode of common sense, what we take for granted. Much of critical social theory has set itself against this common sense—celebrating that which disembeds, decenters, and unfixes. But we argue that these decentering tendencies too often make social theory irrelevant to the worst dangers and best possibilities of our historical times. It has proven surprisingly weak in shaping inquiry and building solidarities for ecological citizenship and democratic reclamation of globalizing economies now escalating inequality, violence, and ecological destruction. Alliance with the margins and the centrifugal makes sense when domination is wholly centralized and emancipation is mere undoing. But how useful is iconoclasm in an epoch so terrorized by overkill, by lust to raze, and then to make the rubble bounce? There certainly are days in which one wants to agree with Nietzsche that the question for philosophy is to what ideas it needs to take a hammer. But perhaps it would be more helpful to sit down and think a bit about what a hammer is for.

Hammers are for building. They are also, as Heidegger noted, extraordinarily interesting—not least in how we think about them least when using them most. Social theory might be less enamored of iconoclasm if questions of building and habitation had not been made to seem boring. A manufactured inattentiveness has veiled these questions for some time. We argue that fear and denial of the labors of recentering are part and parcel of other crises—crises of ecology, inequality, fundamentalisms of identity and religion, gender, violence, democratic authority, knowledge, public space.

A call to recenter social theory should not set up a simpleminded opposition between the negativity of a "hermeneutics of suspicion" (Ricoeur, 1970) and something else, wholly positive that replaces deconstruction with construction. This dualism itself is false—constructed by their placement on that spectral operating table on which they are always already dissected, twinned by the scission that makes each perpetually what the other is not.

This book explores possibilities for social theory to understand itself, intellectually, as ways *to attend to the world* and, practically, as ways to *tend to the world*. We try to meet these intertwined challenges of thought and action, with intertwined images of theory as listening and care. In part, this is an effort to shake loose the self-enclaving of theory understood simply as demystifying and debunking. Listening and care transgress dualisms of subject/object and negative/positive. They are a kind of full emptiness, an open grasping—in which subjective and objective, negative and positive, co-constitute each other. Social theory's long struggle against dualism has taken many forms. But, like many other theorists, we are concerned about efforts to escape subject/object dualisms that seem to more deeply incarcerate theory away from its object and from intersubjectivity. Beyond intellectual questions, political and moral concerns are urgent. Chow describes well the "self-referentiality" that can fold theory back on itself, making it hard for it to encounter its "constitutive exteriority" and the ways in which this self-enclaving of theory is complicit with vicious inequalities of power and wealth (Chow, 2006).[5]

Enclaving and the Loss of a World-in-Common

Theory is not just enclaving itself. It is imbricated in wider patterns of enclaving. A central concern of this book is that enclaving is what neoliberalism looks like when it hits the ground.[6] Of course, the program notes to neoliberalism say just the opposite. Advocates (and many theorists) of neoliberalism describe it as a flattening or smoothing that makes everything more accessible to everything else. Capital flows ever more rapidly in ever more integrated global financial markets that grow by leaps and bounds. Production is ever more fluid and transnational. If you just read T-shirts, you might conclude that global consumerist culture has engulfed the smallest barrios and crossroads on every continent. International trade laws in the last two decades have tilted against national trade barriers (with exceptions, of course, for the politically powerful).

So—products, ideas, images, money, and people zip more rapidly around the world. But, are we closer? Are we more accessible to each other? Are we inhabiting and co-inhabiting more capacious, inclusive, and resilient worlds?

To trot the globe is not to inhabit a world. Even when we are not talking about it directly, world is that to which this book attempts to point—so we should define what we mean. *World is that dynamic mesh of relationships among creatures and their ambient surround that provide durable and livable architectonics for creaturely action and environmental sustenance.* Hannah Arendt might not have agreed with this extension of world to nonhumans, but our understanding of world draws directly from her thinking about humans. Arendt emphasizes that world is a strange mixture of history as residue from past action and history-in-the-making as sheer openness of new possibilities for action (Arendt, 1958). Human world arises in, and out of, history, with all its particularity and onrush, as people find their lives to be at stake in what happens around them. And so, historical events pile up in traces of meaning and matter—forms of intelligible speech, conscious remembrance, unconscious habit and ecological engagement. And world is where this piling up happens, and where it becomes available for us to make and remake individual and collective life in its particularity. *Human world is that durable architectonics of engagement that creates the background that actors need to illumine future and present as coherent settings for action, and into which acts can transmute into remembrance (or habit) that avails past for future action.*

World does something that modernity made deeply unfashionable—it combines contingency with cosmological architectonics. It is contingent because it is made up of the piling up of things, the idiopathic poetics that are the particular residue of particular things, events, gestures, and words that happened. One of the most intense affects of world is the sense of *at stakeness*—that one's life and one's environmental surround are at stake in what happens and what these happenings leave behind. The stuff of world is not the imprint of some abstract order; the stuff of world is particularity, the contingent compost of what happens, or happened or will happen. But world provides powerful architectonics of intelligibility that serve as grounds and experiential endoskeleton for cosmology, as well as rational forms for collective action. World helps to orient us, to give us a sense of where we are, what we are doing, who other people are, and, what we have in common.

World arises from the historicized particularities of social geographies, forms of speech, cultural cosmologies, political bodies, livelihoods, and subjectivities intermeshed with ecology and physical geographies—that make the world livable. And, nonhuman worlding interpenetrates human worlding. World provides another way to think of biodiversity—as human~nonhuman dwelling-in-common in landscapes understood as the sedimentations of particular histories (nonhuman and human).

The notion of world helps us understand and engage with neoliberalism. Neoliberalism is a vast ideological apparatus that claims that market relationships can provide a livable grid for human life on earth. Under neoliberalism, the Market provides the stuff of cosmology and the chronotopes of polity, culture, and subject formation. The neoliberal Market is an endlessly extendable grid of infinite, flat transactability that gives the impression that anybody can get anything if they just play the game right, a game whose outcome is infinite freedom for all even if few get to write the terms of the game. *The Market as cosmology is the un-worlding of human and nonhuman life. Neoliberalism is an ideological war against world in which the few usurp the ability of the many to care for, and care about, the durable architectonics of livability—for their personal bodies, for the places they inhabit, for the planet.*

Social theory began, and has mostly continued, as a reaction against the hegemony of such universalizing grids—forms of rationalization that impose meta-logics, reduce heterogeneity, and provide means of oppression by power and domination.[7] In the past several decades, this has led to such fear of grids, or meta-anything, that many social theorists have repudiated the search for collective frameworks of intelligibility. Against this fear of Big Ideas, we propose an understanding of collective political action and thought as tending of worlds-in-common. These are worlds that help one find orientation within world-horizon and confidence from earth-grounds. Along this way, we approach Bruno Latour's rethinking of political ecology and the dualization of nature and society as if into separate domains—what he calls "bicameral dualization." This bicameralism has paralyzed democracy, neutralized politics, and promoted not civilian relations within the collective but "militarized relations" of subjects and objects (Latour, 2004). Latour suggests a new republic that might re-assemble humans and nonhumans and expand the collective. It might bring the sciences into democracy to allow the search for the "good common world"—with a politics in which nonhuman and human share the same common world (see 54, 93, 127, 226, 231–50).

Defining Body~Place~Commons

Body~place~commons has to do with practices of livability—with the generative powers of embodied life battening, hungering, sating, fearing, enjoying, sensing, resting, and playing within generative matrices co-constituted from earth, air, water, nutrients, energies, and co-evolved creatures. These embodied, lived practices are structured by multiple and heterogeneous temporalities. Some are cyclic, such as ecological cycles and rhythms of seasonal, daily, annual, or sidereal repetition. These ecological and cosmic cycles are not simply out there in the disembodied, machinelike form attributed to them by mechanistic science. They complexly co-author fantastically diverse ongoing creation of earthly forms in the inscriptions of chronobiologies that play such a central role in the co-evolution of mortal creatures—circadian rhythms, life stages from natality to senescence, the astonishingly diverse relationships between generations arising from and inscribed within bodily form, and so forth. But such cyclic temporalities are mysteriously bundled together with often starkly linear temporalities. Whatever we might know about the ecological cyclicity of mortality and natality, the onrush of ecological time can give us some of our most acute experiences of time as an arrow in irreversible flight. For instance, danger floods us with heightened acuity and powers that trigger linear plotlines of flight or fight that are a strange mixture of very old primate neurochemistry, abstract cultural notions about safety and risk, unconscious habits that idiosyncratically sediment out comfort zones from (largely) unconscious daily practices, and so on.

The *matter of our being* as human and social beings should be understood as the creative intersections of body~place~commons. Body~place~commons is the dynamic hinging that lets multiple and heterogeneous space-times hook into each other. This is a complex interpenetration of many different sorts of linear and cyclic temporalities of bodily and ecological rhythms. But, bodily and ecological times are necessarily bound to social time. Social time also has internal paradoxes. The substance of intersubjectivity is a radical openness—a leap, an expectation, a ghostly past. Self and Other co-constitute each other as mirror (becoming oneself only in the gaze of the other), as promise (opening to the other in the future tense, as the hope of a return), as memory (in shared stories), as material (inter)dependence. Culture is the orchestration of these many ecological, bodily, and social space-times—through shared formations of meaning, performance, livelihood, and landscape.

Insights into livability are hard-won these days. Too often, they come under the bitter tutelage of sorrow. To look at "mountaintop removal" is to face forms of annihilation that beggar thought and feeling within us, just as they smash habitations (of human and nonhuman creatures) around us. To save mere cents on a load of coal, King Coal coerces us into hardly bearable labors of mourning—not only for lives and places lost but also for the loss of the *conditions for life*. Dislocations between bodies and their enabling places and commons are systemic these days—in part because we have grown political economies and political cultures that do not put livability into the central frameworks of decision making and planning. Neurochemical sheathes of fatigue, stress, and pain around the bodies of those who must work in outsourced, sped up, "flexible" labor conditions are too often compounded by the stresses of chemical toxicities, the shame and estrangements of migrancy and stigmatization, the dreads and jolts of civic alienation and violence.

Sorrow, whatever its horrors, at least has a kind of moral clarity—a clarity arising in part from the sharpness of its forms of embodiment. Bewilderment and amnesia, in some ways, are more disabling. To question the *social bases of unlivability* requires one to turn into dust storms of distraction and forgetfulness that snatch words almost before one can frame a question or open one's eyes. We argue that there are connections between strip mines and strip malls. Spaces and paces of work, leisure, home, kinship, memory, politics, public life, and civil society discombobulate. The waking insomnia of long commutes, deskilling, the mental gaps and skids of chronic multitasking, and the creep of insecurity are embodiments of intertwined pathologies within existing "models of development" that increasingly spread from blue- to white-collar jobs. These are the new geographies of domination—geographies that ride on the management of places by the few, and the displacement of the many into defensive enclaves, exilic mobility, or sycophantic orbiting of the powerful. The new boss might be the old boss, or then again, it might be a splintered, soft authoritarianism that will not bother to upgrade its panopticon when resistance can be kept on the short leases of subcontracting, short-term hires and long-term fires, the vertigo of courtier masquerade within the crony/pork/industrial complex, or the ventriloquy of faceless whispers—"Outsource? Downsize? Health insurance? Pension? Green card? Deportation?"

Those who are called the poor have often survived with so-called subsistence economies partially in and partially outside of money and markets—getting by and making do—living off the land or scavenging in the cracks of industrial and post-industrial growth and decay. Oscillating between stigmatization and invisibility, such communities can have unofficial histories of stewardship of important gifts for reweaving body~place~commons. Such survival comes from heroic construction, in difficult circumstances, of diverse creative commons of local skills and local knowledges about how to relate to nature as ecological commons and how to build social relations to resist dependence on those forces that would enclose any commons—whether civic, cultural, or ecological. But, such commons-centered communities face growing dangers. Ecological destruction, appropriation, or violence displaces many. For others, external and internal forces fray the civic and intergenerational webs necessary to pass on a way of life. This book is centrally concerned with the gifts and fate of such communities—with their ability to maintain a certain measure of material and cultural autonomy, their labors of mourning, and their gifts for habitation.

Public Space, World, and Commons

We should emphasize the differences between commons, public space, and world—even as we trace their interconnections (see figure 1). The *commons* are the substantive grounds of collective life. We define the ecological commons as the web of interdependencies within nonhuman life and between human and nonhuman life; the civic commons are those social webs of practices through which people tend the ecological commons and reproduce their own ability to tend the commons.[8] *Public space* is the social space in which people contest, ratify, or celebrate the forms and decisions through which social and ecological order is reproduced. It is the performative mise-en-scène that makes such contestation authoritative, binding, and mutually visible. *World* is secreted by, and endoskeleton for, the lived practices of body~place~commons. It is the sensual form of embodied, placed engagement—it is the particular, historicized product of past experience that can sluice the completely novel into being. Who knows what world is

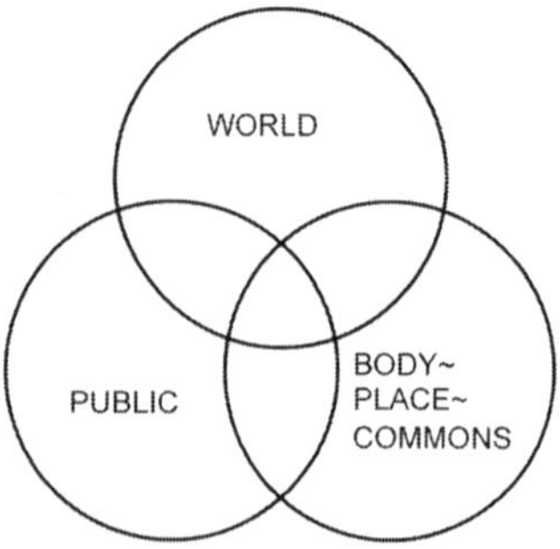

Figure 1. Body~place~commons, public space, and world.

for nonhuman creatures, but for humans it is a complex interpenetration of symbolic and bodily forms. The difference we posit between commons, public space, and world is rather like the old distinctions of nature, polity, and culture—insofar as the first emphasized ultrahuman dependencies, the second emphasized power and contestation, and the third emphasized worldview (placed proportionalities of situation). But the older notions were trapped in dualisms we are trying to dismantle—body/mind, human/nonhuman, agency/structure.

Space-Times of Democratic Public Space

This book can be thought of as a series of reflections on democratic public space—with particular concern to understand the spatiotemporal frameworks of democracy. Almost by definition, we argue, democracy requires *fluency*—the ability to flow easily from one perspective to another, in order to ensure that a question is deliberated upon in an open-ended and egalitarian way. Democratic deliberation also requires breadth and appropriateness of *scope* in space and time. It should have the chronotopic tensility and aptness to be able to change frameworks in order to consider past and future impacts and consequences across multiple sites (not just the powerful and privileged sites that have made themselves central), but also to recenter tenaciously within the particular situations at stake in particular debates. Hannah Arendt's notion of plurality captures both the openness and the groundedness of what we are trying to say here (Arendt, 1958). Plurality for Arendt suggests a complex social and cultural field between humans in which there is a nondualistic relationship between individuation and listening to the other. Plurality is the stuff of democracy—the generative space within public life that catalyses conversations that are open-ended, and in which persons relate to each other as peers, creating a field of intersubjectivity that cultivates originality of individual being (or what we call *particularity* in chapter 6). This book struggles to understand what cultural and political frameworks encourage and sustain plurality. We emphasize that plurality must not simply be understood as social or intersubjective. It must not be framed only as dyadic relationships between persons. Rather, we understand *plurality as communication that illuminates the worlds that are the generative conditions of personhood—including ecological matrices*. This is a greening of Arendt's notions of plurality and democracy.

Democratic public space needs fluency among many times, many scales, many causalities, and many voices. In other words, we need political institutions that are far more *pluritemporal, pluriscalar, pluricausal, and plurivocal.* Instead, we have cascading negative synergies among political institutions (government bureaucracies, academe, civil society, etc.) that escalate fragmentation, specialization, and exclusiveness—making it harder and harder to "connect the dots" between issues, causal impacts, viewpoints, and long- and short-term perspectives.[9] Democracy at any time requires plurality. But cultural and political webs of plurality are peculiarly urgent now as the jaws of greenhouse gases close around our planet, externalities concatenate uncontrollably, and the legions grow of people made superfluous in the global economy and culture. Industrial side effects have so thoroughly slipped loose of natural and civic buffering that we face massive tasks of reclamation of our damaged commons—air, water, soil, systems of mutual support, and so forth. Externalities dangle everywhere, and we have lots and lots of illth to monitor and get under control—if we can.[10]

But it is crucial to avoid dualistic oppositions between plurality and structure. The fluency and openness of plurality is only possible if safeguarded by political structures. And, the nation-state is the only political structure able, we believe, to provide a strong enough vessel for the difficult political contestations that will be necessary to reclaim the social bases of livability—for humans and nonhumans. This reclamation of democratic political structures must operate at multiple scales and in multiple modalities—including the fragile but passionate alliances and conversations that we call the global justice movement. At present, most of these efforts are based in civil society. But, reclamation of other sectors—professional and governmental—is necessary to provide supports and resources for the long haul.

What concrete political practices and structures are needed? We argue for reclaiming the tradition of democratic republicanism, which has been eclipsed by the liberal democratic polity and suppressed by an increasingly imperial corporate state. The notions of liberty in the democratic republican tradition go beyond the negative freedoms of the liberal democratic polity in which the state's primary role is to protect citizens from interference. Republican liberty requires freedom from domination in order to safeguard the positive freedoms that enable citizens to work together to construct and secure the common good.[11] This book joins other efforts to green this republican tradition (Barry, 2006). We are in agreement with Robyn Eckersley that "[a] proliferation of transnationally oriented green states, which are likely to extend and deepen environmental multilateralism, is also likely to provide a surer path to a greener world than the development of a more overarching cosmopolitan global democratic law" (Eckersley, 2004, 202).

What Is Ahead: A Brief Overview

We focus in the first three chapters on the United States because we think it is urgent for American social theory to re-place itself, to reflect critically on its political conditions. Economic globalization is driven by structures that integrate corporate and state powers in ways that have important historic origins in the particularities and contingencies of U.S. history. Excavation of this history is essential to the political labors ahead. American social theory has been deeply shaped by the space-times of the American nation-state. From this base of critical self-reflection, we reach in the last two chapters towards global regional conversations about how to dismantle the space-times of developmentalism in order to reopen democratic transnational alliances to tend the planetary commons and the solidarities it avails and sustains.

The first three chapters explore how the space-times of body~place~commons have been affected by the space-times of the nation state. We argue that the political structures and imaginaries of liberal capitalism and the corporate state have smashed the chronotopes of body~place~commons. Against the liberal polity and corporate state, we seek to reclaim the democratic republican tradition. Republican ideas dominated in America's revolutionary founding and continue, we argue, in grassroots struggles. We emphasize the permeability of civic and ecological commons, economy, and democratic public space in key republican notions of commonwealth, competency, and liberty. Chapter 1 explores "chronotopes of the commons"— developing a feminist, historical, praxical, materialist model of the commons as dynamic articulation of modes of reproduction, production, and social and ecological reproduction that we call the Life Round. We propose a notion of "eco-class" as positionality within these systems of power, authority, and eco-economic capacities—and relate eco-class exploitation with structures of imperial, racist, sexist, and spatial domination.

Chapter 2 looks in more detail at the history of contestation over democratic public space and the commons in the United States from the late eighteenth through the twentieth centuries. It begins by situating citizen action groups across the United States that compose a politics of grass-roots democracy. We see them working between the disappointing realities of a liberal-democratic polity never far from corporate state pressures and the more hopeful vision of a democratic republic felt as both heritage and project.

Chapter 3 looks at the cultural constitution of political subjectivity within the space-times of the nation-state, focusing on the United States. It draws on feminist theory about state, kinship, market, and gender to examine the symbolic mechanisms by which liberal democratic ideologies create an illusory smashing of the chronotopes of the commons and enclosure in mystified notions of "family," "nature," and public life as "consumer republic." This is a denial of (inter)dependence on materiality and the given that fatally weakens national capacity for collective projects of care for habitational grounds of all life and is integral to the later rise of corporate-state American empire.

Chapter 4 turns to John Dewey's philosophy of democracy to search for ways to regenerate public culture with social theory inflected by a post-dualist ecological sensibility. Crises of environmental and social justice are intertwined. Dewey's contribution to an aesthetic ecology of public intelligence is linked to studies by Fischer, Shutkin, and Gottlieb, which show how effective democratic citizenship begins in the commons where body and place meet. Instead of a social theory that postulates "resistance to the present" (e.g., Hardt and Negri), we argue for one that refuses to concede the local with its myriad places of embodiment and struggle.[12]

Chapter 5 examines Merleau-Ponty's revolutionary ontology of human subjectivity in the intercorporeal lifeworld of shifting experiential forms intertwining nature and culture. Edith Cobb's study of the child's cosmopoetic exploration of the environment, the bioaesthetic striving active in both nature and child, converges with Merleau-Ponty's theme of the "durable flesh of the world." Our identification of humanity as a body~place~commons process finds its ambience between Earth and World where horizons of the flesh serve as portals of history and existence. The reification of cultural difference has become central to the post-democratic foreclosure of the political as a generative space for unscripted social expression and growth. It is especially here in the project of regenerating public culture that John Dewey's deepest concerns—his historicized sense of the aesthetic ecologies of public worlds-in-common—finds its ontological landscape where Merleau-Ponty's interwoven structures still never banish the ultimate mystery of the human situation.

Intertwined crises of ecology and democracy make imperative a fundamental questioning of knowledge régimes deeply implicated in corporate globalization. Chapter 6 elucidates Dewey's essay on "Time and Individuality" to move beyond the ontological divides of spectatorial professionalism chained to the logics of fungibility constitutive of the liberal polity. To reverse the enclosure of the commons, or to reclaim the commons, requires an understanding of the implication of professional elitism in the ecological violence besetting our world. This chapter delineates a logic of particularity integral to a feminist materialist approach to the politics of the commons in the cosmogenic, place-infused knowledge enabling democratic agency.

Chapter 7 seeks grounds for political memory and mourning vital for new green public spheres in post-Cartesian ability and courage to embody places and their horizons. Reopening to more reliable worlds for citizen participation and action, the materialization of care promises to revitalize both civic and environmental commons. Social theory begins weakly when it bypasses how people come through particular experiences of the world to move in the direction of the political. Social theory situated in chiasmic fields of embodied co-presence can reweave those life concerns from which politics arise—if it helps reweave aesthetic ecologies of public life in placed sensibilities and horizonal imaginations.

Finally, in chapter 8, we argue for an understanding of social theory as collaborative stewardship of the civic and ecological commons—and reclamation of the democratic public spheres that can ensure such stewardship. We note important ideas arising from the global justice movement—especially Indian critiques of Western developmentalism, the South African "Durban Social Forum Declaration" against the distractions of "identity politics," and Zapatista understandings of global solidarity as "one world of many worlds." Our notion of body~place~commons intwertwines challenges of thought and action in its understanding of theory as listening and care. This is a project of democratic hope that shakes loose of the self-enclaving of theory understood simply as demystifying and debunking. We build arguments for social theory as civic professionalism—oriented by placed, embodied engagement and dialogue within democratic publics. Our notion of participatory reason re-places and re-embodies research and teaching in transdisciplinary collaboration—between social theory, social and field sciences—that breaks down barriers between applied/theory, science/humanities, expert/local knowledges to solve multicausal, multiscalar problems of pressing public concern.

But we begin this journey with the question whether a capitalism increasingly corporate and in recent decades transnational has come to dominate American society and culture. We ask whether corporate state bureaucracies, wherever located, have reconfigured a liberal-democratic polity sometimes reduced to mediating the tensions between essentially imperialist realities and consumerist fantasies. The degradation of the democratic control of the state and most forms of community life is inseparable from something more difficult to see, and that is the stripping and manipulation of body~place~commons modalities of the lifeworld. Modes of democratic republican life, never secure, have been largely supplanted by dualistic schema of space-time that operate to pre-empt the forms of recognition, communication, and cooperation critical for citizen action in public space.

1

Space-Times of the Nation-State and the Effacement of Body~Place~Commons

In the introduction, we spoke about an emergent politics—fragile but tenacious alliances to tend the grounds of livability. *What kind of polity is at stake in this new politics?* This question is hard to answer. In fact, it is hard to ask. Our languages about life grounds have been so debased that they have trouble getting a grip on their political dimensions. In this chapter we argue that the politics of the nation-state have systematically effaced or caged discourses about stewardship of the commons—especially in its embodied, praxical, and emplaced dimensions. We have already emphasized the astonishing complexity and heterogeneity of the space-times of livability. *Body~place~commons* is the name we have given to these generative yet integrative matrices.

This chapter argues that dominant U.S. political discourses have, in effect, smashed the space-times of the commons and selectively redeployed their fragments. Careful stage management of these dismembered chronotopes has been central, we argue, to the construction of an American "mainstream" that mostly denies the space-times of the commons—except for crucial moments when maimed images of the commons are brought out like relics, to magically adorn the nation with spectral moral authority purloined from actual commons. The history of this symbolic construction of the "mainstream" is uneven, contradictory, always incomplete, always contested, with distinctive stages and haunted by stifled alternatives.

This chapter focuses on patterns that seem particularly damaging to democracy and sustainability today. First, we try to undo static notions of the commons (as pre-social natural resources or pre-given natural order) by developing a feminist, materialist, political ecology that emphasizes *dynamic, interactive processes of human and nonhuman production and reproduction.* Second, we use this praxical understanding, to examine relations (from the late eighteenth through early nineteenth centuries) between the emerging American state, democratic public space, kinship and gender, the official economy, and the commons-centered economy—using Dana Nelson's analysis of these issues in James Fenimore Cooper's fiction as a case study.

Official Histories of the State and the "Disappeared" Commons

The effacement of the commons by official discourses of the nation-state creates particular epistemological problems. Scholarly languages are affected by the space-times of the nation-state in diverse and changing ways (Das, 2003, 11; Giri, 2004; Strathern, 2004). And so, our scholarly ways of knowing are affected by the national chronotopes that render the commons hard to see. In an important recent book, Linebaugh (2008) points out that half of the Magna Carta has to do with guaranteeing customary, collective rights of access to the forest commons. However, in most popular icons and scholarly histories the Magna Carta is largely portrayed as the seminal writing that founds *individual not communal rights.* It has been sacralized as an originary moment in a single lineage of constitutional documents that father the negative liberties of the unencumbered self of modernity. The important communal dimensions and positive liberties of the Magna Carta have been made invisible *while in plain sight.* This effacement of the commons radically simplifies historical time, giving the impression of a written, unilinear, and onward and upward sort of history—denying the fact that the written document was but a freeze frame in complex, multilinear, decentralized, place-based contestations and oral transmission of customary practices. Customary practices for managing collective rights to common natural resources tend to be more diversified, contextualized in, and emergent from variegated nonhuman landscapes than the more universalizing disembedding laws of state. The effacement of the commons in origin myths around the Magna Carta sterilizes it—preventing it (and its variegated, diversely placed, oral antecedents and descendents) from providing official legitimation to ongoing place-based and embodied struggles over the commons.

Plumwood (2006) calls this sort of effacement a "disappearing" of ecological being (both our own natural being and the being of nature). The primary mechanism for this is the reconstruction of complex, interactive processes into dualisms. She says such dualisms polarize complex, chiasmatic, and co-constituting relationships into exclusive oppositions and then drop the middle ground—thereby disappearing the most interesting and constitutive parts of nature and our natural being.

The Commons, Economy, and State in Early American History

In a fascinating discussion of James Fenimore Cooper's *The Pioneers,* Dana Nelson (2006) illuminates the disappearance of the commons in American history and gives us critical tactics for its reappearance. Written in the 1820s but set in 1790s, *Pioneers* is a tale of the aged backwoodsman Natty Bumppo, who has ongoing conflicts with Judge Oliver Temple about game that Bumppo shoots on Temple's growing landholdings. The arc of the story is toward consolidation of legal authority in the increasingly wealthy Temple, who as political and legal leader is described as the agent for "systematizing" forces of national laws, transport systems, and rational development. Temple portrays himself as in reasonable and fair opposition to an out-of-date, scofflaw Bumppo. Nelson finds pervasive and problematic dualisms in critical literature on the text. These dualisms have the effect of enclosing Natty Bumppo in a realm of "nature" that is coded as outside and prior to law, society, or—in some readings—civilization. This realm is dehistoricized, and Bumppo is singularized and desocialized. He has largely been figured as an "iconic individual opposed to civilization or as representative of the Lockean State of Nature," one who loses out to the inexorable, linear march of social order, rationalization, and ever more encompassing and universalizing social contracts (Nelson, 2006, 164).

What Nelson does is to approach *Pioneers* with the question of the commons in mind. With this small shift in perspective, tidy dualisms fall apart, and a different drama springs from their interstices—a more interesting, nuanced and passionately historical one. *Pioneers* becomes a searingly detailed exploration of the fate of the commons (ecological and civic) in contestation with the emerging American state and the unequal class systems it veils. Once again, the commons have been hidden in plain sight. And these dualisms construct an ontological terrain in which the constitutive logics of the commons cannot make sense. Extrapolating from Nelson's analysis, we would argue that what these disappearing dualisms have done is to make unthinkable and invisible the *dynamic, interactive, processual nature of the commons*—pushing it outside history, sociality, language, and human material systems. Nature becomes mere background to "America" (T. Steinberg, 2002); "nature" is redefined as mechanistic Other. After the next two sections, we return to Cooper's tale (in Nelson's interpretation) as a kind of allegory for the political ecologies of the early American state, class formation, commons-centered economies, nationalizing capitalism, family, and community. But first, we need to develop an analytic model for post-dualist understanding of the connections between commons, state, modes of (re)production, and public sphere.

A Feminist Materialist Understanding of the Commons

We propose a dynamic materialist definition of the commons as the *substantive grounds of social and ecological reproduction*. We have to take into account the social and agentic nature of the commons—as a weave of *material and significatory practices* (human and nonhuman) that articulate the *mode of reproduction* and the *mode of production* with each other into collective agency—as contested and consolidated in public action. Many current usages of commons are too static. They reduce the commons to mere resources—the static object of a regime of management or ownership of that which is collectively owned or is fundamentally necessary to life itself. In short, they encase the commons on one side of rigid dualisms between human/nature, control/controlled and subject/object—thereby objectifying, mechanizing, and instrumentalizing nature and underplaying human dependence and passivity before nature. Such an approach does not show the commons as socially and interactively constructed in lived practices and contestation. It deflects attention from systemic causal linkages between the commons and other structures of politics, culture, and history. In figure 2, we represent the integration of ecological and feminist economic theory. The bottom arc (the mode of production) is what Wallerstein calls "the commodity chain" (Wallerstein, 1983, 165)—moving from the extraction of "raw materials" from nature to the material production of specific things, which are exchanged within relations of distribution, leading to consumption. We call these *production chains* in order to include nonmarket production.

Ecological and feminist political economics, however, shows that this is only half the story (Daly, 1996; Mies, 1998 [1986]; Mies & Bennholdt-Thomsen, 1999; Waring, 1999). Equally important is the necessary flow of matter through a phase of destruction into a complex processes of material transformation that becomes the basis for renewal or "natality."[1] Both Marxism and capitalism foreground production, making reproduction seem merely to be repetitive processes of repair or naturalized instinct. However, the reality of all material beings (whether manufactured products, ideas, or living beings)

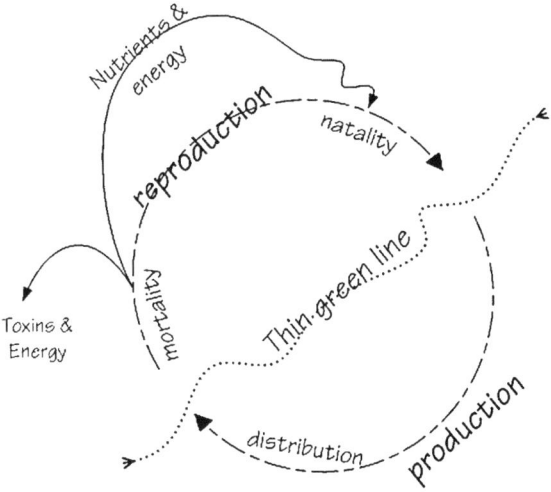

Figure 2. The Life Round.

is that they cycle between creative manifestation and circulation in material form (modes of production and distribution) and creative dissolution and renewal of material form (mode of reproduction).

This model applies to all earthly life—from nonhuman to preindustrial or industrial. The rhythm of manifestation into (restorative or dissolutive) quiescence, and back again, is pervasive in life processes. Circadian rhythms of activity and sleep are widely distributed among very different sorts of living organisms. This circular rhythmicity can be found in micro-neurological cycles, such as the improved cognitive acuity that comes from moments of rest. It is written into our personal life cycles in the knowledge that death is sure as birth. It is built into human bodies and feelings as cycles of emergence and withdrawal, of independence and dependence that require labor and creative thought from others. Subjectivity and intersubjectivity have their own cyclicities in the physical and mental labors of care of the young, old, ill, mournful, distraught, and so forth, for which all societies have their distinctive modes of care and mutual renewal.

Life is maintained at the *thin green line* that balances reproduction against production (see figure 2). The point is not to try to perfectly model the geometry of this line—to impute holistic harmonies or clean homeostatic closures. The point is to recognize that there is some exceedingly complex interplay of productivity and reproductivity that gives each an arcing toward the other—a messy kiltering of disparate cyclic temporalities without perfect or predictable fit, but yet with an astonishing capacity to integrate and iterate durable being with unimaginable becoming. This arcing is not determined by some immanent harmony in nature, but by dynamic processes of mutual engagement, rhythmicity, and interaction that constitute the ruly and unruly interdependencies we call the *commons*. The lifeworld logics of the thin green line are in part ecological and in part cultural. Both, animals and humans develop (at various scales and ways in different species) distinctive repertoires of learned (and, for some species, symbolic) behaviors that help them connect to nature's (re)productivity (through learned knowledge about their habitat and how to use it) and to accomplish their own reproduction (the capacity to bear and rear young in many species is learned from the experience of being parented) (McCarthy, 2004).

Human production chains flow into processes of human reproduction that we call *care chains*, a phrase developed by Arlie Hochschild to refer to the complex and exploitative relationships between paid and unpaid reproductive labor in the global economy (Hochschild, 2000). She focuses on globalizing patterns in which elite and affluent women are able to participate in paid productive labor markets by transferring reproductive labors (of children and other dependents, households, etc.) onto insecure, underpaid (or even illegal) labor markets and services that mostly employ much poorer women, who transfer care for their own children onto women even poorer than themselves—often unpaid kin (Ehrenreich & Hochschild, 2003; Hochschild, 2003). Allison Weir gives an overview of the growing feminist literature on political and ethical philosophies of care, as well as the patterns of inequality and exploitation in "global care chains" that deepen power and wealth imbalances between classes and between global north and south (Weir, 2005), and that articulate in complex ways with the unequal generation of power and wealth in global commodity chains and intercalate racism, sexism, and imperialism. In this book, we use the phrase *care chains* in a more neutral way—to suggest structures of systemic flow between different moments in the mode of reproduction that also articulate systematically with the flow through different moments in stages in the mode of production. These care chains can be exploitative or non-exploitative depending on whether they tend to create inequality in the accumulation of resources, status, power, or authority.

Production and reproduction in this figure require each other. Every object or being entails the destructive release of matter and energy in its production and its necessary destruction—it does not matter that at any one time we cannot define this balance. Manifest being and beings can be recycled into the composting, incubating, and nutritive functions of natality—to become the grounds for the new production of form. Or they persist as waste or toxins (see figure 2). Under patriarchal capitalism social actors in all phases of the mode of reproduction are sufficiently sidelined from decision making about the mode of production that no thin green line can hold. The massive release of wastes, unbound energy, and toxins proliferate risk and chaotic realignments of life patterns at all levels, threatening a radical simplification and reduction of planetary life forms. Industrial capitalism's unimaginable hypertrophy of commodity chains relative to care chains does not cancel out the green logic of the thin green line. Capitalist ideology is based on massive denial of the inevitability of this thin green line, disguising it under the very different thin bright line of the profit margin, which creates the illusion of endless linear progress in productive expansion unbound by the materiality of reproduction. But the ecological law of the thin green line still holds.

Definitions of Ecological Commons, Civic Commons, and Public Space

We propose an ecological feminism that understands political economy to be the systemic articulation of a mode of reproduction with a mode of production within a mode of social and ecological reproduction for which the commons are the substantive grounds. The commons are the substantive goods that enable the turning of the wheel of what Apffel-Marglin calls "biocultural regeneration" (Apffel-Marglin, 2006). We define the *ecological commons* as the web of interdependencies in material processes of human and nonhuman life; the *civic commons* are those social webs of everyday practices through which people engage with and tend the ecological commons and reproduce their own ability to tend the commons.[2] The civic commons can be understood as the *forces of social and ecological reproduction* (that is, a particular historical conjunction of the social relations as well as the means of social and ecological reproduction). *Public space* is the space in which people contest, ratify, or celebrate the forms and decisions through which social and ecological order is reproduced—a space with political, cultural, and social dimensions. It is the performative mise-en-scène that makes such contestation authoritative, binding, and mutually visible.

We believe the above analytic model can help to make visible certain features of American democracy that too often get disappeared. We need to break out of the constitutive spatiotemporal categories of the American nation-state in order to critique it. On one hand, the above analytic model tries to show co-constitutive flows between public space, economy and ecology. This is an attempt to break down the hyper-separation and dualisms that liberalism and capitalism have created between economy, nature, polity and society. On the other hand, the above analytic model tries to make analytic distinctions so that the civic, the public and the economic do not collapse into each other (as Arendt and others have feared for American political culture) (Arendt, 1958), and that the human does not enclose nature (as happens in strong social constructionism). This model takes the notion of economic class—as distinct and usually unequal positions within the chain of production—and turns it into a notion of eco-social positionality—distinct and usually unequal positions within the chains of (re)production.

Eco-class is the term we use for this notion of eco-social position—in order to link the materiality of ecological processes clearly and specifically with economic class formation. *Life Round* is the term we give to these forces of social and ecological reproduction.[3] In this model, politics are shaped in two ways. First, care and production chains can be structured so that they generate chronic inequality between eco-classes in wealth or access to the labor of others. And, at the next organizational level, the material or social organization of the Life Round can be such that there are systemic tendencies to privilege certain positionalities. Second, images of social and ecological reproduction provide exceptionally powerful metaphors for the body politic. Those who are already privileged can turn their power into domination, if they universalize their limited eco-class into cosmological metaphors that provide the stuff of public dramas about "how things really work." This kind of domination gets tricky. On one hand, the ruling group needs to make their eco-class appear to be more important than that of other eco-classes—in order to justify inequality. On the other hand, the ruling group needs to make universalizing claims to give the appearance that it can take charge anywhere along the Life Round. The limited social characteristics of the ruling group and their limited eco-class gets coded and naturalized as a superior force for hooking together and managing all links in the complex articulations of the Life Round. The causality can go two ways. Systemic tendencies in the modes of reproduction and production can (a) give certain groups more resources for meta-authoring of the Life Round, thereby helping to turn material and social power into political and cultural authority, and (b) this authority can allow these groups to change the rules of reproduction and production in ways that benefit themselves.

Male domination under patriarchy follows this ecological topology. Domination is based on the material alienation of one sort of eco-class power from the rest of the commons, while disguising it symbolically as a sublation of the whole into the part. However, while one can foreshorten the circular logic of the commons, one cannot collapse it entirely. It is too deeply written in the structures of life. Patriarchy was a form of sex/gender system that emerged, in some regions, with class society and the state. Kinship and its reproductive functions were domesticated within households under authority of senior males. Senior male patriarchs cornered the official authority to represent these reproductive interests in public space in the authoring of the terms and conditions for social and ecological reproduction—although this cornering is never fully successful and is always contested (Gailey, 1987; Herbert, 1993; Sanday, 1981; Silverblatt, 1987). The very important contributions that reproductive sectors made to real material life were elided and distorted within public representations of collective life and the Life Round. In public symbolism, women and youth become like vestigial appendages of the public persona of males. Under patriarchy, gender difference is artificially mapped along the thin green line—so that they naturalize each other.

Clashing Ontologies of Public Space in Early America: Late 1700s–1830s

The early years of the United States saw important struggles at both levels—over the organization of the material and social practices of the Life Round (and their tendencies toward equality or inequality) and over the foundational metaphors for political space itself. The political philosophy of republicanism central to American Revolutionary thinking continued to predominate through the first few decades of the nineteenth century. Republican metaphors for the constitutive stuff of public space emphasize liberty as the equal participation and dialogue among civic peers where social equality, not deference, prevails. Such peers care together for the *res publica*—the public things—and the commonwealth—immaterial and material common goods. This can be equated with the "first body" of the people that Sheldon Wolin describes as constitutive of "collective identity, of power, and of the terms of power" as active participation of "the people" (S. Wolin, 1981, 11). For this "first body," he says that the "classic statement . . . was the Declaration of Independence [and] its charter, the Articles of Confederation" (11). This is what established what Dietz calls a "polity of citizens."[4] Through the 1780s, the Articles of Confederation kept most powers at the local and state levels where, under the revolutionary republican banner, there was a ferment of experimentation and debate that included multiple, radically democratic, and emancipatory currents despite severe class, racial, and gender exclusions.

We argue that this political philosophy left permeable boundaries between the civic commons and public space, between civic labor and paid labor, between market and nonmarketized material (re)production, because of the centrality of ideas of *res publica* and commonwealth to the metaphorization of collective life and because of the importance of intersubjectivity to the constitution of subjectivity. Its organizational vehicles were the local and state polities where formal governance mixed in complex ways with voluntaristically organized actions to solve practical problems (Tocqueville, 1956), and with community as placed ways of everyday (re)productive life. In other words, these politics created permeable interconnections between civic and ecological commons and the formal structures of the republican state. Republicanism also made permeable connections between thought and action. Experience was an important category of political philosophy. As Wolin says, "the colonists recognized that democracy depended upon making political experience—the true basis of equality—accessible to all" (S. Wolin, 1981, 13), and many of the founders understood practical life experience to be the best preparation for political leadership. In other words, connections between formal political life and daily experience were valued. And the best scale for these connections was local and state politics—where democratic participation could best flourish in democratic decision making that was close to everyday and place-based concerns.

However, by the 1780s and 1790s, the republican polity was in strong competition with a "second body" of the people that was publically legitimated and articulated by ratification of the U.S. Constitution in 1787 and, Wolin says, "such texts as the *Federalist* papers, and Hamilton's great state papers dealing with finance, manufacturing, and the interpretation of the powers of national government" (S. Wolin, 1981, 11). This began with the conservative wing of republicanism. It was promulgated by conservative elites who saw public space as the zone of liberty and civic responsibility among landed, propertied men who were together forging an expansive national economy that would be foundational for the expansion of the American state. Democratic public space was still understood in the republican manner as a zone for action and debate among civic peers, but it was reserved for an elite who *related to everyone else through hierarchical powers*. This is very different from non-elite forms of democratic republicanism. The ontological stuff of this second body politic has a republican core surrounded by expanding managerial and hierarchical structures—inequalities ostensibly legitimated by the greater civic virtues of the elite under conservative republicanism ideologies.

In the first decades of the nation, conservative republicanism was amalgamating imagery and ideology from political philosophies of liberalism—

developing a quite different mix of foundational metaphors for the constitutive stuff of public space. Liberalism is an odd sort of philosophy of collective life, since its key metaphor of human life is the isolated individual. The founders had already incorporated into the Constitution the liberal notion of natural rights of individuals. This gave official underpinnings to strong, ongoing American concerns with negative liberties—collective life metaphorized as a zone of protection between atomistic individuals (leading to many paradoxes as we explore in the next chapter). Antebellum America saw the constitutional system of conservative republicanism incorporating new metaphors of public life drawn from liberal theories for emergent claims to national order and to discredit democratic republicanism. This is what Wolin calls the "second body" of American collective national being that was "primarily and intentionally antidemocratic and [that] can be called a political economy" (11). The liberal ontologies of public life gelled over the course of the nineteenth century, around metaphors of rationality that bound atomistic individuals together in pursuit and defense of individual self-interest (e.g., the market with its economic rationality) or through objective, law-like systems that transcended and harmonized individuals. In chapter 6, we describe these as interlocking "logics of fungibility" that impose fixed laws on objects understood to be infinitely transactable within those laws: the Market, the procedural state (universal legal systems for conflict resolution), the technocratic state (bureaucratic codification and administration based on meritocratic competence), and, at the end of the nineteenth century, the expertise of the burgeoning professions leading to what we call the *technological world picture* (as we discuss in chapter 2).

But, from the beginning, liberal political cultures were double-faced. The public face of liberalism highlighted the equality and freedom of the individual. The very atomism of the liberal subject was used to create the impression of freedom and equality. Free-floating liberal individuals appeared free because they were portrayed to have the ability to keep moving, to author themselves and to refuse the Other's imprint and interference. But, in many ways, this was a sleight of hand. First, it borrowed heavily from images of the republican citizen and republican liberty—which actually entailed quite different forms of subjectivity and intersubjectivity from that of the liberal individual or liberal freedoms. In republicanism, persons and polities are far more embedded in the idiopathic social and ecological contexts than within the liberal imaginary with its extreme emphasis on disembedding and decontextualization. Second, liberal American capitalism bought off white men of all statuses by symbolically associating their social qualities with the "objective" rationalities of the market and the state. This was a collapse of subjectivity into the de-subjectivized forces of universalizing reason imagined as a mysterious sort of logos behind the mechanisms of market, state, and, increasingly through the nineteenth century, science and technical invention. The earlier European association of "reason" with maleness and various forms of European ethnocentrism went through transmutations in the American context that deepened the symbolic associations of public life with masculinity and racialized whiteness. But this only worked symbolically because it stuck together republican and liberal notions that contradicted each other. Nelson describes how non-elite men were increasingly co-opted into the national mainstream (with its covert domination by elites) by appeals to join the spurious equality of an "imagined fraternity of white men" in a national symbolic of "national manhood," which is a pseudo-republican equality. The shift to a conception of the nation as "market" (Wood, 1992) was, Nelson says, a "radical abstraction of male particularity, which glued the (de-individualizing) market ethic of human exchangeability to the Revolutionary ideal of equality" (Nelson, 1998, 252).

In 1787, the Constitution centralized many financial powers that the Articles of Confederation had left with the states. Hamilton articulated the conservative republican view that this could be the basis for national elites to build a great empire based on an expansive national economy. Wolin argues that this is a notion of the polity as constituted from the constant generation of power from economic expansion—a concept of power and polity very different from the republican power and polity of citizens acting together (which was hostile to empire). The national political economic structures for which Hamilton and other conservatives pushed laid the foundations for the markets, transport, and industries that grew so rapidly from the 1830s on. As we see in this and the following chapter, legitimating political philosophies of these massive transformations included evolving combinations of classical liberalism, technocracy, chronotopes of "progress," and competitive and possessive individualism.[5] Liberalism's own program notes applaud its freedoms. But the hidden face of liberalism as a national political culture has actively anti-democratic elements. With its radical focus on the individual, it famously has trouble conceptualizing the collective or intersubjective (Stivers, 2009). It connects individuals together through rationalizing structures (contracts, markets, technocracy, etc.) that might look reasonable, but that actually take unusual time, expense, and labor to construct and maintain. The institutions that are required to manage the social reproduction of liberalism demand heavy expenditure of public goods. But the political philosophy of liberalism has a blind spot for *res publica*, chronically disvaluing public goods and misjudging their political nature, needs, and risks. This is a very dangerous combination. On one hand, it is exceptionally high maintenance—in chronic need of handouts from forces of social and ecological reproduction that are outside its cosmology.[6] On the other hand, it actively disrupts and depletes these commons and the social cultural forms that give them continuity, resilience, and durability. This is partly what Marx called "primitive accumulation"—capitalism's need to seize extra-market natural and social commons, drawing market profit from public or common goods that it does not have to pay for on market terms. Many current theorists of the commons note that this is not only limited to the early stages of capitalism in its associations with imperial predation on colonized natural resources, as Marx thought (Federici, 2004; Goldman, 1998b; Linebaugh, 2008; McMurtry, 1999; Nonini, 2007). Rather, enclosure of the commons is ongoing and systemic; capitalist growth depends on biting the hands of the commons that feed it.

But, even more dangerous is the way in which the marriage of capitalism and liberalism created a public space that radically splits the civic commons from the polity—tending to *smash even the memory of citizens' right to collectively author the forces of social reproduction*. In America, this was a long process of attack on the metaphoric fabric that made up the republican stuff of public life. This national debate intensified in the 1820s and 1830s and continued to the end of the nineteenth century when the increasingly corporatized and imperializing state destroyed the populist uprisings that were seeking to create alternative national macrostructures to serve as forces of social and material reproduction—alternatives that reached directly back to still valued legacies of republicanism (as we explore in the following chapter). As Karp says: "Industrial expansion, which almost all Americans had wholeheartedly welcomed, had ceased by 1890 to be a glowing promise and had become, instead, the source of innumerable burning and bitter questions. The sum of these questions was, in essence, the reassertion of the republican standard in economic affairs. Content no longer with mere industrial growth, Americans now began asking, what *kind* of industrial growth . . . serves the needs of a free and self-governing people" (Karp, 1979, 7).

Natty Bumppo and Judge Temple: Micropolitics in the Enclosure of the Commons

James Fenimore Cooper's tale about the strife between Natty Bumppo and Judge Temple, in *The Pioneers,* can be understood as a dissection of local dynamics on which the above macrostructures pivot. Nelson's analysis brings into clear relief the novel's central focus on the commons (Nelson, 2006). Building on her interpretation, we see Cooper trying to body forth the civic commons as lived daily practices and its changing relationships to the two bodies of the American state that we have discussed.

The novel highlights fundamental questions about the legal and constitutional legitimacy of the nascent second body of the American state. The novel opens on Temple's land, where Temple believes he has just shot a deer. However, Bumppo and Oliver Edwards emerge from the woods with smoking rifles and dispute Temple's right to the deer. Bumppo bases his claim on the rights of the forest commons. Against earlier critical descriptions of Bumppo as stuck in a pre-law, pre-political state of nature, Nelson argues that he invokes, not lawlessness, but a different law and a differing lineage in political authority to make law. As Bumppo says, "There's them living who say, that Nathaniel Bumppo's right to shoot on these hills, is of older date than Marmaduke Temple's right to forbid him" (Nelson, 2006, 163). In fact, Bumppo is right. Even though rendered culturally invisible in plain sight, there are legal rights of the commons, then and now, that have not been fully eradicated by private property laws, as Linebaugh and others point out (Linebaugh, 2008). Like Antigone, Bumppo is resisting not only an instance of legal judgment but its underlying logic and lineage.

The novel documents the existence of a functioning civic commons and delineates its social, linguistic and performative mechanisms. At crucial turns of the plot, the community appears—gabby real bodies of "the people" who throw in their two cents' worth, bruit ideas about, and pull together rough-and-ready judgments about fair ways to distribute resources and what the rules of the game should be. Nelson argues that the novel sets up contrasts between this oral, dialogical, informal civic commons and the monological, closure-seeking, documentary official courts—demonstrating the greater fairness of the former and the covert embeddedness of the latter in unequal special interests. Whatever the de jure status of such civic commons, Cooper seems to be an amused and respectful amanuensis for the ethical principles of working *de facto* commons. He shows the kinds of subjectivities formed by, and forming, such de facto civic commons—the polyphonous civic and communicational skills, the play and contestations, the local and embodied knowledges placed within varied, layered, and sedimented social and ecological landscapes.

Reading Nelson's analysis, we felt a shock of recognition. We know these sorts of voices and this sort of collective action. The social and dialogical forms of this fictional commons echoed similar dramas of de facto commons we have experienced around national forests in western North Carolina (B. Taylor, 2009b), the civic commons of Appalachian neighboring (Hufford, 1997, 2001; B. Taylor, 1992, 2006) in tribal India (B. Taylor, 200ba) and elsewhere (Chung, Kirkby, & Beckwith, 2005). When ethnographers and folklorists approach communities with theoretical frameworks that are open to the possibility of commons, it is remarkable how often de facto commons turn out to be hidden in plain sight (Brown, 1995; Hufford, 1997, 2000; Tsing, 2005)—even now.

The plot of *Pioneers* suggests what we call a "third body" of the American people. Judge Temple seems to exemplify the emergent liberal capitalist logics that would be the dominant stuff of national being by the end of the century. He exemplifies what Nelson describes as the "forces of modernization: capital, federal government, and systematic management" with attendant systems of laws (Nelson, 2006, 162–63). He comes from a merchant Quaker family. Intensely entrepreneurial, he rapidly consolidates his wealth and landholding through speculation, clearings, and "betterments"—setting himself up for the powerful position of county judge and gaining strong administrative powers in future development scenarios and planning infrastructure. His sidekick Sheriff Jones sums up their administrative goals: "everything depends on system . . . I shall sit down this afternoon and systematize the county" (164). Temple presents a public face to "the people" that exemplifies the abstracting, universalizing, masculinist logics of rationalization, which we discuss in chapter 6 as "logics of fungibility." In this role he is the maker of abstract economic space, who encloses and breaks apart the locally embedded places of moral and community economies and ecologies.

However, Judge Temple embodies another persona and drives quite another type of public drama—a form of intersubjectivity we call the third body of the American polity. This is a sort of doppelganger narrative that is also hidden in plain sight. It is the dirty little secret that everyone knows but fears to talk about. It is directly contradictory to meritocratic rationality. The origins of his rise to power are in the ascribed particularities of marriage and feudal privilege in land, not abstract achievement or market-based accumulation of surplus value. His father, the self-made Quaker, married into wealth, allowing Temple to attend an elite school where he formed an aristocratic friendship that "paved the way to most of his future elevation in life" (Nelson, 2006, 165). His rise as a merchant depended on this Royalist friend's money. In the war, Temple manages to gain titles to the abandoned lands of Royalists (including his patron), which laid the basis for his great wealth. In other words, behind the appearance of rational meritocracy, we see a web of cronyistic personalism that is the stuff for building the translocal connections that provide the circuitry for key parts of capitalist expansion. This third body of the American state-in-backroom-deals-with-capital is fueled by the wildly imaginative speculation, fast-talking hobnobbing, male adventurism and boosterism in the personalized networks of speculative investment that Tsing calls "spectacular accumulation" (Tsing, 2005, 59) and an "economy of appearances" in which "boom and bust are intimately related to each other" (55) at conjured "frontiers" of crony capitalism (27). It is the toe-to-toe, have-I-got-a-deal-for-you, don't-tell-anyone-else, whispers-behind-the-hand in bars around capitol buildings small and large all over this land. It is the fevered rim of speculation and appropriation that is the most important thin bright line in this tale.

The political and economic dominance of Judge Temple does not come primarily from his ability to extract surplus value in the middle or end of the chain of production through market rationalities. Rather, it comes from his ability to use personalistic patronage, appropriation, and speculation on the disaster of war and the growing disasters of ecological scarcity to control the primitive accumulation of land, land use planning, and others' rights of land tenure. Judge Temple might seem to get his public authority from being a *master of abstract developmental space,* but his hidden-in-plain-sight doppelganger gets his power from being *a master of place management.* This third body of the people is important from the beginning, and its great competitor is the civic commons of the people. This third body is where we find the thuggish night rider that can be most reliably counted on for the hidden, obscure tasks of clearings and enclosures—to shame, to terrify, to seize, to throw families into the street, to whisper rumors, to whip up factions and hire others to do the bribing, to cultivate dependents and henchmen, to drum up identity politics as a cover for cronyistic networks to dole out the loot, to keep everyone nervous and at each other's throats, to hold handouts in one hand and, in the other hand, a pen poised to sign eviction notices.

Twentieth-century criticism has tended to see Bumppo as outside the law, but we think that Cooper's republican contemporaries might have seen a side of Temple that is not only outside the law, but that threatens its very basis. Perhaps the most distinctive characteristic of republicanism is a fear of dependence. As Viroli describes so powerfully, the political problem with dependency and inequality is that it creates a political culture of deference and conditional largess in which republican liberty is impossible (Viroli, 1999). Temple repeatedly seems to be trying to draw Bumppo into a relationship of dependency and patronage. In the first conflict over who shot the deer, Temple tries to resolve it with what, on the surface, seems to be etiquette. He offers to pay for the deer, thereby, as Nelson says "graciously taking his cake by affording his social/economic inferiors to buy bread" (Nelson, 2006, 163). Bumppo will have none of this. He draws a direct connection between the laws about the commons and the very foundations of the state—when "[h]e invokes his 'lawful dues in a free country,'" (163) not only is Bumppo trying to unmask Temple as outside the "lawful," but he is also accusing him of undermining the very political structures that establish legitimate lawfulness. Bumppo is suggesting that there are highly permeable interconnections between the state, civic commons, and ecological commons—*and that this permeability is essential to vigilant protection of the republic.* He is saying that the shattering of these connections undermines the basis for the Revolutionary new beginnings in increased freedom and morality and better laws. When he "grumbl[es] against the idea that 'might often makes right here, as well as in the old country'" (163), he is clearly associating Temple with immoral domination by brute force in the feudal inequalities of England that is associated with a lawless past. Cooper portrays Temple as trying to seduce Bumppo and Edwards with sweet blandishments to pull them into an immoral and law-disabling web of patronage. This is portrayed as both a regression to a despised past and the advent of a new era in which Temple's kind of development puts others at growing risk of dependency. Bumppo draws a direct line between aristocratic privilege and the new powers of the lords of modernization. Nelson argues convincingly that Temple is invoking what "the staff of *The Ecologist* summarizes as the 'race between growth and scarcity that growth itself creates'" (164). She points out that Bumppo says, "The game is becoming hard to find indeed, Judge, with your clearings and betterments" (163).

Far from being an isolated individual stuck in a pre-law, pre-state state of nature, one can see Natty Bumppo as an articulate voice for aspects of subjectivity and intersubjectivity essential to republican notions of citizenship. He consistently refuses to segregate the polity, the law, the commons and the people—as actual people seizing their rights and responsibilities to speak and act together to keep these connections supple and visible, to confidently address each other as civic peers whatever their economic differences and to call out those who arrogantly set themselves up as patrons with goodies for needy others. This evokes the republican notion of commonwealth (discussed in the next section) that hinges together the political, ecological, and economic dimensions of republican liberty as freedom from dependency.

Commonwealth as the Political Body of the Commons

In republican usage, *commonwealth* signified both the polity and, its material grounds (Boyte, 1989). In our analytic language, commonwealth hinges the democratic body of "the people" together with the commons—understood as the substantive grounds of collective life. As such, commonwealth directly attacks and undoes the notions of property that anchor liberal democracy, neoliberalism, and possessive individualism. Bollier says that civic republicans such as the Anti-Federalists saw "production as a vehicle for family and community well-being, not just for oneself. People are not just producers and consumers but citizens with an active interest in community decisions and the common good. . . . A rough equality and diffusion of property ownership is also considered desirable because it helps thwart any tyrannies of concentrated economic wealth. A society with no extremes of wealth and poverty is more likely to sustain a virtuous citizenry" (Bollier, 2003, 53). This understanding of property excludes that kind of private property that Ruskin would call *illth*—the amassing of property that damages the social well-being of others. It also tames injustice and inequality in a more politically active and direct way. Bollier says that the commonwealth is "an *instrument of the people* for containing the abuses associated with property and the market" (emphasis added). Building on Gregory Alexander's insights, Bollier speaks of an understanding of property that is "not just a commodity to sell in the market but . . . an important tool for sustaining the American commonwealth" (G. S. Alexander, 1997; Bollier, 2003, 53).

In the democratic republican tradition there was a continuum between private property and the commons. This nondualistic hinge is set precisely at the point where liberal democracy creates an ideological chasm, a toggling dualism. In such republicanism even private property has a social dimension, a capacity to affect the common weal. But, the commons are also a necessary dimension of private property—a complementary register of intertwined social and material being. Even the most privatized market cannot function without a commons to manage the property régime itself. A diversity of public assets and services are needed to provide and manage currency systems, the rule of law, education, public infrastructure, and so forth. The ecological commons (air, water, etc.) are foundational of market economies no matter how silenced, or externalized, by the ontological categories of market. Republicanism aggressively counters such atomization of questions of wealth in two ways. First, it strongly emphasizes the commons—making it the moral and social anchor of the polity, not private property. The basis of citizenship and the social order is in the shared labors of common stewardship of common goods, of res publica, or the civic commons. Viroli suggests that the central meaning of political liberty in classical republicanism, the key constituent of sovereignty, is that what concerns "the whole body of citizens . . . must be entrusted to citizens themselves" for active, participatory deliberation (Viroli, 1999, 4).

But there is a second way in which questions of the commons are more integral to republicanism than to liberal democracy. Civic republicanism foregrounds questions of dependency, and this, indirectly but importantly, keeps pivoting the political system back to *concrete questions about the commons*. The commons are, by definition, nonmarket webs of *inter*dependency—creating stable infrastructures for diffusion of risk, resilience, and opportunity within webs of placed and embodied relationships between human and ongoing human creatures. Liberal democratic notions of liberty as negative so pervade our political culture that they sort of swallow up republican notions of liberty, making it hard to see how different these notions are. Viroli says. "According to [republicanism] we are free so long as we are not dependent; according to [liberalism] we are free so long as we are free from interference . . . the central point for classical republican theorists is that dependence is a more painful violation of liberty than interference" (Viroli, 1999, 10). According to republicanism, chronic structures of dependency are grave threats to democracy because they tend to create *cultures of servility and arrogance*. The primary responsibility of a republic, then, is emancipation from conditions of dependency. Viroli aptly summarizes this key distinction: "This classical republican interpretation of political liberty has a wider emancipatory meaning than any liberal one. . . . What worries a liberal is having anyone's freedom of action dominated or controlled; a republican worries about this but worries even more about the dispiritness that affects men and women who lead dependent lives" (12).

Republicanism requires robust, concrete, and practical attention to the material conditions and practices of everyday life. Core liberties are threatened if material conditions generate habits of fearfulness or arrogant domination. General patterns of dependency and interdependency, then, have direct and crucial political implications. Independence of political thought and action is not opposed to the commons (as in liberalism). Rather, it is hinged into the commons in a relation of co-constitution. And, in important ways, that hinge is *dignity*—a sense of personal integrity, security, and honor that is highly charged affectively, as well as the incarnation of abstract political principles in daily embodied practices of livelihood, social interaction, and speech among equals. Of particular importance for efforts to build ecologically sustainable democracy is the concreteness of republican attentiveness to dependency. Viroli responds to scholars who fear that republicanism leads to an anti-individualism, which abstracts the individual into a homogenizing collective identity or communitarianism. He argues that the emphasis on common goods over private goods is not a turn to greater abstraction, but a concern for the concrete things of a shared way of life—a passionate and specific love of a "particular way of life . . . based on the *experience of citizenship*. . . . *The political experience* of republican liberty, or the memory or hope thereof, makes the spaces, buildings, and streets of the city meaningful" (Viroli, 1999: 13; emphasis added).

In the context of revolutionary America, it is important to distinguish between conservative and democratic republican ideologies. Conservative republicanism reserved civic culture and political power in the commonwealth for white, male property owners—with citizenship powers heavily skewed toward big property owners. Early American republican ideologies were gendered, with public civic virtue equated with masculine honor (Bloch, 1987). But democratic republicanism cultivates a hyper-attentiveness to ways in which the *actual geography of lived social interaction and economic practices does or does not cultivate a nondualistic hinging of security with independence*. In revolutionary republicanism, this led to strong concern with the civic commons in its everyday ecologies of material interdependence. For these reasons, in later chapters, we join many green political theorists who have returned to the traditions of democratic republicanism, as they seek ways to re-embed economy and polity within the ecological commons (Barry, 2006; Dobson & Eckersley, 2006; Kuzminski, 2008).

The private/public divide in American political imaginaries is ground zero for a long war against revolutionary republican ideas about liberty, dependency, and the commons. American republicanism saw the foundation of political liberty in the dignity and security that came from *competency*—a livelihood that provided enough to prevent one from feeling dependent on others, and enough security to not fear the future.[7] Unfortunately, in the nineteenth century, the complexity of this notion of liberty as simultaneously *political* and *economic* was fractured and appropriated by the consolidation of a certain kind of national mainstream politics that shattered the connections between political and economic, which were integral to republican notions of liberty and competency. In the next two chapters, we argue that this was done in two ways. First, the economy was sequestered into a mystified separate realm managed by what we describe as a "market machine god." Second, the republican understanding of the connections between politics and economy were mocked as a kind of producer republicanism that was a defensive and dying subsistence farming—caricatured as merely backward, rural, and, above all, *too local, too place-bound* mentality. In fact, as we see in more detail in chapter 2, the populist movements in the late nineteenth century tried to envision and fight for an alternative financial and economic metastructure for the national economy. They were trying to institutionalize a national vision of the nation as a democratic republic rather than an imperial corporate state.

The Enclosure of the Commons and Dominations of Race, Class, Gender, and Empire

One way to understand the specific mechanisms of this symbolic reconstruction is to understand it as multiple deformations of the complex space-times that we have tried to capture with the notion of body~place~commons. Body~place~commons is an understanding of cultural meaning and social being as concretizing, and being concretized by, the embodied, lived practices of particular people in particular places within the enabling limits of the webs of interdependencies that make up the civic and ecological commons. These embodied, lived practices are structured by heterogeneous temporalities—complex interdigitations of cyclic, linear, and arrhythmic temporalities with spatialities that are recursive, planar, topological, and so forth. These heterogeneous bodily and ecological space-times are necessarily but paradoxically bound to social time—which kilters together spatio~temporal~social proportionalities through complex processes of mimesis, projection, introjection, and entrainment of Self and Other.

Culture is the orchestration of these many ecological, bodily, and social space-times—through shared formations of meaning, performance, livelihood, and landscape. The way in which industrial capitalism emerged in the United States had the effect of "unsettling" the country—to use Wendell Berry's powerful phrase (Berry, 1996 [1977]). This was a misaligning of the *cultural* ability to orchestrate body~place~commons that was causally linked with emergent forms of economic extraction and uneven development. It was also a crippling of *political* structures for stewardship of the ecological and civic commons and of the relationship between the health of bodies, the health of places, and the ecological matrix.

National mainstream culture was captured in the nineteenth century by powerful metanarratives that radically split cyclic time from linear time. The American "myth of progress" seized multiple elements of political culture from the Revolutionary period and welded them together into a new paradigmatic matrix that created a new kind of cultural matter. An illusion of the future as boundless and infinite was patched together from magical understandings of the endless creative powers of technology, rational technocratic management, and the Market as a bottomless cornucopia of prosperity (which we discuss in chapter 2 as the "market machine god"). This gained some moral legitimation by equating the endless possibilities of Progress with the utopian hopes encoded in earlier Puritan rhetorics about America as "city on the hill." However, unlike the moral and mortal finitude central to the Puritan commonwealth, the temporality of progress denied all ecological limits—it was the antithesis of the commons. This scaling of time was only plausible because it was ideologically welded to the "myth of the frontier"—a scaling of space as infinite, blank, uninhabited, *without place*.[8]

On this basis we can begin to appreciate the importance of a feminist ecological economics in which the notion of the commons is central to understanding gender domination and liberation—as well as causal connections with racism, imperialism, and the exploitation of nature. It is urgent to understand the long history of these connections in order to build new solidarities in the twenty-first century that can make visible both the political ecological and the cultural dimensions of domination and liberty. We agree with those who would argue that struggles to reclaim the commons will be central to the politics of the twenty-first century (Bollier, 2003; Cromwell, 2001; Klein, 2001; McMurtry, 1999; Nonini, 2007). Capitalist commodification deepens assaults on the commons at all levels. Market logics enclose more and more life forms that were previously taboo or invisible to exchange value (water, air, forests, gift economies of care, genetic codes, professional research, etc.).

It is hard to get semantic or conceptual clarity about this. Our received mystifications hide the commons in plain sight. First, the power and wealth of capitalism is predicated on the denial and erasure of the commons, through ongoing processes of primitive accumulation (Federici, 2004; Goldman, 1998b; Linebaugh, 2008; Perelman, 2000). Therefore, thought about the commons requires a kind of consciousness raising—an undoing of ideological mystifications in mind and heart (Rowe, 2001; Theobald, 1997). Second, many examples of functioning commons have roots in pre-capitalist social formations. In our present political contexts, these are too often dismissed as archaic or utopian. For instance, vibrant global indigenous rights movements have mobilized around the defense of particular commons (traditional knowledge about medicinal plants, various sorts of communalized ownership of land, traditional regimes for collective management of water, forests, etc.). In some sectors of the anti-globalization movement, there has been a call to protect or reclaim subsistence economies that rely on gift economies and the commons.[9] Some would dismiss such efforts as unrealistic or romanticized. We disagree. The traditional imagery that clings to the idea of the commons cloaks and protects potentially revolutionary emergent structures of political economic experimentation that are crucial to planetary survival.

Third, within the identity of women under patriarchy is a taboo against linking their reproductive labor in intimate life with reproductive labor in the public sphere. To think the commons under patriarchy and capitalism is to utter ideas that we have been conditioned to find dangerous. They crack open key structures of exploitation and violence that were hidden within the hegemonic illusions that founded patriarchy—raising desire, sorrow, rage, and hope that we do not yet have the social relations or collective identities to contain (B. Taylor, n.d.). Historical understanding of the centrality of the commons to liberation from gender, race, and ecological exploitation might help to build wider solidarities between localized civic environmentalisms around the world (*Ecologist,* 1998; Guha & Martinez-Alier, 1998; Klein, 2001).[10]

With capitalism, the official logics of public space are abstracted from the circular materiality of the commons and encoded in a universal personhood that was charged with an unmarked white masculinity (Nelson, 1998; Pateman, 2002; Plumwood, 1993). *The logic of the market is ripped out of its proper place in the sphere of distribution to become the basic schema for social and ecological reproduction itself.* In the next chapter, we discuss the "myth of the market" used as a cosmology for the Life Round. In chapter 6, we discuss how market myths interdigitate with other "logics of fungibility"—intertwined rationalisms of market logic, commodification, bureaucratic rationalization, and technocratic managerialism that provide the constitutive cosmologies for economic globalization. These logics of fungibility operate by disembedding beings from the circular logic of the commons—decontextualizing them from ecos, place, social, and historical contexts—to make them infinitely interchangeable within markets or bureaucratic regimes of regulation. Reproductive and ecological processes are externalized, enclosed, and exploited under this form of domination.

The Two Axes of Domination: The Line of Enclosure and the Thin Bright Line

These intertwining forms of exploitation form another axis of domination. In figure 3, we show these two axes of domination. We earlier discussed the thin bright line that is placed over the thin green line—to cover up the mortal limits of personal and collective finitude (the way in which all things, creatures, and dwellings cycle in and out of modes of production and reproduction). This first axis of domination could be understood as a "line of externalization"—projecting negative consequences outside the ontologies of market and state and, as Val Plumwood says, "disappearing" it (Plumwood, 1993) or putting it under "coverture" (Plumwood, 2006). The second axis of domination we schematize as a second line across the Life Round (see figure 3)—this is the "line of enclosure." This is the eco-economic-sociopolitical process that Marx called primitive accumulation but that is actually a chronic underpinning to liberal capitalism. It begins halfway through the production process, where extractive industries draw raw materials from nature and sell them into production. It ends in the zone in which the waste products of production are dumped—where toxins and market externalities are too often left to rot or pollute or left to nature or the disempowered to clean up

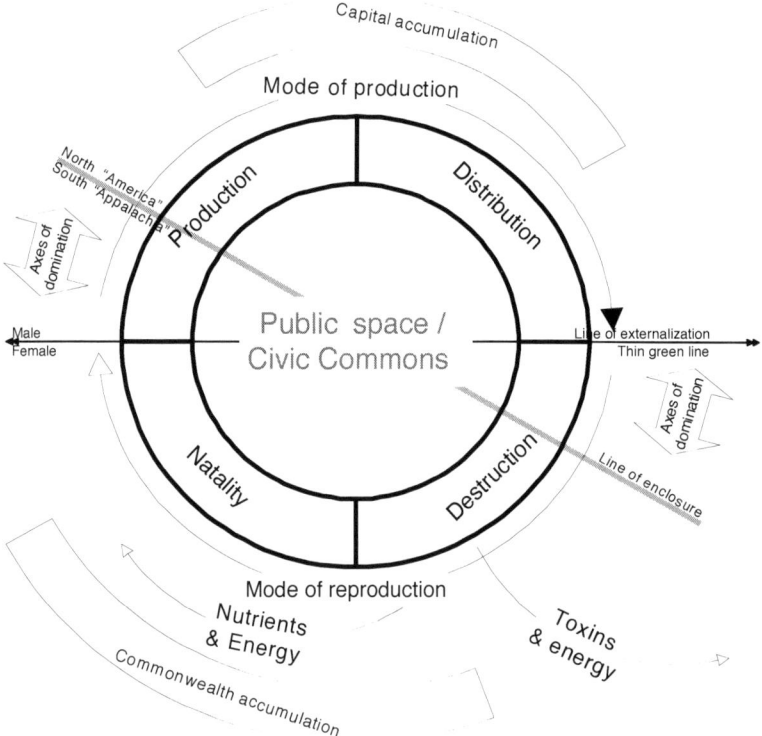

Figure 3. Two capitalist axes of domination.

if they can. From the very beginning, capitalism's insatiable need for raw materials (timber, fossil fuels, agricultural raw materials, etc.) and need for illth dumps have led to a spatialization of inequality that continually regenerates racist ideology and imperialist hegemonies to maintain access to raw material, labor, and consumer markets (Harvey, 2000) and sites of disposal for capitalism's "trash."[11]

Above this axis of enclosure are the geographic regions and economic activities that world systems theory would describe as core. These are the value-adding activities of the final stages of production and marketing, as well as the power-creating economies of violence and war—which are most generative of capital accumulation. Below this axis of enclosure are the material activities characteristic of peripheralized geographic regions and feminized labor—which provide the raw materials for production and retain the least control over ecological destruction. The costs and the labor of ecological and reproductive destruction and renewal are externalized onto actors who were symbolically constructed as Other in public life (the global south, nonwhites, women, national sacrifice regions like Appalachia) who are symbolically constructed as left behind in the linear, progressivist temporality of capitalism (backward, primitive, nonrational, connected with the frightening primal forces of life-and-death) (Reid, 1996, 2005, 2006; Reid & Taylor, 2002). But just as patriarchy enclosed the reproductive and productive labor of women within households, capitalism increasingly encloses all commons into a standing reserve for production and illth disposal. Capital accumulates the most rapidly in the midpoint of the commodity chain where fungibility is highest, lending ever quickening power to the disembedding of power from the ecological and social commons. These two forces of enclosure and externalization converge with the most ferocity on women in the Global South who are triply burdened—with their unpaid labor in gift economies (including civic, human, and ecological reproduction), with sexist discrimination in wage labor and lack of access to unearned wealth, with heavier rates of ecological violence and devastation below the axis of domination (Ehrenreich & Hochschild, 2003; Hochschild, 2000, 2003; Mies, 1998 [1986]).

Global regions (such as Appalachia in the United States) that were locked outside the core of the world system have often been able, paradoxically, to nurture civic and ecological commons that provide an alternative (or supplementary) means of subsistence. Often in mountainous or other fringe geographical areas, nonmarketized biodiversity coevolved with traditions of ecological and artisanal local knowledges and informal economies that allowed oppressed people to survive at least in part as what Gadgil and Guha call "ecosystem people"—sustaining ways of life rooted in local ecologies (Gadgil & Guha, 1993; Guha, 2000; Hufford, 1997). However, the contradictions of advanced capitalism push into remaining pockets of functioning commons—increasing oppression and spurring new forms of resistance in environmental justice and anti-globalization movements (Gadgil & Guha, 1995; Guha & Martinez-Alier, 1998; Nonini, 2007; Schwab, 1994). This way of conceptualizing the commons shows the continuing connections between sexism, imperialism, and the exploitation of nature. The two lines of domination work together. They are a sort of pump of mystification—pulsing together to create symbolic associations between rights to enclose and powers of externalization. They do this by creating webs of symbolic associations between reproduction, nature as passive resources, care, women, racial Others, death, particularizing and contextualizing knowledges, tacit dimensions, and morbidity. They put all this into dualistic opposition to men, whiteness, production, activity, immortality, abstract reason, visibility and actuality.[12]

The Construction of the "Hillbilly" and the Rise of the Corporate State: 1870s–1910s

We have discussed how conservative republicanism ideologies in the eighteenth century and following helped to incubate political and economic structures from which liberal democratic forms and ideologies expanded through the nineteenth century. From the 1820s through the end of the nineteenth century U.S. political philosophies of liberalism increasingly provided the cultural matter from which new forms of national unity were constructed. This cultural reconstruction of national identity projected America as a flat and accessible political terrain open to all citizens equally and governed by fair and transparent rules and included some democratizing elements. But behind the apparent seamlessness of imagined national community, however, were also processes of cultural and economic violence that symbolically constructed Others and then excluded them through repetitions of national rites of purification and pollution. This ideological construction of the modernist body politic was deeply imbricated causally with the emergence of corporate power and the fledging of an American Empire soon to take global wing in the twentieth century.

The symbolic construction of this new cultural matter was linked with urbanizing and globalizing economic forces that were hostile to small-scale farming economies and farmers. The symbolic schizmogenesis of America and its Others have been well studied—especially the complex ways it was constructed out of race, ethnicity, and gender constructed as binary dualisms. In this section, we look at the emergence of the opposition of iconic "America" to iconic "hillbilly"—people who are symbolically coded as "white" (although many are not) and identified with rural wildlands, especially the mountains of Appalachia and the Ozarks and who are portrayed as underdeveloped strangers to American affluence and progress.[13] The America/hillbilly dyad is important to study because it unsettles certain American constitutive dualisms. In many ways, it inverts the whiteness and maleness that are usually veiled within the center's authority. Many theorists have discussed the ways in which the power of racist, imperialist, and sexist authority comes from the ability to remain unmarked—to suffuse its meanings within images of superiority without calling attention to its own material and embodied nature (Brander Rasmussen, 2001; Delgado & Stefancic, 1997; Frankenberg, 1993, 1997; Hartigan, 2005a; Roediger, 2003). The hillbilly icon puts this off-kilter. It is an Otherized whiteness, which is visibly marked with strongly embodied qualities of male violence, natural wildness, genetic degeneration, uncontrollable sexuality, improvidence, and lack of self-disciplined will.[14] Hartigan argues for understanding racializing processes in place (Hartigan, 1992, 2005a, 2005b).

The national Otherization of the hillbilly icon was a *spatial and temporal* reframing of eco-class positionality to push the stereotyped peoples of Appalachia, and other peripheralized rural areas, below the axes of enclosure and externalization cut across the Life Round. Stereotypes about the Appalachian region emerged directly from the unsettling of America (Berry, 1996 [1977]) and the enclosure of the commons discussed earlier. Appalachia became essentialized as a distinctive social body at the end of the nineteenth century (Batteau, 1990). It was marked as different from America in such a way that it could be extrojected as a sacrificial scapegoat—spun off from the mainstream and ritually laden with the contradictions that could not be made officially visible within national public space lest they rip apart the hegemonic order. The hillbilly icon, then, has become one among many toggle switches that flip cyclic from linear time in mainstream politics. The history of the manufacture of this semiotic routing was articulated with structural economic changes in the second half of the nineteenth century, which put corporations at the commanding heights of the national political economy and stigmatized social and cultural identities primarily embedded in local and regional production and supply chains. The pathologies of national space-time that generate "hillbilly" stereotypes continue to discredit and to silence the voices of real people and real communities that were being stereotyped.

Mary Hufford describes entrenched sociocultural patterns that supplant a nation/region dialog with a national monologue (Hufford 2002).

This enclosure of "Appalachia" was an important forge on which the triumphalist linear time of American Empire was early shaped and tempered. It was accomplished ideologically by welding the spatial temporality of the commodity chain to an implicitly expansionist linear time of endless Progress (see figure 4). This concocted linear time is held in place by its inscription on an imaginary landscape where the site of natural resource extraction is equated with the premodern and savage. In the emerging national imaginary of nineteenth-century America, these three forms of linear spatial temporality were also beginning to be equated with lifecycle movements from country to city. The population went from majority rural to majority urban between the 1870s and 1920s. Therefore, the experience of much of the new middle class was of a rural or small town childhood or extended family. This created a subjectivity of urban modernity that was complexly layered with charged affects of attachment to and denial of rurality. All of this was complicated by massive immigration, creating cultural diversities that threatened and bewildered national mainstream identity. For all of these reasons, the question of roots became anxious. The hunger to master new urban and consumerist status and cultural identity jostled with often unmarked mourning and remembrance for lost ways of life.

Chronotopes That Gave Wing to the Corporate State in the Late Nineteenth Century

Harvey describes capitalism's chronic need for a "spatial fix" (Harvey, 2001). Structural contradictions drive geographic expansion for new markets and natural resources. This political economic spatial fix is twinned with time/space dodges in the cultural matter from which national identities are constructed. The last half of the nineteenth century in the United States saw fierce

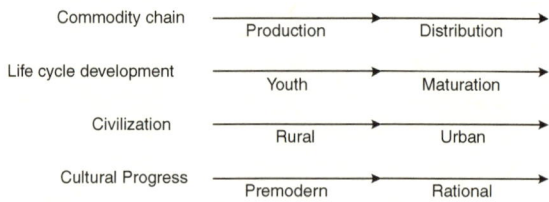

Figure 4. Linear time of economic modernization.

battle between corporate and citizen interests to define and control the cycle of biocultural regeneration discussed earlier (see especially figure 2). We have discussed Sheldon Wolin's metaphor of the two bodies of the U.S. polity (S. Wolin, 1981). The first body binds citizens together with the cultural matter of ideologies of democratic participation and accountability—an understanding of the body politic as emerging from a primarily local sovereignty that is only conditionally bestowed on the federal system. Wolin argues that the second body of the people was the political economy, favored by the landowning elite that ended up dominating the writing of the Constitution and its ratification process. It is this second body that came to be the primary vehicle of corporate power, but the first body politic has often been reconfigured to veil corporate power.

For its first century, American national political culture tended to be anticorporate, because anti-British sentiment was consolidated in rage against the monopolistic political charters of corporations such as the East India Company (Nace, 2005). From the 1870s to 1920s in the United States, however, corporate entities were able to mobilize a rewriting or reinterpretation of national laws to legitimize monopolistic and vertically integrated corporate control of the *metastructures of the national economy*—especially railroads, land speculation, fossil fuels, banking and credit systems, road and other infrastructure construction, and land use planning. This developed from what Edward S. Corwin called the "dual federalism" of the U.S. polity—with two different structures of power for articulating local, state, and federal polities (Corwin, 1964). *Corporate power expanded in the crevices between local, state, and federal authorities.* From the beginning in the U.S. political system, these crevices have been wide and fluid. Originally, the United States was a confederation of many commonwealths, and there are many disjunctures and ambiguities between scalar levels in moral, legal, and political authority. Corporate power utilized these spaces of ambiguity, both as a vehicle and a cultural mask to hide their seizure of power. It is these ambiguous interstices that provided the structural basis for the third body of the U.S. polity—the personalistic web of cronyism that drives the direction and nature of capital speculation and enclosure of the commons that is the most powerful author of the scripts for economic futures. This is the hidden-in-plain-sight gray eminence of the corporate state. It is the boss behind the elected leaders. The liberal democratic polity supplies the legitimating term *lobbyists* and their buildings ring the capitol (cf. Frank, 2008, chap. 1).

The first body of early American republicanism is described often as a producer republicanism—marked by many inequalities, in which production and reproduction were mostly household based. The Jeffersonian ideal casts this as agrarian—tapping into widespread belief that democracy was not possible without most of the population living as independent small-scale farmers. But this was equally shaped by an artisanal, urban, or small town sense of independence from wage labor. Jefferson's fear was that manufacturing would become so profitable that an industrial "aristocracy" would emerge that would subvert democracy because of sheer inequality. That happened within decades of his death, but it went along with something he did not anticipate, which was far more destructive of American democracy as envisioned both in the more radical Articles of Confederation and in the conservative republicanism of the Constitution. The problem was not simply the emergence of great industrial wealth at the end of the nineteenth century. The problem was that corporate structures were able to build monopolistic cartels that centralized power over the *metastructures of social and ecological reproduction*—the political levers of the forces of the Life Round. Populist mobilization against this new national body was not able to combat its rapidly growing powers.

Until the Civil War, the U.S. legal structure was, in certain ways, anti-corporate. Business owners were legally liable as persons—they could not hide from liability behind a corporate veil. U.S. laws said that corporations could only be formed for limited periods of time; were to serve clearly defined and limited public needs (such as building a canal); could not own each other; and required a direct and revocable charter from the state legislatures in which they operated. However, after the Civil War, the new giants of emerging national industries began a long campaign to restructure legal frameworks that would legitimate and expand the powers of the corporation to become the dominant organizational form within economy and polity. The corporate struggle to rewrite the rules of the legal game was, in many ways, an attempt to do an end run around politics. As we discuss in chapter 2, labor and small producers and businesses were creating new organizational forms that were mobilizing strongly against stark new inequalities and the rapid consolidation of wealth in the growing national industrial and financial sectors. In his important history of corporate power, Nace describes how railroad conglomerates led business efforts to bribe or influence state and national legislatures through the 1870s and 1880s to combat the sudden surge of labor and agricultural movements that were strongly anti-monopolistic and anti-corporate. But the most important forum for corporate interests was the U.S. Supreme Court, where they pressed the claim that corporations should be considered "legal persons." In a surreal twist of history, they made this claim under the constitutional amendments that were meant to establish the personhood of newly freed slaves—the Thirteenth Amendment, which abolished slavery outright, and the Fourteenth Amendment, which Nace says "guaranteed all persons 'due process' and 'equal protection of law,' [and] sought to protect the rights of freed slaves" (Nace, 2005, 94). The ambiguous and notorious Santa Clara case of 1883 became the cited precedent for the doctrine that corporations have a personhood that supersedes the actual personhood of business owners and managers—outliving their deaths and deflecting their liability for damage to mere humans and the land. Corporate personhood rests on dubious foundations in late-nineteenth-century claims under the Thirteenth and Fourteenth Amendments. From these contested legal and political origins, corporate interests have made dramatically escalating claims to powers and rights under the Bill of Rights throughout the twentieth and into the twenty-first centuries (Nace, 2005).

Appalachia was a key proving ground for this fundamental restructuring of government into the corporate-state. Once corporations got the right to own each other, industrial empires were systematically built on dense cross-ownership between land, coal, oil, timber, and railroad corporations. Not only did this create overwhelming monopolistic power within industrial sectors, but it also set up almost unbreakable tendencies toward vertical integration and commodification and massive enclosures across modes of production, distribution, and regeneration. The history of Appalachia demonstrates that this was possible because of the overwhelming power of corporations in manipulating the third body of the American corporate state—cronyistic *inter-scalar* relationships between local, state, and national governments. This third body of the American polity created unofficial webs of influence that facilitated manipulation of cultural media and popular anxieties to encourage the creation of national Others. Cultural Others were rendered polluting figures because they were metaphorically associated with the activities represented (in figure 3) under the "axes of domination'—sites or labors that connected them to the cyclic times of Nature and reproduction that threaten the flat, eternal economic space of the Market under liberal individualism.

To a startling extent, corporations have been able *to usurp the future* in the United States—to dominate official and unofficial structures of long-term planning, with special predominance over land use and the meta-geographies of infrastructure and energy systems. Everyone knows about this third body, but few dare talk directly about it. It is the cronyism of elite place-managers who work their deals through personalistic, particularistic, private networks that control the commanding heights of the economy and manipulate government as needed to keep control over the definition of economic structures, land and land tenure, rights of access to the ecological commons, and key constitutive metanarratives of public life—in short, the infrastructures of the Life Round.

For many American citizens, this usurpation has been hard to see, because "quality of life" issues have been so thoroughly privatized. Until recently, the vast natural resources and sheer affluence of the country have disguised the damage done to the civic republic. Middle-class and wealthy people have been able to buy their way into good neighborhoods and the consumer goods that give the illusion of happy independence—creating a landscape marked by what Galbraith called "private wealth and public squalor" (Galbraith, 1998 [1958]). Tragically, this has also led to an increasing greening of inequity—as certain neighborhoods or geographic regions are able to maintain their environmental, cultural, and civic quality of life, precisely because many middle-class or upper-class people owned property and had the political access and sense of entitlement to protect these areas from corporate damage. They have stronger eco-class status within the third body of the American corporate state (although middle-class status frays under twenty-first-century neoliberalism). But regions like Appalachia and other micro- or macro-landscapes culturally identified with Others are where the externalities pile up, suffering vertically integrated cultural, economic, and environmental injustice.

To unfasten the corporate state, we turn to legacies of democratic republicanism that can reclaim commonwealth as substrate of political subjectivity and intersubjectivity rather than the ecologically disembedded market logics or possessive individualism of liberalism. This will require difficult work to claim new grounds of solidarity and to build radically new democratic institutions. As Wolin says: "We need new forms, new scales, new beings. The forms need to be what constitutions truly are: life forms for taking care of a part of the earth and of the beings who are there. That constitution cannot be given; it can only come to be in the concrete actuality of people taking hold of conditions at hand and steadily shaping them to accord with how they think equal beings should live and with what time they should order their lives together" (S. Wolin, 1981, 24).

2

Reclaiming the Democratic Republic

Historical Retrieval and Political Reconstruction

Writing in the wake of the 1973 oil crisis, Wendell Berry commented that the abuse and waste of human energy was as much a problem as the abuse and waste of fossil fuel energy (Berry, 1996 [1977], 388). Today the new activism based on this combined premise is exemplified in several projects. One example is Green for All, the national organization promoting green jobs and environmental justice led by Van Jones of Oakland, California.[1] A movement for greening energy and the economy replaces the human waste and disposability secreted in mainstream policy with guidelines of democratic participation and social creativity. In our view, serious confrontation with catastrophic climate change moves well beyond familiar wilderness protection motifs to mobilize new forms of human and other energies in an expanding dialogue oriented by the toughest questions of political justice and social possibility.

Wendell Berry's argument for decades has been that fundamentally we are all ecosystem people. As he wrote in 1977, "the earth is what we all have in common ... it is what we are made of and what we live from, ... we therefore cannot damage it without damaging those with whom we share it." His meaning is clear: "it is impossible to care for each other more or differently than we care for the earth" (1996 [1977], 123–24). And that is why in trying to protect our bodies and homes we must retrieve the ancient sense of the commons (Linebaugh, 2008). Reopening old questions in new ways is central for revitalizing democratic politics, as activists such as Van Jones demonstrate.

Berry concludes his recent *Citizenship Papers* by recalling us to the old (and new) democratic idea of the commonwealth. Our claim is that the times require setting aside the familiar assumptions of life as commodity, as property, as subject now embedded in the transnational corporate state's all too pervasive forms. We do much better to follow Berry's sense of "life as defined by our own nature and the nature of our home landscapes" and of life as gift and miracle and ultimately as commonwealth. He means that our lives are "shared with all other creatures" and not only with the living. Making much more politically real or effective the world's magnificent (but depleting) variety crucial to the commonwealth sensibility is a challenge of the first order. As Berry tells us, recognizing and acting on this commonwealth takes us beyond, though not as immediately as he'd like to think, "the dualisms of humanity and nature by which some justify their destruction of nature and others justify preserving nature merely as 'wilderness'" (Berry, 2003, 184–85).

Questioning the notion of "global economy" that has prevailed for at least fifty years, as Berry has, brings us into the thicket of political complexity. It is in the middle of this thicket, not its other side, that we should locate the "growing worldwide effort on behalf of economic decentralization, economic justice, and ecological responsibility" (Berry, 2003, 17). His compelling case against the "corporate program of global 'free trade'" and his appealing sketch of a "peaceable economy" evoke political contours unlikely to be retraced without strife or conflict. This is quite clear in our global political context witnessing the rise of "food sovereignty" issues as food riots become more common. How Americans understand themselves crucially configures the possibility of understanding the world food crisis. When U.S.-based corporations such as Monsanto, Cargill, and Coca Cola are put at issue in a country such as India, the veiling of corporate power in the United States is perhaps critical for upholding the fantasy of an entire way of life beyond the ecosystem.

Berry is right to insist that we are all ecosystem people. However, a myth of progress still pervading middle-class life fosters voters who decide not on the basis of where they are but where they want to be (or imagine themselves in a few years). This is one way that the myth of progress has translated into political behavior undercutting both government accountability and cross-class, multicultural alliances that might move toward more fundamental changes. Deepening inequalities eroding most such versions of progress prepare not one but at least two contrasting future political formations. One direction is a right-wing nationalism enforcing new scarcity formulae rationalized by "patriotic" sacrifice. A second possibility is a democratically chosen politics of limits based on a much more decentralized and sustainable energy system. Currently, a fossil fuel corporatist sector, utilizing green-wash tactics, is blurring this key choice as it operates to maintain the post-political forms of elite dominance.

Yet certain realities of catastrophic climate change are exploding into view as certainly as northern Alaskan villages are slipping into the sea. One does not have to be a climatologist or a scientist to know generally why or how these things are happening. It is not that hard to imagine that if polar bears and penguins are marching toward oblivion, we may not be that far behind.[2] After all, we live on what more than one study describes as a planet of slums made up of increasing numbers of ecological refugees. Popular consciousness has amply provided blinders in the United States. But leakage into politics and journalism occurs from the endarkened portals of "national security" studies by what are sometimes called intelligence agencies. Only crackpots eagerly anticipate "resource wars."

Returning to Wendell Berry's historical argument of 1977, he emphasized the *unsettling* of America as many took up the imagery of a chosen people in a land of endless opportunity. Along the way came the capitalist industrialization of agriculture that increasingly is understood as an ecologically disastrous attempt to create a giant food machine that escapes the natural processes and limits of life and its place-worlds. As Berry put it: "If, like the strip-miners and the 'agribusinessmen,' we look on all the world as fuel or as extractable energy, we can do nothing but destroy it" (Berry, 1996 [1977], 94). Banners of progress, prosperity, and development have been flown so vigorously that for most of the last century it was difficult to see a trail of ecosystem destruction coupling with a road to global ecological crisis and nagging questions of empire. Finally, recent work by environmental historians such as Ted Steinberg is penetrating our supercharged commodity culture to provide realistic accounts of episodes such as the "green revolution," while correcting the deficient practice of writing U.S. history "against a stable environmental backdrop" (T. Steinberg, 2002, 268–71, 262, ix).

Grassroots Politics between Liberal-Democratic Polity and Democratic Republic

We want to return our readers' minds to the citizen action politics of grassroots democracy that, among other things, provides important constituencies for the writings of Wendell Berry, Wes Jackson, Barbara Kingsolver, Bill McKibben, and others. By and large, these activists and their groups will be found in eddies just off the mainstream of U.S. politics. Resonant with community concerns and problems, they seek not only more expansive participation but also to redirect the American mainstream toward a more sustainable way of life. What most are trying to advance are an economics and politics of re-inhabitation (Kemmis, 1990, 84–141). Such a politics is hard to conceive much less cultivate in an American mainstream that blends bourgeois liberal tradition highlighting possessive individualist modes of thought, the corporate oligopoly sector of the economy, and a liberal-democratic polity that many citizens consider already bought and paid for. For several years we have been involved in this democratic politics of citizen action struggling simultaneously for community protection and more sustainable forms of life. The groups with which we are most familiar are located mainly in the Appalachian regions of Virginia, West Virginia, Kentucky, Tennessee, and North Carolina. Their counterparts will be found across the country from Oregon and California to New Mexico, Pennsylvania, and Maine.

We think it is accurate to portray most of these groups as on the margins of the mainstream, often participating in the established political processes of the liberal-democratic polity and frequently expecting far more than they "get" from this arena surrounded and dominated as it is by the type of political economy we call the *corporate state*. One of several reasons we name this a corporate state is because the large corporation is as much a political entity as it is an economic entity. The mainstream myth of the "free market" blurs this by encouraging people to make a mental split or reified distinction between the "political" and the "economic" and to assume that the problem of corporate power is automatically checked or even nonexistent. What has happened is that the potentially democratic space between market and state has been foreclosed as corporate power has moved into the gap and been given legal sanction. One challenge we must put forth to our readers is consideration of the extent to which big corporations have shaped the American system of constitutional law to their chief goals and in the process threatened popular capacities for democratic participation.[3] By contrast, the Community Environmental Legal Defense Fund (CELDF) working with citizens and community groups in Pennsylvania and other states (and in Ecuador, as discussed in our final chapter) is giving new life to the legacy of the democratic republic and the vision of a more democratic and egalitarian society than the one that looms over our spirit today. We want to illuminate this legacy and the democratic vision that animates it. We propose that this living memory be taken up by social and political theorists as one vital task for helping reorganize and reorient a citizen-based politics in the United States that can both forge more accountable forms of power and clear paths of popular action for a more sustainable, just, and humane world.

The American legacy of democratic republicanism and its creative reconstruction by John Dewey, Hannah Arendt, and Wendell Berry provides expressive power for helping mobilize citizens determined to confront challenges to both polity and planet. Discussing "writing as an act of hope," Isabel Allende's words seem pertinent: "We dare to think that humanity is not going to destroy itself . . . we write—as an act of human solidarity and commitment to the future. We want to change the rules, even if we won't live long enough to see the results. We have to make real revolutions of the spirit, of values, of life. And to do so we have to begin dreaming them" (Allende, 1989, 55–56). We write to invoke the American dream of a democratic republic even if, in the short run, the most we can expect is restoration of the liberal-democratic polity that might permit serious public reconsideration of the imperialist tendencies of the transnational corporate state. The "American dream" of which we speak is not an academic pipedream. Rather, we have found attractive versions of this vision of a democratic republic animating various forms of citizen action politics in which we have been involved. In Connolly's language the key issue is whether "eco-egalitarian capitalism" is possible. His conclusion is that "progress on this front is possible though not highly probable" (Connolly, 2008, 117). For us the question is whether political strategy infused by democratic republican imagery is the clearest path to eco-egalitarian capitalism as an interim agenda this side of democratic transformation. Democratic transformation does not culminate in restoring the "relative autonomy" of the liberal-democratic polity. Rather, it would entail democratizing its structures and their linkages with civil society and reinstituting policies in a healthier global ecology of relations with other states.

We seek to contribute to an alternative politics for the United States that both cultivates grassroots democracy here and connects meaningfully with the still inchoate global justice movement. Those of us who seek such a politics must dare to dream. We propose a vision blending old and new, tradition and innovation, history and experimentation. In some ways, it is a vision already guiding many of us; in other ways, there are great lessons that will come only with energetic commitment and political experience honestly earned. We envision a cooperative commonwealth of sustainable communities and regions centered by a new multisectoral and multileveled democratic public sphere open to various and competing idealizations of community, region, nation, and new global arenas of cooperation and experiment. Such a politics must be clear minded about the enormity of the American challenge: a transnational corporate state that seems bent on returning to the authoritarian politics of empire. Again, Connolly's terms: "To the extent that inspirational leaders in churches, labor unions, localities, corporations, and public office do not emerge, the growing sense of the fragility of things could intensify a negative dynamic already in motion, increasing the prospect for a fascistic version of capitalism in America" (Connolly, 2008, 115).

If this corporate system of political economy is not rolled back to release public spaces for other civil society structures and initiatives valuing democratic participation and cooperative action, recent trends toward oligarchy and empire will accelerate in growing demands for systematic crisis coordination. It is past time to stop exaggerating the strengths of our liberal-democratic polity to deal with interlocking crises it has helped produce. Some of our most perceptive environmental historians and theorists have pointed out that in recent decades the mainstreaming of the U.S. environmental policy system and some of the wealthiest environmental nongovernmental organizations (NGOs) has included the discarding of the "human bodily side of the environmentalist imaginary" (Sellers, 1999, 31–64).

This cultural and political "body-blindness" is connected with the denigration of local knowledge not only in the policy system but also in education and even in the larger environmental movement. This body-blindness is a crucial element in the technocratic managerial ideologies of industrial capitalism that are part and parcel of the causes of our present environmental crises and are bound up (in complicated ways) with the long history of subject/object dualisms in Western thinking. In the last several decades, this technocratic managerialism—with its attendant body-blindness—has increasingly infected environmental theory, as U.S. environmentalist discourses have moved into mainstream policymaking, while corporations are appropriating green language, if not substantively green action, in the process some call *green-washing*.

Christopher Sellers, trained in medicine and American studies, has provided a fascinating and fresh look at the struggles since World War II in both the environmental movement and what we prefer to call the *corporate state* (he refers to the "liberal state"), affecting especially the intertwined fate of body and place (Gottlieb, 1993; Sellers, 1999). Sellers, drawing on and elaborating the theory of environmental imaginaries, shows how they entail characteristic ways of framing the human body. Going beyond the conservationism of earlier decades, the postwar U.S. environmental movement in Sellers's brilliant historical interpretation was a "grassroots political success" particularly insofar as it saw "the human body as itself environmentally threatened, alongside birds or other wildlife or forests or land." This enabled a political movement "across lines of gender, class, and, eventually, ethnicity and race." However, these "bodily concerns tended to be suppressed as . . . their imaginary as well as their praxis" was adjusted to what Sellers calls "the institutional and cultural constraints of the postwar liberal state" (Sellers, 1999, 33–34).

Our book seeks to provide a more powerful historical and theoretical perspective in which to situate Sellers's insights. He richly documents and charts the political as well as social costs of body-blindness or bodily disenfranchisement in mainstream environmentalism, much of environmental science, and the corporate state system of environmental management. (What Sellers labels "naturalistic human ecology," we would prefer to call a *reductionist, physicalist ecology*). Restating Sellers's attentive discussion of the "environmental justice" groups of the 1990s, we see an emergent development for the recovery and renewal within a broader grassroots globalization movement of body, place, and a world-in-common. We need at once a broader and deeper understanding of what he calls "those bodily concerns that had energized the movement at its grassroots" (Sellers, 1999, 57).

As climate change overturns what seemed to be settled assumptions, we seem to be moving past the mainstream environmentalism that was said to be a largely conservationist, white, male effort to conserve wild areas for recreation and aesthetic and spiritual renewal. That approach drew much of its energy and sensibility from people in a class position to utilize surplus wealth to free themselves from the space-time of industrial production to savor relatively undamaged natural wilds. Little wonder that some Global South writers, from a distance, mistook this approach as the whole of American environmentalism. The newly resurgent citizen politics, however, gets its energy from people who act precisely because they feel trapped by an inability to evade the ecological damage of industrial production and an outrage that that damage has invaded the space of immediate lifeworld/body that the "myth of progress" or the "American dream" had promised them as the payoff for the vicissitudes of work and class.[4] If there is to be a breakthrough in climate change politics here would seem to be its cutting edge.

A figure who has become iconic in the United States of this new sort of activist is Lois Gibbs, a housewife who lived along Love Canal. She began her fight against toxic waste from within a self-identity as housewife and mother. But, shocked by her lack of power as a concerned citizen, she expanded this ethic of private caring into a highly articulated ethic of public action for structural political and economic change. As she wove these various identities together in novel ways, she began to see the mechanisms of the corporate state hidden by the national mainstream. This path out of the progressivist myth of the national symbolic and its divisions of work and family/leisure/nature, is one that more and more people are traveling as capitalist production cuts closer to the lifeworld.

The leaders of these new environmentalisms are people who see economic space falling in harmful ways over particular places that people experience as constitutive of who they are. They have energized, expanded, diversified, and radicalized environmental politics. These leaders are much more likely than earlier national leadership to come from, and to speak to, people of color, women, the disaffected young, and working-class communities. The point of rupture, then, that engenders this new politics comes when the two thin lines that we have described fall in contradiction in a place from which a person cannot run because it is inextricably woven into their identity or existence. Academic "realists" cynically defending the liberal-democratic polity of consumers and established elites shortchange this new politics of democratic hope. The placed, embodied, and engaged citizens caring for a world-in-common suit the vision of a democratic republic.

The Democratic Revolution and Capitalist Bypass Surgery

From monarchy to republicanism to democracy is the drastically simplified history of our political system, as told by some of our most interesting and esteemed historians.[5] They thus accommodate mainstream myth partly by refusing the concept of "liberal democracy," which requires attention to troubling issues in an ongoing politics of inequality rooted in tensions of capitalist economy and a liberal-democratic polity. Claiming such a monopoly on "democracy" for the dominant system feeds both a messianic view of "America" and a tendency to marginalize any sort of "populism" that challenges the framework.

Andrew Shankman's study of the struggle to fuse egalitarianism and capitalism in Jeffersonian Pennsylvania is on the mark in suggesting that here is the "crucible of American democracy" (Shankman, 2004). How historians, young and established, settle their accounts is a small matter at a time when an oligarchical politics is not only integral to unprecedented forms of socioeconomic inequality but also is making a shambles of various claims to democracy including certain academic ones. The desire to maintain egalitarianism in the presence of capitalism of some type has indeed fed numerous struggles often involving the meaning of democracy itself. Scholars who appreciate the increasingly illusionary aspects of popular versions of the American dream might well confront the tragic limits of our liberal-democratic polity unable to slip the boundaries of a corporate consumer culture fueling catastrophic climate change ultimately impacting the whole planet. Yet several seem to think a more convincing apologetic for the existing system and a more inventive appeal to its elites may work.

How the latest forms of corporate power relate to democratic politics will not be understood without critical, self-reflexive attention to global labor and resource markets and to the role of global investor classes that provide both financial and cultural/ideological support. Social and political theorists as well as grassroots activists must get to a new clarity about these issues. One of the most promising scholarly developments is work that engages historic republicanism's concern with chronic structures of dependency discussed in the preceding chapter. Impressively Michael Thompson (M. Thompson, 2007) argues that (a) a democratic society cannot sustain itself under conditions of extreme inequality, and (b) political renewal today must go beyond notions of equal opportunity and individual rights and instead resuscitate republican traditions of social equality, civic virtue, and democratic creativity. Reform liberalism has facilitated "serious gains in the areas of race and gender," but the wellspring for replenishing struggles against persistent economic domination and class hierarchy fogged over by "culture wars" is elsewhere. If the mainstream environmentalism we described above is dead, then it died with that type of liberal reform that fantasized a post-material way of life that did not need inequality on its agenda.

In Thompson's view and ours, the retuning of democracy has its most vibrant forms in "the political impulses of the American republican tradition that inspired the critique of inequality and sustained the discourse for well over a century as capitalism continued to mature and develop" (M. Thompson, 2007, 194–96). Ironically, one of the ways liberal individualism's hegemony has been advanced is by exaggerating its popularity in the past. When reform liberalism's roots in the classical liberal tradition are obscured, our reactionary liberals tend to become more intolerant and romantic and reform liberals more insecure and self-righteous, but the salient fact is that both have inventive ways of dodging issues of power and justice. And today needed historical clarity is sacrificed when the term *liberal* is employed as an ideologically broad canopy while *populist* becomes another omnifarious term of largely negative reference. The overall effect is to suspend critical concern with ways that corporate capitalism generates unaccountable configurations of power that are the flip side of the everyday domination that accompanies abusive forms of socioeconomic inequality. The political orientation and self-understanding we seek is grounded by historical knowledge that locates the democratic heart of the new nation without ignoring or getting stitched into the capitalist bypass surgery it has undergone.

The 1787 framers' successful effort to structure the new republic is too often identified with the democratic revolution of the eighteenth century that was inseparable from "the development of an autonomous public with its own 'opinion,'" to use Charles Taylor's words. That new model of public space was not at all a *government* realm to be opened to larger numbers of people. What is innovative, even revolutionary, is *the space of public discourse itself,* a bounded space of common recognition and concern, "a new force in history" (C. Taylor, 1990, 108–9). Michael Warner's brilliant study of eighteenth-century American "republicanism as metadiscourse" makes exactly this case by not collapsing this emergent public sphere into the classical politics of elitist virtue (soon to be ended by a modern liberal conception of interest politics). When he writes that the new "print discourse made it possible to imagine a people that could act as a people and in distinction from the state" (Warner, 1990, xiii), he accounts for a radical/conservative tension in American egalitarianism that depictions of the liberal-democratic polity as progressive modernization typically obscure.

The fact is that some of our most influential and brilliant historians share the liberal phobia for "populism" or "mass politics." Their role as keepers of the "official hermeneutics" generally has been shared by political scientists fretting over the difficulties of containing democratic theory within familiar American boundaries. Warner joins Goodwyn and Lasch in recognizing, however, that the "modern nation does not have citizens in the same way that the republic does." As he puts it, you "can be a member of the nation, attributing its agency to yourself in imaginary identification, without being a freeholder or exercising any agency in the public sphere" (Warner, 1990, 173). Lasch made it very clear that American liberals would do well to replace the progressive notion of history with a new understanding of populism. He granted that as time went on and "large-scale enterprise crowded out small producers, petty-bourgeois movements became increasingly defensive and allied themselves with some of the worst impulses in modern life—anti-intellectualism, xenophobia, racism." Reform liberals, instead of fixing on this and culturally enclaving themselves as "the civilized minority," should realize that this "same tradition of plebeian radicalism gave rise to the only serious attempt to answer the great question of twentieth-century politics: what was to replace proprietorship as the material foundation of civic virtue?" (Lasch, 1991, 531). A democratic republic has to have a politics seriously addressing this question.

While Warner is careful not to make too much of the late-eighteenth-century republican paradigm of print discourse, he does disclose a fleeting moment of democratic promise and public virtue that was overwhelmed in the next century by the social formation of private liberal subjects caught up in the opportunities of frontier market society. In short, he does not make the mistake of putting all his democratic eggs in the basket of emerging "liberal society" the limits to which Louis Hartz (Hartz, 1955) refused to forget even as some of his readers were to label him a "consensus historian." Liberal democratic politics at its best has worked to constrain elites while promoting hope in the main chance for the many. Still, never more than in this time of global ecological crisis do we need to remember that this is just one form of democratic politics, granting its historical weight in the United States. Both before and beyond the limited democratic advances of the Jacksonians we need to remember that this new, only potentially democratic public space quickly became the site of struggles to inaugurate new forms of domination as well as existing ones based on race, gender, and so on. *The displacement and domestication of the democratic revolution has been going on since it began.* Most of the framers of the 1787 Constitution were conservative republicans determined to contain this new democratic movement.

John Kasson's important study of nineteenth-century America begins here in its documentation of conservative republican efforts over several decades to institutionalize and legitimate new capitalist technologies. The 1830s and 1840s saw remarkable radical republican critiques from Seth Luther, Orestes Brownson, and others that resonated in worker resistance and protest at Lowell and elsewhere (Kasson, 1977, 86–106). As Eric Foner has said of the general era bridged by the Civil War: "The ideologies of nineteenth century labor and farmers' movements, and even early-twentieth-century socialism itself, owed more to traditional republican notions of the equal citizen and the independent small producer than to the coherent analysis of class-divided society" (Foner, 2002, 123).

Nevertheless, the century saw not only the cultural and political turmoil of such conflicts but also institution building increasingly led by capitalist elites. The new system's legitimacy in much of public opinion turned especially on the vision of America's destiny as "nature's nation" merging with the history of a "rapidly developing industrial power" (Kasson, 1977, 174). The century's last decade witnessed the translation of this mythos into 1896 presidential politics by industrialist Marcus Hanna for the victorious William McKinley, portrayed as the "nation's protector of order and . . . 'advance agent of prosperity'" (Kazin, 1998, 43).

It must also be remembered how this mythos was embodied in the White City opening at Chicago's World Fair in 1893 and also symbolized the triumph of a white racism in American society. Racism was not merely a regional problem but a massive social reality pervading the political dynamics of what has been called *modernization* (Trachtenberg, 1982). That such an American polity shaped mainly by conservative republicanism, institutional racism, and liberal capitalism for a hundred years would prove resistant to democratic transformation by the Populist movement is less surprising than the ambivalent role of subsequent reform movements in midwifing a system prone to the "sorrows of empire" (Johnson, 2004).

Chalmers Johnson has provided a more than adequate examination of Woodrow Wilson's anti-colonial imperialism, stressing the idealistic grounding given to capitalist expansionism (Johnson, 2004, 47–51, 189). Amy Kaplan's brilliant analysis of the struggles with U.S. imperialism of Mark Twain and W. E. B. Du Bois must also be noted. Mindful of the limits of Du Bois's politics in the era of Wilsonian Progressivism, Kaplan retrieves his powerful analysis of "the racial formation of class in America as part of the global anarchy of empire" (Kaplan, 2002, 193–212). Studies by Kaplan and the late Michael Rogin help us to understand that the national unity Wilson sought in war included the white supremacy reflected in D. W. Griffith's *Birth of a Nation* (1915), the film premiering at the White House. Rogin's insight into the anti-Populist dimension of the "intertwined racial, class, and imperial histories that lie behind *Birth* helps illuminate the political repression of labor that was so acute before 1935" (Rogin, 1987, 341, 66–67). The biracial Populist alliance was never strong or secure and ultimately failed, but its democratic potential disturbed ruling elites and those determined to shape another American future.

As Rogin puts it, Wilson, defending the war against the Philippines and joining his novelist friend Reverend Thomas Dixon, linked "the racial question at home to America's world mission abroad" (Rogin, 1987, 194). (Rogin and Kaplan both probe the varied connections and occasional deviations involving Griffith, Dixon, and Wilson). What Kaplan shows is that the "international perspective on whiteness" in Du Bois's 1920 work *Darkwater*, "its imperial cartography," is vital for a fuller understanding of the idea of the "wages of whiteness" set forth in his monumental 1935 study of black Reconstruction and its aftermath. We must set aside some of the complexities

Kaplan and Rogin examine, but it is sufficient for our purposes to emphasize that the U.S. road to empire is cemented in both corporate capital's drive to control labor whether in West Virginia or Guatemala and in the political limits of racialized policies mired in a regenerate national identity.

By the 1920s the elite-dominated process linking technology, abundance, and capitalist democracy had not only paved the way for the recasting of consumption as a cultural ideal but also for an increasingly commodified politics reproducing the citizen as another consumer. It is a much more complex story than space allows, but Alexander Hamilton, Tench Coxe, their heirs, and contemporary apologists suggest deep elitist roots for the ongoing problem of democratic façades for corporate cultural domination. Understanding the problem, however, may depend on appreciating how New Deal reform ended up facilitating both the corporate state and a more fair and equal (but still racialized) consumer culture. In some ways the latter strengthened what Dewey called "democratic publics," but the overall result has been more of a parody than anything else.

Alan Brinkley's work documents what should not be glossed, and that is the reformers' "accommodation with modern capitalism" by 1945. Earlier in the Depression years, breaking with the laissez-faire liberal faith in the market, these "progressive" exponents of liberal reform had confronted corporate power and socioeconomic inequality by espousing forms of government intervention aimed at individual and community protections while trying to "balance" competing blocs of power. Most importantly, Brinkley has illuminated how and why "the reform liberalism of the New Deal years gave way to the consumer-oriented liberalism of the postwar era" (Brinkley, 1995, 8–10, 265–71). Thomas Ferguson, utilizing Gramsci's concept of historical blocs, has traced a multinational (capitalist) bloc from 1918 into the late 1970s, helping explain the role of new information technologies and global markets in the restructuring of the corporate state-dominated system (Ferguson, 1989, 7–24). Ira Katznelson's analysis of the Democratic Party's failure to launch cross-race, class-based policies due partly to an expert-oriented "interest group pluralism" also illuminates its vulnerability to the Right's charges of "special interests" since the Carter-Reagan years (Katznelson, 1989, 202–4). It might be said that the Clinton administration became ground zero for the convergence of multinational liberalism, corporate multiculturalism, and consumer culture.

It has become easy in contemporary America to forget or neglect the role of multiple civil society movements in breaking through and altering the boundaries of the liberal-democratic polity. Installing the civil rights movement into the great American museum of status quo celebration rituals, the rights-based liberalism described by Brinkley tends to create different scales for weighing Diversity and Inequality. Perhaps no one should be surprised at the degree of capitulation to corporate restructuring of the economy and the corporate state's turn to neoliberal globalization. But the commitment to Economic Growth (and the idea of consumption as its key) in a fossil fuel–based system is dead-ending in imperial disasters, new levels of economic insecurity, and an unprecedented global ecological crisis.

In the postwar context including pervasive Cold War apologetics, the polity's national security sector "forged intimate partnerships with the corporate world" (Brinkley, 1998, 93). (Bring to mind the 1950s U.S. interventions in Iran and Guatemala.) For David Harvey, writing in the Bush-Cheney years, this is the core institutional domain of the "new imperialism" that operates, however successfully or not, to intertwine "territorial and capitalistic logics of power" (Harvey, 2005, 145). Political realism and historical credibility are absent in the notion that the liberal-democratic polity has suffered from a deficit of elite power that is partly alleviated by the projection of mass consumption into this century as surely as it became predominant in the last. The intellectual foolishness of "republicanizing" the consumer culture and its identity politics should be clear.

Democratic Struggles and Corporate State Modernization as "Progress"

What is needed instead is a focus on the transnational corporate state centrally implicated in a catastrophic climate crisis cracking windows onto persistent global as well as national issues of class, race, and gender. Professional cynicism has its affinities with that curious combination of notions of "consumer sovereignty" and "mass society" embedded in corporate attempts to engineer consent, even to manufacture public opinion, one of the most conspicuous projects of twentieth-century America. Depoliticizing aspects of this capitalist utopian "consumption" project have taken a variety of forms including the post-1989 wave of "cold war triumphalism" that occasionally seemed to give impetus to academic capitalism (Schrecker, 2004). This intellectual mood, reaching far beyond the American Right, has poorly served democratic discourse regarding increasingly conspicuous realities of unequal power and elite-skewed policies of our transnational corporate state. In any case, the last half of the twentieth century saw a deterioration of public space and the marginalizing of public discourse as the corporate state both grew to live off of the liberal-democratic polity and reconfigure it as a new weapon of constitutional inequality. One example is the NAFTA trade policy regime and its contribution to what is sometimes described as "trading democracy" Gill, 2002). The corporate state's trade policy regime allows overruling democratically legislated public policies because they are deemed violations of "free trade." American elites have oversold globalization even as its links to accelerating ecological crisis have become glaring. Charges of "protectionism" and "liberal" nostalgia for the territorial state should be set aside in favor of vigorous attention to forms and issues of democratic space.

What is called *globalization* trails a long history, but it is the globalizing or neoliberal policies distinctive of a transnational corporate state that is overwhelming the liberal-democratic polity, setting it unmistakably on a historically familiar road of empire. Some of our political ancestors of a century ago came to see the key issue as one of "republic or empire." Our own time not surprisingly has seen a flurry of studies and tracts renewing this debate amid even more troubling circumstances, not least of all the links between the political and social clout of the fossil fuel industry and global warming. The propaganda to which we refer, increasingly coated in green wash, has scored in right-wing "populist" and evangelical Christian circles, although there have been countervailing tendencies in both groups. "Is God green?" has become a serious question increasingly asked in church circles sometimes competing with a resurgence of apocalyptic fatalism. And the traditional social justice question "How much should a person consume?" is, in the same circles, garnering a greener sensibility.

But those Americans who think of themselves as "progressives" need to confront Lasch's suggestion that there is no cultural or political mileage in "a distrust of everything but science" and an "ingrained irreverence" linked to a disposition "to see the world as something that exists only to gratify human desires" (Lasch, 1991, 527). Lasch saw himself writing in the wake of an exhausted progressive tradition that needed a new understanding of the populist tradition grounded in some ways in the republican tradition we have been discussing. When Tim Luke, building on Lasch's historical analysis, refers to the same grassroots groups we have been discussing as advancing a "populist social ecology," he draws exactly the lines of political choice we have in mind.

Adapting Luke's terms: from the 1890s to the 1990s and today, struggles with an eroding quality of life, disempowerment, and a growing "awareness of limits" has moved them in a populist/republican direction. The guiding principles were (and still are) "notions of widespread competence, shared governance, and ordinary ownership—ideas that progressive new class managers contained with their utopias of consumption and clientage from big business and big government" (Luke, 1999, 224). Academics and other members of the professional middle class have begun to detect the extent to which corporate state narratives of modernization as progress often conceal an anti-ecological arrogance abusing both technology and communities while weakening cultural possibilities for pursuing alternative modernities. Our contention is that the professional resort to imagery of political containment and technocratic progress only accelerates democratic decline and ecological disaster.

There are several reasons for this state of affairs, but we might do well to recapitulate three main arguments to this point. First, is the degree to which since the early nineteenth century the *market myth* increasingly has held sway in various forms of American culture, generating a "market metaphysics" that keeps rebounding to crudely limit what is called *mainstream politics.* Second is a *corporate state* system of political economy advancing unevenly through the decades since the late nineteenth century but by the 1980s engulfing as never before the liberal-democratic polity. Third, more often than not this corporate state has generated a cultural horizoning of professional worlds that insinuates the political *need for elite power.* It is more subtle and complex than an issue of managerial ideology. In recent decades professional participation (usually as junior partners) in the Global Investor Class has compounded the problem. The democratic reconstruction of professional life is an important dimension of the struggle for democratic spaces attuned to the lived ecological experiences and possibilities of communities whatever their geographies.

The last several decades of the nineteenth century saw the drafting of the first chapter of this massive system of power as intellectuals as different as Mark Twain, W. E. B. Du Bois, and John Dewey came to understand. Those decades generated a cultural and political crisis that favored narratives of national Progress either have ignored or misconstrued. Nevertheless, by 1890 "the richest 1 percent of Americans received the same total income as the bottom half of the population and owned more property than the remaining 99 percent" (Foner, 1998, 117). As early as 1889, the Arkansas Populist W. Scott Morgan described the scene in these terms: "Monopoly is wielding a greater power in the government than the people. While general discontent prevails, the masses of the people who suffer all the evils of class legislation have been disunited, and charging each other with being the cause of their ills" (Pollack, 1967, 31). In our own time, when growing inequalities in the United States as well as the rest of the world are unmistakable, some social theorists such as Craig Calhoun and Timothy Brennan are beginning to question the academic investments that apparently make it difficult to see corporate globalization for the "class legislation" it mainly is! The looming global ecological crisis as well as the global jobs crisis should be even more compelling.

The late nineteenth century was the period of emergence for a corporate state system of political economy based on the corporate capture of the environmental commons and the displacement of local communities as a significant realm for participating in the civic commons. Writing from a producer republican and Christian socialist perspective in 1894, Henry Demarest Lloyd's *Wealth against Commonwealth* clearly captured the key issue of corporate power's challenge to democracy itself. Historian Ray Ginger documented many years ago that this period saw the political collaboration of Lloyd, Governor John Peter Altgeld, Florence Kelley, and Jane Addams of Hull House (Ginger, 1965, 133). Lloyd was inspired by Wendell Phillips, who had died in 1884 and who left with us a powerful address making the case for scholar-agitators as the lifeblood of the republic. Lloyd's work for a political alliance of farmers and factory workers drew upon the great insight he found in Phillips's view of the essential continuity between the abolitionist movement against slavery and the movement for labor's rights. The Populist/Labor cause foundered especially in the domain of racial and ethnic tensions while national reconciliation was to be worked out on more reactionary auspices as we have indicated.

Critical remembrance of this great struggle against corporate power for a democratic republic was seldom easy in a twentieth century so caught up in the ideology of modernity embedded in the grand narrative of corporate state modernization as Progress. Nevertheless, we would do well to recall Lloyd's view that "free trade" not be used as a cover for imperialism. As he said, "Trade that exchanges the products of slave labor, whether of plantation or slum, cannot be free" (qtd. in Pollack, 1962, 96–97). One year after *Wealth against Commonwealth* was published, the newly formed National Association of Manufacturers met in Cincinnati (1895) to lobby for "government help in opening foreign markets" (Beatty, 2007, 388). The dance with empire may not have begun in the 1890s, but it did begin to acquire some uniquely American steps as the new century opened. Uncertainty and ambivalence about colonialism in public opinion would seem to be a political link to the notion of "making the world safe for democracy." Noreena Hertz of the Cambridge University business school has made the important point that talk of "spreading democracy" often conceals the liberal-democratic theme of "market economy" that often translates into the American art of making "politics out of money" (Hertz, 2002, 99–103). So it is well to remember that while the liberal-democratic polity has generated anti-imperialist critics and reformers, this has not prevented it from serving corporate state projects in brutal ways. Indeed the confusion of democracy with capitalism is a longstanding problem in American culture that has to be addressed. This corporate state has drawn upon peculiarly American versions of the bourgeois-liberal tradition and the technological world-picture, a complex process that has legitimated (or, in Gramscian terms, "hegemonized") integral structures of a complex class society, authoritarian technics, and consumer (or mass) culture.

Today, the privatization of public policies and the corporate appropriation of state agencies is so rampant that familiar terms such as *government-business partnerships* seem antiquated. The language of concentrated economic power assisted by state intervention and coordination seems less adequate than even a few decades ago. The fast capitalist metamorphoses of the "political" and the "economic" are raining new forms of unaccountable power on much of the world and America. But the cultural/ideological raincoats that outfit Americans for living in the era of "disaster capitalism" are among the most amazing constructions known to humanity. They help explain why one of our best legal scholars could write: "No socialist economy has ever had the command-and-control capacities of the American corporation" (Mitchell, 2002, B13). This is an enormous problem in our public culture and is only compounded when academics, especially historians and political scientists, become averse to examining "the role of ruling elites in the country's evolution" (S. Fraser & Gerstle, 2005, B13). In the 1950s the noted conservative journalist Walter Lippmann was more candid about the need for elite power. His "public philosophy" of 1955 made the case for getting "mass opinion" in place to pave the way for political leadership and what in that era was called *national purpose*. When academic liberals claim the issue is leadership, they should instead be focusing on the problems of democratic space and the conditions confronting citizens. Silliness about "consumer freedom" has various sources and is highly implicated in the popular American confusion of democracy and capitalism on which corporate power thrives.

The development of the American corporate state has been inseparable from the construction of a consumer culture that has enfolded a reconstituted citizenship and a new ideology of citizens as consumers, that is, "voters." Political scientists such as Schaar and Garson have indicated how, during the last third of the nineteenth century, capitalism became equated with America itself. "At the very time when the free enterprise system was being swallowed by the corporate system, the ideology of free enterprise became identified with the spirit of Americanism" (Garson, 1973–1974; Schaar, 1981, 295). Schaar makes this point in the context of an analysis of American amnesia for the Lincolnian conception of covenanted patriotism based on an informed citizenry's dedication to founding principles in the Declaration of Independence and the Constitution. Garson and Schaar may be read as documenting the reduction of republican citizenship to the rituals of a voter-oriented "citizenship" as nationalist ideology.

In John Schaar's view, we need a patriotism that weakens the principle of nationalism and strives to break its connections with the state (Schaar, 1981). Schaar's analysis of the corruption of patriotism by nationalism and the cult of progress refused to see the political imagination of the nation inevitably reduced to statism or tribalism. Thirty years later it is clear that the latest cult of progress typically takes the form of a "globalism" rationalizing ever more placeless, vacuous shells of republican citizenship. The lopsided debates over NAFTA and the WTO provide recent measures of how deeply the Lincolnian ideal of republican citizenship has been submerged in "consumer freedom," a corporate state baptismal pledging allegiance to the market machine-god. However, as John Berger recently reminds us, the "consumer is essentially somebody who feels, or is made to feel, lost, unless he or she is consuming. Brand names and logos," he adds, "become the place names of the Nowhere." Most importantly, he is saying we are losing places as territories of experience (Berger, 2007, 119–27).

Over sixty years ago, Karl Polanyi predicted that the faith in a self-regulating market would move humanity toward the "demolition of society" and the annihilation of "all organic forms of existence" (Polanyi, 1957 [1944]: 73, 157, 163). In John Berger's comments on "some photos taken in the Red Cross shelter for refugees and emigrants at Sangatte (near Calais) by Anabell Guerrero" we find a lesson in the expendability of what we call *body~place~commons*. The photos give account to "how a man's fingers are all that remain of a plot of tilled earth, his palms what remain of some riverbed, and his eyes are a family gathering he will not attend" (Berger, 2007, 120–21). The question that too many mobile academics don't want to ask is exactly the one Berger insists on asking: "Where are we?" Call this system of power whatever you will, Berger says, "Its aim is to delocalize the entire world." "Its ideological strategy," he contends, "is to undermine the existent so that everything collapses into its special version of the virtual" hooked to the goal of endless profit (42–43).

The unspoken premise of "citizenship" modeled on Consumer Freedom is the expendability of landscapes, places, the commons, and their forms of life. The great ecological threat of this corporate state system of political economy that keeps trumpeting "consumer freedom" is increasingly recognized by topnotch environmental scientists. For example, James Gustave Speth says in a new book: "We are rapidly hollowing out nature, ourselves, and our society... [leading to] a ruined planet" (Speth, 2008, 236–37, cf. 225–30). Speth also detects a new consciousness and hears emerging a new movement for fundamental change. Our central effort is to cultivate the ground these seek beyond the disastrous dualisms of the transnational corporate state.

Dualist Horizons of the Transnational Corporate State

The crisis of civil society partly reflected in expanding political alienation is directly related to the exploitive plans of corporate managers and their junior partners and functionaries in the corporate state. At the core of the pluralistic processes of corporate state planning in the transnational era is global economic space, a shroud drawn over the world as a resource object. What must be confronted, however, is the extent to which transnational class rationalizations of the extension or remodeling of this functionalized space draw upon the ideological treasury of the technological worldview.

Moreover, the objectivist fantasies of "technological progress" of this transnational class are projected from a subjectivist posture the constitution of which must not be overlooked. What is involved is a positioning of the subject that reflects the covert myth of the phoenix self: from the ashes of the civil society it is helping raze, the transnationalist anticipates flight into postcommunality. The phoenix self and the postcommunal society—the magnetic poles for the global dreaming emanating from our corporate state's body-machine complex—have been forged from popular narratives of freedom and progress. The historic-specific cultural horizons of the technological world picture and liberal individualism are grounded by the corporate state body-machine complex out of which they are evoked as the operative or instrumental categories of *official* knowledge. The transnational capitalist class (Sklair, 1991, 6–8, 238) of symbolic analysts is situated here and working from this context generates and deploys the texts, models, and images of global economic space just mentioned.

In the technological worldview, the lifeworld of being is compartmentalized in realms of "nature" and "culture," and economics is constituted as one more technically "rational" tool aimed at facilitating human mastery. This ontological dualism characterizes jointly the structure of modern Western capitalism's "natural order" as well as the bourgeois subject whose instrumentally "rational" behavior fuels the economic machine and its functionalizing logic (Reid, 2001b). In the United States the nineteenth-century institutionalization of the technological world picture and the growing hegemony of liberal individualism became pillars of the twentieth century's corporate state. Social policies developed largely under the sway of these cultural/ideological horizons have generated political struggles marking their instability and inadequacy as hegemonic frames. But it is the complementarity, the dialectical nexus of these horizons, that we want to emphasize.

Atop this political culture was an ideological layer that had as its core ingredient a liberal myth or ideal of self-enclosed subjectivity including the enclosed body (essentially male as a matter of historical fact). Its operational terms were caught in Tocqueville's analysis of the prevalent "philosophic method" in the Jacksonian America of liberal capitalism in its heyday. His identification of the self-enclosed Cartesian ego is followed by an emphasis on a pervasive instrumentally rational approach to the world (Tocqueville, 1956, 143–83). As technology developed, popular orators of antebellum America such as Daniel Webster invoked a "rhetoric of the technological sublime" to reconcile American imagery of the "machine in the garden," assuring the citizenry of the democratic results of its capitalist auspices (Marx, 1964; Porter, 1985, chap. 3, 312–13). Remember, however, that the public mind in this era made a rational distinction between anti-*corporate* and anti-*business* sentiment, with the former targeting legislatively established monopoly privileges that could only be justified, if at all, in terms of service to the common good. But that is just why the coupling of democracy and capitalist technology in the public mind was so ominous. Ted Nace's important study (Nace, 2005) of the "corporate revolution" that took place between 1850 and 1900 describes how and why the antebellum system of control over what Jefferson called in 1816 "the aristocracy of our monied corporations" gave way. Our own purpose here is to have excavated the ideological roots of twenty-first-century images of a "Consumer Republic" in conservative republicanism. Our argument is to discard such a camouflage for the transnational corporate state as worse than useless for critical, democratic social theory.

The corporate state institutionalized, through highly contested terrain from roughly 1880 to 1970, a system of largely authoritarian technics affected partly through the magnificent bribe of "consumer freedom." The institutional anchoring of the technological world picture in the bureaucratization of modes of instrumental rationality steered by managerial elites has never been a smooth process. American mainstream politics and corporate management have resonated with the rhetoric of "progress," "growth," and, more recently, "environmental management." As the system has hurtled from one impasse to another, the hegemony of the monopoly sector has involved much more than the profit-oriented hierarchical control of the mode of production.

What social theorists once described as the industrialization of cultural life in an expanding consumerism has been dynamized by the informatics of the "new" corporate state in transnational operations throughout the global system. The control problems in this new system for those at the highest levels of power have, alas, led some academics and pundits to suggest it is really one big power puzzle somehow signaled by the Marx and Engels prophecy: "All that is sold melts into air." It would be a mistake to overlook what Neil Lazarus (Lazarus, 1991, 114) has termed "the enduring *systematicity* of capitalism" by fixing on the postmodern ethos of this new cyberculture disseminating from and to projects of global economic space. This is one electronic "fix" from which some postmodern theorists can get unhooked if not unplugged through recuperative modes of civil society and democratic politics. But in the roaring 1990s the appeal of the academic market for some seemed too great to resist the lure of postcommunal professionalism. John Dewey's model of civic professionalism seemed antiquated and unfit for exciting experiments in "self-fulfillment." Community struggles to maintain social ecologies were so many distractions from the professional calculations of academic markets.

When the Calvinist saints such as the Reverend John Cotton preached a "certain deadnesse to the world" amid diligent attention to business, they also counseled earnest efforts of public duty. Contemporary consumer culture encrusts its believers in an electronic shell of rationalized and sensationalized world imagery generating a numbness at once for public life and genuinely intimate life. Perhaps Merleau-Ponty's rereading of Weber provides needed historical insights into the ontological dichotomization of life and thought at the core of bourgeois-liberal culture: the subjectivization of existence and the objectivization of world ascetically and parasitically abstracted from a larger, encompassing, and open-ended experience of society and nature. Merleau-Ponty's "Weberian Marxist" reading of this history, this "strange object . . . which is ourselves," this "historical matter" with its "unique fiber of human choices" (Merleau-Ponty, 1964a, 193–210) recovers our right to judge the past and to question the master tale of history working according to the external model of the Market, the global social order's salvation by a machine-god.

The Progressivist Left, Objectivism, and the Lure of Globalization

It must also be said it is past time to set aside another master tale of history, what appears to be an effort of ideological resuscitation that would see in globalization's garb not a capitalist wolf but the socialist lamb of revolution. Perhaps this helps explain why some "progressives" sometimes have such an ambivalent relationship to liberal "internationalism." Most know it has not been a reliable guide for a democratic left unwilling to set aside its historical knowledge of imperialism. It is not surprising that many post–New Deal, baby boomer liberals have found neoliberal (i.e., corporate-dominated) globalization an irresistible lure bolstering their favored cosmopolitan self-image. It is not only the Right that has been quick to dismiss opposition as "protectionist," "isolationist," and "anarchist." What is amazing is that some on the Left have acquiesced to the "necessity" of economic globalization apparently hoping that *their* old "internationalism" may have found a new vehicle. It is a rather long, bumpy ride they seem to think we should take to the "global economy" and the best "objective conditions" presumably when the revolutionary transformation of this system will be possible. In this view, "globalization is unifying the world into a single mode of production and a single global system and bringing about the integration of different countries and regions into a new global economy" (Robinson, 2004, 15).

That indeed is one long-range direction of what is called globalization. We agree that transnational capital "has become the dominant, or hegemonic, fraction of capital on a world scale" (Robinson, 2004, 21). However, the "global economy" projected by this transnational capitalist class spells ecological and political disaster. If we grant that the "still emerging transnational phase of capitalism is qualitatively new" (5), why would this require that the political terrain of opposition be understood as already having transcended the "nation-state phase"? Does "capital's liberation from the nation-state" (39) as an issue permit only a reactionary politics? William Robinson continues: "In the emerging global capitalist configuration, transnational or global space is coming to supplant national spaces" (92). He should have said "dominate" national/local spaces, but to do so would have required him to problematize his understanding of the grounding of the "new transnational social forces" (130). But the placeless, disembodied imaginary of Global Economic Space depends upon the theorist's adoption of a modernist assumptive framework we prefer to call the *Archimedean Fix*. Postmodern intellectuals are right to be wary of constructions of "the People" that render an ultimate universality. It also will no longer do to follow Marx in thinking being in the form of a determinate totality supposedly avoiding the ambiguities of the perceived world.

Robinson claims that "the U.S. military apparatus is the ministry of war in the cabinet of an increasingly globally integrated ruling class" (Robinson, 2004, 140). After assuring the reader that TNCs (transnational corporations) have interests in military expansion, he concludes emphatically: "*The empire of capital is headquartered in Washington*" (140). Robinson's world-historical approach leaps to a politics of "global struggle" because power is no longer "mediated and organized through the nation-state" (178, 175). There is no need to reflect on political relations involving a historically specific organizational form that is "becoming transcended" (142). Robinson professes a "concrete interaction of agency and structure" that is "open-ended and not predetermined." But his resort to the category of "global civil society," not surprising given his total bypass on questions of historical public spheres, only underlines a structural determinism that over-relies on "the systemic logic of transnational capital and its power" (143, 175, 175).

Hobbling along with Hardt and Negri and their central image of an empire with no center (Robinson, 2004, 175), Robinson only suggests a totalizing politics for a new "global society." Yet before closing his brilliantly speculative study, he suggests that popular oppositional forces may indeed wish to "struggle to win state power" (177). Reminding them of the structural power of transnational capital, he is nonetheless clear that a national alternatives approach may not be very effective. For us the question is certainly not whether to maintain a traditional Leftist notion of "state power." The issue is put succinctly by Adam David Morton in his recent study of Gramsci: "One cannot afford to impute a singularly transnational logic to the domains of hegemony and resistance at the expense of local context and texture" (Morton, 2007, 199). Rather it is whether engaging the state "as a relation that can be transformed" (Robinson, 2004, 177) is sufficient for a new politics working out sustainable configurations of global civil society, nation, region, and place. Hardt and Negri and also Robinson fail to provide critical ecological scrutiny of the notion of "global economy" that relates importantly to their structurally determinist approach to questions of political agency. Robinson's final formulation shifts the focus back to a globalist politics for a *"democratization of global society"* that may well concede too much political space of the near future to the anti-globalist far right (178).

Undoing the Archimedean Fix and Regaining Political Terrain

Social and political theorists might well begin from M. K. Gandhi's premise that we must embody the truth we want to see realized in a new world, the changes we seek to persuade others to help us make. If we all begin in the body~place~commons nexus, how are we to conceptualize its *political* terrain? In social theorist Zygmunt Bauman's search for politics and public space, he refuses to forget or junk "the republican model of the state and of citizenship" (Bauman, 1999, 8). He treats the model as a key to cultivating agency and vision and to the democratic movement of issues, particularly a basic income as universal entitlement essential for rebuilding institutions of civil society that enable public participation. But the language of "models" would be misleading were it not coupled with great sensitivity to the tasks that take a society's historicity seriously. On this note we come back to American society where the corporate capitalist reprocessing of culture has magnified the problem as perhaps nowhere else on the planet.

Bauman makes a crucial distinction between *nation* and *republic* and emphasizes their tensions rather than peaceful cohabitation (Bauman, 1999, 163). As he says, the nation needs "nationalism" to which it must be added that in U.S. politics every major move toward empire has enlisted a virulent version rejecting core values of any democratic republic. He goes on to the historic link between republics and the ideal of the common good that always has seemed foolish to liberal individualists except in some quantitative (aggregative) form. The republican emphasis on freedom as enabling power rather than negative liberty is always jeopardized in a culture saturated with liberal individualism, especially when the latter has degenerated to daily celebrations of "consumer freedom."

"Politics must catch up with power," Bauman says, but he also is aware that we would be foolish to try to wish a "new internationalism" into being. Structural determinism on the Left is a problem when it feeds on the naïveté of liberal internationalism while short-circuiting patriotic radicalism for a democratic republic that is a working partner of the global justice movement. The political passivity of a number of academic radicals and liberals is not eclipsed by their shared references to "global citizenship." Nevertheless, political fragmentation must be fought, for there can be little doubt that corporate freedom from political control feeds on it. Neither will it help to fix on the defense of "community" especially if it promotes, intentionally or not, enclaved, essentialized identities whether or not these are rationalized as the necessary basis of "multiculturalism" (Bauman, 1999, 190–201).

Instead of railing on about the real problem of "identity politics," perhaps we might think of this beleaguered scene as one of *fragmentary postmodern populism*. Instead of adding more scornful variations on "populism," in the manner of many pundits, reform liberals, and academic leftists, perhaps it is time to consider a historical lesson from the main era of corporate state founding. Indeed we might find that recently grassroots political activists already have learned more than they or we seem to know. If the historical Populists made significant strides in organizing what Larry Goodwyn (1976) calls a "movement culture," then today we may have some of the material conditions for a new globalization discourse that is at once more critical and constructive. There is in the works an alternative globalization movement that addresses both new forms of socioeconomic inequality and the concerns of more marginalized groups while recognizing that equality as a democratic ideal in an era of drastic climate change must be pursued with a new sense of limits much more widely acknowledged by contending groups.

It is also important not to overrun critical analysis of the institutional setup that from William McKinley and Mark Hanna to George W. Bush and Karl Rove has produced and thrived on cultural segmentation and political fragmentation. The U.S. corporate state has been built and developed in the matrices of a longstanding liberal-democratic polity, the contradictions of which it has given increasingly acute expression. As Alan Wolfe once put it, the "history of politics in capitalist society is the history of the tensions between liberal and democratic conceptions of the state" (Wolfe, 1977, 9). In this historical process of modern Western politics, one of the most fundamental battlegrounds has been the "public sphere" and the possibility of a democratic public sphere, illuminated in the work of Jürgen Habermas and others. A central theme of these studies of advanced capitalism is the depoliticization of the public and its manipulation by industrial public relations and state administration (cf. C. Boggs, 2000). The development of the corporate state, to a great extent, has entailed the undermining of the conditions for a democratic public sphere.

The "populist moment" so brilliantly analyzed by Larry Goodwyn has left us with at least a glimpse of some of those conditions. One of the points he made was that in forging a "movement culture" the Populists went a long way in developing an independent media apparatus. He points to the National Reform Press Association, intellectuals such as W. Scott Morgan, and thousands of small, struggling newspapers (Goodwyn, 1976, 351–86, 236–37, 498). Today there is little doubt that Internet communication provides citizen activists across the globe with similar services and opportunities. Nor can there be any doubt about our version of the Populist problem of the link between the corporate media and the narrowed boundaries of mainstream politics. Flying under banners of "free trade" and "economic progress," corporate globalization gets favored media treatment in contrast to its critics, whether in, say, the World Social Forum or political leaders south of the United States such as Andres Manual Lopez Obrador or Evo Morales. Yet alternatives to neoliberal globalization continue to strengthen in the Americas and elsewhere. The Seattle protest against the World Trade Organization (WTO) in 1999 may offer a glimmer of a new movement culture, yet one that may still benefit from the history of the failure of the Labor/Populist alliance that drew so much energy from Henry Demarest Lloyd and others.

As Alexander Saxton (1990, 368) has stated, "American Marxists, whether native or foreign-born, had acquired their radicalism in the European tradition from which Jacksonian egalitarianism on the one hand, and the problems of a racially and ethnically divided labor force on the other, were conspicuously absent. Perceiving the Producer Ethic mentality as naïve or hypocritical, they gave short shrift to the notion of common interests shared by industrial workers and agricultural producers." Saxton goes on to point out that the Republican Party in 1896 moved into this gap "with its dramatic shift to cultural pluralism and its promise of rising wages—even for Hungarian and Italian mill hands—to be buoyed by rising tariffs. The proclivity of Peasant-Traditional mentalities to reproduce client-patron models in cross-class relationships dovetailed with this Republican initiative" (368). Saxton is not offering a lament for the egalitarian producer ethic that was to be rearticulated in a corporate state version of Americanism that was used in the 1920s to beat down workers such as coal miners in West Virginia. Among the minority of scholars sympathetic to Populism, even the late Christopher Lasch noted that it came up short as political theory. Lasch, however, did not throw out the baby with the bathwater.

Once we have deconstructed the mystical uses of artisan egalitarianism in corporate consumer culture, the residue of republican producer sensibility that remains may still be relevant to the project of reconstructing democratic agency. What the Democratic Left might remember here is Lasch's criticism of the anti-Populist "politics of the civilized minority," its inadequacy as political theory, and his point that keeping class issues out of politics has been a mainstay of the American Right and its strategists from Mark Hanna to Karl Rove (Lasch, 1991, 412–75). Perhaps even more important is Lasch's argument that the Populists were committed to the principle of respect and "always rejected both the politics of deference and the politics of pity" (106). The substantive issue in the 1890s has been put very well by Tim Luke: "Localist, communal, entrepreneurial, populist forms of everyday life, then, were marginalized in the Gilded Age by finance capital and big technoscience as nationalized, corporate, monopolistic, elitist systems of lifestyling remade the economies and ecologies of most North Americans' everyday lifeworld" (Luke, 1999, 6). Elitism in twentieth-century American politics took various forms. If the welfare policies of reform liberals sometimes tended toward a politics of pity, more recently it seems quite clear that corporate globalization often promotes a new "politics of deference" toward the global investor class.

The aim of our analysis is to traverse the gap between academic and professional subcultures and the more explicitly political subcultures animated by concerns for social justice and a healthier environment. We seek to show how an agenda starting from the body~place~commons points to shared projects of a democratic public sphere and a more sustainable world. These intertwined projects are inseparable from the struggle for a democratic republic in the United States and a global justice movement that will not have to fear imperial domination as the structural meaning of American policy.

On all too many campuses tough issues in the politics of corporate globalization raised by the Zapatistas, the World Social Forum, and Peoples Global Action get little attention even though there is much talk of "global citizenship," "multiculturalism," and so on. Citizen action organizations with names such as the Ohio Valley Environmental Coalition, the Community Farm Alliance, and Kentuckians for the Commonwealth are connecting these global-local issues and are increasingly questioning national and state policies in this context. To understand the political passivity of many academicians (including some academic Marxists) we have to go deeper than terms of contempt such as "populist" to the modernist mindset we have called the Archimedean Fix. The traditional Marxist counter to intellectual detachment by emphasizing the "materiality of the world" is not sufficient when the latter is embalmed in modern Western dualism and reified in the structural laws of global capitalist economic space. If this is the only game in town and place is ultimately a troublesome theoretical category scaled by an Archimedean theorist, then the earth's doom hastens while academic analysts seem to be somewhere else.

We would replace the academic capitalist sub-ideology of postcommunal professionalism with a civic professionalism grounded in what Henry Bugbee called the "sacrament of coexistence" (Bugbee, 1961). Starting from home is the ecologically responsible path to global citizenship, and academic migrants need not be homeless. If democracy is a vital concern of professionals in American society, they will have to find new ways of joining citizen action groups in the fight for public space and genuine public dialogue. There is no getting around Bauman's point that "the endemic instability of the lifeworlds of the overwhelming majority of contemporary men and women is the ultimate cause of the present-day crisis of the republic..." (Bauman, 1999, 180). What we hope to advance are projects in which intellectuals re-embody and re-place themselves working from the body~place~commons terrain of a democratic republican imaginary connecting with the struggles of a global justice movement that surely needs better help from the United States than it often has had. The political perspective we propose is a democratic republic of sustainable regions providing alternatives to such trade policy regimes as NAFTA and CAFTA in the form of new global regional projects coordinated increasingly by an advancing global justice movement.

3

De-toggling "Consumer Republic" Dreamworlds

The grassroots struggles of the global justice movement are partly a negative project—an effort from a steeply disempowered position to dislodge market logics as the dominant circuitry in national decision making. But this struggle is also a positive project to re-open and reclaim other logics as the constitutive stuff of the national body politic. In this chapter, we examine challenges in both the negative and positive labors of rebuilding democratic public space.

Within the diversity of the global justice movement, there are growing calls to put collective stewardship of the civic and ecological commons at the center of public life. These struggles open new moral and political grounds for citizenship. Against liberal notions of citizenship that abstract persons from embodied, emplaced participation in common worlds (as bearers of abstract rights, reason, interests, etc.), this call for justice embeds political subjectivity in practices of co-constitution between person, ecology, polity, and economy that emphasize interdependence. This battle is an unequal clash of modalities of spatiotemporal enframing. This is an active process of cultural creation, not some blind propulsion from structural processes. It involves complex synergisms of space and time, so we use Bakhtin's notion of "chronotope," which he describes as "the intrinsic connectedness of temporal and spatial relationships that are artistically expressed" (Bakhtin, 1981 [1930s], 84).

National political terrain in the United States is steeply slanted at present against democratic participation by citizens.[1] In the place where democratic public space should be are commodified, fragmented, and corporate media-driven zones of communication where citizen participation is more apparent than real. The semiotic fabric of these national zones of communication is woven and rewoven from a limited number of dramatic scenarios that set boundaries to what can and cannot be talked about in public deliberation, who speaks, how they speak, and how they are heard.[2] The effect is to sequester the commons from democratic debate—caged in faux-sacred zones like "tribal" reservations held separate from reigning regimes of private property. But, in fact, the private property regime depends on the moral legitimacy of the civic and ecological commons—selectively deploying sacralized icons of the American commonwealth in orchestrated displays of national history and possibilities.

Toggle Switches between Contradictory Chronotopes

These delimited fields of permissible national speech are what we called the *mainstream* in chapter 1. American mainstream politics constitutes a sort of semiotic circuitry that routes and reroutes conversations in preset ways that have a specific history. In this chapter we continue the exploration of this semiotic circuitry and its history. The mainstream ability to reroute public deliberation comes from a set of symbolic devices that function as something like toggle switches that flip conversations back and forth between contradictory time-space frameworks. By definition, toggle switches shift energy flow from one discrete state to another. *This toggling between incompatible and discrete spatiotemporal frameworks is the antithesis of the spatiotemporality of body~place~commons that serves as hinge, not toggle*. Body~place~commons is a fluency between multiple and disjunct temporalities. As we discussed in the introduction, this fluency is carried by, and created from, praxical enmeshment in worlds scaled to creaturely proportions and hinged into the worlds of human and nonhuman others. But, world is that substrate of political subjectivity that fades into invisibility under the fluorescent glow of dominant mainstream national political culture. Mainstream political space, we would argue, has been constructed to create precisely that spatiotemporal disorientation we feel when world fades—just as shopping malls are structured to disorient just enough to lock our attention on prepackaged displays. It is not enough that—disoriented—we can turn to shopping mall maps, seeking that orange dot with its chipper proclamation—"you are here." At right angles to, and silenced by, the certainties of this brisk little dot are the complex, intermittently speakable processes of embodied, emplaced, many-horizoned worlding—which provides *that substrate of hereness, that gyring of mute, loquacious, uncontainable bodily being* that the orange dot must suck into itself in order to have anything to say.

It took a long time to hardwire these semiotic toggle switches into American national political culture—two centuries in fact. The history of this symbolic construction is contradictory and complex. This chapter pulls out patterns that deeply damage democracy today. First, we explore the political terrain of mainstream politics that specifically *toggles off the spatiotemporal frameworks of the commons*. Second, we consider the corporate creation of mainstream toggles to unhinge body~place~commons using a recent campaign by the "Oil and Natural Gas Industry" as a case study. We analyze how this ad campaign discredits the legitimacy of the U.S. legislative government in energy policy formation and symbolically transforms American citizens with a polity-in-common into isolated, scared child-adult units.

Chronotopes of Development and the Public/Private Divide

The boundary between private and public in America is and has been heavily patrolled by seemingly simple dualisms—home/work, female/male, family/state, given/voluntary, unconditional/conditional. Feminist social theory has illuminated multiple ways in which this border is fictional, co-constitutive, or permeable.[3] Its simple geographies do not accurately map complex practices of people's actual lives. But this phantasmal border is a necessary fiction because it helps to prop up other fictions that legitimate the corporate state and empire. In this chapter, we consider how the private/public divide serves as a crucial toggle switch for unkiltering the democratic passions and identifications of care for, and within, body~place~commons. It has had a crucial role as a kind of master switch for splitting the pluralisms of the world-in-common into fractured pseudo-worlds—such as the "real world" of work, the "empire of love" (Povinelli, 2006), "politics as usual," casino world with the Big Win always rising, and "nature." This creates hallucinatory landscapes in which it is hard to track persons, creatures, places, things, and ideas through the entanglements and unfolding happenings that, in reality, constitute them and without which they cannot be understood as citizens in a commonwealth.

This phantasmal boundary of public and private is an historical construction. Beneath the veneer of simple dualisms, it wires together political contradictions that have piled up from several centuries of contestation over the meanings of the American republic. This history matters greatly now because it has left behind a political landscape that discourages citizens' participation. To connect their lives with wider worlds, citizens have to go against long-term forces that enclave them from the political. To act civically, citizens have to bushwhack their own way out of their homes in order to connect their personal paths with others, in an often bewildering landscape without intelligible paths, let alone public signposts,. The politics that we are calling an emergent global justice movement is often dismissed as too "local," as mere NIMBYism (not in my backyard). But we would argue that this is precisely the point, that this stubborn bushwhacking is an important political labor in itself—rebuilding an intelligible and walkable civic landscape between home and the public square. The exhausting labor of rebuilding political terrain across the private/public divide is not a sideshow of global politics, but a key battle ground in a two-century war of position in literally house-to-house battle. This battle is connected to wider political struggles because it is waged at a primary site for destruction of chronotopes of worlds-in-common.

Such contemporary struggles carry on political legacies of the democratic republicanism of the eighteenth century. This republicanism was marginalized, if never completely suppressed, by the hegemonic ascendancy of liberal democratic ideologies by the mid-nineteenth century, leading to the consolidation of the corporate state (and empire) in the late nineteenth century, devolving into hollowed-out notions of the "consumer republic" in the twentieth century.

Ecological Realities and Economic Fantasies

It must be one of the great ironies of U.S. history that a nation so blessed with nature would fall captive to a mechanistic model of societal development premised on an expendable "environment" as a vast resource object. As Tocqueville noted long ago, most Americans—dedicated to the "practical" side of life and an instrumental rationality—gave little time to a more reflective approach (Tocqueville, 1956). And for more than a hundred years, they have been able to count on the society's economists for a justifying rationale. Social theorists refer to "the almost total naturalization of 'the economy' that has taken place in public discourse over recent decades" (Gibson-Graham, 2006, 53). The society/nature dualism underlying this familiar formulation should not block the historical point made earlier that it was a mechanistic model of nature that was appropriated by a capitalist economics that is inherently anti-ecological. Authors Gibson-Graham brilliantly analyze how "capitalocentric discourse [has] colonized the entire economic landscape" (55). Even more importantly, they emphasize that this landscape is ripped out of its historically varied, living geographic, and ecological context and is subjected to the "imaginary functionings of 'a self-contained and dynamic mechanism'" (54, quoting Timothy Mitchell). Their project of constructing "a language of the *diverse economy*" is fundamental to repoliticizing public discourse in the United States and anywhere that neoliberal ideology has been installed. In chapter 5, however, we explore Merleau-Ponty's point in one of his last lectures that it is a "poor dialectic" that leaves nature in ontological silence, in the realm of the "objective" and a dualistic conception of "materialism" (Merleau-Ponty, 1970, 62–66). The fetishization and naturalization of the "market machine god" (Reid, 2001b) makes it seem as if production, like a perpetual motion machine, can operate forever from its own self-subsistent logic—the very thin bright line that is the profit margin leading to capital accumulation. Capitalism has always had an extraordinary capacity to create the illusion that the thin green line of biocultural regeneration does not exist—even as capitalism depends utterly on it.

At the heart of this book is the question of citizenship. What does it mean to talk of ecological citizenship? It is our contention that Merleau-Ponty's notion of the "flesh of the world" can take us beyond a citizenship based in decontextualized abstractions of "natural rights" to concepts of citizenship that recognize that we are dwellers on the land, that make us, once again, natives of the Earth (as we explore further in chapter 5). To speak of "dwelling," is to invoke Heidegger's powerful development of this concept.[4] In the modern world, the constituting of personhood in images of landscape has often been associated with reactionary political movements, and emancipatory movements have tended to invoke notions of personhood disembedded from the concrete and autochthonic. In trying to reground politics in ecological awareness and embodiment, one must always be aware of the problematic history of organicism and organic analogies—which can too easily be used to enclose the arbitrary and oppressive within the seeming inevitability of a falsely purified "natural order." But, by saying "natives to the Earth," we invoke both the cautionary image of nativism as well as Hannah Arendt's notion of natality (Arendt, 1958). Her notion of natality avoids reification in a chiasm of matrix and individuation, of personal creativity and collective generosity—as glory of originality is engendered by the capacious theater of public space and always reappropriated history. So, we would argue that the danger in ecological and organic analogies is not inherent but is in the reifications that freeze and fracture the chiasmatic complexity of the co-inherence of Earth, Others, and Self.

But this project must take place within history. And the history almost all people are now within has its political embodiment as public, within the time of the nation-state. To be politically efficacious, a project of transformation must move through this space-time—harvesting what is helpful and shaking down reifications along their internal lines of fracture and cross tensions. The citizenship that was instituted by modernity and liberal, procedural democracy ties its moral appeal to processes of logical abstraction. Its foundational notions of natural rights are symbolically constituted by decontextualizing selves from the givenness of (gendered, raced, propertied, etc.) bodies. Feminist theories of public space and recent debates about identity versus class politics in North America have shown the complex ways in which the citizen is symbolically produced as an abstracted, universalized ideal out of the messy materiality of particularity and difference.

The process of symbolic purification that disembeds the citizen as a bearer of rights from the contingency of given identities works by, as it were, stacking dualisms so that they prop each other up—hiding the irrationalities and instability that would be obvious if any one dualism had to stand alone.[5] These dualisms are familiar: voluntary/involuntary; subject/object; male/female; white/black; rational/emotional; mind/body; middle class/working class; human/animal; new/old; urban/rural; free/dominated; culture/nature; space/place. Elizabeth Povinelli brilliantly unsettles the equation of freedom with social disembedding. She argues that the social imaginaries of "liberal settler colonies" constructed a dualistic opposition between "genealogical societies" (e.g., putatively kinship based, constrained by social and natural "givens") and "autological societies" (based on the self-constituting subject) (Povinelli, 2006; see also N. Fraser, 1993; Hirschmann & Di Stefano, 1996).

The dualism of space/place is key to hegemonic control (Casey, 1993, 1997, 2002). The question of ecological citizenship pulls up the tensions submerged in this dualism's hegemonic power. Some of the most helpful thinking about these questions is to be found, not among scholars, but among activists who are building a new kind of citizen politics that forces them to weave together identities as political actors and identities as dwellers within place (G. L. Boggs, 2000). It is hard to know what to call this emergent political process. Mainstream environmentalism in North America has often dismissed it in the past as NIMBYism. Within the national imaginary, it is seen as "public" political action that seems to spring from "private" domains. In this construction, these activists respond to environmental threats to home, neighborhood, and that which is classed as "recreational resources" for consumption in "leisure" (public lands, heritage spots, built or natural landscapes that are increasingly bundled within the increasingly commodified notion of quality of life, etc.).

Mechanics of Mystification:
Metanarratives of Nation, Gender, State, Market

This work of mystification was built up from the nineteenth to twentieth centuries through metanarratives of nationhood, gender, and place. The secret to success in mystification is to fold contradictions almost, but not quite, out of sight—so that people feel authorized to "skip over" them (in Heidegger's phrase). Never completely denied, yet never fully present, they float spectrally in public and private awareness, making people feel barely conscious complicity in their own duping. Narratival transmutation is an excellent way to do this—welding deep desires into oppressive macrostructures. These narratives are stacked on top of each other in order to make these dualisms seem to make sense. The narratives of market, nation, and state that are foundational of ideologies of liberal individualism, the technological world-picture, and economic and scientific "progress" flow, like laser beams, in parallel narrative temporalities—lending potency to each other.

What is important about this for our discussion of ecological citizenship is how this relates to the balancing of reproduction and production that is basic to an ecological economics. The genius of this national symbolic and the source of its world-conquering, world-devouring "success" is its ability to (quite falsely) equate the thin green line of the lifeworld logos with the thin bright line of the capitalist profit margin, as we discussed in chapter 1. Reproductive processes—human and ultrahuman—are pushed off the edge of time into the detemporalized realm of the family and nature as the grail that grounds and energizes the quest but is never included in the logic of the quest. This is like the "gynesis" that Jardine describes in which "woman" emerges symbolically as an after-effect of masculinist narratives (Jardine, 1986). Similarly, the zone of the reproductive—family, wildness, noncommodified cycles of life—is the prize to be savored in leisure outside of public action, historical identity, and power struggles. This zone is necessary because it is where it is made to appear that pure value—that is, use value—springs up, like an eternal fountain that flows backward to salve and heal the injuries of power, history, exchange value, and male violence.

These metanarratives are falsely sutured together to create the national semiotic circuitry that officially effaces body~place~commons. It is able to do this because it seems to hold together two very different temporalities, but it actually veils their contradiction. They are held together in public space by the toggle switches built into mainstream politics that function to fracture complex spatiotemporal frames and then to flip between frames in a shell game that prevents public debate within the pluritemporal and pluriscalar fluencies necessary to a commonwealth. Within history are the (masculinist) narratives that use unilinear time to hold apart dualisms that would collapse if brought too close together: old/new; nonwhite/white; primitive/modern; violence/equality, irrationality/science, and so forth. These narratives of economic and social progress, liberal individualism, technological mastery, democratic triumphalism, male competition, and imperialism are each one like dioramas with robotically repetitive actions. The unilinear flow of time guarantees precisely that purification of given and natural identities into the decontextualized universal Self and Other from which citizens, in procedural democracy, are constituted. The problem with this tidy picture is that it disguises the fact that the end products of these narratives—seemingly universal selves—need the dark, primitive, natural others that they seem in their self-contained dioramas to always be vanquishing. Because of their very abstraction, these end products need to keep returning to the originary point to mine it for new nourishment and vitality—a process that bell hooks describes as "eating the Other" (hooks, 2000). This salvific and violent return to originary Otherness pervades the national symbolic of the United States (Slotkin, 1996 [1973]).

The cruel brilliance of this metanarrative is the way in which the market logic sits, in plain sight but almost invisible, at the end point of these narratives. It thereby provides the symbolic mechanisms that join dehistoricized Nature to the world of action in time. The majority, which is in fact marginalized by these narratives, has been bought off by the consumerist dream that work within the system gives the monetary ticket to buy the space of home and leisure, which gets its meaning and value from things that "money can't buy." The North American frontier myth, with all its evocation of premodern self-subsistence outside of the discipline of labor markets and within an always resilient and lavish ecos, has been joined with the North American suburban imaginary that is the Atlanta's apple that has settled down the American worker and other potential malcontents. The remarkably adroit algebra of this national symbolic is repeated night after night, on American television, with astounding rigor in advertisements for Jeep Cherokees, SUVs, and so forth. against the radiant backdrop of the Big Sky and rough land of cowboy country. This toggling between putatively "historical" and "natural" as if they were separate states of being actually disguises the extent to which this ideology naturalizes history (in the mechanistic teleology of the myth of progress) and traps "nature" in a reified cross-section of "first discovery" and "exploration"—the "autological" self (Povinelli, 2006) discovering itself as in, but not of, the frontier upon whose cornucopia it is utterly dependent. This strange dyadism parallels the "intimate event" of two decontextualized selves discovering each other in the mini-social contract of "romantic love"—which Povinelli says functions as the ontological anchor for liberal democratic ideology (Povinelli, 2006). The "intimate event" seems to solve, but actually covers up, the constitutive contradiction of possessive liberalism—it cannot explain the grounds for solidarity except by an endless regression of "free" contracts among atomistic individuals (Stivers, 2009) who lack constituting authority to constitute collective sovereignty (see Arendt, 1965, chap. 4).

Big Oil Sits Down with Us at the Kitchen Table

These mechanisms of mystification are on vivid display in a massive public relations campaign by the energy industries to position themselves as political actors within American mainstream conversations. These ads now blossom all over TV, newspapers, and the Web and invite readers and viewers to www.EnergyTomorrow.org with its nonthreatening, dot-org-ish sheen of seemingly noncommercial and civic disinterest. You would think we would have noticed these ads from the "Oil and Natural Gas Industry" when they first appeared in our newspaper—given how consumed we are with questions about energy, climate chaos, and social justice. But the visuals of these ads are such that our eyes skipped over them at first, as if we already knew they made a kind of sense—maybe not *our* kind of sense, but, some kind of industry-centered coherence. It was only after a long double take that we looked beneath the cultivated ordinariness of the pictures to see the weird layering of contradictory stories beneath—precarious piles of meanings about "America," "middle-class Americans," "energy futures," Congress, family, "We the People," and so forth.

In this section we unpack these ads, finding that they exemplify wider processes in the capture of democratic public space, its reconstitution as "consumer republic," and the effacement of the space-times of the commons. These wider processes accelerated in the last several decades of the twentieth century. However, they had roots in the "dual horizons" (the dialectics of subjectivization and objectivization) that we discussed in chapter 2. Academic apologists for the "consumer republic" see it as a more or less adequate replacement for, or adjunct to, the liberal democratic polity. The "consumer freedom" to choose between commodified products and lifestyles is equated with the negative liberties of the market and the procedural rationalities of rights and due process within a well-run liberal polity. But, as we pull these ads apart, we discover a strange, jumbled stratigraphy within the iconography of the "consumer republic"—with disturbing mixtures of magical protections and thuggish dangers. Folded alongside images of the happy atomized subjects of so-called consumer freedom are disjunct husks of the liberal democratic polity and uncanny fragments of radically *inter*subjective stuff—gift economies of family and kinship, numinous relics of the republican "We the People." But what we focus on here is the insertion of bits and pieces from the third body of American politics — mutterings of threats, fears, and obeisances spilling out from the hidden corridors of capital's circuitry as sheer cronyism.

A recent full-page ad appeared in our *Lexington Herald Leader* (see figure 5).[6] At the top of the page is a picture in which the white and pastel color scheme enframes the domestic scene so tastefully that the first impression is of a perfect American couple and baby in an American dream home. Suburban trees and greenery show unobtrusively through the window, and at the center of the picture is a Martha Stewart–like, studiedly natural arrangement of branches as if just gathered in a happy yesterday. This hetero-perfect normality is like a soothing gel over the ad. But a second glance brings out big white words hovering like Casper across the bottom left of the picture, "Who really pays when Congress taxes oil companies?" Cued that something is wrong in paradise, the gaze is drawn to the weeping baby in the visual center of interest in the picture. If someone is paying, it must be our children. Somebody is going to have to pay. Someone is weeping. But does anyone care? The second plane sets off reverberating anxieties, and, these anxieties are concretized in images of basic primate susceptibilities. This second level moves onto red alert and suffuses the page with anxieties of care and dilemmas of reproductive labor.

But what chains of care surround this distressed child? Here things get ambiguous. On third glance, it is hard to tell where things actually are headed. There are no definite visual clues that things are not unraveling. We cannot see any mutual gazes. It is true that the (apparent) father is looking at the boy. But, how strangely his jaw is clenched— a grimace that could be either tender solicitude or teeth-baring rage. If you think about it, you could imagine all kinds of scenarios here. The child might quiet down under the charm of tender paternal shushing. Or be thrown across the room by a boyfriend who snapped. The woman is also hard to read, not least because we cannot see most of her face and have no clues as to what she is looking at so intently outside the frame of the picture. Is she smiling? Is she about to throw hot coffee at her husband? Is there a bear at the window that is the real danger? All we know for sure is that the baby is looking at us, to create the only mutual gaze of the picture. The child's eyes pull us into the picture, creating a confused sense of responsibility—like watching a child being hit by someone near to us in the supermarket aisle and not knowing what to do next. This picture is hemorrhaging reproductive risk, guilt, responsibility, and insecurity. It suggests urgent but illegible futures.

Figure 5. 2008 Ad from the Oil and Natural Gas Industry. Reproduced courtesy of the American Petroleum Institute.

This ad is about energy policy in the U.S. Congress. The actual contest is between a huge energy sector and the national legislature—but it is carried in the symbolic vessel of an anonymous home at its most vulnerable. Why have crucial dramas about our collective energy future been so radically privatized?

We see three reasons for this. First, this seems to be an example of what Berlant calls the "infantile citizenship" (Berlant, 1997) pervading the American national symbolic in the last several decades—childlike images of good citizenship that resort to the most innocent, idealized, and unthinking roots of collective being or responsibility because of "the contradictions threatening 'adult' or 'full' citizenship in the political public sphere" (29) and practical civic labors. Second, this also seems a turn to what Povinelli calls the "intimate event" (Povinelli, 2006)—the heterosexual romantic bond used as a numinous image of intersubjectivity in "liberal settler" polities that have trouble finding symbolic ways to convey the connections between the persons who have been atomized within liberal imaginaries and polities. The "intimate event" is one of the few forms of relationship that is already highly charged emotionally, so it becomes almost a necessary symbolic vessel for anything that truly matters. So impoverished are the affects and meanings of public life that a big collective problem does not seem to look important or real, unless one can show its impact on private life and extra-market householding.

But we see a third reason for this privatization of talk about collective energy challenges. The infantilization of citizenship and the collapse of common adulthoods into a mystified "intimate event" can be linked with the *active attack by the third body of the American corporate state on the civic commons and on direct links between citizens and the state.* This ad goes directly at the complex hinging of disjunct temporalities that make body~place~commons what it is. This hinging happens in the embodied, daily practices of particular people in particular places within enabling limits of webs of civic and ecological interdependencies. The key characteristic of body~place~commons is the power to *kilter heterogeneous temporalities of cyclic, linear, and arrhythmic temporalities with spatialities that are recursive, planar, topological, and so forth and that integrate sedimentary forms of retention with capacities of protention toward the unexpected, new, or the maddeningly or wonderfully same-old.*

This ad goes to the rhythmic heart of body~place~commons. It stakes a claim to the intimate pivots of everyday kiltering in body~place~commons— that mysteriously constant and unitive juggling of the disparate times of creation, destruction, and care through which we make our lives habitable and hospitable to human and nonhuman others. The visuals of this ad demonstrate the odd mix of heterogeneity and integration in the chronotopes of kiltering. It seems to be morning, with the woman sucking in her caffeine and perhaps trying to block out the wails long enough to make a mental list to get her through the day in some sort of linear fashion. So, the picture conveys the feel of the habitual, of night turning into day and circling back to night and home in dependable rounds of time and space. It suggests people trying to maintain a workable hinge between private and public life, to balance labors of care with whatever labors of productive work the man at least seems dressed for.

But kiltering always thrums with unkiltering. Kiltering is the ability to juggle stuff that you did not see coming or that just slipped out of your grasp. Kiltering is not control of past, present, and future. Kiltering is learning from what happened, imaging what might happen, and sluicing partially legible, partially conscious pasts/futures into a way to meet what actually is happening. This ad puts the newspaper reader at the "fourth wall" of a TV soap opera, where the camera and the studio audience get a close look at the juicy infrastructures of the private life of kiltering. It suggests multiple and disjunct possible outcomes and scenarios, leaving us with the sense that these people might be about to pull their day and their lives together, or might just lose it. It evokes the partial legibilities and tensional fields of what Stewart calls the "ordinary" and the "everyday" (Stewart, 2007):

> a shifting assemblage of practices and practical knowledges, a scene of both liveness and exhaustion . . . the varied, surging capacities to affect and to be affected that give everyday life the quality of a continual motion of relations, scenes, contingencies, and emergencies. They're things that happen . . . they move through bodies, dreams, dramas, and social worldings of all kinds . . . a reeling present . . . composed out of heterogeneous and noncoherent singularities. . . . Attention is distracted, pulled away from itself. But the constant pulling also makes it wakeful, 'at attention.' Confused but attuned. (1–3)

> For some, the everyday is a process of going on until something happens,
>   and then back to the going on.
> For others, one wrong move is all it takes,
> Worries swirl around the bodies in the dark.
> People bottom out watching daytime television.
> Schedules are thrown up like scaffolding to handle work schedules and
>   soccer practice or a husband quietly drinking himself to death in the
>   living room.
> We dream of getting by, getting on track, getting away from it all, getting
>   real, having an edge, beating the system, being our selves, checking out.
> But first we take the hit, or dodge it. (10)

Big Oil's Protection Racket

The picture in this ad inserts itself like a knife into the joints of body~place~commons. It is astonishingly intrusive. It creates an oddly generic but urgent image of everyday practices of life, but it encloses them in a fantastical "home" that is brutally open to the corporate gaze and disembedded from nondomestic civic space or the ecological surround. The only visible social glue between the humans here seems to be the gift economy of generativity within family. This ad looks over the edge of the market economy, grabs some powerful affects from the nonmarket moral economy, and, then uses these nonmarket powers to weld "home" to industry in a relationship of infantile dependence. The unspoken visual messages of the picture dominate two-thirds of the full-page ad and revolve around the vicissitudes of care chains.

The written text in the bottom third of the ad is reproduced below:

> We all do . . . in more ways than one.
>
> Tens of millions of mostly middle-class Americans have an ownership stake in the nation's oil and natural gas companies through pension plans, IRA accounts and mutual funds. All of them invest heavily in oil and natural gas stocks, enabling the industry's strong earnings to help support Americans' financial security.
>
> Every day, Americans count on the oil and natural gas industry to deliver the energy they need and to invest in securing energy they'll need in the future. The industry has delivered on both counts. Since 1996, the U.S. oil and natural gas industry has invested nearly $1.2 trillion to keep Americans and the economy moving. Strong earnings make all this possible.
>
> So when Congress increases taxes on oil and natural gas companies, it's really taxing Americans' economic futures as well as targeting their livelihoods and their energy future.

The written text is organized according to a completely different logic. It seems at first that it uses only market metaphors to describe the stuff out of which intersubjectivity is made: "Who really pays . . . ?"; "middle-class Americans have an ownership stake in the nation's oil and natural gas companies"; "the industry's strong earnings . . . support Americans' financial security"; "Strong earnings make all this possible." But it takes only a moment of reflection to see that this market rationality is irrational even in its own terms. In fact, ordinary Americans do not have much of an ownership in energy industry, and what they do have is extremely unevenly distributed, making this ownership more a measure of financial insecurity for most rather than what the ad describes as "Americans' financial security." It confuses the role of stockholder with the role of consumer. Ordinary Americans face Big Energy not as owners but from the very unequal position of consumers facing massive restructuring and escalating insecurity and prices in fossil fuel global markets.

The overt messages of this text are bizarre and illogical. However, behind this overt level is a meta-level that makes sense but in a chilling way. The meta-message of the text is in the first fabricated dialogue. "Who really pays when Congress taxes oil companies?" "We all do . . . in more ways than one." This ad is trying to use market metaphors to construct extra-market, collective subjects. The most important collective subject is a diffuse "we" that somehow seems to be a national collective body associated with diffuse solidarities of American-ness. This solidarity is established by common victimhood—the sense that somehow someone is taking something from us. Somewhere there is a piper that we all unfairly have to pay. So, that screaming face is our face. From the get go, this "we" is dualistically constructed against the government, which is taking from us what is ours. The Congress in these ads is constructed as Other, as Bad Daddy, as not owned by "us," not producing that which contributes to "our" well-being. As we discuss toward the end of this chapter, these ads systematically try to sever the bonds between "Americans" and their government by enclaving and ridiculing the legislative branch—a process related to what Nelson describes as an increasing "presidentialism" (Nelson, 2008).

It does this by attacking the very notion of commonwealth that we discussed in chapter 1—the placed, embodied, praxical matrices that connect citizens with each other and rhythmic exchange of energies with the nonhuman ecologies. It goes to the rhythmic heart of the temporalities of body~place~commons and, slices them away from the formal polity and the informal civic commons. Into the site of this dissection, these ads graft another body—a corporate system of energy exchange. This is the third body of the corporate state whose historical origins we discussed in chapters 1 and 2. Its logic is nothing like the disembedding abstract reason of the liberal market. Its logic reaches back to the feudal intersubjectivity of Judge Temple and those he can bring into dependency and subservience. The "we" of this ad is the boss and his minions. The stuff of this ad is dependency and isolation. Its energy is the promulgation of insecurity, fear, and a culture of low hopes. It turns the face and heart of the ordinary people to yearnings outside the economic sphere. The message from the boss is to do whatever it takes to get what you can from the system so that you can retreat into the safe enclave of your home. Value only the fragile chains of care in fragile circuits of privatized space. But, says the boss, work with me to keep this fictive "we" alive, and at least I can promise you the security of how things already are. Cry—and Big Daddy will take care of you and yours—maybe. Do not imagine that ordinary adults have any collective powers as a people outside of the body of the economy. Above all, do not imagine these collective powers as political, elected, or representative. And remember, I, the existing corporate being, am too big to fail. You rise and fall with me.

At the meta-level, this ad is a discursive apparatus for creating a collective subject—a diffuse corporate personage, which vertically integrates modes of production with clientalistic domination of care chains—to dominate the metastructures of social and ecological reproduction. Before the mere "Americans" scurry back into their privatized retreats, they should make sure to hand their futures over to this entity, and everyone will pretend that we are covered by its unitive being. This is what Plumwood calls "coverture" (2006). By infantilizing ordinary Americans under corporate coverture in the faux public of mainstream discourse, this collective subject bestrides the landscapes of the civic commons and democratic publics and, dominates the levers of time. Jardine describes masculinist discourses that chronically produce "woman" as a kind of aftereffect of what are essentially male dramas—a process she calls "gynesis." This ad could be called a process of "bossesis"—the use of market, liberal democratic, and republican discourses to generate the collective subject of the third body of the corporate state—almost as an after image from discourses that would seem to preclude this kind of feudalistic domination. This "we" is the internalized drama between an inner child and an inner boss. It is the fake conversation between the fetishized home and the fetishized "market machine god" that the myth of progress figures as offering an eternal cornucopia of endless plenty to an eternally dehistoricized "family"—as long as they remember who is boss.

But, most importantly, these ads suture mainstream toggles into the fluent hinges of body~place~commons. The effect is to disrupt the sense of dignity, liberty, and competency that were key to republican hinges between polity, public space, and commons. The dualisms of mainstream toggles provide gears to insert the corporatized "we" into the intimacy of everyday, ordinary, private life practices. But, as importantly, they provide a tool kit for enclosure and privatization of care itself—disvaluing and disrupting the affects and meanings of citizenship as care for public life and commonwealth.[7]

Beyond Neo-Liberal Globalization and Transnational Elitism

The enclosure of the commons and of care that began in the nineteenth century has, a century later, been enshrined in a neoliberal theology of privatization, deregulation, and manufactured insecurity backed by dominating forms of transnational corporate power. Americans are waking up to realize that corporate media dreams of globalizing prosperity are turning into the nightmare of an American dream in reverse. As Holly Sklar puts it, the reality is "an increasingly low-wage workforce instead of a growing middle class." Unlike many European countries, the United States has been on a low road to economic globalization, and the economy's decayed infrastructure and public school system are just two of several glaring results (Sklar, 2006, 4). Today, as reports indicate, almost all the growth in household income and wealth has been accruing to the richest 20 percent. Mark Hertsgaard sums up the situation: "Increasingly, the United States is dividing between a small, fabulously wealthy elite and a growing, struggling majority who must work hard simply not to fall behind" (Hertsgaard, 2003, 139).

More and more middle-class Americans are experiencing what the working poor have had to confront during the fifty years since Louis Hartz argued that the United States epitomized the "liberal society" (Hartz, 1955). While Hartz exaggerated the impact of the bourgeois liberal ideology, there can be little doubt about its hegemonic role in the dominant system of political economy in the United States. A few years ago, social theorist Zygmunt Bauman wrote: "What liberal society offers with one hand, it tends to take back with the other; the duty of freedom without the resources that permit a truly free choice is for many a recipe for life without dignity, filled instead with humiliation and self-deprecation" (Bauman, 1997, 196). Middle-class anger and frustration simmer while the classical liberal ideal of "equal opportunity" pursued on "a level playing field" seems to fade from reach. It is an open question how many are vulnerable to the endless right-wing scapegoating of the most exploited groups (e.g., Mexican migrant workers) as somehow responsible for the unlevel field.

As Christopher Lasch has put it, "the history of American politics in the twentieth century can be seen as the history of disenfranchisement and of the creation of new structures from which popular participation is increasingly missing. On the other hand, we also inherit a legacy of democratic political traditions that makes it extremely difficult to govern in this manner" (Lasch, 1980–1981, 190). Updated in the language of political theory this means: "there is a growing contradiction between the tendency towards globality and universality of capital in the neoliberal form and the particularity of the legitimation and enforcement of its key exploitative relations by the state" (Gill, 1995, 422). In other words, globalizing capital "cannot operate outside of or beyond the political context" of evolving structures marked by a particular society and its history. Moreover, we need to confront the ways that the resurgent neoliberal market metaphysics, beyond mere ideological veneer, sometimes become infrastructural to various popular modes of authority, identity, and most American anti-politics traditions.

A new democratic theory has lessons to learn from the Right's approach to an American political culture of anti-authoritarian egalitarianism as an aspect of middle-class integration into the corporate state, a process increasingly made uncertain for many by "globalization." Some of these elements of traditional belief operated in the Reagan Right's politics of romantic nostalgia. Many in our middle class are perplexed by a double paradox in American political culture. A romanticized version of this outlook figures in our reactionary liberals' fear of a strong, rampant "Welfare State" that, curiously, some of our reform liberals have believed in sufficiently to ratify their sense of liberal reform as the Grand March of Democracy. As white-collar workers watch the corporate destruction of their pensions and other benefits, the consolation of scapegoating "welfare queens" wears thin. The political capital Bill Clinton claimed for his "welfare reform" (said to steal conservative thunder) pales while the hold of corporate capital on his party strengthens, inhibiting its oppositional role in the Bush-Cheney years. If this seems to suggest a schizophrenic aspect to the interplay of "right" and "left" in mainstream politics, perhaps the American polity exhibits a "systematic ambiguity" relating to a myth of the nation as an egalitarian social democracy (the American dream) and an ideology of the state as a bourgeois liberal democracy (fostering "equal opportunity").

It is not enough to declare the latter's intellectual and moral bankruptcy. It is not even enough to castigate professional academics for working to rationalize and reconcile tensions in these mythic and ideological features of what political scientists once extolled as the great American "civic culture." It is the theoretical auspices of critique to which we call attention. The question is whether these provide conceptual access to historically grounded mythopoetic structures of feeling and orientation from which a politics for alternative modernities is possible. That is why we have highlighted the pluralistic eco-logics of social struggles for a democratic republic in an American history that sometimes we are reminded is not dead by the perverse forms its return takes. Leaving this territory of experience to the Right assures that!

But so does intellectual acquiescence in the destruction of places and their commons and the de-worlding of citizenship.

Indeed, sometimes it seems that American political scientists and historians are in a competition to incorporate and integrate elements of market metaphysics and political ideology to refurbish the dominant system's legitimation. Their resort to notions of "democratic consumerism" and a "consumer's republic" has deep roots (Hanson, 1985; Cohen, 2003). To call the current system a "consumer republic" is to refresh the central myth that a democratic America has solved the problem of political authority by giving it over to public opinion. The popular distaste for traditional forms of political authority was thought to be vindicated somehow in a civil society of unique "diversity," although it took a bloody civil war in one century and a bloody civil rights struggle in the next to get to a broadly acceptable "multiculturalism." Never mind that the manufacturing of public opinion and the structuring of the process of consent by corporate power marked increasing domination of civil society. Only such a thoroughly dominated and fragmented society would present the recent spectacle of overwhelming popular support for a national health care system ignored by decision-making elite maintenance of an increasingly expensive, wasteful, and inadequate corporate-dominated policy.

We take this as more evidence of citizens' interest in the public good that is demeaned not only by corporate advertising but also by cynical academic labels such as a *consumer republic*. However, before another historical probe we should bear in mind the larger assumptive frame immediately holding up such a politically inflated or flattering portrait of American corporate consumers. Today's fashionable balloon term is the *global economy*. Deflating it by critical scrutiny, we often find problematic assumptions not only about how far it benefits the world's peoples but also about large-scale production, colossal technologies, and American leadership. How rational are these approaches when we consider that sustainable policies confronting extreme forms of climate change suggest different scalar models for a post-carbon world?

The classical liberal notion of the market as a "system of natural liberty" arose as an ideological response to a crisis in authority or social order. That it has been revived today in globalized garb may be a sign of long-run weakness in corporate state legitimation, although this could depend especially upon the role of the new middle classes in the universities and other professional domains. The growing interest in "sustainable communities," "alternative media," and "social citizenship" both retrieves and projects the precarious promise of new social movements in their struggles for genuinely political discourse, action, and democratic change. We contend that these fragments for a movement need to be linked historically to the quest for a democratic republic.

It is not only our reactionary liberals who obscure the field of power within which civil society organizations operate. Questions of power and justice, of authority and responsibility, find little traction in a globalization discourse partly impoverished by the extent to which universities have promoted a *global economy entrepreneurialism,* to use the language favored by academic administrators. The impact of the "market" in American social and cultural life is at once a matter of institutional power and ideological service, influencing professional opinion and public discussion. Recently, sociologist Raymond Morrow observed that "the academy no longer knows how to conceptualize its demands for autonomy coherently." He contends that what "might be called the *disenchantment of academic authority*—carried about in different ways by the right and cultural left—has culminated in a tragic polarization between epistemological relativism and a dominant positivism that undermines new alternatives" (Morrow, 2006, xxvi–xxviii).

Many academicians in U.S. universities and colleges have only very slowly, if at all, begun to ponder the political implications of what Carl Boggs calls "global anti-politics" in this brave new world order. There seems to be a high degree of quiescence to the fact that, in his words, since the 1970s "the public sphere in many nations has been shrinking steadily and dramatically" (C. Boggs, 1996, 9). One might expect the academic professions to be undertaking more serious efforts to help reconstruct public spheres for more relevant and effective forms of public discourse and citizen action. Vapid academic talk about "civil society," "social capital," and "global citizenship" can be replaced by collaborative projects with local and regional citizen action groups. Academics are not stuck with the plight of the character in Thomas Pynchon's *Gravity's Rainbow* who says, "we have learned to stand outside our history and watch it, without feeling too much." Whatever its basis or rationale, the latest form of academic capitalism we call *postcommunal professionalism* is slowly being vacated by those coming to understand that the possibilities of justice in the global ecological crisis are bound to a movement for democratic change that has replaced the imperialist gaze with commitment to the intrinsic visibility of the world of ecologically interdependent life.

Excavation of the Pathological Pseudo Public Sphere of the "Consumer Republic"

Democracy needs vibrant public spheres in which citizens, from all walks of life, can debate, celebrate, and care for public well-being and the common life. In this section, we describe the contradictions of the pseudo public space of the "consumer republic" that act to pith national political culture of the chronotopes needed for common talk about what is of common concern. This creates problems in reasoning collectively about danger, equity, and ecological and human security—an oddly systemic stupidity in a country with considerable civic and communicational capacity in many ways. These anti-public discourses are made to seem coherent, by rhetorical strategies, which use a rag bag of historically sedimented political ideas and images to present the appearance of sense in what is, substantively, nonsense. The hegemonic discourses of "consumer republic" carry semiotic bits and pieces of earlier political discourses of liberal democratic and democratic republican chronotopes and values—to drape themselves with the forms of legitimacy, competencies, desires, and loyalties that they are, in fact, undoing.

A good example of such political rhetorical sleight-of-hand appeared in a 2007 full-page ad on energy policy in our local newspaper from the "Oil and Natural Gas Industry" (see figure 6).[8] The bottom third of the page is made up of text that urges readers to contact their representatives to oppose energy bills in Congress that sought to encourage conservation and renewable energy and to decrease reliance on fossil fuels. "IT'S 2007, NOT 1977" blared the banner headlines, followed by "Congress is playing '70s style energy politics. What about America's energy future?"

This text is made alluring by the nonverbal messages covering the upper two-thirds of the page. In the following analysis, we try to disentangle the veiled contradictions of this ad. We conclude that it serves to legitimate the corporate state by deploying a phanstasmal "consumer republic" that allures by eliciting and soothing contradictory structures of feeling in everyday life. Ontologically anchored in invocation of the dailiness of personal experience, this imagery of the consumer republic is strengthened by textual association with the moral authority of (vestigial) emblems of the democratic republic and with the rational and bureaucratic efficacies of the liberal democratic polity.

Visually, the ad is self-consciously constructed as a pastiche, as if thrown together out of the happenstance of life on the go. Two-thirds of the page are filled with images of odds and ends of everyday life in the 1970s—a rabbit foot on a chain, a note scribbled 9/24/77 8:00 A.M., images of disco dancers, stack heels, 8–track tape, and other passé techno-artifacts—all tossed, as if randomly, onto a shag carpet. A large, central photo shows a Pontiac Le Mans with its hood up, almost hidden behind a handwritten sign "OPEN for SERVICE. SORRY NO GAS." The hodgepodge nature of this assemblage is important. It evokes the architectonics of everyday life in several ways. The seemingly randomness and sedimentation of ordinary objects suggests the

Figure 6. 2007 Ad from the Oil and Natural Gas Industry. Reproduced courtesy of the American Petroleum Institute.

contingent unfolding of events falling athwart each other and then piling up in the forgotten corners of life. This ad evokes the chronotopes of the junk drawer—a midden heap of what once was brought together in the bustle of one day leading to another. But apparent chaos evokes a certain kind of coherence—the aura of authenticity emanating from documentary archives. By gathering together the effluvia of daily life, this pastiche presents itself as witness to the tracks of time. The gathering of times past does more than re-present lost things. It embeds them in a stratigraphy.

This stratigraphy, we would argue, is one of the linear times of the "consumer republic"—constructed from the irresistible movement of "style" endlessly devouring itself—like a necessary cosmic principle of ourobourus. The first sentence of the text makes explicit that this ad organizes itself around temporality as the linear movement from bad to good: "The 1970s was a bad decade for fashion, hairstyles and, especially, energy policy." This sentence sends one's eyes back to the top of the page, into a rummaging around in the junk drawer of now exoticized images of what (given the demographics of newspaper readers) is probably the personal and familiar past of many readers. The "badness" of these images is now imputed to be as self evident as Descartes' *cogito*. Lurking behind this, however, are other more ironic and amused meanings. The playful allure of this ad comes from covert implications that this might be "bad" *now*, but it was not "bad" *then*. The 1970s hair, the hot pink on yellow colors, and so on is "bad" because it is enforced by that specter of Universal Otherhood that is the eye of fashion—the construction of self through the imagined gaze of the imagined *contemporary* other. Commodified fashion only exists in the simultaneity of mutual affirmation of stylistic mastery. Chronotopically, it is flat both temporally and spatially—a grounding in the immediacy and simultaneity of the lateral gaze from nowhere and everywhere. In the world-making powers of commodification, the fads of fashion are a sort of qualitative equivalent to the quantitative mesh of the Universal Otherhood of the market. The Invisible Eye of commodified style is like the Invisible Hand of the market in the self-constituting nature of its authority and scope. Its reign is inevitable if one stays within the constitutive terms of its realm. However, this very absoluteness makes relative its authority and scope. It has no grounds but itself. It cannot (officially) create its own state of exception.

The written text in the ad is reproduced below:

> The 1970s was a bad decade for fashion, hairstyles and, especially, energy policy.

So why are some in Congress playing '70s-style energy politics, pushing the kind of gasoline price controls and energy tax hikes that led to gasoline shortages, long lines at the pump and increased imports?

These schemes will increase the cost of energy for American consumers and businesses. They'll curtail access to America's plentiful domestic energy resources and restrict advanced energy research.

The U.S. Department of Energy predicts Americans will need 28 percent more energy by 2030. It's time for energy policies that ensure future generations have the energy they'll need at home and on the job.

Tell Congress you oppose new energy taxes and price controls. Because it's time for real energy policies, not old-fashioned energy politics.

The written text in figure 6 begins by making explicit the normative and linear chronotopes of the realm of fashion. Then, it quickly appropriates this space-time/good-bad logic to make it the endoskeleton of political economic history with the following trumped up syllogisms (1970s:present as good:bad, and, fashion:energy policy, therefore, the energy policies of the 1970s = bad). Having annealed the "progress" of consumerist goods to the necessary "progress" of government policy, this ad is able to cover up the specificity of actual history behind the generic and linear time of generalized "progress" ("a bad decade for . . . hairstyles and, especially, energy policy"). In the second paragraph, the specificities and messiness of history are further encased into aestheticized simplicities of time understood as shifting fads. The rather ungroovy "energy policy" of the first sentence is recast, in the second sentence, as "some" in Congress "*playing '70s-style energy politics*"—as if the debate about decreasing carbon emissions was a fashion faux pas, and as if the common life was a playground where our main worry should be not to submit our bodies to (consumer) public gaze while wearing anything like polyester leisure suits, which seems to be what "some" elected leaders are doing.

The first paragraph sets the assumptive frame of space and time that makes it easy in the second paragraph to rewrite history, reverse or muddle chronology, and derange geography. In fact, the decade's most dramatic "gasoline shortages" and "long lines at the pump" were not the results of congressional "gasoline price controls" and "tax hikes," but the results of the Arab Oil Embargo of 1973. This political event resulted from Arab anger at U.S. support of Israel in the 1973 Arab-Israeli War. The long-term trend to increased imports was driven primarily by exhaustion of once massive U.S. oil resources. Price and tax policies, through the decade, were not simply driven by Congress but were a very complex mix of presidential, legislative, and industry maneuvering and contestation that shifted over three administrations. President Nixon was a key player in the Emergency Petroleum Allocation Act of 1973, which initiated the strongest price controls. This complexity is dismembered and devoured within the pre-abstracted chronotopes of simple linear time, and, the political space of a highly simplified "America"—with highly simplified, pre-set dramas among a few stock characters. In fact, domestic politics so thoroughly absorbs geopolitics that the rest of the world is present only by vague implication in the caution against "imports."

Spatial and temporal frameworks are simplified by reduction into chunks of time and space. History is chopped into decades. This becomes something like an efficient system of containerization. Once the "'70s" has been constructed as an abstract vessel of abstract time, just about anything—politics, global scramble for natural resources, war, consumerist bric-a-brac, government policy, you name it—can be tossed in and trucked out, down the highways to some dump site for the ontologically passé. In case anybody has missed this message, it is made explicit in the last sentence of the ad—"Because it's time for real energy policies, not old-fashioned energy politics." This completes the trussing together of disparate linear times that was started at the beginning of the text. The first sentence nailed the past to the bad. The last sentence nails the past and the bad to the unreal. The chronological, the normative, and now the ontological are welded together. They are partly held together by a process of stacking linearities that is also a ranking of dualisms. The syllogisms prop each other up (bad:good :: past:future :: unreal:real) and take authority from their alignment with the seeming indubitability of the irreversible arrow of time.

This consolidates the overt chronotopic infrastructures of this text and that constitutes the *overt and official* chronotopic endoskeleton of the pseudo-public of the "consumer republic." Giddy temporal flight is the engine of these infrastructures (new! real! good! chugs the little engine of progress), but, this kind of temporality leaves behind a strangely un-geographized geography—space deposited as if a kind of residue of time. The middle paragraph assesses the "needs" of "Americans" for "energy" and spatializes this onto a shattered geography that is segmented only into "at home" and "on the job." This un-geography includes no commons, no shared space of public appearance—not even a mall.

The girders of consumerist space-times might be infrastructural to this text, but the "republic" part of "consumer republic" is only established by drawing in bits and pieces of quite other political ideologies. It is into the middle of the text where remnants of the liberal democratic polity are hauled and tacked on—lending the appearance of "republic" to what has so far been structured as if a playground of consumerist style. The statement that "The U.S. Department of Energy predicts Americans will need 20 percent more energy by 2030" evokes an image of impartiality and science as arbiter and guarantor of predictive rationality. The future is now encased in the panoptic, forward-looking gaze of technocratic reason that is in turn encased within the calm authority of a rationalized, bureaucratized government agency. This magisterial gaze is mirrored by a perfectly mastered objective world in which "energy needs" can be perfectly known and predicted. This suggests that society and nature are made up of forces that can be analyzed and pre-known because they are immanent with regularities of Newtonian clarity and universality. This is vitalism. It is grounded in a superstitious notion of the generative capacities of nature and society as vital essences that grow from their own immanent nature. This is a notion of civil and ecological "growth" that exactly mirrors the economic "growth" imputed to capital markets. It imputes mechanistic inevitability and necessity to economic expansion. But, this economic "growth" is actually driven by the actual social relationships of investment, their boosterish dreams, and all their apparatus of political and material might—what Tsing calls "spectacular accumulation" (Tsing, 2005, chap. 2; see 59).

This technocratic and bureaucratic gaze appears to annihilate alternative futures. It also annihilates ecology and politics. It assumes the steady expansion of energy needs, because it assumes the steady expansion of consumerist markets and industrial production to meet the "needs" that are being instantly created and instantly devoured in the Saturnine maw of capitalist time as "progress." Actual ecological and political temporalities tremble, frighteningly, on the edges of this page—with all their recursivities, unpredictable concatenations, synergism, and just plain messy heterogeneities, boundary jumping, and boundary making. It is interesting that both of the cars in this ad are positioned so that we cannot see their tailpipes. But, surely, that does not wipe out all awareness of what is coming out. Cigarette ads airbrushed smoke for decades from the glamorous glow of their cigarettes, but that did not keep it forever beyond congressional purview.

In its short text, this ad manages to strategically appropriate key sectors of the liberal democratic polity—rationalized bureaucratic policy and regulation, technocratic science, possessive individualism, negative freedoms, interest group politics, and professional managerialism of nature construed as standing resource. "Politics" is linguistically tamed and turned into "policy." The subtitle says "Congress is playing '70s style energy politics. What about America's energy future?" This belittles politics—casting it as a mere "playing."

It infantilizes Congress—making the elected representatives of the people an immature and despised Other unable to care for America's future. It effaces an understanding of politics as democratic contestation that is essential to the health of a democratic republic. The text goes on to say that the Congress is "playing" "politics" and "pushing" "schemes," when it is "time for" "real energy *policies* . . ." not "*politics.*" The first and last sentences create something like ontological bookends that hold the ideological structures of this text together—recontaining mere, unruly "politics" within the sedate authority of "policy." As we shall see in following chapters, this has been a key rhetorical move of the liberal democratic polity. It is a process of removing collective and participatory democratic debate about issues of common concern from the democratic public sphere, to sequester them within professional and bureaucratic institutions. There are three problems with this feature of the liberal democratic polity—as we discuss in detail in later chapters. First, the twentieth century has clearly demonstrated that government agencies are liable to capture by the industries they are mandated to regulate. Second, professions and universities are increasingly vulnerable to corporate influence. Third, the fracturing of government agencies and professions into specialized mandates and disciplines tends to dismember thought, making it hard to do the integrated analysis and judgment that is appropriate for reality (in all its multi-dimensionality, complexity, and heterogeneity).

This corporate text also manages the open-ended contestation of democratic politics by encasing it within "interest group" schemas that are foundational of liberal democratic ideology. The only type of intersubjectivity in the text of this ad is in the mode of "interest group" relationships—collective subjects who possess interests that define the scope of their action in public space, delinking it from collective, open-ended debate upon questions of the common good. This is because the only social actors in the main body of this written text are "Congress" (coded as "scheming," negative actors), "consumers," "businesses," and "future generations." Citizens are strikingly absent (so far). The agency of these actors is predefined, because their roles are predefined—limited to defending "needs" and getting "access" to "resources." This mise-en-scène constructs actors as *bearers of self-interest*. There is one sentence that suggests something like generativity, in the call for "policies that ensure future generations have the energy they'll need." This one sentence cleverly scoops up a key common phrase from discourses of sustainability to decorate itself in the borrowed plumage of green morality—very much going against the grain of this ad's stylistics. But the unborn potential victims (of "Congress" it seems) are themselves no more then need-bearing, interest-bearing, abstract individuals. The semiotic apparatuses of this text tend to squeeze shut dialogical spaces—with one exception. At the very end the grammar shifts to the second person, and for the first time hails a "you" who is accorded powers of action. But this is a predetermined and administered space of dialogue—"Tell Congress you oppose . . ." It would be interesting to know how much this ad cost to conceive, design, and distribute and to know the ratio between that cost and the average monthly salary of the average citizen reading it. But one can be sure that a lot of marketing firepower bears down on the eyes skimming the newspaper—falling subliminally, for most readers, into the drowsy bodily textures of caffeine and distraction that separate the night's oblivion or insomnia from the harried overwork of day. It suggests the agentic space-times of citizen participation. It is, however, but the façade of dialogue and free speech. It is indelibly marked by vast inequality in the available resources for constructing voice and the terms of the conversation in the public square.

In any event, this appropriation of emblems of rational dialogue, expertise, and governance from liberal democratic ideology is primarily ornamental. It grabs up tokens of legitimacy and competency that are needed to cover up the inadequacies of the "consumer republic." These bits and pieces of liberal democratic rhetoric are like flying buttresses on medieval cathedrals—heavily ornamental and structurally necessary to prevent collapse. The DOE prediction is not science; it is fake science on a leash. The imagery of government regulation and technocratic managerialism bestow gravity to pseudo-public ceremonies of pseudo-participation. They do not authorize free-ranging public debate about energy policy understood within complex ecological and social geographies of citizens inhabiting shared worlds.

Tucked into the lower right-hand corner of this ad is what we read as its political linchpin. In the realm of spectacle, of virtual commodified space, this is the least important corner—where the eye falls last. But if you take this ad as a manifesto or a letter to the public, this is where you look to find the signature, the revelation of the unique inscription of the author. And it seems that we should read it both ways—both as a sort of abject remainder, an unimportant margin, and as the authorial voice proper. For, as it turns out, a quick glance suggests a moving living hand. One's eyes are arrested by the first line: "THE people OF AMERICA'S." "People" is in a strong cursive font—dramatically suggesting that constitutional "We the People" through which the revolutionary popular will was instituted as foundational of the American republic. It is as if the free people all got together the night before to sign this letter to themselves so they could reread in the morning. There are some very confusing transubstantiations going on here. One corporate body is morphing into another in ways that seem grammatical but do not make sense. What people is this exactly? Well, the full "signature" is "THE people OF AMERICA'S/OIL AND NATURAL GAS INDUSTRY." How is this "America's" industry? Who owns whom? Is nationalization of "America's plentiful domestic energy resources" implied? Or, has Big Energy just eaten up the people's body?

On one hand, this seems to be a sacred relic of the body politic of the democratic republic. It suggests the self-authoring of the collective general will in the constituent assemblies of a free people. It is the only place where any notion of citizenship is suggested. But it is not the citizens of the rough and tumble debate of a genuine democratic republic (all that has been safely cleared away by the fashion police who are making the streets safe for good fashion). Those sorts of citizens are diverse, particular, gabby, and opinionated; this is the abstracted, cleaned-up Citizen representing the incorporated, collective body in its constitutional propriety. However remnantal their representation, the "people" need to be there, however, *because no other authorial voice carries sufficient moral power to anchor the legitimacy of this document.* The specter of the democratic republican polity still haunts. This is especially true when questions of entitlement to the civil and ecological commons are raised—which is inevitably the case with energy industries, which have vast powers over infrastructure of all sorts, as well as that heating and cooling of habitations that bears so intimately on bodily comfort and our sheltering from ecological extremes. And so the "Oil and Natural Gas Industry" actually has the last word in this document, but only by appropriating the signature of "We the People." This is, then, the imprimatur of the corporate state—engulfing the governing structures of the republic, rewiring the symbolic circuitry of public life, and dressing itself up in weird corporate drag as "We the People."

4

Regenerating Public Culture
Ecological Ontology for Democratic Publics

The ecological havoc our world is experiencing is integrally linked with the structural forces that increase inequality and weaken democratic publics. These publics require a stronger civic commons if what has been thought of as an environmental commons is to be restored to healthier conditions and rewoven into less destructive forms of economy and social life. The last century's prevailing notions of "development" and "environment" have failed. That is why the challenge now is configuring a post-dualist ecological sensibility as a political search for institutions of fundamental change in the political and economic status quo.

If we want to live in a peaceful, cooperative world led by democratic republics, then the public understanding and practice of certain civic labors is vital. Strengthening of the civic commons is integral to protection of the environmental commons. If the environmental commons are the substantive goods in common that are the sustaining grounds of life, the civic commons are the institutions, collective memories, social networks, and skills that enable and inspire individuals to engage with each other in stewarding the common good. Such collective labor for the larger good requires some form of collective imagination that enables awareness of self and other (human or nonhuman) as inherently valuable. But, beyond this, it requires perceptual and social infrastructures that nurture the ability to see self and other as *emergent from* and *dependent on* the supra-individual matrix that supports both life and individual. Central to such civic labor, is a nondualistic understanding of individual/matrix. Such a nondualistic understanding of self/other-in-matrix is central to political and ecological imaginations that are decentered from ethnic, species, class, gender, or other domination and solipsism.

John Dewey's Democratic Theory

John Dewey's work as a whole is a powerful call for such a nondualistic understanding of individual-in-matrix, and few have better understood its connections to democracy. But, it is in his philosophy of art that Dewey describes most specifically the central importance of the aesthetic dimension of public culture to overcoming crippling dualisms of Western modernity that vitiate participatory engagement—individual/world, nature/culture, ends/means, leisure/work, art/science, aesthetic/ordinary. Reading Dewey's aesthetic ecology in this light requires going beyond reductionist, individualist philosophies of art and politics that think within the categories of self, other, and dyadic experience. Rather, one must turn to ideas like John Dewey's notion of public intelligence—considering the matrixical conditions of public life that provoke and sustain nonreified ecological consciousness.

Dewey's writings on art have not been much utilized in the philosophical work for civic environmentalism. We argue for their relevance to the key goal of overcoming the segmentation of life ushered in by modernity and buttressed by these dualisms. Second, we look at the implications of Dewey's aesthetic ecology for an "environmentalism of daily life" that challenges the false dualisms of neoliberalism and of technocratic professionalism that undermine place-based forms of life and knowledge. Third, we draw on Dewey's aesthetic philosophy to suggest ways to rebuild democratic public space at the nexus of body, place, and commons.

Before probing Dewey's thought more deeply, we wish to consider the highly compatible study of the politics of local knowledge offered by Frank Fischer, who also enlists Dewey in a similar way. Both Shutkin and Fischer rely on *The Public and Its Problems,* whereas we are interested in a wider range of Dewey's work during the last thirty years of his life (Fischer, 2000; Shutkin, 2000). In particular, that later work offers a mature vision of the vital entwinings of art, nature, and social critique, or what we choose to call his *aesthetic ecology of public intelligence*. At the beginning of his invaluable study, Fischer (2000, 1, 6–8) says the question is "Can the democratic process be rescued from the increasingly technocratic, elitist policy-making processes that more and more define our present age?" A few pages later, Fischer enlists John Dewey's argument from his 1927 study *The Public and Its Problems* (1991 [1927]). That book might be characterized as describing the path not taken by a system of political economy that constantly reorganizes platoons of specialized experts charged primarily with narrowing the democratic relevance of technical knowledge in favor of elite dominance instead of fostering public enlightenment and participation. Fischer's account of "participatory inquiry as civic discovery" and some of its forms of emergent practice may indeed be understood as "the methodological extension of Dewey's call for a more collaborative relationship between citizens and experts." Dewey certainly would have applauded Fischer's documentation and analysis of various, viable forms of citizen participation in complex environmental decisions. Fischer's examination of community inquiry, participatory research, and the "discursive institutions for environmental policy making" are major contributions to democratic theory and critical ecology.

However, Dewey's philosophy of democratic communication, knowledge, and community was more revolutionary than Fischer's ideas of "collaboration" and "methodological extension." It is true that students of Dewey's political theory are divided on whether he was a liberal democrat or a philosopher of radical democracy. We think Dewey's radical democratic politics are illuminated by some attention to his later work. For example, in the 1927 essay Dewey's concluding Emersonian reference to local life in "the lap of an immense intelligence" recalls his earlier comment that the "prime condition of a democratically organized public is *a kind of knowledge and insight which does not yet exist*" (1991 [1927], 219, 166; emphasis added). The question we wish to take up is whether Dewey's work—especially from his *Experience and Nature* of 1925 to the end of his life in 1952—provides a more radical foundation for the participatory inquiry central to Fischer's postpositivist perspective and to Shutkin's emerging paradigm of civic environmentalism. What we want to show is that *Dewey's radically ecological understanding of the aesthetic dimensions of experience and public intelligence is especially pertinent to grappling with interrelated crises of environmental and social justice*. A number of scholars have pointed to Dewey as an exemplar of "civic professionalism," but we think a much more substantive engagement with his work is needed.

Dewey's Aesthetic Ecology for an "Environmentalism of Daily Life"

In 1962, ten years after Dewey died, Henry David Aiken pointed to the importance of *Art as Experience* (Dewey, 1934) as a signal effort to move pragmatism beyond scientism and moralism without falling into aestheticism (Aiken, 1962; Dewey, 1934). Later in the 1960s we find John J. McDermott following Dewey in arguing that "we would do well to view the economic and political questions as, at bottom, aesthetic" (McDermott, 1976, 52). In *The Culture of Experience,* McDermott proposed an *"aesthetic ecology"* that begins with the basic problem formulated by Dewey in 1934, *"that of recover-*

ing the continuity of aesthetic experience with normal processes of living" (10; emphasis added). In short, McDermott suggests that the anaesthetizing of these processes is fundamentally a political and economic problem.

By the end of the twentieth century, the dominant system of power in the United States had effectively instituted a bifurcated politics of jobs versus environment, of work versus place. Robert Gottlieb's critical historical analysis (Gottlieb, 1993, 2001) of this segmented politics and its consequences provide a fundamental perspective on the challenges to movements for socioecological justice. For instance, the representation of "workers" has been increasingly confined to atomized "jobs," sometimes requiring the destruction of the remnants of community life. The rationalization of this process in eastern Kentucky and southern West Virginia by energy conglomerates such as Arch and Massey is but one example.

Organizations representing "the environment" have been accorded greater legitimacy when middle-class citizens have acquiesced to accommodative measures, detaching matters of leisure from those of work and community. We have already mentioned the problem of mainstream environmentalism's elitism. Gottlieb has demonstrated how this bounding of environmentalism in the United States reflects its domestication by a corporate state that in its current transnational phase is systematically disrupting if not destroying all placed forms of community experience. Almost always, inferior and transient jobs are offered to workers, as governors and mayors repeat the neoliberal mantra of "global competitiveness." Gottlieb makes the key point for us in these words: "Environmentalism as a form of consumption and a language that separates the social and the ecological stands in contrast to an environmentalism of daily life within an evolving social order" (Gottlieb, 2001, 45).

Dewey's aesthetic ecology of public intelligence provides one powerful way of understanding and advancing this "environmentalism of daily life." Dewey's concern for the future of democratic publics is clear in *Art as Experience,* where political aesthetics weaves the connections of environmental health, meaningful work, and civic experience. Too often in the twentieth century, the politics of work failed to effectively raise questions of experience and participation, as labor representatives settled for modest economic securities in a "social contract" that was largely shredded by the 1980s. It was in that decade that one leading political scientist (B. Gross, 1982) portrayed the possibility that our beleaguered democratic polity might be transformed into a "friendly fascism." We believe that this threat should be taken quite seriously as we engage a question with which Dewey was especially concerned during his last twenty-five years: Is it possible to reconstruct a democratic public that is capable of transforming the transnational corporate state that has been suffocating our traditionally liberal-democratic polity by reshaping it as an instrument of sheer corporate power? It is from this explicitly political perspective, and with special attention to Dewey's contribution, that we want to make a conjoint case for civic professionalism and civic environmentalism.

William Sullivan's 1995 study *Work and Integrity* is right in contending that there is a crisis of professionalism, that we have a lot to learn from the Progressives' struggle for a civic professionalism, that today professionalism must be reinvented, and that we should look to John Dewey as an exemplar of civic professionalism. But we need to do more than extol Dewey's "faith in the power of democratic participation" (Sullivan, 1995, 232). John Dewey's "civic professionalism" should not be split off from his politics or political theory. As Westbrook has shown, John Dewey "[b]y the thirties . . . was not arguing for 'social intelligence' as an alternative to politics but for a radical politics that incorporated social intelligence into its practice" (Westbrook, 1991, 526).

Thomas Alexander, while making no mention of McDermott in his 1987 book, points out that "Dewey's is one of the first explicitly ecological views of nature and consequently of knowledge" (T. Alexander, 1987, 101). We find in Dewey, as they do, a theory of practical rationality crucial for the development of a postpositivist university that has as its lodestar a democratic public. As Sullivan puts it, the "critical step in this direction lies in the rehabilitation of nonformal modes of rationality which do not screen out the practical, moral, and historical standpoint of both the subjects and the objects of knowledge" (Sullivan, 1995, 171). It seems very doubtful to us that this "rehabilitation" can be accomplished on any significant institutional scale by sermonizing the business and political leaders of the corporate state including most administrators of our corporatizing universities.

Bruce Wilshire's book *The Moral Collapse of the University* demonstrates the role of the epistemic regime of positivism in our crisis of professionalism and higher education (Wilshire, 1990, 201–54). What Reid argues is that we also have to understand the role of scientism and positivism in producing forms of knowledge and policy that exemplify and legitimate the organizing principles of corporate capitalism, regardless of our personal intentions (Reid, 2001a, 2001b). Sullivan's concern with "professional integrity" needs to be more strongly informed by his analysis of how the professions took up "positions within the new national economic order *according to that order's own organizing principles*" (Sullivan, 1995, 58–59; emphasis added). Of course, what Richard Sennett calls the "autonomy" of professionals has varied historically and from field to field (Sennett, 1981). But it is from Sennett rather than Sullivan that we clearly understand that professional "autonomy" is fundamentally an ideology of class society legitimating a form of authority "without love" or nurturance (84–121). Technocratic tendencies in the professions are structured by the "dualist horizon of the corporate state" (Reid, 2001a, 35–38) based on the nature/culture dichotomy that keys the dialectic of space and place in which the former invariably dominates the latter. The postcommunal thrust of the professions caught up in the globalizing processes of the transnational corporate state is at the heart of the crises of the civic and environmental commons.

In Dewey's *Experience and Nature* (1925), he says art "is the complete culmination of nature and . . . 'science' is properly a handmaiden that conducts natural events to this happy issue" (1929 [1925], 290). The smashing of the integral vision of art and science is one and the same as the ontological destruction of the lifeworld and its institutional dismemberment in the slaughterhouse of the technocratic university. (Academic folklore awaits its Kurt Vonnegut, although Jane Smiley's *Moo* is suggestive.) As Dewey went on to say, the "separation of science from art, and the division of arts into those concerned with mere means and those concerned with ends in themselves, is a mask for lack of conjunction between power and the goals of life (311). In his last twenty-five years, Dewey devoted much energy and imagination to dismantling the sacrificial altars to the market machine-god that are being rebuilt today, under neoliberal auspices, on some of our campuses (and not only in economics departments).

John Dewey did not just espouse a theory of social intelligence; he was a philosopher of "public intelligence." Unlike many political scientists he did not simply consider public opinion in American society as at one and the same time a given force and an elite tool; Dewey pursued a critical theory of the formation of public opinion. He would agree with Frank Fischer's call to experts to consider themselves "specialized citizens" and categorization of the good citizen as a "local expert" (Fischer, 2000, 41–46, 147–69). Perhaps the most important statement in Dewey's classic essay *The Public and Its Problems* (1927) is that: the "prime condition of a democratically organized public is a kind of knowledge and insight which does not yet exist" (Dewey, 1991 [1927], 166). What we have discovered in a number of Appalachian contexts are communities whose experiences of place as a reliable life rhythm have been disrupted, even traumatized, leading them to appeal to first principles of the body politic. Infuriated that corporate state officials would justify their exploitation as necessary because they live in a "national sacrifice area," coalfield

Appalachians increasingly have sought remedies on various paths of democratic citizenship. Roughly twenty years ago, the Appalachian Alliance task force—exemplifying democratic resistance and reconstruction—examined mineral and land ownership patterns and followed through with publicity, policy advocacy, and community organizing for years afterward. The Alliance experience provides one durable model for a democratic public sphere project (Reid, 2001a, 519). This project of critical regionalism exemplified Dewey's point that: "Communication of the results of social inquiry is the same thing as the formation of public opinion" (Dewey, 1991 [1927], 177).

Retrieving the Political from Body~Place~Commons: Cues from Dewey

But it is on Dewey's *Art as Experience* that we wish to focus. The great problem for Dewey in this study is the "chasm between ordinary and esthetic experience" (Dewey, 1934, 10). His first working premise is that "life goes on in an environment" (13), and one of his initial targets is a sort of aesthetic individualism that among other things impedes communication between "humanists" and "social scientists." Dewey moves quickly to the key problem of the institutionally based dualisms that mechanically structure compartmentalized forms of life experience. He is clear that the denial of the body and the confinement of the senses are centrally involved in the industrialization process he witnessed over so many decades.

The test of institutions lies in the forms and qualities of the human experience that they allow or encourage. Because human energies provide the nourishing fluids for institutional life, Dewey labors to illuminate the aesthetic organization of energies in relation to everyday experience. His discussion may be connected with Teresa Brennan's recent critique of political economy and psychology, which describes "an interactive energetic economy" (Brennan, 2000, 41). For Dewey the disordering of experience too often results in a consequent loss of "*the power to experience the common world in its fullness*" (Dewey, 1934, 133; emphasis added). This power is *grounded* in rhythms in nature—"a universal scheme of existence, underlying all realization of order in change" (150), cosmopoetic forms interlacing world and subconscious life at the deepest levels.

Listening to West Virginia mountaineers narrate their experience of valleys, mountains, and streams before and after traumatic strip mining or mountaintop removal, we find examples of the "living natural energies" central to "interactive energetic economy" (Teresa Brennan, 2000, 52, 41). The loss of agency here is exactly the loss of holistic experience described by Dewey, a process resulting from the destruction of both environmental and civic commons.

As Dewey argues, "Whenever the bond that binds the living creature to his environment is broken, there is nothing that holds together the various factors and phases of the self" (Dewey, 1934, 252). It is the breaking of this bond that is key to the dualistic structuring of life experience. From Sam Shepard's film *Paris, Texas* to William Leach's study *Country of Exiles* (Leach, 1999, 58–90), a people historically dislocated or disoriented in what Leach calls a "vast landscape of the temporary" is an image flickering on the edge of political despair. Leach goes straight at those versions of academic cosmopolitanism founded on the irrelevance of place.

However, social theorist Manuel Castells argues that the "network society" finds power and knowledge increasingly configured in an ahistorical *space of flows* reflecting the "organizational capacity of the dominant elite" deployed, of course, by professional managers and experts. The spatial and social segregation of such groups, tending toward transnational identities, positions them at odds with the great majority of people living in scattered places where in everyday experience a contrasting logic is primary (Castells, 1996, 415–69). He forces everyone's attention in his observation: "Articulation of the elites, segmentation and disorganization of the masses seem to be the twin mechanisms of social domination in our societies" (415). In this work, Castells makes too sharp the disjuncture between the space of flows and the space of places and underestimates political capacities for redirecting flows of power. (We illuminate why this is the case in the chapters that follow). But Castells himself soon came to realize the political promise of "grassrooting the space of flows" and went at least so far as to allow for the "coexistence" of the two spatial logics (Castells & Ince, 2003, 58). Our ongoing argument is that the political fact of the domination of one logic does not resolve the ontological issue.

In Thomas Alexander's very insightful work, he shows us quite convincingly how Dewey and Merleau-Ponty provide complementary theories of the living body as a medium for expressive activity, and that as "the body becomes 'encultured,' to coin a term, so culture becomes embodied" (T. Alexander, 1987, xix, 143–46, 221–22). As Alexander puts it, for Dewey "[e]xperience is the on-going world of nature culturally inhabited" (270). John Dewey's aesthetic ecology of democratic publics is one way to grasp why it is so important for academic work to recognize and negotiate the gaps between the space of flows and the space of places. In the next chapter, we connect Dewey's thinking with the work of Merleau-Ponty, Edward Casey, and Jeff Malpas to develop a theoretical language for the civic commons as infrastructure for the aesthetic ecology of democratic publics.

Dewey's key understanding of culture is "that organized body of activities by which human beings are meaningfully present to each other" (T. Alexander, 1987). While shared, participatory endeavors and dialogue are fundamental for community, it is "[t]hrough the culture of nature [that] the community appropriates itself as art" (267). Alexander's renderings help us understand Dewey's point that the sense of relation between nature and humanity "in some form has always been the actuating spirit of art" (Dewey, 1934, 339). As Dewey put it, the "barriers that separate human beings from one another" may be undermined by artistic expression that re-weds people and nature and reminds persons of "their union with one another in origin and destiny" (270–71). It is in this sense that Dewey speaks of "experience in its integrity" (274). What Dewey lamented as the isolation of art and the failure to adequately acknowledge it as a "power in human association" (348) is part and parcel of the tragic loss of "integral elements of experience" (337).

In Dewey's view, as long as "art is the beauty parlor of civilization, neither art nor civilization is secure" (1934, 344). What should not be ignored is Dewey's connection of this state of affairs to those conditions preventing "the mass of men and women who do the useful work of the world" from realizing freedom "in conducting the processes of production" and in developing "a richly endowed . . . capacity for enjoying the fruits of collective work" (344). He was writing in the midst of the Great Depression, at a time when the global jobs crisis was less obviously linked to global environmental crisis, as is the case today. The past twenty-five years of economic globalization have too often entailed intertwined processes of disinhabitation and subjectivization: a growing world of thinned-out places and ecological refugees. A citizenship capable of dealing with the social and environmental crises that beset our world must be situated in the aesthetic ecology of bodies, places, and times that Dewey's later work described. While social hope has its roots in the commons where body and place meet, it springs from their cultivation in political tasks of public discourse and action. Our universities need to be relocated from the global economic space of transnational corporations to the global regional publics and bioregions where a politics for a sustainable world-in-common is emerging. Tenured faculty operating as academic tourists need to understand that as re-placed public intellectuals practicing participatory inquiry they do not have to keep buying into an unsustainable professionalism twisting in the winds of cynical reason and looming deanships.

If "nature is gone for good" (Jameson, qtd. in Hardt & Negri, 2000, 187) and the production of subjectivity is nothing but a project of external power, then it is not only Dewey who is passé. If Hardt and Negri are right, the United States indeed may be the seat of a new empire. However, grassroots environmentalists, following Emerson, Thoreau, Wendell Berry, and Barbara Kingsolver, are not ready to give up on the empire of Nature. Max Horkheimer (1974 [1947], 101–26), lecturing at Columbia in the 1940s, fearful that "nature's tongue has been taken away," predicted nevertheless a "revolt of nature" that could play havoc with the new empire and drive us all back upon the local of not only survival but new beginnings. History, we might speculate, would finally install the American Adam amid the ruins of the myth and its products. Today our political options are wider, and so we think it is foolish to fantasize ourselves as "nomadic revolutionaries." Instead of preaching "resistance to the present" (Hardt & Negri, 2000, 393), our grassroots environmentalists are finding fertilizer in their various time zones to cultivate new institutional blends of the familiar and the innovative in a process of democratic change. John Dewey's aesthetic ecology of public intelligence is another contribution to the political imagination capable of forging an ecological politics for and from our world-in-common. As Milenko Matanovic recently wrote, "Just as a gardener uses the compost of one season to stimulate the growth of the next, the artist takes part of the old disintegrating world and uses them as fertilizer for cultural change. Out of the chaos of the old, new order is created" (Matanovic, 2002, 14).

Dewey's Pragmatism and the Politics of American History

Examining the politics of identity in U.S. history, social theorist Norbert Wiley has argued that the "pragmatic coalition . . . saved American democracy in the early twentieth century. At the very least, it looks as though citizenship rights and civil liberties would have diminished if Social Darwinism had not been checked by pragmatism" (Wiley, 1994, 141). The core cultural configuration for this coalition, according to Wiley, is the classical pragmatist theory of the self that he describes as dialogical, social, egalitarian, and so on. He attempts to show how in the democratic movements of U.S. politics around the beginning of the twentieth century it came to replace the "faculty psychology" of the founders at a time when corporate capitalism was being legitimated by an amalgamation of frontier individualism and social Darwinism. Wiley recognizes that by the end of the twentieth century a new resurgence of global capital and transnational corporate power had worsened both economic inequality and identity tensions (142). Subtle new biologically reductionist forms of social Darwinism in academic and consumer culture are now at work in league with neoliberal justifications for "free trade" and "global competition." Wiley's own response to what we think is a new crisis of democracy in the United States is a neo-pragmatist theory of the "semiotic self." However, our concern here is to make a deeper probe of Dewey's democratic pragmatism, taking into account the views of one of his most astute contemporary critics.

No American historian writing today has probed so thoroughly as John P. Diggins modern America's problematic structure of authority. His liberal-realist critique of the socialization of authority and its elevation of the principle of public opinion to the detriment of viable political governance reflect a view of authority as the "intellectual expression of power." Diggins's adamancy on the role of the "theoretical intellect" is illustrated in his criticism of Richard Sennett. Driving hard and fast a rather familiar academic liberal distinction between knowledge and opinion, Diggins accuses Sennett of reducing authority to emotions and of resorting to a hermeneutical approach of "turning authority over to the people." His 1979 essay poses the issue: "Can society be sustained by opinion alone?" (Diggins, 1979). His argument with Sennett answers with a resounding "No" (Diggins, 1982, 376–80; Reid, 1990; Sennett, 1981).

But is the question falsely posed? Is there always in modern societies a dialectic of knowledge and opinion that takes hegemonic and alternative forms? Does Sennett "reduce authority to emotions and perceptions," or does his populist-anarchist and hermeneutical approach offer a candid and more democratic response to the inextricable role of consent in the practice of modern authority? (see Sennett, 1981, chaps. 5 and 6). Isn't the post-Enlightenment recognition of interpretation as an integral part of social process an acknowledgment that the genie of traditional political authority as "the right to rule and the duty to obey" (Diggins, 1982, 376) is not going back into the bottle? Statist projects, whether of the conservative Right or the social-democratic Left, lacking legitimacy, have vacillated between aristocratic restorationism and pseudo-populism.

Is it any wonder that this process has enhanced the durability of the classical liberal myth of the market in a society where socialized authority increasingly has been subject to technobureaucratic appropriation of the structures of political action? What does the Democratic Left have to learn from the elitist "realism" of reform liberal or conservative restorationist laments for "traditional political authority"? Perhaps there is much to learn whether we are considering the despair of a democratic populist like Christopher Lasch quoting Philip Rieff on "sacred order" or whether we are taking a second look at the Diggins confrontation with Sennett, Dewey, and Rorty (Reid, 2001a, 530–35).

Diggins's argument with Sennett may now be read as a skirmish preliminary to his important commentary on and extension of the Niebuhr-Dewey debate. Diggins's lucid review emphasizes what Niebuhr has to teach Dewey, and by extrapolation the relevance of the theologian's Christian existentialist-realism for comprehending the dilemmas of contemporary liberalism. Niebuhr's superior knowledge of evil and the "specter of power" is pitted against Dewey's passionate belief in self-realization and "intelligence as an instrument of control" (Diggins, 1994, 9, 216, 285–91, 297, 441, 481).[1] Beyond his extremism on self-fulfillment, Dewey "purged from political philosophy the one idea that had made community actually work—the idea of authority as the right to rule and the duty to obey" (Diggins, 1993, 120). Diggins' trial of pragmatism's promise is brilliantly concluded with a ruling on the Dewey legacy, Rorty, and the "illusions of poststructuralism" enlisting his most credible witnesses, Niebuhr and Henry Adams. Dewey and now Rorty are situated before "the spectacle of power and evil" and put to the Niebuhrian measure, a "pessimistic wisdom of tragedy and irony" (Diggins, 1994, 481, 434) that becomes a bath of skepticism washing both the solidarity projects of the pragmatist and neo-pragmatist. Diggins's move is to question the poststructuralist resort to social authority by demonstrating Niebuhr's case for an ineradicable subject (combining essentialism and modernism) as well as the "possibilities of human agency" (439). It is a courageous effort to show that the theorist of politics is unable wisely to dispense with theological categories of guilt and grace. Anticipating the criticism of ontologizing power and evil, Diggins comes up, with O'Brien's help, a pithy statement by Edmund Burke chastising radicals who fail to "acknowledge that the wicked inventiveness of power eludes its passing representations" or transitory modes.

Perhaps Diggins is right to reject the political paths to solidarity as they are designed and confronted in his valuable study. Nevertheless, there remains the problem of a liberal pluralism magnified by the appeal and dread of solidarity. Some might see here a Christian-existentialist-realist version of a very familiar liberal concern with the possible excesses of communitarian politics. Is the political authority appealed to here not only that of a "procedural republic"[2] but also an American liberal-consensus version of "sacred order" (as "new world order"?) that entails an undue tribute of reason to power? As our procedural republic has generated a more fearful moralistic politics of pseudo-community, has this provided reified, seldom convincing images of a "democratic" state? We doubt that Diggins would deny that our corporate state's veil of liberal pluralism leaves us with the agony and the anger of unanswered questions or issues of justice. It seems pertinent to ask if he is not saying that it is important for intellectuals to entertain such suspicions but recognize that not much can be done politically with them?

On the eve of the Great Depression, John Dewey's philosophy took a "profoundly radical turn": he "extended the community of investigators to include the democratic public itself" (Diggins, 1994, 236). Diggins knows too much about the public's opinions in U.S. history to let Dewey get away with that. Dewey, he says, failed to face up to "political reality," an intellectual luxury not available to our best politicians such as Lincoln. Diggins's criticism of Dewey is made by moving from a realistic view of Lincoln's time and leadership to an idealized (i.e., abstracted) picture of Peircean science outside the corporate state. The trouble with Dewey is that he took democracy too seriously and did not leave alone the sleeping dogs of mass belief. Dewey should have learned from Peirce that critical inquiry and rational discussion are confined to professional communities. Dewey kept raising questions about the social conditions of inquiry when he should have been concerned with "the autonomy of science." Critical studies in the philosophy, sociology, and politics of science do not yield such a facile contrast with Dewey.[3] Nevertheless, was not Dewey's point that, yes, social order might be jeopardized, but how else could a democratic society develop?

Diggins contends that Robert Westbrook "considers Dewey's greatness to lie in what may be his weakest area . . . his mushy sentiments as a political philosopher." Diggins does not dispute the link (made by James Miller as well as Westbrook) between Dewey, Mills, and the early New Left idea of "participatory democracy." He thinks that if Dewey had faced up to the American democrat's sorry record including "his" tendency to reduce community to real estate, Dewey would not have "read into politics values that once were found solely in religion." It seems that radical democratic illusions in politics are enough to spook even a part-time Nietzschean skeptic into the liberal loft of the "procedural republic"—a narrow perspective on the "constitutional system" coupled with a remarkably generous view of how it "works." In Diggins's account of recent times, "the advancement of women and minorities has succeeded not because of democracy but because the courts intervened and imposed over the democratic process a new rights-based culture that would have confounded Dewey."[4] What is striking in this comment is the reference to "the democratic process" as well as a legalistic account of political struggle. The latter recalls Attorney Morris Liebman's defense of the procedural republic against the Reverend William Sloane Coffin's case for civil disobedience protesting U.S. Vietnam War policy.[5] The SDS Port Huron Statement that opened the decade in question can hardly be accused of such mushy sentiments about "the democratic process."

Dewey, Raymond Williams, and the Academic Left

The ambivalent reaction of reform liberals to the Port Huron idea of "participatory democracy" exemplifies the tendency to make law do the work of politics. Today, when a democratic transition to a green economy is urgently needed, it is well to remember this history and the question of whether we can learn from Dewey's extension of the community of investigators to include the public itself. The Second New Left, partly engulfed by the counterculture, was vulnerable to what become a persistent dialect of scientism and subjectivism. Dewey's democratic professionalism and his ecological ontology were lost in the process. A generation later they were still missing among postmodern academics retreating from the streets, sometimes preoccupied with "subjectivity as such."

Reform liberals and others have been divided for many years on Dewey's case for participatory democracy when in the 1920s he challenged Walter Lippmann's elitist-realist argument for containing public opinion's role in government decision making. Historian James Livingston has revisited the debate, making the interesting argument that Dewey "understood the new scope and significance of cultural politics better than Lippmann" (Livingston, 2001, 53). But Livingston bypasses Dewey's politics for a culturalized version that is recast as the "subjective" basis for a socialist transformation made possible by the "socializing imperatives of the new corporate order" (82). The large modern corporation and corporate globalization are presumed to provide objective conditions for socialist development. Forcing Dewey's theory of the "social self" into such a progressivist historical framework not only misses his ecological ontology but also dumps his democratic political theory.

When Westbrook refers to Livingston's thesis that "the pragmatists forecast a postmodern self . . . located in time rather than space" (Westbrook, 2001, 60), it is important to appreciate Livingston's self-conscious subject-object dualism and how it connects with his treatment of Dewey's thinking about the Local, which Dewey averred might be the only absolute. Livingston's readiness to dismiss Dewey's "homage to local community" (53) not only reflects his way of privileging time and history but also serves as a marker for dis-placing and depoliticizing Dewey's citizen-agent, which has become a reified prototype for postmodern subjectivity. The "integrity of the self" or "moral personality" (Livingston's terms) wait on historical development of the structural context of life for which historicist socialism keeps the keys promising "a passage beyond class society" (1994, 275–79). In what follows, we want to show both Dewey's pragmatic theory of the self situated within a theory of democratic culture and its significance for critical alternatives to academic "whistling in the dark" toward globalization and the subjectivization it promotes.

As Westbrook documents, Dewey "was not only a democratic collectivist but also a persistent populist" in a project that may be understood partly as the reconstruction of the democratic values of the producers' republic (Westbrook, 2005, 96, 134). Neither in Dewey's 1926 essay on "corporate legal personality" nor later did he discard his concern with "the limitation of corporate power" (Dewey, 1926, 667). His critical review of jurisprudence did not conceptualize a "social self" divorced from his emerging thinking about democratic publics grounded in public space beginning in local communities. Dewey "argued in 1926 that questions about the nature of corporate personality were not only about corporations and the state but about people" (d'Errico, 1926, 102). Peter d'Errico's analysis confirms our point that Dewey's illumination of a legally relevant "social self" was not devoid of his concern with cutting back corporate encroachment on potentially democratic space. The Herculean aspect of Dewey's effort to overhaul the doctrine of corporate legal personality is best understood in relation to the development of public intelligence and its capacity to employ what he termed the pressure of social facts. To present him as clearing a path in the academic history of ideas for a postmodern social self engaged in identity politics mocks his democratic political theory. Livingston's postmodern subjectivity is an idealized configuration cut loose from its enfeebled eco-logic that is now projected as a ghost no longer even having a carbon footprint as it hovers over the frequent flyer lounges essential to the academic market. It is as if frames of democratic change can be constructed from the ungeographies of spectacular accumulation discussed in the previous chapter. (In our next chapter we seek to illuminate with Merleau-Ponty's help the formative infrastructure of conservation and becoming in democratic action).

Drawing on a particular version of feminist theory that concedes too many issues in spatial politics, Livingston's cultural politics pursues a Gramscian "war of position" that regrettably misses the Italian radical's attempt to work beyond a certain Marxian base/superstructure dualism (Livingston, 2001, 9, 54–55). Gramsci and Dewey are allowed a marginal relevance in the current stage of identity politics while we search our corporate age for directions toward "a transnational, postimperialist future" (114).

The postmodern subjectivization of Dewey's approach to culture and democratic action is not the way to find a concrete universal for the politics of diversity and *justice* in a global or any other context. Strangely, instead of Raymond Williams's neo-Gramscian cultural materialist approach, Livingston turns to a postmodernist view of cultural politics entailed by his favorable labor endorsing Judith Butler's poststructuralist feminism. He expects this elastic culturalism to help us be "at home in the divisions of historical time" (Livingston, 2001, 185). The metaphysical pathos of this Augustinian reference to time confirms his attempt to rely more on William James than on Antonio Gramsci. Whatever the problems with his historical rendering of James, we would question Livingston's Marxist-progressivist concept of the "socializing imperatives of the new corporate order" (82). It seems a back-handed way of providing historical sense to the democratic promise of pragmatism. Livingston suggests that understanding Dewey is one way that the U.S. Left can find in our history "a tattered but still legible map of a transnational, post-imperialist future" (114). But Dewey's ecological ontology for the theory and practice of democratic action did not wait for corporate capitalism to enable or authorize concepts of knowledge, power, and justice for the reconstruction of civil society.

Livingston's effort to put James and Dewey to work for a cultural politics supposedly configured in Gramscian terms falters early on when he misconstrues a statement on culture, class, and language by Raymond Williams. Livingston quotes out of context when he argues that Williams is making a linguistic turn in cultural history. While it is true that a linguistic approach to culture has been very influential in American cultural studies, it has not developed from a careful reading of Williams's work. His intention was reconstructing a certain Marxist concept of a "dominant class" in order to show that a selective tradition (illustrated by the American term *mainstream*) is neither simply "the product of a single class" nor one exhausting the alternatives of a "transitional society" (Williams, 1966 [1958], 319–21).

For a much fuller presentation of this cultural theory, Livingston could have consulted the 1977 book by Williams entitled *Marxism and Literature*. Four years earlier, Williams had offered a profound interpretation of Gramsci's theory of hegemony in *New Left Review* (Williams, 1973) that challenged de-materialized notions of culture in both cultural studies and Old Left circles. His nondualistic treatment of the material dimension in the social process of culture, instead of discarding the concept of class, sketched a stronger and more flexible one just as global capital was ushering in a new era of cultural fragmentation. Livingston's warning about certain forms of abstract totalization can be applied to his own Archimedean thinking about the future presuming historical stages that oversimplify alternatives. Williams's understanding of structures of feeling and creative practice in *the interplay of dominant, residual, and emergent elements* offers an approach to culture and politics that does not reify or value language and difference or allow "diversity" to marginalize issues of justice, equality, and ecology.

This brings us back to the U.S. transnational corporate state's consumer culture. It is one of the crucial borders often blocking cultural (not just "intellectual") contributions to public life and a vital public sphere where ecological action for sustainability could materialize appeals to "community" and "self-realization" that too often tend to be moralistic and vacuous. A democratic left must stay on this border, working against temptations to cynicism, withdrawal, and symbolic violence to transform it on all sides toward a more democratic culture. We should have learned from the 1960s that you cannot fight technocratic scientism or corporate power with liberal subjectivism repackaged in a "radical" rhetoric of "liberation" from the "System."[6] And in the 1990s we might have learned from the Zapatistas that if we are going to "open a crack in history," our political words must become "bridge and stone and maize and tree and the hope of tomorrow" (Marcos, 2002, 216, 283).

As Dewey came to realize, the liberal-democratic polity was not only an emerging site of corporate state hegemony but also part of a democratic heritage facilitating the pragmatic replenishment of a pluralistic civil society.[7] John Dewey may have been playing for bigger stakes than Diggins and all the "symbolic analysts" who blink as a globalizing corporate state continues to raze civil society to make way for new regional shopping malls and a consumer culture that only a few political scientists still confuse with a "civic culture." Dewey refused to bet on the procedural republic and on the professional elites, for both were being reconstituted in ways at odds with America's democratic aspirations. Dewey's rhetoric of "neighborly communities" seems quaint today, but he had in mind Tocqueville's "little republics," the continued decay of which he knew had drastic implications for the hope of a democratic Republic. Livingston's view of pragmatism as a "postrepublican alternative" hinges on the questionable assumption of the ongoing socialization of markets and a problematic stance toward what is called *globalization*.[8] Questioning the wisdom of such a historical leap, we take the more pedestrian view that Dewey not only confronted corporate power in the industrialization process but increasingly recognized that the dispersal of power from the state to society (detected by Tocqueville) was more importantly a democratic opportunity than mega-corporate destiny. The incorporation of America and the struggle for democracy remain intertwined.

When Dewey wrote in 1927, "the prime condition of a democratically organized public is a kind of knowledge and insight which does not yet exist," (Dewey, 1991 [1927], 166) he laid down a political challenge to the professions that public intellectuals dare not ignore. As for the academic gatekeepers to the professions, their universities by and large are moving in a direction opposite to "where" democratic action is. Blinded by technocratic ideologies that regularly privilege corporate spatial planning over place-based forms of life, more thoughtful scholars grow increasingly uneasy with the anti-democratic uses of certain types of research. "Terrorism" as ideological justification for at least some forms of the U.S. military/industrial/Congressional complex increasingly sags even in a political mainstream reeking with corporate money. The widespread repression of dissenting expressions of alternative approaches to "globalization" is not going to be swept under the rug of "counter-terrorism." The World Social Forum of recent years remains a shining example of a Deweyan public sphere as a project of democratic projects. Nevertheless, we have to bear in mind reasons for the tardiness of many U.S. academicians in recognizing this challenge.

As legal scholar Richard D. Parker indicates, there is a strong "Anti-Populist sensibility" (Parker, 1994, 65) in American intellectual circles directly related, we might add, to what the late Christopher Lasch described as "the politics of the civilized minority" (Lasch, 1991, 412–75). However, as Parker has put it: "Our attitudes toward the political energy of ordinary people shape our sense of what are the constitutive problems of our democracy" (Parker, 1994, 4). Dewey was not afraid to harness the "political energy of ordinary people." In the growing din of corporate propaganda about "free markets" and the incessant corporate branding of cultural experience, questions about the compatibility of "globalization" and democracy are being raised with new vigor and depth of insight.

Media-based activists such as Naomi Klein are both reporting and shaping a new politics not only fighting the "international rule of the brands" and the "privatization of our collective rights as citizens" while aiming at the reclamation of the commons and a Zapatista world with many worlds within it. In her brilliant treatment of "brand bombing" and "identity marketing," Klein is clear that what is at stake is genuine public life. "The argument against transforming education into a brand-extension exercise," she writes, "is much the same as the one for national parks and nature reserves: these quasi-sacred spaces remind us that unbranded space is still possible" (Klein, 2002b, 105). The chief significance of her "no logo" argument is the way it undercuts the myth that corporate consumption choices realize "democracy," a mainstay of the ideological warehouse for the pseudo-populist masquerading of American corporate power. The farcical notion of the United States as a "consumer's republic" actually promotes the pollution of democratic public spaces. What we have been trying to show from John Dewey's work is that what is at stake is the aesthetic ecology of public intelligence.

John Dewey's Aesthetic Ecology of and for Public Intelligence

Dewey's pragmatic theory of the self as a democratic agent is very definitely part of what we have in mind. But as Thomas Alexander has shown, Dewey's concept of the self is situated within a theory of democratic culture as one that organizes "stable horizons of care" nourishing forms of social imagination vital for generative (generational) participation in public intelligence (T. Alexander, 1995, 153–54). The temporal structure of this participatory, communicative process fundamentally enables the meanings of selfhood and social action. In his 1939 essay "Creative Democracy—The Task before Us," Dewey identified democracy as "belief in the ability of human experience to generate the aims and methods by which further experience will grow in ordered richness." He concluded by saying that "the task of democracy is forever that of creation of a freer and more humane experience in which all share and to which all contribute" (Dewey, 1993b [1939], 244–45). When you go back to his thoughts roughly twenty years earlier, you find him proposing roles for philosophers and others in "the use of intelligence to liberate and liberalize action" (6, 37, 46–47). We think that John Dewey connected art and politics. He outlined an *aesthetic ecology of public intelligence* that links his writings about democratic publics (Dewey 1991 [1927]) and creative democracy (Dewey 1993b [1939])—as we explore in a 2003 article that elaborates on insights of John J. McDermott's from some years ago (Reid & Taylor, 2003). Dewey's insights illuminate global justice movements that struggle to move beyond environmental violence and ecological displacement to the celebration not only of place-based forms of life but also of "genuine care for common experience," to use McDermott's Deweyan language (McDermott, 1976, 91). We hope to illuminate the emerging forms of these politics in encouraging a more holistic understanding of the local in various confrontations with transnational corporate power.

In 1927, Dewey stated that the "outstanding problem of the public is discovery and identification of itself" while also commenting that in "no two ages or places is there the same public" (Dewey, 1991 [1927], 125). He saw the challenge as one of merging "free social inquiry" with the "art of full and moving communication" (184). Those who would make the mistake of identifying Dewey's political aims and values with the liberal-democratic politics of the New Deal miss or ignore key points elaborated in such works as *The Public and Its Problems* and *Art as Experience*. In the former he writes: "The prime condition of a democratically organized public is a kind of knowledge and insight which does not yet exist" (166). Dewey's essay of November 1935 titled "Liberty and Social Control" makes clear he did not ignore or slight the problem of the unequal distribution of power. Conceptualizing liberty as "effective power to do specific things," he highlights the question of power's distribution and the connection between the system of liberties and existing systems of restraint or control. There are always varying systems of social control, but the trouble in 1935, he observed, is that "it is exercised by the few who have economic power, at the expense of the liberties of the many and at the cost of increasing disorder" (Dewey 1993a [1935], 158–60). Seventy years later, in the United States we think this is an accurate and fair statement of the basic problem, although we have to emphasize that new dimensions of power are raising the challenge of finding new or alternative forms of a democratic public whether "provincial" or "cosmopolitan." To repeat what we hope is obvious to most readers: we need various forms of democratic publics including what we have called *global regional publics*.

Dewey's critique of the corporate capitalist process of industrialization was relentless and included the way in which the sciences were being institutionalized and misused. His examination of art as experience is an attempt to bridge the "chasm between ordinary and esthetic experience" by illuminating the aesthetic as a key infrastructural modality in the logic of practical judgment. He is not at all content with depicting a traditional utopian function for art but resituates the aesthetic dimension of experience in work and the everyday understood as tensional landscapes. The threat or problem of the corporate mentality is never lost from view. Consequently it is ludicrous for C.A. Bowers to claim that "Dewey's view of democracy requires a process of colonization" because, for example, the "rapid merging of scientific research and corporate values is only the latest manifestation that the method of experimental inquiry that Dewey placed so much faith in can be used in destructive ways" (Bowers, 2003, 36). As James Campbell's excellent book *Understanding John Dewey: Nature and Cooperative Intelligence* demonstrates, this is a gross misreading of his approach to democracy as cooperative, experimental inquiry (Campbell, 1995). Oddly, when Bowers calls for "radical educational reforms that replace the current emphasis on promoting forms of education that expand the economy with regenerating the capacity of cultural groups to live in more self-sufficient and interdependent ways" (Campbell, 1995), he reflects precisely Dewey's concerns (as long as certain issues are kept in focus). We would argue that Bowers reads Dewey's philosophy and politics through the lens of Richard Rorty's reform liberal/social democratic reduction of Dewey (Bowers, 2003, 26, 28).

Our reading of Dewey's philosophy and politics has been enhanced by several astute and penetrating recent studies, especially those by Alexander, Campbell, and Westbrook. Thomas Alexander's very timely contribution documents Dewey's efforts to "formulate an ecological ontology and with it an ecological view of experience in which the aesthetic context of inquiry is acknowledged" and, we might add, re-conceptualized (T. Alexander, 2002, 22). We have to shed our intellectualized and dualized notions of knower and known if we are to grasp our knowledge—and so logic—existing or active "within a noncognitive temporal framework, arising from experiences which are noncognitive and passing into experiences that also are noncognitive" (19). Alexander shows how Dewey worked to situate knowing in a "creative ecosystem" distinguished by "change, plurality, possibility and mutual interdependence" (21).

This and the earlier work of scholars such as John McDermott lend support to our approach or what we call Dewey's *aesthetic ecology of public intelligence.* Dewey's notion of public intelligence should help us understand the matrixical conditions of public life that provoke and sustain nonreified ecological consciousness. Following Dewey, Alexander has claimed that the democratic community "realizes that it is ever in danger of losing itself, of becoming hidden from the possibilities of the present or from its own inherently unfinished and problematic nature" (Alexander, 1987, 273). Our claim is that today, confronting both the threat and challenge of economic globalization, various forms of democracy must be re-imagined in ways facilitated (though not at all completed) by Dewey's aesthetic ecology. We are painfully aware that Dewey, in trying to restate his theory of inquiry, sometimes capitulated to the reigning scientism (Kaufman-Osborn, 1991, xii–xiii; Stuhr, 2002, 282–84). Nevertheless, we find in his arguments for recasting the relationship of art and science and in the thrust of his work toward what Alexander calls an "an ontology of environed or ecologically situated being" (T. Alexander, 2002, 5) some vital considerations for the social theory of intellectual roles in globalization struggles.

Our task is not to blame Dewey for not anticipating the enormity of what Arendt was to call "the political integration of technical power" (Young-Bruehl, 2006, 150). Rather the question for us is whether Dewey (and others) offers the outline of a democratic approach to science that helps advance an alternative to corporate state modernization. Instead of rummaging the vast corpus of his writings, hooting at his encomiums to Sir Francis Bacon, we spotlight his quest for forms of inquiry, knowledge, and communication facilitating growth of democratic publics. If democratic public debate is not a viable answer to thoughtlessness and bureaucratic capitulation in science and technology, then what is? Have we not had enough of instrumental calculation clouded over by metaphysical pathos? For example, we learn in *Fortune* magazine for October 30, 2006, that the lower part of the upper class is increasingly hostile toward the super rich because the success of the latter is seen as out of reach. There are political scientists quick to argue that such conflicts of interest grease the wheels of the liberal-democratic polity while providing traction to sub-ideologies such as meritocracy. In such contexts as this the significance of democratic republican alternatives is unmistakable.

John J. Stuhr makes the key point that Dewey's philosophy was "a sustained effort to help forge a democratic culture" (Stuhr, 1998, 85). Dewey's critical reconstruction of American liberalism made clear that the liberal-democratic polity was not the culmination of the project. Stuhr also rightly observes that Dewey's methods and ideals are rejected by many philosophers who basically have made peace with postmodern capitalist trends, even neoliberal globalization. They would do better to consider Joseph Margolis's argument for the philosophic promise of the convergence of Deweyan pragmatism and Merleau-Ponty's phenomenology. In his view and ours, their work converges by undercutting philosophical "oracular privilege" in favor of ecologically situated inquiry recognizing "the contingency of the cultural formation of our cognitive powers" (Margolis, 1998, 249–50). This "extraordinary convergence" of what is "similar in Dewey and Merleau-Ponty may be what will be surest in the philosophy of the twenty-first century" (250–52).

Robert Westbrook's *Democratic Hope* describes Dewey as a "democratic collectivist but also a persistent populist" carrying forward some of "the radical impulses in producer-republicanism" (Westbrook, 2005, 96). This is our view of Dewey's political philosophy, and we have tried to extend it in readings of the 1927 and 1934 texts as well as relevant insights from scholars such as Thomas M. Alexander. "Reconstructing the democratic ideals of the producers' republic" by instituting bottom-up democratic planning is one of several projects already sought by a number of citizen action groups. Among other perspectives, we hope to have cast more light on Westbrook's argument for rejecting the notion that the "pragmatists forecast a postmodern self... located in time rather than space" (60).

We are especially concerned to encourage a rethinking of the role of the professions insofar as they operate in the dialectic of space and place (Harvey, 1996, 29–30, 324) to promote anti-democratic aspects of transnational corporate power. There will be those who insist that Dewey's horse of science long ago left the barn of democratic possibility, that the daunting institutional realities of corporate state science, technology, and media are simply too overwhelming. On the other hand, the question may not be whether Dewey's conception of science is outdated but whether it has persisted even if in limited, tattered forms in grassroots politics such as what once was called the "environmental movement." The least we can say is that these beleaguered democratic publics have been able to enlist and even produce some Deweyan-type "experts." We refer to people with scientific credentials who work as civic professionals with citizen action groups. We want to mention two conferences exemplifying this collaboration between political activists and civic professionals.

The first is the Coal Summit that took place June 20–22, 2002, in Charleston, West Virginia, focusing on the human and environmental impacts of coal. Scientists such as Orrie Loucks, Ben Stout, and Joel Schwartz joined activists from several states to blend an amazing variety of experiences and types of knowledge at a time when the Bush-Cheney administration was boosting the coal industry and denying the reality of global warming. The second is the Genetic Engineering Action Network's November 15–17, 2002, national conference held in Louisville, Kentucky. This conference brought a remarkable probing of biotechnology's risks to the environment, biodiversity, and human health, as well as its socioeconomic and ethical consequences. Kentucky's Community Farm Alliance kicked off the conference by organizing a public debate on the question "Is biotechnology right for Kentucky?" Appropriately on one side you had the dean and faculty members from the University of Kentucky's College of Agriculture matched on the other side by poet-farmer Wendell Berry, biologist-environmentalist Martha Crouch, and farmer-activist Dan McGuire. Social and political theorists seeking evidence of synergy between grassroots organizations and civic professionalism need only attend a few conferences and debates such as these, although they might also become more familiar with the citizen action organizations that utilize expertise on a regular basis.

Before depicting corporate state science and technology as a phalanx they might also discover the front lines of ecological blowback and advancing socioeconomic inequalities that help explain why Tom Friedman's flat world is already shaking and that, whether or not TV network news tells us, we are already "living in the long emergency" (Buell, 2003; Kunstler, 2005; Speth, 2004). Social and political theorists with more direct political experience might be better positioned to detect growing academic and professional disenchantment with the glorification of speed and intertwined myths of limitless knowledges and borderless world markets. Our search for an ecological ontology for political alternatives to globalizing knowledge regimes continues.

5

Merleau-Ponty and the Flesh of the Political

The corporatized, globalizing university is one of the vehicles deploying the dualist horizons of the transnational corporate state. Prevailing versions of academic professionalism that have rationalized the growing elitism of this fixation on global economic space must be replaced by a civic professionalism that takes its organizing cues much more from surrounding regions and their placed communities and local eruptions of the crisis of the global commons. Such a reorientation requires the undoing of dualisms that drive academic behavior even as crises of climate chaos accelerate. If universities are to retrieve and renew the project of cultivating public culture and discourse, a post-dualist ecological sensibility not wired into spectatorial professionalism and transnational elitism is crucial. As Merleau-Ponty put it: "After all, the world is around me, not in front of me . . . the question is to make space and light, which are *there,* speak to us" Merleau-Ponty, 1964a, 178). It remains to be seen whether we can find ways to slow down, think, and regain trust in nature's living being and the intrinsic visibility of the world.

Merleau-Ponty and the Enveloping Earth

We begin by highlighting the fundamental role of Merleau-Ponty's work in rethinking these problems and issues of body, place, and knowledge in environmental science, policy, and politics. As Merleau-Ponty said, "nature . . . is not simply the object, the accessory of consciousness in its tête-à-tête with knowledge. It is an object from which we have arisen, in which our beginnings have been posited little by little until the very moment of tying themselves to an existence which they continue to sustain and aliment" (Merleau-Ponty,

1970, 64). In the working notes of *The Visible and the Invisible*, Merleau-Ponty writes of "the mind as the *other side* of the body" and of "Nature as the other side of man (as flesh—nowise as 'matter')" (Merleau-Ponty, 1968, 259, 274). He also wrote of "Logos. . . . as what is realized in man, but nowise as his *property*" (274). Earlier he had commented that "It is by the flesh of the world that in the last analysis one can understand the lived body" (250). This flesh is the "invisible hinge upon which my life and the life of the others turn to rock into one another, the inner framework of intersubjectivity" (234). He says that flesh is "the formative medium of the object and the subject" and the "concrete emblem of a general manner of being" (147). It is through this formative dialectic that our lives open "upon a natural and historical world . . . it is our involvement in Being" (85).

John O'Neill, in *Making Sense Together,* translates this as "time's body," the "collective focus of seeing and being seen" that is our "natural light," "the time our senses need to become human, to speak, and to think" (O'Neill, 1974, 37, 80, 37). Alphonso Lingis contends that the "concept of flesh emerges as the ultimate notion of Merleau-Ponty's thought . . . a prototype for Being universally" (Lingis, 1968, liv). We might better observe that in his 1959–1960 lectures on nature, Merleau-Ponty was stating: there "is a Logos of the natural esthetic world, on which the Logos of language relies." As he went on to say, we may consider language "as a resumption of the logos of the sensible world [leading into] [m]atrices of history" (Merleau-Ponty, 2003, 212, 219). (Bear this in mind when we come to Edith Cobb's research.)

Along this path Merleau-Ponty interrogated the kinship between the being of the earth and that of our bodies (*Leib*), a kinship that in his last lectures extended, he noted, "to others, who appear to me as other bodies, to animals whom I understand as variants of my embodiment, and finally even to terrestrial bodies." At this point, he admitted that we can resort to the idealizing projections of modern physical science including the pretension to be an absolute observer. "But such an idealization cannot provide its own foundation, and the sciences of the infinite are experiencing a crisis" (Merleau-Ponty, 1970, 122). As he had observed in another lecture, "nature itself has become explosive" inasmuch as modern science and technology "range before us energies which are no longer *within* the framework of the world but are capable of destroying it" (103).

During the summer before he died, Merleau-Ponty wrote: "Scientific thinking, a thinking which looks on from above, and thinks of the object-in-general, must return to the 'there is' which underlies it; to the site, the soil of the sensible and opened world such as it is in our life and for our body—not that possible body which we may legitimately think of as an information machine but that actual body I call mine, this sentinel standing quietly at the command of my words and my acts. Further, *associated bodies* must be brought forward along with my body—the 'others' . . . who haunt me and whom I haunt" (Merleau-Ponty, 1964a, 160–61), even as we haunt (and are haunted by) a wild being—the seedbed of the perceptible—which, in its primordial historicity, enables cultural renewal including the reordering of the sciences.

Human Development and the Grounds of Ecological Citizenship

It is interesting to recognize that during the years Merleau-Ponty was lecturing at the College de France—including courses on the child's relations with nature and with others—and working on *The Visible and the Invisible,* in the United States Edith McKeever Cobb was pursuing her study of childhood imagination, focusing on the child's body as a field site "where the powers of nature and human nature meet" (Cobb, 1977, 89). This extraordinary participant-observer of children's world-building play discovered that "child and nature were engaged in some corresponding bioaesthetic striving" (16). Cobb's 1959 article anticipating her only book—published in 1977—provided the basis for Reid's 1977 *Dialectical Anthropology* reading of her work in connection with the phenomenological studies of Merleau-Ponty and Erwin Straus. She has detected and illumined "a preverbal experience of an 'aesthetic logic' both in nature's formative processes and in the gestalt-making powers of the child's own developing nervous system, aesthetic powers that overlap meaningfully in these moments of form-creating expansion and self-consciousness" (Cobb, 1969 [1959]; Reid, 1977). Cobb's account—at once ecological and phenomenological—of perceptual expectancy, exploration, organization, and integration helps us understand the lifeworld as ecosystem and a common (though open-ended) human project. Her insights into the dialectical intertwining of the "child's morphogenetic impulses" (Cobb, 1969 [1959], 19) and what she described as "a universal aesthetic logic in nature's formative processes" (34) illuminate the "biocultural continuum" (53) grounding the possibilities of a cross-cultural environmental ethics (Cobb, 1977).

Exploring the "child's ecological sense of continuity with nature" (Cobb, 1977, 23), Cobb's work helps document "how we are living portions of the vast historical continuum that is nature" (100–101). It is her ecological redefinition of human individuality, however, that deserves special note. Her friend Margaret Mead came to understand Cobb's analysis of the child's "cosmopoetic exploration of the environment" (30) as identifying a basic need, "an intrinsic human need for understanding of the natural world" (Mead, 1977,

8). The political significance of Mead's point must not be submerged. In one of his College de France lectures on literature and politics, Merleau-Ponty remarked that "to be human is a political position" (Merleau-Ponty, 1970, 18). The political implications of this ecological need were clear enough in 1977 but are unmistakably so today when the earth itself would seem to be simultaneously for sale and in unprecedented danger. Reid's 1977 article concluded that "the ecology of creative childhood imagination" discloses what O'Neill once dubbed a "prepolitical suffrage" (O'Neill, 1970, 72, 82) that is vital for the critical theory of social change because it promises the inauguration of new political norms.[1]

Rereading Cobb's work at that Merleau-Pontian intersection where coexistence is a matter both of history and transcendental geology, we find new ways to make room for children in the house of truly serious ecological citizenship. Responsible adult accounting for body, place, and commons involves—in Merleau-Ponty's language—recognizing that the horizons of the flesh attain durable forms from the Earth and from historical remembrance as collective reactivation. In this sense cultures have a concretely transcendental dimension. The urgency of green concerns with the intergenerational claims of future generations must be felt in this context. We have to track the claim of future generations to a structure of needs rooted in lifeworld's generative possibilities requiring a commons that is simultaneously ecological and civic. What is to be avoided in the quest for new political norms is tacking on a "children's rights" amendment to a shabby contract that only duplicates the atomized personhood being reproduced daily by systems in thrall to global capital. "If the 'prepolitical suffrage' of the '*Lebenswelt* logos' is to be 'counted' in public affairs, then it can only be through the renovation of the language, and meaning, of the body-politic" (Reid, 1977, 126). In this era of globalizing capitalist economies initially marked by the ascendance of transnational corporate power, our new century confronts awesome tasks of political renovation. Social theory has to be clear about the ideological functions of human rights based on the capitalist dialectic of universal otherhood and perpetual inequality. Exposing the neoliberal lie of an "any day now" unified humanity is inescapable.

Transversal Politics and Merleau-Ponty's "Secret Order of Embodied Subjects"

We pause to warn the reader that ours is not a Deep Ecology effort to portray the body~place~commons level of lifeworld experience as a realm separable from the biocultural continuum that includes human and nonhuman plurality, social conflict, and political struggle. It is not an argument for awakening experience anterior to all traditions and political systems. In Merleau-Ponty's essay "Everywhere and Nowhere," he describes the unending, unhappy tasks of a concrete philosophy that tries to "restore to each experience the ontological cipher which marks it internally" (Merleau-Ponty, 1964b, 157). To enable a setting from which "the relationships between Orient and Occident" may be thoughtfully engaged, we must be open to the challenge of remembering or "rediscovering the existential field [in which our institutions] are born" (138–39). This move provides access to "the unity of the human spirit . . . [that] already exists in each culture's lateral relationships to the others, in the echoes one awakens in the other" (139). As Hwa Yol Jung has put it, Merleau-Ponty's search is for those "lateral universals" that allow "interpretation *across* cultural boundaries" (Jung, 1993, 223). We refer to the exact but always uncertain process that allows political communication in, for example, the World Social Forum. We strive to illuminate the question of what ontological configuration of nature, selfhood, and communication is involved in the empowerment of constituent groups in their intercultural search for truly critical ecological alternatives to the world projected by such entities as Exxon-Mobil, Monsanto, and Archer Daniels Midland.

In even more philosophical language, it is world as an ontological problem on which we focus especially due to the extent to which, in the American context, the problem of citizenship reflects a constitution of worldlessness produced today by the interplay of economic globalization and cultural subjectivization. In chapter 7 we move from philosophy to social criticism as we examine efforts of Hannah Arendt and Christopher Lasch to deal with this problem. For now, however, it is Merleau-Ponty's approach to institutions as a struggle against reification with which we are concerned. Taking up tasks left by Weber and Lukacs, Merleau-Ponty blazed a trail overcoming objectivism and scientism by recovering a phenomenology of historical choices. In 1955, in the midst of the Cold War and under attack from some on the Left, he explained why "history does not work according to a model [but] is in fact the very advent of meaning" (Merleau-Ponty, 1964a, 200). Reworking several texts of Max Weber, Merleau-Ponty "renews the concept of historical matter" by disclosing "the unique fiber of human choices" within historical struggles while never blinking at ever-present contingencies. Rather than deduce a politics from a dogmatic philosophy of history, he probed living history's capacity for "intelligible nuclei" with their "dialectical facts of adumbrative significations," institutional nodes and niches with "various accesses or, if you prefer, various likenesses" (202–10). Along this path he reopened "the Marxist idea of a meaning which is imminent in history" (Merleau-Ponty, 1970, 38) as well as problems in the philosophy of consciousness (39) and was led to a clearing well beyond familiar dualisms of materialism/idealism.

Breaking from "an ontology which leaves nature in silence" (Merleau-Ponty, 1970, 62), still evading dualistic resorts to nature and history, he refused to forget; we might say he remained awake to "the flux of the natural and historical world" (108). Merleau-Ponty—following Husserl's last manuscripts—came to speak of an originary truth dwelling "in the secret order of embodied subjects" (83), of lifeworlds sharing the earth/seedbed of "preobjective spatiality and temporality." Against any charge of romanticism, he warns that in addition to forging innumerable political ideologies ignoring our shared terrestrial roots, we have promoted the technical spirit to make nature itself explosive. But this leads our own discussion back to the question, wherever science, technology, and politics are institutionalized, of how we understand our subjectivity (and nature) or what Anthony Steinbock appropriately terms *generativity* (Steinbock, 1995, 192, 208, 257–70).

Dispensing with the constituting subject of modernity and a certain phenomenology, Merleau-Ponty reveals an "instituting subject. . . . [that] exists between others and myself, between me and myself, like a hinge, the consequence and the guarantee of our belonging to a common world" (Merleau-Ponty, 1970, 40). Here, we contend, is a key contribution to the struggle against reification as a problem of the social world. The world of institutions is rooted in the earth as "the matrix of our time . . . [and] space" and the institutional ideologies are divergent historical versions of time that all presuppose "our proto-history as carnal beings compresent to a single world" (Merleau-Ponty, 1964b, 180). Hannah Arendt's concept of natality finds its power here, where care for the world generates creative arts of renewal. It is along this Merleau-Pontian path that we hope to reinforce Hwa Yol Jung's claim that "[w]e are in dire need of 'geophilosophical' ideas in which the earth is not just one element among other elements but the encompassing element of all elements" (Jung, 1999, 283).

We are especially interested in "transversal communication" that has its praxis in "a new topography of intersubjectivity as a we-experience" (Schrag, 2002, 389–93). Social theorists would do well to catch up with and account for the political practice of increasing numbers of "transversalists," for it is certainly not only academicians who are cutting or reaching across "ethnocentric universalism" (cf. Jung, 2002, 13). The transversal encounters experienced between regional groups of the global justice movement need not be understood as dispensing with coordinates of time and place, whatever is the case in the frequent traveler lounges. Rather, they somehow generate dimensions of the lifeworld vital for embodying ecological citizenship and moving toward a politics for our world-in-common. At the same time, we join scholars such as Jung and Schrag in appreciation of postmodern contributions to "dispelling the ghosts of a subject-centered and theory-grounded universalizing rationality," as Schrag has put it (Schrag, 1992, 155). Those who would enlist Foucault to warn against Husserl's insular construction of the crisis of European thought and its resolution might also consider that Husserl in the unpublished, late manuscripts, on the reading of Merleau-Ponty, was moving beyond phenomenology as constituting egology and its affiliated modern Western conceits. Several capable scholars, have cultivated this post-Husserlian approach offering a nonfoundational understanding of body/nature/time/world that ontologically limns, one might say, a critical political ecology. The last thing we want to do is to bog this discussion down in arcane philosophical debates regarding the later Husserl.

Democratic Theory and the Durable Flesh of the World

There is time for the brief mention of James Mensch's critique of the Derridean "self as an absence" that proceeds from an invaluable reading of the later Husserl and Merleau-Ponty writings (Mensch, 2001, 20–21, chap. 6). Mensch argues against Derrida that Husserl came to see self as a place of presence due to its embodied functioning or world-dependent temporalization (retentional and protentional in its lifeworld shaping). Husserl's eventual understanding of embodiment as temporalization and of the latter as "an openness rather than a pregiven unity" is where we must leave Mensch's interesting study. (His path to "ethical selfhood" pursued with and beyond Levinas unfortunately must be set aside.)

Edward Casey's work (Casey, 2001) is especially illuminative of place and landscape as they shape the world-presencing self crucial for democratic agency. The amazing circuit of body~place~world must be understood as having geography as well as history. Casey has dared challenge geographers and the rest of us to reconsider our intellectual compulsion to treat place in terms that are purely spatial as if we were "out there" looking down with mighty ideational weapons. In Casey's work, Merleau-Ponty's instituting subject lives at least from birth in an intercorporeal field where place and self are co-ingredients. Their co-ingredience puts into open-ended play intercorporeal matrices or space-time schema in a field of experiential dynamics magnetized by both conservation and becoming. We find in the "durable flesh of the world" a key for democratic theory.

Merleau-Ponty, unlike Derrida, sought to show "how subjectivity is indissociably, at one and the same time, *both* seeing (corporeality) *and* writing (language)" (Madison, 1997, 101). In this philosophical understanding of the subject-object relation in perception as the reversibility relation and of the self as a bodily place of presence and horizonal experience, we find a promising way of situating the body~place~commons nexus. We agree with Gary Brent Madison's argument that reversibility is all that is needed to conceptually account for alterity. "Otherness," he says, "is that without which the embodied subject would not be a subject" (Madison, 1990, 31). We turn to Barbaras for a formulation of Merleau-Ponty's phenomenology of life or "an analysis of the sense of being of living beings" (Barbaras, 2005, 221). What is rendered here is the ontologically revolutionary thesis and co-evolutionary understanding that "vision becomes possible because of *the intrinsic visibility of the world*" (226, emphasis added). Barbaras's reading unfolds this powerful theme bridging Merleau-Ponty's lectures on nature and the working notes for *The Visible and the Invisible*. In the former, the philosopher had contended that nature "has a meaning . . . is the autoproduction of a meaning" (Barbaras, 2005, 222; Merleau-Ponty, 2003, 3). This will spook only those addicted to the prevailing concept of subjectivity that leaves them teetering on the edge of a deep ecological pit.

Barbaras follows Merleau-Ponty's interrogation of the sensible world that acknowledges the "silent persuasion of the sensible" (Merleau-Ponty, 1968, 214), which helps render an assumptive form or inter-corporal schema of perceptuality, in one lecture mentioned as: "Universal-lateral of the co-perception of the world" (Merleau-Ponty, 2003, 218). This sensible world thus "forms our bond with the other . . . makes the other be for us" and yet remains ambiguous and transcendent, as Merleau-Ponty puts it in the working notes to *The Visible and the Invisible* (Merleau-Ponty, 1968, 214). For nature may be thought of "as a leaf or layer of total Being" rather than as "a separate power of being," to use Merleau-Ponty's lectures (Merleau-Ponty, 2005, 221–22).

"The flesh designates," Barbaras says, "exactly the point of articulation of nature and culture, of their passage into each other" (Barbaras, 2004 [1991], 265–66). Describing their relationship as chiasmic, Barbaras says that for Merleau-Ponty "the natural world always envelops the cultural world, which nevertheless always expresses and envelops the natural world" (266). He reminds the reader that Merleau-Ponty early on suggested that it is "in the body of the other [that] the world begins to reach expression" (266) and that the body of the other is "the first cultural object" (Merleau-Ponty, 1962, 348). Barbaras thus observes: "It is this space of the natural environment where the horizon of a culture is primed" (Barbaras, 2004 [1991], 265–66).

Put another way, from some of Husserl's later manuscripts, Merleau-Ponty takes up a geohistorical lifeworld and, moving into what he calls the "field of experience," reminds the reader "from the midst of being": "I the seer am also visible" (Merleau-Ponty, 1968, 110–14). Not taking space here to ponder scholarly differences of interpretation (e.g., between Mallin and Steinbock) we move to appropriate some of their terms for our own tasks of social and political theory. Merleau-Ponty is our guide in seeking to comprehend better "what the being of the world means" (6). It is his inquiry into the lifeworld as the interwoven (interweaving) matrix of earth-ground and world-horizon that we claim to follow (cf. Steinbock, 1995, 97–122). Michael Steinberg recently argues that often "we try to live in a world in which suffering, aging, and death have no place" (M. Steinberg, 2005, 33). It is not just that the body is silenced under capitalism but that historically and today the commons is enclosed (robbed) and people displaced (cf. M. Steinberg, 2005 on Federici, 192). To speak of the body~place~commons as the horizon of intellectual responsibility is to take a political position on what the being of the world means for humanity.

A politics for our world-in-common has to take aim at the links between globalization, subjectivization, and worldlessness. Quoting Mallin (possibly against himself), "To say that something in particular is on the horizon is not to deny its presence and reality, but only to affirm its distinction at this moment from those situations that have achieved a high degree of determinacy." He goes on to note that for Merleau-Ponty "the world consists of a fabric of interwoven structures" (Mallin, 1979, 36–37). As for the institutional context of political change, instead of fantasizing totalizing revolutionary ruptures, social and political theorists should take into account two points made by Lefort. The first is that Merleau-Ponty recognized "a principle of conservation in becoming." The second is that understanding ourselves to be situated in history, we are charged with "preserving a memory of the mystery of our situation" (Lefort, 2005, 376–77).

Caught up in the horizons of the flesh, we are opened onto a natural and historical world and a style of being that is informed by, but not exhausted by, a culture (Merleau-Ponty, 1968, 84–85, 148–49). Recalling our earlier effort to sketch the history and geography of the American idea of the democratic republic, we would project along this ontological path not a single way of being but the historically specific, always indeterminate, flesh of the political.

Taking our cues from Claude Lefort, our search for the political as generative space refuses indulgence in the fantasy of an organic society. Those U.S. social theorists and political scientists much enamored with ideas of community should consider Lefort's argument that we paraphrase as follows. The role of society in a democracy is not that of a communal body; it is rather a medium for generating public structures of space-time schema that permit work on common concerns, allowing decisions without closing debate. Those who would make community a terrain without contestation, perhaps longing for a harmonious political order, are off the democratic path.

But Claude Lefort has more to say about the problem of democracy that exposes a crucial incapacity of "liberal thought" inclined toward skeptical reduction of any "public" or "people" to "interests" or "opinions." It is in this intellectual milieu that we find the postmodern temptation to resort to a new kind of totalism by replacing what Lefort calls "the fiction of unity-in-itself with that of diversity-in-itself" (Lefort, 1988, 232; Dallmayr, 1993, 116). Sheldon Wolin's magisterial study of Tocqueville permits us to situate this postmodern detour already mapped by the new *post-democratic* despotism that has emerged in American society and politics. It is a despotism that is "enveloping rather than domineering"; instead of regimentation there is privatization and a murky system of elusive power channeling the everyday experiences of "stunted individuals who have embraced lives emptied of political responsibility" (Wolin, 2001, 569–70). Our argument, however, is that while Wolin is right to see the transnational corporate state producing a post-democratic "culture of privatism, isolation, and . . . consumerism," numerous grassroots groups have kept alive the culture of participation that at least promises a democratic movement.

Hopefully this intellectual labor advances the project of a social and political theory that has no need of a theory of culture to "become a primary technology for disarticulating difference from inequality" or politics as a "commitment to new subject positions instead of to more just societies" (Michaels, 2004, 17, 177). We fear that there is much to Michaels's contention that "the Left today obsessively interests itself in a set of essentially liberal issues—from racism to gay marriage—as a way of not interesting itself in the problem of economic inequality" (181) and to Ortner's concern about the suppression of economic class in American social theory (Ortner, 2006, chap. 3). Five years before the disputed election of the first Bush-Cheney administration, Michael Lind suggested Americans might see a "right-wing multicultural regime." He found already in place "a plutocracy tempered by tokenism," a system obscured by multicultural liberalism that compounds the familiar problem of a fragmented, ineffective majority exploited by a loosely unified elite, his largely "white Overclass" (Lind, 1995, 252, 183). A fundamental critique of corporate globalization and a multiscalar theory of democratic change and citizen agency would have facilitated more critical engagement with issues such as NAFTA in the 1990s.

Alas, it is all too clear that corporate-dominated globalization is creating a world of increasing socioeconomic inequalities, stripped-down places, and growing numbers of ecological refugees. These intertwined problems involve more than economic policies such as the privatization of people's water around the world. Even more insidious is the way that the dominant form of globalization promotes subjectivization, a process undermining popular access to modes of collective, public action. It is against such atomization of personhood that we propose a re-embedding of subjectivities within the intersubjective life grounds of body~place~commons—to claim ecological citizenship as a basis for reclamation of public life and collective action. There is now a growing body of interdisciplinary literature (cf. Kahn, 1999; Kahn & Kellert, 2002; Goodenough, 2000; Nabhan & Trimble, 1994) on the intertwining of place and human development, the child's need for nonhuman nature, and the reciprocity of place and person in experience. We fear that the contemporary possibility of understanding better than ever before the matrix or nexus of body, place, and commons is directly related to the degree to which it is threatened. But there is an emerging transnational politics especially from the grassroots level for a world-in-common that finds its life-ground, however remnantal, here. The geomorphological dimensions of democratic space are fundamental.

Deep Ecology and the Political

From Edith Cobb and Merleau-Ponty, we may find a beginning in the recognition that the culturing of the body, the child's body, must inaugurate the pre-political suffrage of our vital and necessary participation in the world's flesh of time's body. Deep ecology has begun a process of resituating ecological citizenship in the nexus of body and place. However, in the following, while we recognize the contributions of deep ecology, we argue that it does not move toward a sufficiently political economic analysis of the roots of the body/place nexus in politics of the ecological and civic commons. "Deep ecology" has emerged as a critical response to technocratic managerialism, but we argue that it does not go far enough because it does not attend sufficiently to body, place, and politics—especially as these are understood as different modes of *engagement with the world within history*. Theorists such as David Abram, Neil Evernden, and Monika Langer richly articulate the embodied phenomenology of our lived being as ecological, yet they sidestep history and power. This move is particularly curious in theorists who have a thick sense of the sensorily grounded experiential flow. (A curious deflection, if one stops to think about it. Having gotten one's feet wet in time, does one not fall "naturally" into history?) It is as if the (much needed) turn to the senses and embodiment is too easily shifted to a strangely "abstracted concrete"— sliding into idealized practices of sensation in a purified "natural," practices that do not fold clearly into praxis as historical action.

This curious sideways slip suggests an undertow of submerged hegemonic meanings. In the following chapters, we offer an understanding of the body~place~commons nexus in a political ecology as an alternative to "deep ecology" theories that falter in the face of transnational corporate power. Our current institutions of higher education, in the United States and elsewhere, are key players in maintaining the "body-blindness" that is a central prop of technocratic managerialism and its attendant blindness to place, politics, and history. Against this, as a necessary part of our struggle for a sustainable and equitable world, we propose institutional transformation of academe toward "place-based" scholarship and teaching in partnership with "local knowledges" in collaborative defense of the civic and environmental commons.

In his 1988 *Environmental Ethics* article and more recent book *The Spell of the Sensuous: Perception and Language in a More-Than-Human World*, David Abram has offered a remarkably creative, compelling, and lucid reading of Merleau-Ponty's discoveries and their significance for what he calls "the movements toward an ecological awareness" (Abram, 1988, 1996). Merleau-Ponty's "*Lebenswelt* is identical to the biosphere of a truly rigorous ecology," as Abram put it (Abram, 1988, 119). Abram ably renders Merleau-Ponty's understanding of thought and speech taking form upon the infrastructure of a living perception already engaged in the world and from "the play between the esthesiological body and the expressive physiognomies and geographies of a living world" (116).

But a "truly rigorous ecology," if cultivated in Merleau-Pontian terms, must also be a political ecology. Today, as never before, our diverse "ecologically aware" groups are engaged in a political search for what Merleau-Ponty called those forms of historical action that "constitute a step into the public duration and inscribe themselves in the human memory" (Merleau-Ponty, 1970, 29). The movements to which Abram refers are at the forefront among those of us increasingly realizing that relevant ideas of global justice entwine dimensions of equity and ecology. While Abram's published work does not indicate familiarity with Cobb's work, he no doubt would agree on the common, general direction of Merleau-Ponty's thought and Cobb's reflections on her studies. But, alas, when we contemplate the child's growth as a matter of participation in society and politics, the problem might seem to be one of worlds upon worlds. In his 1996 book, Abram shows us why it is so difficult to "walk out of our heads into the cycling life of the land around us" (Abram, 1996, 272). He talks about our "progressive forgetting of the air" and the "eclipse of the earth"—our loss of meaningful connections with the enveloping earth.

Yet Abram offers a surprisingly shallow explanation for what he calls the loss of "our organic attunement to the local earth" (267). In what is perhaps his strongest formulation, he describes us: "Transfixed by our technologies, [short-circuiting] the sensorial reciprocity between our breathing bodies and the bodily terrain. Human awareness folds in upon itself, and the senses—once the crucial site of our engagement with the wild and animate earth—become mere adjuncts of an isolate and abstract mind bent on overcoming an organic reality that now seems disturbingly aloof and arbitrary" (267). Failing to situate "our" technologies in political economy would seem to make them at once "aloof and arbitrary" yet pervasive in our experience. Abram has a bioregional vision of a society of "largely self-sufficient communities," but he seems to think we can get there without a politics. Political and economic problems are dismissed as "forces," "abstractions," and "ephemeral entities" (267). Bypassing the politico-economic problem does not seem a persuasive way of reaching the sensibility and solidarity that he seeks. Politics, as Merleau-Ponty also helped us understand in deeper ways, is about connecting what the poet Adrienne Rich describes as "the pain of any one's body with the pain of the body's world" (Rich, 1986, 100). Today, there is something hollow and inadequate about academic discourse about "the pain of the body's world" that at no point mentions Exxon, Dupont, Monsanto, the Mitsubishi Group, Union Carbide, or the World Trade Organization.

A notion such as Abram's "collective perceptual disorder" does not refer us to a malady that will be remedied by herding people under a big tent for ontological revival. Those of us in the academic professions must beware intellectual conceits that obscure the way in which prevailing ideologies of professionalism make it difficult for us to remain true to our embodied experience inasmuch as Merleau-Ponty taught us that the world is not what we think but what we live through. Reid was concerned, in 1977, to remedy and reconstruct the Frankfurt School theories of subjectivity and reification in light of Merleau-Ponty's understanding of our instituted existence grounded at the deepest levels by those basic meaning-structures that are the invisible hinge of the interhuman world and history (Reid, 1977). The point was that we must avoid then popular Left myths of the "iron cage" that overly reified the systemic nature of the interlocking rationalizations by corporate domination, bureaucratic governance, technocratic scientism, and pacifying consumerist culture. In part, the point was the now somewhat hackneyed post-structuralist argument that there are fissures and contradictions within the interlocking systems of rationalization—economic, governmental, intellectual, and psychological. That is true, and it is important to open up and unsettle these spaces of contradiction and disjunction. More important, however, is the argument that there are universal structures to the lifeworld that can provide the basis for renewed public spaces and reclaimed collective action—structures immanent within the processes that link body, place, and commons within the shared histories of common life on the earth in relationship among humans and other creatures. It is the universal constituting formative processes of this body~place nexus that provides common grounds for what we are calling *ecological citizenship*.

A number of us, including Neil Evernden, have followed Merleau-Ponty on this path beyond proliferating managerial ideologies to the core of the environmental crisis. Making our way through a largely corporate-steered culture of denial with its technological fantasies of crisis management, we are able to see, in Evernden's words, that "We *are* the environmental crisis"; "it is inherent in the context of our lives" (Evernden, 1985, 128). Nevertheless, this does not necessarily mean that we have to take our politics from the Advertising Council of our Transnational Corporate State! Less obvious are the problems with what is called *ecological science* in our increasingly corporatized system of higher education and its prevailing forms of academic professionalism. One of the dilemmas confronting "environmentalists" making this journey is that the development of *ecology* as a "science" by and large has become entangled in what Evernden calls "resourcism and reification" (22). As Evernden observes, "the issue of habitation is central to the environmental movement" (19). However, what is usually regarded as ecology "can help one to criticize inefficient exploitation or destructive utilization of nature, but it cannot help illuminate the experience that inspires one to be an environmentalist" (22). Deepening his reflections in the 1992 study *The Social Creation of Nature*, Evernden notes that the "ordering that makes the world seem comprehensible also makes most of it inaccessible" (Evernden, 1992, 119).

In Evernden's deep ecology perspective, what is needed is a cultural transformation, a "liberation of nature." (His failure to mention Herbert Marcuse's ideas in this context would seem to be deliberate). In the more recent study's formulation, what is called the *environmental crisis* "demands not the inventing of solutions, but the re-creation of *the things themselves*" (Evernden, 1992, 123). While he clings to the hope expressed by Walker Percy that "a sparrow can be recovered under conditions of catastrophe" (132), Evernden's most troubling theme is that increasingly there is "no place" for the experience of "the genuinely *ultra*human being of nature" (121).

While both of Evernden's studies garner and elaborate what he refers to as the "environmentally positive" insights of Merleau-Ponty, Heidegger, and Portmann, we find in David Abram's work a "philosophy on the way to ecology" that is much more thoroughly and persuasively grounded in Merleau-Pontian inquiry. Yet the landscapes that Abram and Evernden so thoughtfully talk about recuperating are abstracted out of any earthly realm of political economy in which they might in fact to be found. In Abram's words, the "recuperation of the incarnate, sensorial dimension of experience brings with it a recuperation of the living landscape in which we are corporally embedded" (Abram, 1996, 65). At some point, we have to engage the possibility of "a rejuvenation of our carnal, sensorial empathy with the living land that sustains us" as a political problem or challenge. The fact that "nonhuman nature seems to have withdrawn from both our speaking and our senses" at some point needs to be understood as both an issue of ecology *and* equity and ways in which they are institutionally intertwined (92). The argument is simply that we will make little progress toward a sustainable earth unless we can forge a politics recognizing that social and natural emancipation co-determine one another.

Monika Langer's 1990 article "Merleau-Ponty and Deep Ecology" offers a brilliant synthesis of the French thinker's work underlining its centrality for ecophilosophical inquiry (Langer, 1990). However, no attention is paid to Merleau-Ponty's discussion of the concept of *institution* as a way of dealing with certain problems in the philosophy of consciousness. His approach to the subject "not as a constituting but an instituting subject" and his remarks about duration, sedimentation, and action are relevant to the problems over which Langer's analysis stumbles (Merleau-Ponty, 1970, 39–40).

Langer's grasp of Merleau-Ponty's new ontology does indeed enable "us to see more clearly why there can be no question of any dichotomy between 'nature' and 'culture,' nor any conception of 'environment' in the traditional sense." She is right that what Merleau-Ponty's philosophy articulates "puts us on the path to resolving that 'environmental crisis' that we *are* as long as we cling to our old ontology" (Langer, 1990, 129). Langer does admit that "clinging to the old ontology" is not only a philosophical fixation in the academy but also a matter of destructive lifestyles. But no reference whatsoever is made to corporate capitalism's construction of consumers and such patterns as the dualization of work and community life. Rather, we are told that the "Cartesian/scientific paradigm . . . lies at the source of our current ecological crises" (128) and that a radical paradigm shift plus a Deep Ecology process of "Self-realization"—especially as advanced by Merleau-Ponty's philosophy—provides the solution.

Eliminating our estrangement from our world, ourselves, and other people, Langer suggests, "requires that we affirm the prereflective, prepersonal dialogue between the phenomenal body and preobjective world, instead of continuing to negate it" (124). The point needs elaboration for, as Reid argued in his 1977 *Dialectical Anthropology* piece, this dialogue and its meaning-structures must at some point be understood as *instituted* in Merleau-Ponty's sense rather than constituted (Merleau-Ponty, 1970, 39–45). The question is one of generating social modes of affirmation and finding ways of institutionalizing them. Indeed, we have a number of "pilot projects" on which to build. The political issue is whether we can begin bodying-forth some of the institutional changes necessary for a more sustainable world. The political problem is that not only are these projects and our related efforts marginal to the hegemonic consumer culture but also that the transnational corporate state operates to further that marginalization in various ways.

Beyond Political Fragmentation:
Democracy, Justice, Sustainability

In chapter 4, we discussed strategies for reclaiming and renewing public spaces with notions of ecological citizenship grounded in body~place~commons. Corporate globalization cuts deep into the lifeworld of community life. Against "globalization from above" and the mantra of "free trade" dictated by a market machine-god, there is an increasingly well-organized "globalization from below"—interlocking, still inchoate, collaborations among numerous grassroots networks in resistance to corporate globalization. Based on the premise that "another world is possible," a central aim of "globalization from below" is to reclaim the environmental commons and restore its various local forms under public control. Some social theorists dismiss the diverse and often localized struggles of this new citizen politics as overly localized "militant particularisms" that do not grapple sufficiently with underlying macrostructures of the global economy, o, that are unable to build coherent multi-issue or class-based alliances. However, there is a growing body of scholarship that seeks to theorize this new citizen politics as creating the basis for a coherent movement that can transform environmental politics.

William Shutkin labels this new politics a "civic environmentalism" that understands that environmental problems emerge from problems at the heart of our political economy, and that change can only come through integrated work on multiple issues simultaneously—economic justice, identity politics, equity between rural/urban and between regions, knowledge systems and cultural identity, and public infrastructure (Shutkin, 2000). Whether we call this "civic environmentalism" or simply "joined-up thinking," it should be clear that we agree with those who stress "the pivotal importance of environmental justice to sustainability policy-making" (Agyeman, Bullard, & Evans, 2003, 332). In October of 1991 the People of Colour Environmental Leadership Summit adopted a list of "Principles of Environmental Justice" that in retrospect is a "line in the sand" pointing toward new democratic movements that some scholars argue require "just sustainabilities." In fact, Julian Agyeman's 2005 study of Alternatives for Community and Environment (ACE)—the organization Shutkin helped launch—makes the case for a broad social movement that is not "just" about environmental sustainability or the narrowly focused "civic" energy going into such efforts (Agyeman, 2005).

Various studies of these emerging movements beyond liberal environmentalism have contributed much to our ability to engage the multiple intersections between crises of inequality, injustice, technocracy, corporatization, and the pervasive assault on place and thinning of public participation. Toward the end of the last decade, veteran *New York Times* journalist and now independent writer Philip Shabecoff set out to engage "a broad spectrum of thoughtful and informed people within and without the environmental movement." His book, based on numerous interviews, offers a very important assessment and prognosis of our worsening ecological predicament. Despite its notable achievements, by the end of the century the movement "had not yet adequately prepared itself to meet the current and coming challenges, to transform a future that now seems filled with danger" (Shabecoff, 2000, xii).

A careful reading brings the key problem to the fore: the failure to "recognize and acknowledge that the decline of the environment is *not* an issue distinct from other flaws in our society" and that environmentalists "are in the same boat with other groups of Americans who are thwarted and victimized by the status quo" (Shabecoff, 2000, 190). While Shabecoff is clear about the pattern of locally based grassroots organizations trapped in struggles with immediate problems such as toxic waste dumps, his criticism of the narrow, myopic, and politically timid role of mainstream environmental groups is more compelling. He offers a comprehensive reform agenda for a broader, more inclusive movement and for American society and politics. But he also makes an intriguing suggestion at the end of chapter 4 on environment, community, and society. "Concern about and love for place can make environmentalism a unifying force" (81). Much later, in discussing political strategies, Shabecoff elaborates that because "people do care deeply about concrete environmental issues where they live" (127), a place-based approach is vital for engaging the translocal levels of environmental problems, including issues of power and responsibility.

Shutkin's book of the same year claims that this is beginning to happen in what may be loosely regarded as the environmental movement. As we have said, his contention is that "Civic environmentalism is the emerging model of social and environmental activism" (Shutkin, 2000, 238). He emphasizes the links between the civic life of communities and environmental conditions, between civic health and environmental quality, and "the environmental consequences of civic decline" (120). Yet there is a curious tension between Shutkin's unflinching diagnosis of what he calls "the great divide between democracy and environmentalism" (120) and his contention that civic environmentalism "is becoming the trend among mainstream environmental organizations" (239). (It should be added that, in his view, these mainstream organizations have not yet done enough to engage or implement the goals of civic environmentalism.) He is clear that the promise of civic environmentalism lies in "a holistic approach to environmental problems in that those problems and their solutions are seen as inextricably linked to social, political, and economic issues" that he synthesizes as "civic issues" (22). What is not clear is how far and how deep "civic environmentalism" will be able to go, considering what he presents in a remarkably penetrating analysis of how the rift between the haves and have-nots "is driven by two main forces: professionalism and global capitalism" (38).

The increasing inequalities and insecurities within the United States and between countries of the South and the North, brought by economic globalization and the dominance of multinational corporations, have been documented by numerous studies. It is Shutkin's focus on frequently unacknowledged impacts of professionalism in American society that we will maintain. "Professionals are ... detached from the destiny of wage-earning Americans, their fate hitched to the forces of modern capitalism and their lives ensconced within exclusive work, residential, and leisure environments" (Shutkin, 2000, 39). Shutkin's concern with professionalism's notable costs to democracy may even provide more evidence that the transnational corporate state systematically promotes "postcommunal professionalism" (see Reid, 2001a, 520–35). While Shutkin may be a bit glib about how we are to find "the proper mix of collective will and social capital" (Shutkin, 2000, 141), he does emphasize the difficulties of transforming mainstream environmentalism. We might agree that this environmentalism "is evolving from an essentially elitist movement" (xiv) to a more democratic movement oriented particularly by notions of "sustainable community" as long as it is recognized that the stakes include two contending political visions.

We have noted Shutkin's awareness of John Dewey's general relevance to the fundamental argument that "participation in the civic environmental model validates the expertise of not only professionals but ordinary people" (Shutkin, 2000, 129–30). There is growing recognition that a transformation in American politics is needed that is at once local and global. But there probably needs to be more sober thinking about various forms of transition. Here again we would attempt a broader view by referring to the "civic commons" or the challenge of reorganizing and restructuring public spheres for local-regional transformation that, from their diverse ecological grounding, contribute to innovative forms of global action. To engage current forms or policies of corporate state elitism and nationalism, fueled mainly by corporate power and global capital, requires increasingly coordinated efforts on all these fronts.

Cosmogenesis and the Ecology of Democratic Space

We are arguing for a public space that is emergent from the particularities of collective civic labors grounded in local and everyday struggles and in the placed nexus of body, self, and commons. The semantic architectonics of such a public space cannot derive from rationality *simpliciter*—whether Habermasian communicative rationality, Weberian rationalization through differentiation from the lifeworld and personal narratives, constitutional codification of citizen rights and deliberative codes, or neoliberal market logics. However, this is neither a complete abandonment of universalizing notions of citizenship nor a collapse into simply local and incompatible "militant particularisms" (Harvey, 1996, 32). Rather, we are pointing toward a kind of secular mytho-poetic world-building power that is essential to the imagination and instantiation of a civic commons. This capacity springs from aesthetic human powers and encompasses *and feeds* scientific and other logical endeavors.

We call this power *cosmogenic agency*—or the labor of conjuring a "cosmos" out of "universe" and of "consenting" in Ricoeur's sense (Ricoeur, 1966, 346) to one's constitution by and in the matrices of world and mortal time (B. Taylor & Reid, 2000). Within the space-based logics of universe and the universal, the relationship of individual and matrix is "flat" because the individual can be infinitely resituated and rotated insofar as it can be relocated according to calculable coordinates—which are themselves infinitely replicable in all locations where those calculative logics obtain. Several studies by Bruce Wilshire cast much light on why such spatialized perspectives miss or obscure what he terms "the behavioral flow of the mimetic and the communal" (Wilshire, 1991 [1982], 186). In a more recent study, he puts it this way: "Body-self is mature when it knows viscerally that it is both a unique center of agency *and* bound indissolubly into the unimaginably vast, regenerating world" (Wilshire, 1999, 150). The key problem of political and personal life with which we are now concerned is that we "have lost [our] bearings in the sensuous matrix, and in the local and cosmic surround, and so we rattle around in nihilism, unmet primal needs, assorted addictions" (240). We emphatically agree with Wilshire, and in fact the Merleau-Pontian theme of this chapter focuses on "the sensuous matrix, and . . . the local and cosmic surround." Here and later in chapter 7 we strive to open social theory up to what Wilshire calls "the sustaining numinous experience of body-self and local environment nesting in the everything else" (Wilshire, 1999, 240).

In cosmogenesis, the relationship of individual and matrix is deep and full. It is simplest to say that this logic is the logic of place and narrative. But given the disvaluing of place and story that is foundational of Western modernity, these words (even with the recent explosion of theory about them) scarcely capture the nature of this kind of thinking and its centrality to humanness (or nonhuman ecological processes). The cosmogenic relationship of individual/matrix is deep because of its temporality. Place is not a neutral location within interchangeable space/time coordinates. It is a nexus of multiple and unfolding chains of events, and multiple pasts and futures are enfolded into immediate reality. The sedimentation of stories transform interchangeable spaces into *a* place, drenched with a particular history and signified concretely through sensory forms that evoke, provoke, and intensify thought but always exceed and evade it. It is deep and full because there is a tenacity of connection between the individual and the matrix (unlike in universalizing and space-based logics). It is tenacious, in part, because of the emotional power of sensory and kinesthetic forms that seize our attention at all neurological levels, from the cerebral cortex through primate modes of ambulation and prehensility to much more primitive and affectively charged mentations including smell, foregrounding and backgrounding of sight, and constitutive and unconscious locational orientation. But it is also tenacious and full because of the complexity and volume of metonymic condensation of matrixical forces and meanings into the identity of an individual—such that displacement can radically reweave or disrupt individual identity.

Paradoxically, for place-based logics, the relationship of individual to matrix can be labile, responsive, and resilient, because it is synergistic, fluid, and interpenetrating. Unlike the fixity and inertia that Teresa Brennan (Brennan, 2000) describes in the political economy and psychology of global capitalism, the agency of cosmogenesis is *both matrixical and individual*. Merleau-Ponty has helped us walk back into time's body (John O'Neill's term)—our formative medium grounded by the kinship between the being of the earth and our bodies. This kinship is central in the late Edith Cobb's brilliant rediscovery of children's world-building play where "child and nature [are] engaged in some corresponding bio-aesthetic striving" (Cobb, 1977, 16). Cobb's research demonstrated that to neglect the geographies of childhood is to misunderstand the roots of human creativity. Cobb's studies of the ecology of self-hood, linking place and human development, support Jeff Malpas's argument that "our existence [is] fundamentally an existence in and through place" (Malpas, 1999, 198).

But Malpas raises a question that we think Dewey and Merleau-Ponty help us begin to answer: What politics would "do justice" to this crucial feature of the human condition? In the preceding chapter, we resituated John Dewey's later philosophical development toward an "aesthetic ecology" in order to show how it grounds and enriches a critical, democratic place-oriented politics. We should never underestimate "place-bound particularisms," but neither should we continue to pay intellectual homage to what David Harvey has called "the postmodern death of justice" (Harvey, 1996, 324, 341). Grasping the centrality of place for human development does not require obscuring the political geography of difference, but it does point toward human norms that limit or check both "geographically fragmented notions of justice" and those differences that are "poles of world historical systems of domination" (358–65).

Corporate globalization from above has accelerated the process Dewey described in 1927 as "the dislocation and unsettlement of local communities," which he linked to the most urgent problem of the public: "to find and identify itself" (Dewey, 1991 [1927], 212, 216). Discussing "the problem of method," Dewey remarked that the "local is the ultimate universal, and as near an absolute as exists" (215). What we are attempting to show in this chapter is that *Merleau-Ponty's chiasmatic rendering of placed experience hinging body and world enables both Dewey's insight and a politics grounded by transversal solidarities.* Our notion of public space as grounded in cosmogenesis retrieves a holistic understanding of the Local by placing it at the nexus of the civic and the environmental commons where a new politics must be situated.

To put the "local" in cosmogenic perspective is to re-introduce its "globality" in terms of ecological realities and possibilities. This theoretical move is crucial today in order to unprejudice the ecological action agenda at a time when "global economic" priorities are claimed at every policy turn. Rather than fall back, as U.S. social theorists often have, on an abstract concept of "community," matrixical rendering of the Local as democratic culture or possibility opens onto stable horizons of care and transversal cooperation. The interdependencies of civic and environmental commons are best recognized and served in the social theoretic illumination of the generative capacities of public space. The challenge to social and political theory is outlining a politics that is unafraid to assert the dimension of universality that is caged by a global capital machine that spins out replicas to clutter lost political space on an overheating planet.

This brings us to a supportive formulation by Slavoj Žižek, condensed as follows: "Globalization is precisely the name of the emerging postpolitical logic which progressively precludes the dimension of universality that appears in politicization proper" (Žižek, 1999, 201). Jodi Dean has illuminated Žižek's critique of new forms of political subjectivization that channel political energy into pools of culture that leave "the economy as a kind of unquestioned, taken for granted basis of the way things are" (Dean, 2006, 116). Her courageous and brilliant study does more than help us understand why, for Žižek, "politicization *is* universalization" (122). It also documents his engagement with the role of university discourse in fostering political and cultural fragmentation and the social theoretic phobia concerning "the universalizing move proper to politics" (103). Žižek's critique thus understood converges with our earlier argument (drawing on Claude Lefort) that it is time to end social theory's postmodern detour into the dead-end fiction of diversity-in-itself. We indicated how and why this new totalism has legitimated cultural fragmentation and a disastrous political subjectivism analyzed in perceptive studies by Wolin, Michaels, and Lind that clarify the ways increasing inequalities reinforce post-democratic despotism. In other writings we have offered a complementary perspective (e.g., on Appalachian studies) that helps explain the political misallocation of considerable academic energy.

Our argument for the "cosmogenic" dimension of democratic public space is not a theme of deep ecology, granting some related contributions from that bailiwick. Our deep ecologists often seem inclined to forget Merleau-Ponty's point that "it is a question of grasping the *nexus* . . . of history and transcendental geology, this very time that is space, this very space that is time . . . which makes them be a historical landscape and a quasi-geographical inscription of history" (Merleau-Ponty, 1968, 259). A kind of amnesia for the history and politics of wilderness may well be fed by a philosophic proclivity to treat consciousness as constitution. We are unable to follow them in ignoring the political problem that consciousness is instituted, "already engaged in the world, in definite situations in which its resources are never merely its own" (O'Neill, 1970, 81). Our political life between violence and utopia ceaselessly engages collective questions of justice and injustice, truth and deception, unable to quit a fundamental "ambiguity of virtue," in O'Neill's rendering of Merleau-Pontian politics (81–86). If human life itself has a utopian moment, then body~place~commons is its always threatened, never fully realized register that keeps history open beyond the extravagant claims of liberal-democratic politics steered by global capital.

6

Participatory Reason and Democratic Professionalism

In this chapter we consider connections between knowledge, state, and ecos. The negative project of this chapter is to link our critique of dualisms of knowledge (in chapters 4 and 5) with our critique of the toggling space-times of the liberal and corporate state (in chapters 1 through 3). Our positive project is to show how Dewey's notions of "public intelligence" and the "aesthetic ecology" of public life can undo the segmentations of modernity that cut expert knowledges off from the placed, embodied reasoning needed to reclaim republican democratic publics able to provoke and support stewardship of the commons. With his notion of "flesh," Merleau-Ponty untoggles the web of dualisms (of thought, polity, and ecology) inaugurated by Western modernity. In this chapter, we connect the enfleshment of public intelligence with emerging forms of knowledge in the global justice movement—which emphasize participatory research and planning. These emergent forms of public intelligence catalyze new connections between research and action, local and expert knowledges, and new institutional forms for collaboration between sectors (civic, artistic, scholarly, governmental, etc.).

Participatory reason is the name we give to forms of knowledge emergent from and embedded in body~place~commons. In this chapter we argue for forms of participatory reason that ally community-based citizen thought (usually called *local knowledge*) with new forms of civic professionalism and participatory governance. We approach participatory reason from four angles. First, we explore concrete examples drawn from India and Appalachia of the vicissitudes and promise of participatory reason. Second, we critique recent theoretical efforts to undo the dualisms of modernity—including post-dualist green political theory and social theory arguing for "flat" epistemologies. Third, we consider the entrenched institutionalization of dualistic thought in the technocratic and bureaucratic toggles that fragment economy, polity, and ecos—to deeply inscribe the lines of externalization and enclosure into the Life Round and, thereby, to interlock class, gender, racial, imperialist, and ecological violences (as discussed in chapter 1). Fourth, we look more specifically at the metadiscursive combination of these dualisms into *logics of fungibility* that provide essential toolkits for the toggles of neoliberal globalization. To replace these logics of fungibility, we propose *epistemologies of participatory reason* and *ontologies of particularity and transversality*.

Recovering Place-Based Knowledge: A Story from Northeast India

The Apatani, a tribal group of about forty thousand in the Indian state of Arunachal Pradesh, are known for their system of growing fish along with rice in very productive paddy fields in a high valley of the eastern Himalayas. Tourists visiting the hard-to-get-to, beautiful Ziro Valley are regaled with tales of this agriculture, and much else, as examples of ancient folkways. On a visit to Rajiv Gandhi University in Naharlagun in 1997, however, we learned from Dr. Pura Tado of the Political Science Department that it was, in fact, a recent creation. We offer this tale of how fish came to paddy as an exemplar of participatory reason.

As described by Dr. Tado, the fish cum paddy system evolved gradually in the 1950s and 1960s. A village-level agricultural extension agent urged the Apatani to start fish ponds. Several farmers experimented, without much success. It seems that it was local people who first suggested that it did not make sense to build new ponds in the midst of already existing, laboriously hand-hewn, terraced paddies. However, when they experimented with putting the fish in the paddies, they faced problem upon problem—requiring one small inventive solution after another. First, the fishlings ate up the young rice plants. Gradually, after experimentation, the Apatani figured out how to introduce fishlings at the point when the rice plants were strong enough to withstand their gnawing. It also took years of experimentation to find the right plants and small creatures to introduce into the paddies, in the right amounts and mixtures—to provide food for the fish without harming the rice—all with exchange of ideas and mutual support between the local people and this unusual village extension agent.

This is an inspiring tale. If this pattern had been duplicated around the world in the 1950s and 1960s, we might now live on a much healthier planet.

Somehow, at the heart of this success was a long-term partnership that brought together an outside government expert with a local people who not only maintained their ways but also participated actively and creatively in technical innovation that improved material well-being, while reinforcing local culture and an indigenous ethic of sustainability. What were the micro-processes in this partnership that encouraged holistic and multisectoral development? Too often, government agents come in with a "blueprint"—a fixed plan developed by experts.[1] This is the sort of linear thinking for "progress" that replaces, rather than builds from within—which was embodied in much of the Green Revolution. Too often, such approaches introduce alien factors that destabilize local culture and ecosystems, such as an invasive weed (or the first rice-devouring fish in the paddies). When this happens there are imbalances between innovation and local context. However, in the Apatani example, local people were able to keep control over the relationship between thing and context. The secret of their success was in the way that they kept designing micro-experiments — placing and replacing the new thing (the fish) in a variety of local contexts (multiple reinventions of the paddy)—until they got a relationship between thing and context that satisfied them. This is innovation that arises from iteration. It shows a reversibility between thing and context, between thought and action—which is like the reversibility in Merleau-Ponty's notion of flesh. The iteration pivots on a hinge, not a toggle. It shows the pluri-fluencies of time and space that we discussed in the introduction. It shows the connections between democratization and participatory reason.

The infrastructures of this creativity enmesh with the infrastructures of body~place~commons. It recognizes that human being emerges from the interplay of diverse yet overlapping forms of bioaesthetic growth grounded by a body~earth hinge of changing persons and places. Today, the fate of humanity hinges on the claim, a necessarily political one, that human life requires a lifeworld facilitating the ability to weave levels and facets of reality into integrative coherence, such that the earth recovers its generative status as place, not merely economic space. The *bija satyagraha*, noncooperation movement against patents on seeds and plants (a coalition of more than two thousand groups including Vandana Shiva's Navdanya) clearly indicates how food democracy is central to this struggle (Shiva, 2000a, chaps. 2, 5, 7).

Let us look closely at this because it is the point where culture meets agriculture, folk ways meet expert ways, global meets local. What is it that makes something folk rather than expert? Again, the dialectic of thing and context is all important. To gather something within folkways is to establish a dialectic of thing and context in the way in which the Apatani established a relation of accrual between fish and paddy. This dialectic between fish and paddy resonates with the cosmogenic agency of culture making in general. In Apatani society, there is tight articulation between paddy maintenance, kinship and clan structure, the elaborate and ingenious irrigation systems, gender (women are the primary farmers and paddy builders), religious ritual (closely tied to agricultural cycles and landscape), political and juridical order (clan governance co-exists with the local Indian state in politics in Ziro Valley), and so on. Because of the slow way that the fish were introduced, with a strong degree of local control and creativity, these multiple horizons of socio-cultural-political systems could keep alignment with agricultural innovation. It is important to note that this local reality is not a simple harmonious world. Apatani society is shot through with its own local tensions—including inequalities of gender and landownership. But, these inequalities are open to contestation and rethinking within Arunachali democratic public spaces—which are a rapidly changing mix of traditional tribal assemblies, new civic spaces (many driven by women), and the Indian nation-state, in all its complexities (B. Taylor, 2002, 2009a). Such a place-based approach is a more sustainable alternative than the industrializing shrimp farming tied to global export markets in other states of India, leading to overharvesting, inequality, displacement, and ecological damage. The ecological violence typically present in the latter development is the direct product of the sorts of political asymmetry between eco-class positions around the Life Round that we discussed in chapter 1. More resilient, sustainable, and equitable development paths in Arunachal are integrally linked with new forms of community-based planning, civic empowerment, and participatory research (Agrawal, 1999; B. Taylor, 2009a) and struggle on a difficult terrain shaped by labile interactions of neoliberal globalization with local, regional, and national economies.

Phantasmal Globalization and Disembedding Knowledge Regimes

In this section, we examine rationalities of state, market, and science that valorize disembedding—as ways of knowing and valuing. In earlier chapters, we discussed three regimes of thought as linchpins of the ideologies that legitimate globalization. First, a fetishized market logic claims to embody a logos of reason and efficiency that can be endlessly redeployed between places and sectors without weakening its potency. Second, the ideal of the liberal democratic polity is a proceduralism that grants political authority according to bureaucratic rationality and legal code, but too often simply provides managerial "blueprints" that displace democratic representation or contestation. Third, hyper-specialized professionalism (that understands truth to arise only from academically certified methodological purity) can strengthen the universalizing logics of global economic space and disvalue claims rooted in the lifeworlds of body~place~commons. These forms of power and knowledge operate by giving the appearance of being able to know the truth by disembedding the object and subject of knowledge from their matrices of being in the world. For instance, markets can give the appearance that the value of a forest can be calculated on world markets that disembed it from local use values or nonquantifiable ecological interdependencies. The professionalized bureaucracy of national forest departments can serve as a standing guard that removes such sales from public debate, scrutiny, and awareness (while also veiling the complicity of government regulatory bodies with globalizing timber industries). Such a disembedding from politics is accomplished by an ontological disembedding of the forest from nature and from local and bioregional human history, through a reconstitution of the forest as an object that is defined to be only properly visible through the gaze of the professional forester—into what Hufford calls the "spectacular forest of innumerable rotations" (Hufford, 2001, 31).

If the professional forester is anxiously bound to systems of professional status and reward that encourage methodological perseveration rather than field-based, open-ended intellectual encounter with the forest, the intellectual practices in the bureaucratic construction of the forest will have a systemic tendency to top-down, easily quantified analysis according to the safest, most replicable, and least self-critical methods. This intellectual self-enclosure is compounded when social relations, daily practices, and spaces segregate professionals from contingent and open-ended encounters in diverse local publics or collective civic endeavors. Under such conditions, governmental regulatory bodies are particularly susceptible to the influence of corporate interests that have a vested interest in any mode of valuation and analysis that enables extraction according to predefined ontological categories most analogous to market valuation.

The form of such corporate/governmental/professional complexes vary by sector relating to human and nonhuman well-being—such as roads and transportation, land use planning, environmental reclamation and stewardship, art and cultural heritage, education, public health, and so forth. Within sectors, the distinctive patterns of intersection among government, business, and professional are the product of complex and distinctive histories of interaction among state, markets, experts, the general citizenry, and civil society activists particularly concerned about the matters regulated by that sector. Social theory should reflect carefully about these historical patterns. Even slight changes in these interrelationships can put into motion trajectories of democratization or de-democratization that can have profound impacts over time on whether ordinary citizens are able to participate in democratic deliberation, and to shape the terms of planning for the future (B. Taylor, 2009b).

Mary Hufford discusses the way in which official languages can annihilate aspects of forests that are not on the predefined, cognitive grids of the "spectacular forest of innumerable rotations" of official government regimes of property ownership or public lands management (Hufford, 2001). The rotation of the forest through multiple, officially authorized perspectives was more dependent on shifting bureaucratic mandates or political struggles than on an ongoing chiasmic dialogue of human and nonhuman. She gives an example of the annihilating power of such official perspectives in discussing the struggle of a local community to protect their watershed and forests from mining. The "reciprocating forest" of the local knowledge in this community was symbolically constructed as a forest with streams that were known across multiple temporalities—seasonal and generational. These streams might dry up in some times of the year, or in drought, but they still were understood as "there" by their constitution in stories going back to grandparents and beyond. Hufford cites John Gaventa (Hufford, 2001) for the description of an incident in which one government official, standing beside a visibly flowing stream, consulted his maps and said to the citizens arguing for its protection, "there's no stream here" (Gaventa, 1993).

Such conflicts are not only about specific ecological management techniques or values. It was also an epistemological conflict about what spatiotemporal frameworks to use to understand the forest and the forest/human relationship. *Too often our official ecological regimes foreground space-based epistemological frameworks in their symbolic construction of the forest and background site-specific learning.* For instance, Taylor argues that the U.S. Forest Service management plans tend to emphasize *space-based epistemologies* that lay abstract grids over forests with categories of assessment according to predefined, mostly quantified grids of abstract qualities—such as the number of board feet of marketable timber, species by market value, and discrete zones for discrete modalities of human use predefined by outcomes (B. Taylor, 2009b). However, in ethnographic fieldwork on environmental conflict in western North Carolina, Taylor found that citizens foregrounded *place-based epistemological* frameworks in their struggles against clear-cutting in national forests. In the speech of local residents, Taylor found such vernacular forests to be symbolically constructed as a complex and recursive layering of multiple temporalities—past, present, and future in almost topological entanglements. In one grassroots struggle against clear-cutting on public lands, a primary concern was that the Black Mountains' forests were vulnerable because of past events (overuse, landslides, acid rain). Repeatedly and unsuccessfully, local citizens asked the U.S. Forest Service to increase the *temporal depth and complexity* of government assessments and analysis. But, they also wanted more flexible *spatial frameworks*. They asked for environmental assessment and planning to be more *site-specific*—calling for place-based monitoring, training of personnel, and analysis of outcomes into official procedures. The citizens requested strongly that government planning should include analysis of past events in the ecological and social history of a particular forest in debates about possible future risks and benefits (B. Taylor, 2009b).

However, Forest Service actors were limited in their ability to do place-based management or thinking by the inflexibility of their official roles. They lacked the institutional structures to focus on a particular forest ecosystem across long ranges of ecological and social time. Historical, ecological, and site-specific views exceeded the temporal mandate of primary planning protocols—which were broken into five- to fifteen-year plans strongly shaped by standardized national practices. In addition, their knowledge, personnel systems, and institutional culture did not emphasize ways to track natural or human impacts over long periods of time in particular ecosystems or to reward officials who might try to accumulate such place-based ecological or social knowledge and skills (Hayes, 2007; B. Taylor, 2009b). We should emphasize that in these contexts, the citizens' local knowledge was not antiscientific—in fact, you could make a convincing argument that this perspective was *more* scientific insofar as it led to empirical questions about what was happening in the actual forest under question, rather than the forest imagined within the bureaucratic protocols of the Forest Service. From the point of view of the citizens, the official management systems tended to fragment the "real" forest—smashing it into the small time frames and aspects that were permitted by bureaucratic managerial protocols.

The Fragmentation of Knowledge and Crony Capitalism

One of the successes claimed for modernity has been the production of knowledge that has improved the lot of humans and improved the world. But this progressivist picture changes if one applies a "through-put analysis" to modernist production of knowledge—asking, as ecological economists ask of industry, "But what happens to its products after they are produced?" A tragic byproduct of the displacement of academics from public life can be inattention to the ways in which epistemologies circulate once they leave academe. We are concerned with the way in which academic methods (which might work well in delimited, well-thought-out contexts of scholarly application) can provide conceptual equipment for enframing public deliberations to decrease pluralistic and real-world deliberation. *If one looks at environmental and social planning structures from the point of view of people and places affected, fragmentation of knowledge becomes a significant political problem.* Figure 7 represents how, far too often, official frameworks of causality, time, and space appear to citizens when they try to steward the habitability of their lives and communities. One axis signifies the degree of *multicausality*—starting with highly flexible and multicausal ontologies and extending to increasingly narrowed and monocausal models. The other axis signifies the degree and flexibility of spatiotemporal frameworks—starting with those that integrate multiple times and spaces and extending to narrow spatiotemporal frames. Figure 7 represents *local knowledge* as the most flexibly integrative of multiple causal factors and spatiotemporal patterns. We use local knowledge to refer to knowledge about ecological or social phenomena gained through the habitual patterns of people's everyday lives. Local knowledge about particular forests, streams, or species, for instance, is gained from repeated encounters with the same places or phenomena over long periods of time—enabling people to share knowledge about the same thing, through changes of seasons or shifts in human or ecological patterns. Local knowledge is often patchy, nonsystematic, and inaccurate. But the trajectory of local knowledge is toward integration of spaces, times, and causalities. Against the integrative tendencies of local knowledge, figure 7 suggests that government and professional expertise are caught in trajectories of fragmentation of knowledge (in disparate frameworks of space, time, and causality). Government agencies evolve with competitive and contradictory mandates and fragmented protocols for assessment, planning, and regulation.

Against this is a process of the *greening of inequity*—a systemic tendency under economic globalization for the most powerful individuals, neighborhoods, and regions to be most able to protect those places that matter most to their perception of their quality of daily life. Boutique projects of proactive, holistic, green planning often primarily provide amenities for the privileged and educated as well as excellent green-wash for corporate interests with good public relations programs to distract from un-green global supply chains and externalities (Adamson, Evans, & Stein, 2002; Karliner, 1997). More powerful communities can afford professional planners and resources for proactive, long-term, integrated planning—creating an unequally distributed regime of *place managers* able to buffer the local places that matter to the more fortunate from the intensely displacing and dis-integrating pressures of economic global markets on the holistic embeddedness of community quality of life.

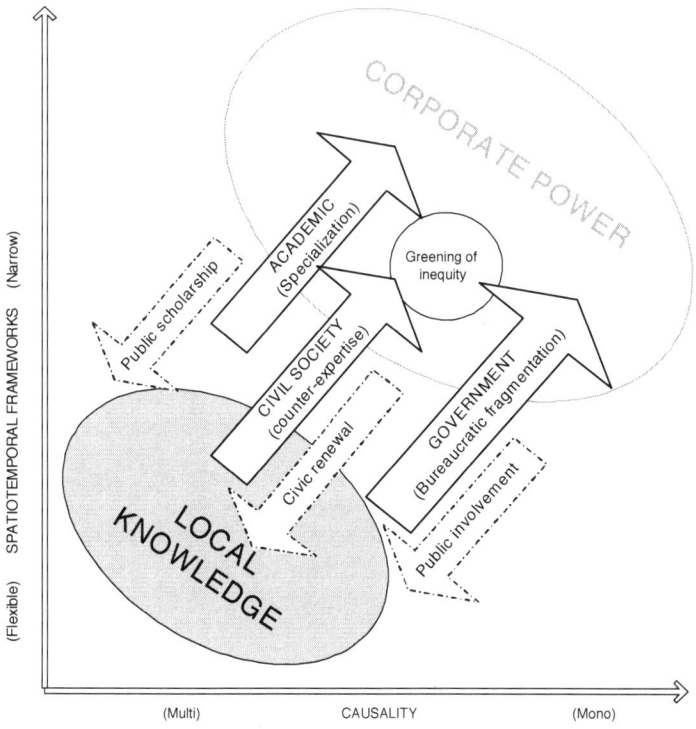

Figure 7. Space-times of local knowledge.

Figure 7 suggests that governmental fragmentation is mirrored in academic tendencies toward specialization—a dominant disposition that is weakly countered by far less well funded efforts at interdisciplinary, applied, or public scholarship aimed at community-based, place-based, population-based, or participatory application of specialized expertise (Fischer, 2000) in support of burgeoning movements for civic renewal nationally (Sirianni & Friedland, 2001) and regionally (Fisher, 1993; B. Taylor & Cook, 2001).

Finally, corporate interests play a shadowy role. If particular agencies are influenced by corporate or elite fields of power, fragmentation and specialization in the regulatory and planning process become useful tools for special interests to bracket out or deflect citizen's more holistic interests and integrative ways of thinking or to create a disorienting, constantly shifting shell game of spatiotemporal dislocation that fosters the interests of power elites.[2] For a community to enter this political terrain is like a patient entering a huge hospital without a medical chart, or like someone inadvertently entering an amusement park's multiply distorting hall of mirrors.[3] The dangers and demoralization of such political dismemberment are greatest for low-income communities that lack access to protective place managers.

These disembedding ideologies are in an uneasy relationship with regimes of sheer might. Both state-sponsored militarism and subnational terrorisms create their own forms of global audiences in which violence is the currency in which "success" is calculated. Neoliberalism also converts the seeming unreason of bloody struggles for sheer power into the curious "reason" of a resurgent social Darwinism. The idealized laws of competition within a fetishized market are elided with the so-called facts on the ground of neo-imperialist displays of sheer might. For instance, this is the logic that declares agribusiness a more "efficient" economic player than small family farmers in the games of market rationality. This economic frame ignores the political closeness of agribusiness to the levers of power (national and international) that write the metastructures of markets—such as global trade and food aid policies that are influenced by U.S. geopolitical interests and sheer might, the vertical integration of production and distribution markets to favor big players, official and unofficial manipulation of legal and illegal immigration flows, and displacements of agricultural workers.

What is fascinating about these regimes of sheer might is that they operate in very confusing ways, through both the second and third bodies of the U.S. state (which we discussed in chapters 1 and 3). Sometimes the same corporate actor will hold up to the citizen the public mask of the second body ("Your home is going into foreclosure because you are an irresponsible player in the housing market. The invisible hand of the market always leads to reasonable outcomes."). But, in the second act of the same drama, this same corporate actor will speak through the mask of the third body, in the voice of muffled, thuggish threat ("Congress has to give us $700 billion or else the entire U.S. economy goes down with us. There is no alternative."). Contradictory logics are deployed selectively under conditions of dialogical irreversibility and monologue—the corporate voice has much more power than the civic voice to pick which act and which mask to wear, or, when to enter and when to exit. Hufford has a good description of these monological and irreversible qualities in the public voice of what she calls "King Coal"—the web of linkages between the coal industry and all levels of the U.S. government (Hufford, 2004b).

Dis/Embedding as Inadequate to Undoing Modernist Dualisms

We have focused on disembedding, but this critique of disembedding is only useful up to a certain point. To understand how globalization works, it is helpful to watch for these moments of disembedding that can function as an ideological toggle switch that authorizes the public redefinition of places, persons, and beings from one (putative) ontological state into another. However, to locate the problems of globalization primarily at the site of a toggle between embedded and disembedded can reinscribe some of the problematic stories that modernity has told about itself. (This is, in fact, what too much postmodern theory has done.) It can be complicit with the divide that modernity creates between itself and the premodern in which the premodern is seen as a simple acceptance of embeddedness within the given or a sacralized cosmic order. Povinelli describes this as the symbolic construction of the "genealogical society" that modernity needs to anchor its own self-constitution as "free" from the matrixical. This dualism of embedded/disembedded may take the form of imputing romantic isolation to eco-centered, premodern cultures that are assumed to elide subjects into social, ecological, and cosmological orders that are collapsed together and taken as an immutable moral template. Or it can lead to a postmodernism that finds freedom in the escape from the given and a displacing of intellectual responsibility rationalized by a spectatorial professionalism built on the death of the subject.

The vision of globalization as primarily a process of disembedding does not problematize the fetishized dualisms that enable it. It thereby lends reality to spectacles of globalization—making a false contrast between the global and the local. Globalization, then, seems to take place always somewhere else in an autonomous sphere that is everywhere and nowhere—what Tsing calls "globalization as blob" (Tsing, 2005). Accordingly, contestation against globalization always seems to be "local" and to be somewhere where globalization is not.

To find libratory notions of self, knowledge, polity, and ecos, it is crucial to problematize and move beyond these ontological divides. We need to find ways to not suggest that certain *modes of thought* are inherently bad. The question is what *modes of relationship* are enabled by our practices of inquiry and action. One must not create reified and dualistic moral oppositions between modes of thought—good/bad, place/space, concrete/abstract, narratival/rational, care/justice, female/male, premodern/modern, humanities/science, art/science. We would argue that the key question is whether the mode of engagement between knower and known is one that *allows the knower to hold fast to a particular being in its manifestation as an existent in the fullness and career of time.* Giroux has a good discussion of the pedagogical issues and challenges in this context in *Beyond the Spectacle of Terrorism* (Giroux, 2006).

Social Theory, Flatness, and the Critique of Meta-Levels and Unitary Selves

From its beginning, social theory has questioned whether hierarchical regimes of knowledge and power were hidden behind the apparently democratizing Reason of Western modernity. A recurrent concern has been that universalizing knowledge produces multiple layers of knowledge—as abstraction and generalization (seem to) generate meta-levels of thought of ascending degrees of orderliness, clarity, and law-likeness. One concern has been that this multileveled ontology creates hierarchical and imperializing epistemologies—as when positivist science sidelines or forecloses more hermeneutic, messier epistemologies by claiming ascendancy based on greater clarity and order. But another concern has been that this cognitive hierarchy has elective affinities with other hierarchies (gender, race, ethnicity, caste, etc.) and forms of domination such as those of state, empire, market (Giri, 2002; Grewal & Kaplan, 1994; Mudimbe, 1988, chap. 1; Plumwood, 1993).

Two kinds of complicities in power and knowledge hierarchies are particularly relevant here. First, we agree with those who argue that régimes of expert knowledge are directly complicit with rationalizing state and corporate bureaucracies facilitating the global circuitry of expansive markets that are the prime cause of those growing global inequalities dwarfing those of earlier imperialisms. Second, problematic kinds of subject formation are complicit with these systemic patterns. Social theory has given much thought to how the meta-levels of universalizing reason hide within apparent objectivity a universal Subject—the god's eye view positioned to surveil messy particularities—which carries covert meanings of male, whiteness, sovereignty, escape from nature, and the body. This empowers certain social actors by disempowering others. It also hardwires the subject/object dualism into multiple channels in the circulations of power and authority. Martin Jay describes Merleau-Ponty's critique of the *pensée au survol* as suspicion of that "high altitude thinking which maintained the Cartesian split between a distant, spectatorial subject and the object of his sight" (Jay, 1989, 52–53).

In reaction against entangled hierarchies of knowledge, state, market, and empire, some social theory, especially in the last several decades, has tried to dismantle levels within epistemology and ontology, for fear of meta-levels that purport to control and to transparently encompass and sublate "lower" levels. Closely related to this are efforts to dismantle the notion of the subject out of fear that a notion of unitary selfhood requires the perfect adequation of the *pensée au survol*—selves that author themselves from some Archimedean vantage point like an ideal cartographer, and selves that can be known because they are adequated to their objects. All of these concerns have led to an interest, in social theory, in flatness—theories of knowledge that put knowers and known in a common ontological scale.[4]

This book turns away from flat ontologies and epistemologies, which we feel do not grapple with key constitutive forces of domination. Rather than a flat ontology, we propose a folded ontology, in two senses. First, we propose body~place~commons as ruly and unruly generative matrices that are manifolds of ontologies—multileveled, flat, but mostly curved/ing and (un) folded/ing. For example, in the phenomenon of hunger (and what in our world is a more important topic than that?) mechanistic causalities intercalate with more recursive causalities—as when the recursive, emergent cycles of animal learning about how to get food intersect with the brute linearities of causal chains of energy transfer in the cellular dynamics of metabolism. Second, body~place~commons has imminent architectonics that provide something like a meta-level, a certain kind of lifeworld logic, but one that provides purchase, not vantage, on its mostly wild, occasionally domesticated, heterogeneous, constituent temporalities—what Latour might call "pluriverse" (Latour, 2004; see also Giri, 2002; Katz, 2001).

This chapter argues that body~place~commons provides a site from which to think about the folding, unfolding, and enfolding of manifold ontology that is not at all like the *pensée au survol*. Several political, intellectual, and moral possibilities follow. First, as a way to kilter multiple knowledges, the architectonics of body~place~commons is immanently dialogical and open in texture—giving it elective affinities with democracy, empowerment, and tolerance. Second, as a way to understand across, and with, many differences, body~place~commons is transversalizing, not universalizing, in the traditional sense. In part, this is because it is in the pragmatist genealogy of "good enough" truth rather than perfect truth—lessening needs to dominate differences it moves between. It is composed of habitational logics that look for simple recurrent patterns in the mutual transformations of creatures inhabiting worlds and worlds transmuting under the tooth of time. The simplicity and recurrence of these patterns give them a kind of cognitive power— a power that outweighs its fuzziness as merely good enough truth. Third, this approach argues for new alliances between social theory and science. In many ways, social theory emerged over a century ago as a repudiation of science's claims to *pensée au survol*. Our argument is for a turn toward science, but a critical turn. At the end of this chapter, we call urgently for building far stronger institutional and intellectual alliances between social theory, the field sciences, and public arts and humanities, and between local and professionalized knowledges—in movements for civic and ecological renewal arrayed against conjoined hegemonies of technocracy, scientism, and globalization.

Constitutive Rhetorics of Green Public Space

Philosophies are not just simple statements about the world. Their epistemological architectonics contain rhetorical forms that determine what kind of subjects can speak, to whom, how, and about what. Green political theory has powerfully critiqued dominant Western thought for putting nature outside of democratic public space—as fully objectified and controllable through instrumental rationality—a managerialism that seems to foster ecological unmanageability and to be integral to various anti-democratic oppressions (Plumwood, 2006). However, de-centering public space to include nature is also problematic. Saward surveys recent attempts to create theoretical justifications for direct political representation for nature (Saward, 2006). Deep ecology is notorious for assuming unmediated apprehension of the interests and value of nonhuman beings and systems (Reid & Taylor, 2003). Plumwood suggests that hidden within the apparent generosity of deep ecology is an architectonics of monologue in which the first-person singular sweeps everything into its orbit, and that liberal instrumentalism spins nature out into the far reaches of the third-person impersonal (Plumwood, 2006). In both, "nature is subsumed by the enlarged Self" put, like the premodern wife, under "coverture" (66–67).

But Saward argues that even more nuanced and self-critical efforts downplay the complexities, slippages, and gaps *within representation,* both as political and cultural. He says that Eckersley's argument that there should be "proxy" representatives of nature in legislatures (Eckersley, 2000), Dryzek's "listening" to nature (Dryzek, 2000), and Goodin's "political representation" of nature's "objective interests" (Goodin, 1996) create a "uni-directional" human/nonhuman relationship that assumes unmediated grasp, and that singularize and objectify nature's interests (Saward, 2006, 186–91). Dryzek says we should redesign political units to fit bioregions that "should promote, and in turn be promoted by, awareness on the part of their human inhabitants of the biological surroundings to sustain them" (Dryzek, 2000, 157). Saward says Dryzek has a naive notion that this would bring people "close to nature" through "day-to-day contact with particular aspects of the ecosystem, and therefore in a much better position than distant managers or politicians to hear news from it." Saward says this is still too "Rousseauian." It taps, he says, into deep "Garden of Eden" metaphors in a false vision of politics "relatively free from the corrupting artifice of aggregative representative institutions as we know them" (Saward, 2006, 191).

We need to undo subject/object dualisms if we are to find theoretical models for democratic representation of nature that incorporate Saward's call for complex understanding of the gaps and mediations in human representations of nature, with Dryzek's argument that some ways of life are "closer" in human/nature interfaces than others. Only then will we be resituated to re-place—within reality-based democratic deliberation—the political atomism and fragmentation of liberal democratic polities and anarchic market forces. We are not presupposing professional autonomy in this process.

On the brink of catastrophic climate change, the historic bloc of corporate globalization and transnational elitism may expose a weakening link between professionalism and the corporate state, thus enabling a repositioning of professional work. What we are proposing is more attention by green political theorists to the role of the political rhetoric of civic professionalism in shifting from space-based logics of fungibility to place-based logics of democratic public inquiry. Based partly on an Arendtian understanding of the issues, Christopher Lasch's contribution to a renewed sense of world-enabling civic and ecological action offers important lessons.

Political Ecology, Democratic Agency, and the Mystery of Time

In his essay "Time and individuality," Dewey opens up some crucial questions that move his thought outside the dualisms of modernity, rather than into the false exits of the premodern or the postmodern. This essay draws interesting parallels between a mechanistic scientific cosmology of Nature and a progressivist notion of history. He argues that the premodern and the modern notions of time share a similar hunger to impute greater reality to the immutable.[5] He says that the classical hunger to escape the "tooth of time" and its destructions led to philosophies in which "change, and consequently time are marks of inferior reality, holding that true and ultimate reality is immutable and eternal (Dewey, 1962b [1938], 142). However, he sees Enlightenment philosophy and mechanistic science as simply displacing this hunger for the certain and the immutable while sharing "the conviction that the ultimately real is fixed and unchanging" (142).

While nineteenth- and twentieth-century scientific philosophies of cosmic evolution made change and time central, the threat of the impermanent was simply displaced because the "locus of the immutable was shifted to scientific natural law, but the faith and hope of philosophers and intellectuals were still tied to the unchanging" (Dewey, 1962b [1938], 144). The hunger for the perfection of the immutable was displaced from beings and world onto the laws and their final progressivist products that embodied the redemptive goodness of that which came before. Such modernity must constantly originate itself at this hinge of disjunct temporalities where Knower and Known incessantly disembed themselves from the worldly flow of time into a temporality within which thing and self are decomposed into pre-known qualities that can be laid out on eternal templates.

To move outside of such modernities, Dewey notes Whitehead's process ontology and subatomic physics. In a fascinating move, he takes indeterminacy to signify not the deconstruction but the possibility of what he calls the "individual." He says Heisenberg's principle does not give scientific substantiation to doctrines of the arbitrary or unconditioned free will. Rather, its actual "significance is generalization of the idea that the individual is a temporal career whose future cannot be *logically* deduced from its past" (Dewey, 1962b [1938], 151–52). Most importantly, he says, "If we accept the intrinsic connection of time with individuality, [individuals] are not mere redistributions of what existed before" (153). There are two reasons for this. First, unlike the decrees of Newtonian mechanistic science, the qualities of things turn out to always be *relational* (e.g., even mass turns out to be relational to position, velocity, time). Second, potentiality is an imminent, nonreducible quality of things. By this, Dewey does not mean an Aristotelian notion of potentiality as the imminence of a *fixed* end that the individual actualizes. Rather, he means an *emergent* quality of co-creation between individual and world that appears at a hinge of "interaction" that is an open, synaptic site characterized by uncertainty, indeterminacy, and contingency, yet can be known after the interactions have occurred. What makes this a deeply ecological view is that this quality of individuality characterizes human and *nonhuman beings,* and the co-creative unfoldings of evolution.

But, above all, it makes a continuum between the human endeavors of art, work, and science. It does not exalt a technocratic science because science does not reside in a separate sphere either epistemologically or ontologically, nor can its methods of thought be cleanly separated from the practices of art, material work, or embodied and social action in general. There are two reasons for this. First, science does not have a deeper ontological access to the constitutive nature of things because the important qualities of things cannot be predefined, without encounter with the thing in particular moments in its matrixical interactions. In fact, in many ways aesthetic practices are necessary to the knower's ability to grasp emergent qualities of the thing and their sedimentation from past events. Second, Dewey understands the reality of a thing or being to be a mystery, yet a potential object of science. And, the nature of this mystery is in the sheer being of the thing in time—a positionality that is continuous with the mystery encountered by artist or mystic. He says, "The mystery of time is thus the mystery of the existence of real individuals" (156). Dewey thereby reinscribes humility and awe into the scientific endeavor—experiences that are markedly present in the experience of many scientists able to do unalienated labor, yet that are radically proscribed in the meta-ideologies of most institutionalized science.

Particularity and Participatory Reason

Dewey's word *individuality* has problematic connotations of political and economic individualism. Therefore, we recast it as *particularity*. We argue that our most urgent intellectual challenge is to nurture and weave together multiple modalities of thought and imagination that can grasp and engage with *particularity*. This labor is fluid across the labors of community activist, scientist, anthropologist, artist, or politician. To encounter the world in its particularity is to encounter beings as mortal. To be mortal is to be actual and material within the flow of time. That is to say, the reality of mortal beings is in their stubborn presence in the present—yet this present exists as emergent from multiple past events and chains of consequences, as inherent in a matrix of simultaneous and contemporary events, while mysteriously pregnant with multiple but incompatible futures. To be mortal is to have everything at stake in the present but never contained by the present. It is in the present that things happen, where the significance and consequence of multiple pasts actualize, and a future can take hold. Beings as particular are beings that are a unique nexus of intertwined past events and entrained future consequence—the coming together of that unique configuration is what gives it the stamp of actuality. The paradox of particularity is that it derives equally from determination (what happens emerges from what happened before) and from contingency (multiple chains of consequences fall athwart each other to have effects that could not be anticipated from within any one strand of events).

Particularity can be understood with what Taylor calls "participatory reason" (Reid & Taylor, 2000, 461–63). Participatory reason is the ability to hold fast to particular beings within the flow of mortal time, using whatever cognitive, symbolic, ethical, affective, machinal, or sensory means are necessary to keep self and world in a relationship of mutual apparency. The particular is often confused with the unique or the concrete. These confusions then oppose particularity to the general, the universal, and the abstract. These are false oppositions. In our current historical situation, what opposes thought that is apt for *particularity* is thought that seeks only *fungibility*.

Logics of Fungibility, Technocracy, and the Corporate State

Logics of fungibility reduce beings to an assemblage of predefined traits. Beings, then, become infinitely interchangeable with each other. Such an encounter with a being is a process of assaying its constituent traits according to preknown formulae as to the elemental natures of those traits and pre-established methods for trait identification and measurement. Systematized, these protocols for assaying traits can, in turn, be assembled into a limitless world picture that creates a logical grid across which things can be interchangeably moved along a static circuitry of commensurability and difference. The dominant logics of our historical epoch are logics of fungibility. The hegemonic powers of market logic, commodification, bureaucratic rationalization, and technocratic managerialism derive from their ability to legitimate and implement global systems for the extraction and manipulation of labor, surplus value, natural resources, and desire in order to accumulate wealth and power. Their power comes from their ability to so glamorize logics of fungibility that the reduction of things to the infinitely interchangeable appears to be a form of liberation and empowerment.

The historical development of the periodic table of the elements exemplifies the efficacy of logics of fungibility—and continues to lend them prestige and legitimacy. By demonstrating that there is a viewpoint from which one can reduce matter to discrete elements, it legitimated a certain kind of essentialization—the attribution of an essence to substances such that they can be preknown as necessarily displaying a fixed array of traits. This was joined to two other processes. First, this essentialization was a kind of brickmaking factory for the reconstruction of nature as machine regulated by a layered hierarchy of natural laws. Second, the mechanistic reconstruction of nature begun in the seventeenth and eighteenth centuries flowed into extraordinary increases in human productive capacity in the nineteenth century and the first half of the twentieth century. Husserl's point is still relevant that the success of mechanistic and positivist worldviews in popular culture had to do with "[t]he exclusiveness with which the total worldview of modern men, in the second half of the 19th century, let itself be determined by the positive scientists and be blinded by the 'prosperity' [he uses the English word] they produced" (Husserl, 1970, 6). It is a historical accident that logics of fungibility were constructed at the convergence of these three different processes—essentialization by predefinition of traits, hierarchical causal laws, and economic and technological transformation. It is crucial to differentiate between the three because they pose different ethical and political challenges.

Let us start with the problem of essentialization, since social theory has expended much effort over the past three decades in combating essentialization as a prime force of domination. The linguistic turn in social theory led to an unfortunate conflation of the positivist essentialization and metalogics discussed above *with any naming of any entity as enduring over time*. Derrida and others drew on Saussure to argue that the relationship between signs and their referents was arbitrary, labile, and driven by immanent characteristics of language. Unfortunately, the problems of linguistic representation engulfed reflection about whether there are unitive and durable beings (including selves) and what stuff might constitute them. In much social theory, the unmasking of essences became equated with the labor to demonstrate that no one entity can be zipped into one word with nothing hanging out and no room to move and change. But to say this is to argue from within the logic criticized. Who ever thought that language was a set of pre-labeled, pre-measured body bags? Well, really only positivism in its extreme form. But positivism is a strong example of the long tendency in Western modernity that Adorno critiques as trapped under the "law of identity" requiring adequation of subject and its object (Adorno, 1983, 1997). If we look at the history of the law of identity, we find more geohistorically specific and dangerous problems than are engaged by much of the critique of representation in social theory. Unfortunately, the battle against essentialization has increasingly and unnecessarily become a debate about representation in general—a "baroque" (Sanbonmatsu, 2004) debate that is displaced and disembodied from sensuous living struggles to attend and tend to the particularity alimenting and secreted by sensuous living creatures.

To say that the problem is how things are named is to skip over what is distinctive and most dangerous about logics of fungibility. The power of fungibility is the way in which it constructs a label for a thing guaranteeing that it is an entity that bears a fixed repertoire of traits. These traits are not just any sort of characteristic. A trait is selected because it is an indicator that the thing will behave in a predictable way. In other words, such a trait is really a marker of repetitive dramas that one can definitely provoke the thing to do. Hydrogen is hydrogen because (a) it can be identified as that which has a set of characteristics that (b) are predictive of hydrogen-like reactions to (c) other things with traits that similarly predict patterns of reaction. This way of essentializing could best be called *elementalizing* because it reduces things to entities that can be put onto a common grid of mutual interactivity like the periodic table of the elements. The form of the grid and the qualities of its elements construct each other. Nothing can be put into the grid that does not already embody its terms. Because elementalization is produced by reduction, it naturally produces hierarchies of law like regularity. It is the same process run in the opposite direction.

This hierarchy matters not simply because it is a meta-logic, but because of its extraordinary power to turn complex beings into fungible items by provoking controlled dramas. It is here that technocratic science, markets, and bureaucratic government conjoin. It is for this reason that the political ecology of fungibility poses far more urgent ethical and political dilemmas than questions about representation posed as a general feature of human engagement in the world. The key problem of our age is not so much that things are slippery and cannot be easily or safely lassoed by words. The key problem of our age is the political economy in which markets, technocracy, and bureaucratic governance displace democratic public space with hegemonic regimes of interlocking and ever expanding grids that pre-label things and beings according to elementalizing categories that ontologically containerize them as entities that are infinitely exchangeable and substitutable—and that kick anything off the game board that does not act according to a small repertoire of actions. It is not a panopticon of observation so much as the construction of a gameboard that one can navigate only through mimetic obedience to a grid whose logic is not accessible from one's position within it. To cast this only as a problem of representation or as a problem with the meta-logics of modernist science is to overlook the social relations that determine who gets to play the game, and who makes the board it is played on (Latour, 2004).

Role of Experts in Chronotopic Reframing of Citizen Concerns and Debates

We came to these concerns about science and transdisciplinarity through a long loop outside academe. We have sat through many hundreds of grassroots meetings over two decades (on topics including strip mining, water quality, public health, community forestry, cultural heritage and identity, toxins, air quality, biodiversity, and local food economies) In such meetings, questions about science keep coming up. Particularly astonishing were similarities between different parts of the world in questions citizens raised about the scientific frameworks that they encountered in régimes of social and environmental planning that affected their lives—régimes that brought together academic and professional forms of knowledge with official government systems of regulation and management. Whether sitting in a community hall in the rural U.S. South or a women's self-help group in northeast India, we heard echoes of the similar concerns—suggesting that something structural is going on, a grassroots interrogation of the limits and negative consequences of forms of knowledge built into current forms of the nation-state.

On one side, grassroots citizen's organizations argued for *place-based and integrative* kinds of knowledge. On the other hand, regulatory and policy systems often appear to them to be on trajectories of increasing fragmentation, at least in terms of the causal and spatiotemporal frameworks that government applied to assessment, management, and planning. This happens across three dimensions: causality, space, and time—creating big gaps between grassroots and official ontological frameworks for constructing the objects under contestation (whether local watersheds, forests, children's bodily health, etc.). Taylor has argued that grassroots civic action and discourse tends to frame questions and solutions as multicausal, multiscalar, and multitemporal—out of concern for real-world risks and consequences that might affect them and the places and people that matter to them (B. Taylor, 2009b). However, government action and discourse, at its best, often appears in public contestation to narrow and fragment the spatiotemporal and causal frameworks around questions and solutions. At its worst, these constrictions of space, time, and causality can be seen as ways to shut out citizen voices and empower economic elites—by creating a kind of shell game in which the matter under discussion is continually reframed within spacetime frames that exclude real-world causal patterns and consequences and pressing questions of habitability and life stewardship. Diverse grassroots imaginaries can show similar high levels of anger when official perspectives fracture community concerns—as if holding a shattered mirror up to realities that the communities experienced as integrative.[6]

This shattering of matrices for time, space, and causality compounds the difficulties citizens face in conceptualizing, deliberating, and acting on collective concerns, hopes, and possibilities (see figure 7). To engage in contestation about the well-being of their bodies, places, and the commons on which they depend, citizen organizations typically have to develop "counterexpertise" (Fischer, 2000) to match the specialized skills and mandates of the government agencies with which they deal. Again and again, we have observed the exhausting amount of intellectual labor that citizen organizations must do to break multicausal local realities into component issues, reconstruct them into appropriate technical or bureaucratic languages, and reframe and repackage their analyses according to the contradictory and limited time frames of disparate government agency planning protocols.

Contrary to the displacing ideology of much official science, grassroots concerns about the lack of accurate and sufficiently field-tested science arises directly from the *place-based* nature of these struggles. Place-based matrices of political action do not necessarily oppose feeling and reason. Rather, they can provide durable chronotopic frameworks for weaving them together with laboriously gathered scientific understanding. One might expect "local" voices and perspectives to focus on trying to get power brokers to see, not "as a state" (J. C. Scott, 1998), but in terms of citizens' lifeworld experiences, human needs and values, stories, and material interests. Instead, careful and passionate lifeworld reframing can arise together with arguments for more and better science—even in "conservative" ideologies that might seem "antiscience" in American national politics. In such struggles for the habitability of local and regional places, flaws in reason and data in environmental management seem to be discussed at least as much as the concern that community values and stories are being neglected by power brokers.

Professions, the Fragmentation of Knowledge, and Displacement from Particularity

Professions rose in the late nineteenth century based on guild-like systems for certifying the caliber of individuals and programs in their ranks. The great strength of this system came from its democratic nature, insofar as it encouraged excellence through lateral identity formation among peers. It also, remarkably, created large numbers of stable, middle-class jobs that were, to significant extent, organized around logics of the commons. Despite recent enclosure of ideas as private property in heavily corporatized parts of the contemporary university, most of academe, most of the time, has treated the knowledge it produces as an intellectual commons—accessible to other scholars and the general public (with appropriate recognition of authorship) in support of intellectual inquiry and the public interest. Despite their competitiveness, the daily practices of professional life within such a commons-centered livelihood have, at their most democratic, produced a fabric of intersubjectivity that nurtures subjects with capacity for, and pleasure in, plurality—open-ended speech among peers engaging a world-in-common with courage, creativity, and a sense of personal security. As Peirce insisted, the freedom and integrity of scholarly inquiry can only arise from, and be secured by, a "community of inquiry" (Westbrook, 2005).

Despite the vicissitudes of professionalism in a world increasingly dominated by private interest ideologies, this world still retains ideals that promise a measure of personal dignity and meaningful work for something greater than one's private interests. A democratic and mutually empowering fabric of life based on labor for an intellectual commons also provides certain kinds of security for professionals as workers, which most workers lost when they were displaced from the civic and environmental commons that supported other livelihoods. Professional bodies have been able to secure high wages through archaic guild strategies vis-à-vis the state, including monopoly control of whole sectors of more or less artisanal work—although this negotiating power has plummeted in recent decades in professional sectors not connected with high capital accumulation industries. The increasing vulnerability of professions and expert knowledge to enclosure within logics of fungibility is directly proportional to the collapse of stewardship of the commons and public assets as a key role for government.

Having noted democratizing features of professionalism, we now turn to negative tendencies. Foremost in most discussions of modern knowledge systems is the problem of fragmentation. The proliferation of disciplines and subdisciplines based on ever-increasing methodological and epistemological specialization has had the effect of chopping the world up into bits—which are then divided up among disciplines in a way not unlike the European scramble for Africa. Critical social theory has produced large and eloquent literature critiquing these trends, from Husserl's last anguished book (Husserl, 1970) through the efforts in recent decades to found interdisciplinary social theory and cultural studies programs. Never successful in shifting the centers of power and funding streams, inter- and transdisciplinarity continue as guiding goals for many efforts within academe.

In addition to this fragmentation of the world, we see ways in which displacement and disembodiment were unfortunately (and unnecessarily) built into professional subject formation. This creates an unworlding of professions, a tendency toward postcommunal identity (Reid, 2001a). In important ways, the intersubjectivity of professional disciplines was made out of the shared stuff of common methodological training and evaluation and common disciplinary objects of investigation. Professional expertise then produces, as a sort of byproduct, a chronic haunting by a collective subject—the imaginary community of others who use this expertise and before whom this expertise is performed. It also, as many have noted, reconstructs the world according to the logic of one's own expertise—a sort of spectral collective object, predefined according to one's own intellectual tools.[7]

This pushes toward professional practices that have the internal logic of fungibility, even against the conscious intention of practitioners. When disciplinary epistemologies freeze into nonpluralist, fixed protocols, then the collective disciplinary subject is hooked into a mimetic relationship with a collective disciplinary object—which has displaced world. The relationship between Collective Disciplinary Subject and Collective Disciplinary Object then is in danger of losing precisely the slippage that is constitutive of plurality and of the best of modernity. At its best, modernity allows a kind of playing around in the relationship between subject and object. The doubt of modernity is best when it is not completely systematic, a sort of serious play within self-conscious (self-disciplined) boundaries—a messing about, trying now this and now that in aligning, un-aligning, and misaligning subject and object: "How do things look if I (we) move from this perspective to that?" "What happens if this factor is added (or subtracted), emphasized (or backgrounded)?" This is a nondualistic play between distanciation and re-alignment of subject and object.

However, when disciplinary epistemologies or methodologies become fetishized rituals in the court of the Collective Disciplinary Subject, free inquiry becomes more lever than hinge. World remade as Collective Disciplinary Object becomes just something that is predesigned for expertise to move about, according to its own constitutive and predesigned logic. This evinces arrogance of Western modernity at its worst—like the grand claim of Archimedes that he could move the world if he could find just the right lever. It also embodies the logic of fungibility, whether or not the disciplinary world-levers involved are quantifying or positivistic. The interpretive humanities and social sciences can fall into this as easily as the "hard" sciences—when they, as collective bodies, are levered into the world in such a way as to reduce the world into constituent elements and to containerize and circulate those elements. And this reduction of the Collective Disciplinary Object inevitably involves a reduction in the Collective Disciplinary Subject as their mimesis binds them into a hall of mirrors without slippage. Husserl pointed to such a dynamic when he said, "Merely fact-minded sciences make merely fact-minded people" (Husserl, 1970). On the other hand, professional disciplines can reclaim the best of modernity by re-placing and re-embodying themselves and their labor within emergent global justice movements to reclaim the right to steward the commons. As Tim Luke puts it, "populist resistances are about recollectivizing people and things by finding alternative modernities in modernity to serve more people more fairly more locally" (Luke, 1999, 237).

Recovery of Critical Sovereignty

The ideal of professionalization was to create protected zones around communities of inquiry *to protect the sovereignty of open-ended, critical discovery.* Insofar as disciplines have been able to function as something like democratic republics organized around stewardship of a defined intellectual commons, this has worked well. At its best, the fabric of mutuality in a community of inquiry nurtures plurality that in turn produces methodological and epistemological pluralism, criticality, and creativity in work. These features of subject~world relationship are integrally related to forms of (inter)subjectivity that discourage servility and arrogance and encourage a passion for thinking. It is important to note how affect affects intellectual agency. The best guarantee that thinkers will not grovel their talents before Power and Money comes when the pleasures of thought and the joys of conversation among thinkers are strong and relatively free of the fears endemic to chronic self-abasement and self-reconstruction before a spectral Collective Disciplinary Subject or before a boss in an unsatisfying and scary job.

If there is a freezing of the playful distantiations of modernity and a chilling of the open-ended and pleasurable mutualities of egalitarian plurality and shared world, the Collective Disciplinary Subject falls head over heels into the vicious circles of the Paradoxes of Sovereignty that we discussed in chapter 1. This is the result of a distinctively modern vicious circle: no system of order can ground itself, yet modernity recognizes no system of authority except itself. Arendt says that the "predicament of all modern political bodies, their profound instability[, is] the result of some elementary lack of authority" (Arendt, 1965, 159). The result, she says, is a distinctively modern need for distinctively modern absolutes. The absolutism she describes in politics is analogous to absolutism in knowledge. If the Collective Disciplinary Subject stakes its rights to define the Collective Disciplinary Object, in the perfection of its epistemic world-levers, it is perilously close to the dynamics Arendt imputes to the French Revolution. The absolutism of the decapitated Sovereign reappears in the absolutism of revolutionary self-founding (Arendt, 1965, chap. 4).

It is this absolutism, we believe, that is the mainspring of the *pensée au survol*. To try to undo this absolutism by decapitating anything that sticks its head up and that appears meta is to set up a process, metaphorically speaking, that keeps barricading the doors against Sun Kings, while Bonapartes crawl in the windows. It is the cult of epistemic levers that sucks us into the paradoxes of sovereignty—in which Subject is always dualistically opposed to Object (or vice versa). We propose replacing and re-embodying this phantasmal twosome within a third—world as metonymic entanglement of diverse spatiotemporal modalities of multiply unfolding becoming in, and from, the manifold of particular being. If we cannot do this, academe will literally be fiddling while the planet burns. To hold fast to disciplinary epistemic levers will be to trap ourselves in an endless process of self-understanding based on how we enframe the world.

There are two dangers. One is the blueprint thinking in which a reductive academic model is projected onto the world. At best, the blueprint will be both wrong and irrelevant so that it does not affect anything much. At worst, it will remake the world in its own image. One of the horrors of the moonscapes of mountaintop removal is the sensation that one is looking into the face of the Collective Disciplinary Subject of technocratic science and neoliberal economics. But the second danger is the danger of what Sanbanmatsu calls "baroque theory" (Sanbonmatsu, 2004). This is theory that uproots itself from world and repots itself in carefully and consciously delimited theoretical frameworks. Unable to move beyond the limits of its pot-bound epistemic base, it implodes in hypertrophy of entangled forms—ever more elaborate twists entrapped in too small and rigid a framework for its forms of life.

Geographies of Uneven Development and Unequal Chronotopes of Public Deliberation

If the world-displacing epistemic levers of professionalism only hurt their practitioners, it would be a bad but not world-altering thing. However, the chronotopic displacements of professional knowledge have provided crucial semiotic apparatuses for toggling the space-times of corporate capitalism and its capacity to dominate national imaginaries. The timeframe within which we encounter a thing or being is a crucial factor in how we constitute it. Within the media of advanced capitalism, we increasingly experience things and beings in a "spectacular" mode (Harvey, 1990). They rise up before us in an "eternal now" that contains their visible meanings with ever denser webs of commodified codes of self-referential meanings carried by "floating signifiers" displaced from historical particularity and human plurality (Curtis, 1999). Commodities not only fetishize and hide the class inequalities of their production (as Marx argued); they also hide the imperialist spatialities of their production (the global division of labor that externalizes ecological wastes, toxins, and exhaustion onto peripheralized regions, workers, and ecologies) (Harvey, 1996; Rogers, 2005; Schwab, 1994).

In a commons-centered, democratic political economy, beings and things would appear to us as an oscillation between a coming into being and a going out of being. They would tend to carry the aura (and the marks and scars) of particular pasts and possible futures. A political economy in which political and social actors are equal through all phases of the commons would create the material conditions for an ontology and epistemology formed around the rich, concrete particularities of the particular histories of things in oscillation between being and nonbeing. For instance, agribusiness deflects and ferociously attacks public knowledge about the real conditions of animals in factory firms and mechanized butchery, just as carefully as they disguise the real conditions of migrant farm workers. However, there is a burgeoning around the world of grassroots efforts to create direct exchange between food producers and food consumers. For instance, the Community Farm Alliance in Kentucky (a grassroots alliance of small family farmers; see http://www.communityfarmalliance.org) is campaigning for L.I.F.E. (locally integrated food economy)—including community-supported agriculture, farmers' markets, dependence on local produce by government institutions and private businesses, community gardens, and safeguarding of heritage seeds and native plants (B. Taylor, n.d.).

As is true globally, the language of this activism is suffused with an understanding that such material changes would bring about and require epistemological and moral changes — as people revalue the contingent, local, and imperfect beauties of products, places, and relationships that are not symbolically perfected by a mass culture industry and that are marked by the productive and reproductive cycles that form them. Such an ontology and epistemology would not abstract itself from habitat. Such a reason is different from the logics of fungibility that have been exalted and rewarded under patriarchal capitalism. We call it *participatory reason*—a way of thinking at the nexus of multiple causal and shaping forces that must be understood in their *particularity*. This requires understanding living beings over long periods of time in those habitats in which they create their being through all phases of the commons. For instance, new forms of civic environmentalism globally are developing creative new forms of participatory action research as part of citizen efforts to monitor the healthy forests, watersheds, biodiversity, public health, and so forth (Edwards & Gaventa, 2001; Fischer, 2000). This scaling up of so-called local knowledge is an important mobilization against the dominance of technocratic and professionalized knowledge regimes. It emphasizes field-based, long-term, ground-truthed knowledge of *particular* habitats or beings through seasonal change, unique and multicausal local histories. To reclaim a Deweyan heritage of this sort of democratic and participatory reason will require political struggles within higher education to bring poetics and field sciences together in place-based, action research and pedagogy. It also requires the deflection of prestige and resources from the now dominant technocratic research that is increasingly fueled by nonpublic, corporate entrepreneurialism.

Our contention through this study has been that the ecological imperative and need for limits of our epoch makes unmistakably urgent what Gibson-

Graham call recognition of "economic being-in-common" (Gibson-Graham, 2006, 98). Drawing on Dewey and Merleau-Ponty as we have, we also are concerned with what Gibson-Graham call "an ethical praxis of being-in-common" (88). We share their concern for democratic spaces of autonomous negotiations over interdependence and its varied meanings in building community economies. We concur with their postdevelopment vision that aims at de-essentializing economic logics, cultivating diversity, and reclaiming and enlarging the commons. We certainly agree on the need for "a larger world in which to start where we are" (196).

However, we have worked to find and to configure theoretical auspices with intercorporeal, praxeomorphic, horizontal dynamics providing working edges for a new, multiscalar, democratic politics. The issue we have to raise is—in Jean-Luc Nancy's words—what if "world" is "one in which things can genuinely *take place*" (Nancy, 2007, 42). It would be too easy to slide off the ontological plane of political practice. In fact, Gibson-Graham's account of practice registers surprise at "the ways that we are all already in a space of commonality" (Gibson-Graham, 2006, 160). Even "small changes in place" (196) may suggest a deeper praxis with transpersonal roots invigorating postcapitalist imaginations seeking alternative economies.

We are embodied in and surrounded by a visible world. We see ourselves seeing; our "vision commences in the things," Merleau-Ponty noted. He also speaks of this world as "intermundane space" — shared with others but owned by no one, which is exactly why recent decades have echoed with talk of the politics of experience. When things genuinely take place in the world, we are moving—as Merleau-Ponty speculated—not back into the "politics of the subject" but in that sensible field where it is possible for history to garner structural but still fluid coherence from a praxeomorphic logic reactivating a "transcendental geology" of forms distinctive to the human body and its world-in-common (Merleau-Ponty, 1968, 271, 269, 258–59).

The question is whether Gibson-Graham (Gibson-Graham, 2006, xxxiii–xxxiv) exaggerate the ontological space of nonbeing in their determination to negatively ground subject and place. In February 1960, Merleau-Ponty observed that the "problem of negativity is the problem of depth," and that time, taking place, is chiasmic institution-building (Merleau-Ponty, 1968, 236, 184, 267, cf. 105–55). Tracking his notes to June 1960 where we find his reference to a "quasi-geographical inscription of history," we are able to understand place not merely in terms of a "politics of becoming" but as a reversible interworld of "*formulated* structure" and horizontal Being allowing institutional change and transformation (236–59). Political action is possible because "an anonymous visibility inhabits both of us," opens us "upon a natural and historical world," marking our co-involvement in Being, where we "cannot judge the powers of life by those of death" (142, 85, 84). So it is that Edward Casey says landscape is the transitional domain of place and space, self and other, and why every landscape, unlike space, has a horizon (Casey, 2001, 417–18).

If we are not to privilege the more academic or formal rationalities and knowledges in local politics of becoming, we need this way of reopening to the pre-reflective, pre-subjective origins of our world-in-common. Intellectual capitulation to the corporate capitalist politics of Speed and its disregard for Place is irreducibly a political act. Virilio tracks these connections between politics and chronotopes when he speaks of "political fluctuation where 'terror is the realization of the law of movement' (Arendt), [is] outside all effective localization. . . . We are witness to the beginnings of a remarkable event: *the decline of territorial politics . . . this disintegration on the way to generalization . . .* what is *common* is today disqualified by the immediacy of what is not (Virilio, 2005, 189–90) [And where the audiovisual pressure of "the industrial exploitation of speed" (132)] represents "the *decline of the unity of vicinity* and through it, the expression of the next stage in the decline of territorial politics" (189–90).

Above all, participatory reason is thought that attends to the conditions of its own generation. The central attunement of participatory reason is to what Heidegger called truth as *alethia*—where knowing is a kind of turning that foregrounds one side and thereby backgrounds other sides. This turning back and forth, between foreground and background, between thing and context, between particularity and matrices, is the infrastructural generativity of participatory reason. Recognizing that particularity is always emergent, it becomes very interested in the conditions of emergence on which it depends. Its natural habitat is the "field"—ambulatory exploration that puts the embodied scholar within the unfolding places that are the portals to and sedimentations of events. In her powerful explorations of ethnography as a "field science" (C. O. Davis, 2000, introduction), Christopher Davis gets at the topological folding and recursions of time and space in embodied, placed thinking that recognizes that "stories about places are makeshift things" (20). This is a way of thinking that tries "to retain the instability of the new; that is, rather than allowing it to be dissolved in pre-existing categories of comprehension, we will make of it the foundation for further thought . . . those forms of thought that . . . can be defined as systematics or sciences of—(un)anticipated outcomes. In these sciences, exemplified by therapeutics . . . war . . . and farming, each application of a principle is also an experiment with it" (10).

There is a great deal of lip service to local knowledge, but have we thought deeply enough about how much we would have to change if we were to build partnerships between local and expert knowledges? The call for new forms of community/academic partnership and a revaluing of local knowledge can be seen as important efforts to combat technocratic managerialism and its ecological and political abuses. What is local knowledge? Too often, local knowledge is thought of as what uneducated people do. We would argue that local knowledge is better thought of as thinking that is placed, embodied, and integrated in the tending of the civic and ecological commons. It is thought that is rooted in particular lives, grounded in locales and histories. It is thought that cannot escape from givenness, from the tooth of time as it is inevitably experienced within unfolding personal and collective stories.

What this says to us is that we social theorists can rediscover and resituate ourselves amid the historical thick of things where we find terrain for surprising horizons of political imagination and action. But we will have to unchain ourselves from the dog of alienated politics if we are to generate ideas that reinvigorate the flesh of political struggle and sensibility. Public cultures are regenerated in the soil, the historical matter cultivated by ideas, better yet visionary practices emerging in those places that make time for democratic sensibilities capable of opening up historical possibilities. Social theory can play a crucial role in tending that intersection of world, public, and body~place~commons that we described in the introduction as necessary portals to democracy. The *pluritemporal, pluriscalar, pluricausal, and plurivocal* fluencies of emerging forms of participatory reason and emerging forms of green democracy incite and nurture each other.

7

Translocal Politics, Ecological Hermeneutics, Democratic Struggles

Wendell Berry begins "Elegy," a poem in *The Wheel,* his eighth collection of verse:

> To be at home on its native ground
> the mind must go down below its horizon,
> descend below the lightfall
> on ridge and steep and valley floor
> to receive the lives of the dead. It must wake
> in their sleep, who wake in its dreams. (Berry, 1982, 5)

In a world of global refugees and displaced workers, the relationship of many to their "native ground" is highly problematic. A few years ago, historian Leon Fink turned his attention to a struggle of poultry plant workers to organize themselves in western North Carolina. His study examines the Laborers International Union of North America effort that brought together Mayan refugees from the Aguacatan valley of war-torn Guatemala, Mexican workers, and a diverse group of local allies (Fink, 2003, 54–78).

Perhaps Fink's most fascinating chapter is entitled "How the Dead Helped to Organize the Living." He provides an account of a burial society formed by the Aguacatecos, the largest group of workers, reflecting their commitment both to returning the deceased to native ground and to their grieving families in Guatemala. Burial rites helped institute solidarity and community, or in the labor historian's words: "the dead not only make demands upon the living but also some times serve as their most efficient community organizers" (Fink, 2003, 78). To return to the poet's perspective, we might note the capacity of political consciousness to draw upon the power of the ancestors and for the dead, in a certain sense, to live on in the dreams and political action of the living.

Even before NAFTA was implemented in 1994, a global regional labor market was under construction to restructure Appalachian economies such as east Tennessee. Highlander Center (HC) near Knoxville has facilitated grassroots responses to challenges such as environmental devastation, labor organizing, and sociocultural conflict. HC has assisted Save Our Cumberland Mountains (SOCM), one of Appalachia's oldest citizen action organizations, which arose to fight strip mining. SOCM's interest in a wider spectrum of regional community issues made it attractive as an ally to Citizens Against Temporary Services (CATS), which had formed in the late 1980s in response to corporate restructuring undermining workers' lives and their communities. It was an early sparkplug for the Tennessee Industrial Renewal Network (TIRN), which more recently continues as TERN, the Tennessee Economic Renewal Network (Weinbaum, 2004, 176–259). In the early 1990s, a band of these worker-activists filmed their journey to the Mexican border—one of several cross-border exchanges—in search of new forms of labor solidarity (Ansley, 1999, 154–56).[1] Some of the Tennesseans became part of the great Seattle WTO protest in late fall 1999. The global movement for economic justice continues and now incorporates what may be even more stubborn issues of climate justice or ecological equity.

Global and regional community-based movements for socioecological justice are versed in the arts of weaving mourning and memory for more durable tapestries of public life. For fifty years the protection of family cemeteries has been one of the most poignant concerns of rural Appalachians who have lived amid mountains being stripped for coal. Many communities and families impacted by mining have stories of destroyed cemeteries (see powerful examples in Hufford, 2004a). Threats to others continue as a focus of political action (Bady, 2008, 13). In Kentucky, state capitol funerals for mountains have been conducted by Kentuckians for the Commonwealth in order to dramatize government collaboration in environmental destruction. From our own political experience, we turn to one example of ecological mourning and protest. Hinton, West Virginia, artist Carol Jackson has created a cardboard cemetery remembering the hundreds of streams destroyed by mountaintop removal (MTR), which is better named Mountain Massacre Mining. Public meetings in West Virginia organized by groups such as the Ohio Valley Environmental Coalition have included this method of raising questions of energy policy and the true costs of coal.

At a Charleston, West Virginia, rally at the state capitol we assisted Carol in putting up her memorial for the event. Imagining the extinction of streams, hollows, and living communities in this re-creation of a public space forged by grassroots environmentalists (some with direct experience of the destruction mentioned) was a powerful lesson in "aesthetic ecology." Jackson's memorial in effect reweaves the civic and ecological commons in a public space by provoking collective remembrance of aesthetic ecologies that have been lost but remain vital for ongoing political action. Retrieving democratic republican politics is partly reconnecting in experience aspects that the corporate state has dismembered and spectralized.[2]

Memory and Mourning—Place, Nation, and Democratic Republic

Drawing upon Frederick Buell's keen formulation, we seek "a way of dwelling actively within rather than accommodating oneself to environmental crisis" (Buell, 2003, 206). We fully agree with him that "Perception of deepened environmental crisis . . . does not have to lead to political passivity, to calls for inhumanist authoritarian solutions, or to trying to walk away from the damage. Dwelling in crisis that is firmly perceived as such, coupled with the exploration of a new economy of feeling, opens up a very different set of possibilities for care, commitment, and doing all one can" (208). Buell's important study gives particular attention to the genuinely new, emerging literature focused on environmental mourning. It is a process very familiar to those of us active in the field of Appalachian politics where mourning for damaged or destroyed mountains and streams is often performed in political theater making an appeal not only to legislators but public conscience.

There is an academic tendency to presume that building cosmopolitan institutions necessarily contributes to a more democratic social life. Yet this may be based on failure to critically consider, as Craig Calhoun has put it, that cosmopolitanism is "now largely the project" of global capitalism and transnational corporate managers. The qualifying word is *critical* because top academic administrators and program directors usually know "where the money is" and often have been exempted from critical scrutiny by faculty. Given the accelerating power and influence of global capital, there can be little doubt about the need for more cosmopolitan institutions. However, if this project is to be a democratic one it must, to use Calhoun's words, "put down roots in the solidarities that organize most people's sense of identity and location in the world," where global capital does not dictate politics as liberal individualism and an abstract or formally procedural concept of rights. His point is that an academic mentality ensconced in "frequent traveler lounges" may generate a lot of moralism about what the world needs but little in the way of democratic action on problems that concrete communities face including tendencies toward exclusive localism (Calhoun, 2002, 102–9).

What we call the *dialectic of globalization and subjectivization* is clearly at work in the fast capitalist, high-tech life of postcommunal professionalism that promotes intellectualizing fantasies of a bodiless, placeless existence. This amounts to hiding behind electronic masks where serious work is presumably confined to the *"globalized* time of generalized interaction" (Virilio, 1997, 70) as if set in abstract parameters of economic space disconnected from placed communities (Reid, 2005). Professional mobility and the anti-historic time of global corporate media are two powerful forms that reinforce intellectual complicity with what Virilio calls "the death of geography" (Virilio, 1997, 65). Our insistence on increasing and improving civic professional participation with nonacademic people caring for places means, among other things, that the academic market must be decoupled from this tide sometimes called *corporate globalization*. Transforming the academic market is perhaps an incremental or piecemeal process that must be part of *a movement to reclaim public universities*. Yet our situation already is one of deep environmental crisis posing enormous tasks of memory, mourning, and social and political renewal. More concretely, academic institutions and programs have a responsibility to carry memories (living archives) of once beautiful, expansive habitats of region and community. What we call a *critical ecological hermeneutics* has many starting places and surely depends on our post-Cartesian ability and courage to embody places and their horizons opening toward both historical political worlds and zones of a global commons under siege as never before.

Freedom is possible only within a commons-centered, democratic political economy. This would free us from false dualisms (subject/object, universal/concrete, self/other) that cripple our agency by reifying our relationships to the world in ways that fuel domination (especially gender, class, and race). Capitalism has an astounding capacity to make the direct production of products seem to be the only real work. Global immiseration of those who do that labor of "caring" (Hochschild, 2003) is driven by the increasing colonization of the lifeworld as described above, which drives increasing numbers of workers into the labor market as they are displaced from gift economies or are ecological refugees (Guha, 1990). This floods the job market with increasingly desperate workers. The only long-term way to fight these structural tendencies is to develop a concerted political platform to fundamentally change power along the axes of domination through both externalization and enclosure (see figure 3 in chapter 1). The primary need is to change the legal definition of who can function as a collective actor and collective representative of the interests of persons doing labor along each phase of the cycle of the commons.

Efforts to re-regulate and deconstruct the legal personhood of corporations and global financial entities are crucial (Nace, 2005). Also important is the effort to create new legal and collective entities to protect and express the interests of those stuck below the axes of domination. Civil society organizations, which (claim to) represent the interests of the global South, youth, women, mothers, victims of violence, and nonhuman beings at least introduce these positionalities into global imaginary. It is most important, however, to develop collective entities, for new forms of ownership and direct political representation—these are bigger tasks than can be managed by civil society alone. There is experimentation in this area. For instance, Bollier surveys emerging models for institutionalizing collective and equitable ownership of the commons and commonwealth—including public domain patents, various forms of land trust, joint management and ownership models, and public asset development (Bollier, 2003). These new forms of politics and economics require recognition that the most important site of value creation is not in the zone of capital accumulation but in the zone of commonwealth accumulation (see figure 3). We need new ways of recognizing, conceptualizing, and institutionalizing the generation of public and common goods and assets. Above all this is a process of reclaiming democratic control over the temporal horizons within which we deliberate about our needs and obligations to care for the bodily grounds of our (and others') being in the hereness of particular places and convergent ecologies. To refer to ecological citizenship is to speak of citizens *embodying* their particular *places* of ecological experience with common concerns grounded in the life *commons* leading to expansive spatiotemporal horizons of responsible action.

Perhaps a few summary observations are in order. First, memory, mourning, and action as vital forms of human experience are charged in important ways by multiple processes of place-destruction and reclamation and by those cosmopoetic energies that reground places. Second, much of human experience today in all areas of the world including the American context is affected by the politico-economic destruction of or damage to place. The transnational corporate state's drastic delocalization of experience shifts it into a virtual Nowhere that is then filled with, for example, the reality-TV subculture. Third, the fate of the most (or more) meaningful forms of democratic politics is significantly connected with the prospects of an emerging global justice movement struggling on planetary terrain dominated by economic globalization shaped by corporate policies and neoliberal ideology. Fourth, what we call *ecological hermeneutics* works not from a Derridean self as absence but from a postfoundational selfhood thriving or not, embodied and emplaced in an indeterminate field of centering and decentering experience. We also contend that such a hermeneutics must manifest itself as a form of political theory refusing acquiescence in the "death of geography" marked by the "gradual dematerialization of the earth's horizon" (Virilio, 1997, 65, 43). A critical political theory must start from somewhere and today has no choice but to work amid the earthly ruins of global capitalism and human strife with the "refuse of the dialectic" (D. Gross, 1992, 135). Memory, mourning, and a placed sensibility are integral to this endeavor.

As our study has labored to make clear by this point, several contributions have been made and many remain to be contributed to a social and political theory aiming at a more hopeful and democratic future. We are trying to clarify an agenda that, among other things, gives particular attention to the tasks of an ecological hermeneutics searching for structures of historical action composing the global justice movement out of its constituent groups. Of course, such an approach or perspective must engage obstacles to cross-boundary collaboration and especially concepts of nation, nationalism, and nation-state. Already we have explored some of the evidence of *vital growing edges between global regional places and various forms of democratic public space*. Theory must engage ways in which the temporal structure of political action is shaped by the placement of human experience. How are we to understand and reformulate certain notions of the "dialectic of space and place" in light of such an ecological hermeneutics? In their pioneering study confronting the gaps between environmentalism in the North and the South, Guha and Martinez-Alier have outlined the transregional project of a cross-cultural environmental ethic based on "building blocks" of diversity, sustainability, and equity (Guha & Martinez-Alier, 1998, 91). From Merleau-Ponty and Dewey, we have worked toward *the ecological ontology best suited to advance the project and the public intelligence informing it*.

Those of us sharing Hannah Arendt's concern for world-care to reverse modern Western world alienation have every reason to situate ourselves in a truly ecological hermeneutics of democratic political discourse and action. Few of us lack experience with the academic/professional configurations of knowledge, authority, and identity that block or hinder institutionalization of such efforts. They are one reason we have much to learn from the memory-mourning-place triad in our urgent search for a more just and democratic world. By this time, we should have had more than enough of the "wasted lives" linked by Bauman to a "liquid modern culture"... [that] looks... like a culture of disengagement, discontinuity and forgetting" (Bauman, 2004, 117). We might begin by joining Arendt in questioning "life as the highest good" (Arendt, 1958, 313–20) if we are to escape professional enclosure in the structure of our minds (and unnecessarily narrow academic-bureaucratic roles) and act on and out of experience of a world-in-common. She proposed that we must "think what we are doing" as inhabitants of the earth as opposed to adopting the perspective of the Cartesian-Newtonian world in which "dead matter" was made the standard of intelligibility. From Erwin Straus, Merleau-Ponty, and Marjorie Glicksman Grene, there is a challenge to social theory, in the latter's words: "To know ourselves as knowers, we need to know we are alive.... *how we are ourselves out there with things and others*" (Grene, 1995, 67, 83; emphasis added). In his remarkable poem "Remorse for Any Death," Borges writes that the dead person "is nothing but the loss and absence of the world." Those of us that are left are like robbers, for "we have shared out like thieves the amazing treasure of nights and days" (Borges, 1972). The poet thus reminds us to seek solidarity, sustainability, justice!

As we would put it—much like Subcommandante Marcos, who once referred to the WTO as a "death train"—our neoliberals want a world for sale that they can parcel out like thieves. The tracks on which their train operates echo with more than the convulsions of a commodity economy, for the grid laid across the earth spells what Hans Jonas once termed "the ontological dominance of death" (Jonas, 1966, 12). This is how youthful social majorities are being robbed. Meanwhile, our American young await a politics of prophetic memory of the "amazing treasure of nights and days" (Borges, 1972). But we must first learn political arts of mourning and social renewal, curing the American version of the "inability to mourn" that the Mitscherlichs examined in postwar Germany (Mitscherlich & Mitscherlich, 1975). The way forward begins as we reopen ourselves to the expendable landscape. In Jean-Luc Nancy's words, the challenge is "reopening each possible struggle for a world, that is, for what must form the contrary of a global injustice against the background of general equivalence" (Nancy, 2007, 54).

Walter Benjamin's understanding of Charlie Chaplin's film performances provides a clue to world-forming tasks crucial to democratic political space. Susan Buck-Morss's thoughtful account of Benjamin's deep interest in childhood play is her context for eliciting his insight, one that recalls our previous discussion of Edith Cobb's work. "Chaplin rescued the capacity for experience by mimicking the fragmentation that threatened it" (Buck-Morss, 1991, 269). Benjamin is clear that political space for social transformation will not be "accomplished contemplatively" (270). In our language, these tasks of memory, mourning, and democratic renewal are praxeomorphic struggles for aesthetic ecologies enabling public intelligence (see chapters 4, 5, 6). When such struggles bear the eco-cultural depth and debts of our histories, they bring to institutional spaces a living historicity from diverse sources capable of regenerating human hopes and dreams.

Critical Ecological Hermeneutics

The theorist loads the dice against ecological agency when the "subject" is not re-placed, recognizing that, as Heidegger once said, "place always opens a region" (qtd. in Malpas, 1999, 157). Refusing Heidegger's nostalgic romanticism without discarding his concern that the world was becoming a world-picture, Leslie Paul Thiele (Thiele, 1995, 187–91) rightly observes that this points toward bioregionalism. Of course, what we wish to stress is the ontological primacy of dwelling, even if admitting we may remain standing for a good while in the shadows of the corporate state's technological rationality and its resourcism. The question is whether a politics of worldly dwelling—working with "the poetic-historic character of the world" (Murray, 1985, 105)—can stop positivizing increasing homelessness (in whatever form) and expand the commons while trimming the more violent enframing policies and tactics of the transnational corporate state. What we might learn from Thoreau and Wendell Berry (and if not Heidegger, certainly Dewey) is that reopening the everyday is a work of both time and place. We might learn, too, that mobility (as market reduction of labor to another resource) may undercut as well as highlight the political challenge of Difference (Thiele, 1995; White, 1990). The new politics we are proposing needs Dwelling from both transcendent modalities: lifeworld as world-horizon and lifeworld as earth-ground (see Berry, 1995, 13–45; Steinbock, 1995, 104). An ecological hermeneutics works in the chiasmatic interplay of these earthly and worldly modalities.

As Michael Murray (Murray, 1985, 104–5) once explained, we can critically appropriate Gadamer's fusion of horizons because horizon "determines the ground as a particular region, a lived geography, a native land, and it brings together an experience of earth with an experience of the divine." When Murray insists on "the linkage of horizontality with the dimensions of ground and measure," we understand this as a praxeomorphic fusion of horizons that enables the great political issues of power, responsibility, and co-existence. Rather than leaping to ideological forms either of the nationalistic or the cosmopolitan, we would reclaim more viable alternatives beginning with the endowments of enabling regions and the practical possibilities of neighboring. It is from these places that we can build a translocal politics intending to transform nations into democratic republics and insular regions into global regional publics that know what justice is and the terrains that provide its roots.

What we have called the *dualist horizon* of the transnational corporate state has been institutionalized into the fabric of academic and professional knowledge and identity. To undo these dualisms in our lives and work will require more than replacing one type of knowledge with another. We must find ways to help forge a new politics with a sustainable vision viable in both local and global contexts of action. As Terence Ball argued in 1995, "The problem with contemporary 'identity politics' is that while it supplies some with a place to stand initially, it provides no one a place to stay.... The politics of identity offers, as it were, a homeless shelter rather than a home" (Ball, 1995, 296, 273–96). In our view such a politics fits the form of a liberal-democratic polity. We hope to have shown that such an approach can be a distraction or a dead-end turn from a grassroots citizen action politics growing out of a democratic republican tradition.

Is part of the academic problematic of recent years a postmodern intellectualism that, missing these lessons, has prematurely proclaimed an "academic cosmopolitanism" and "global citizenship" that threatens to fall into the new transnational elitism intertwined with corporate globalization? Are stratospheric approaches to solidarity finally getting the critical reconsideration they deserve? Recent analyses by Timothy Brennan (Brennan, 2006) and Craig Calhoun (Calhoun, 2002) are motivated by this chief concern and contention and confirm William Leach's argument at the end of the 1990s, that an "unprecedented alliance against place" had emerged involving corporate executives, academicians, and postcolonialists. By "denigrating place and fostering everything connected to mobility and choice," liberal, left-wing cosmopolitans, Leach claims, "actually fortify the context for more market expansion" (Leach, 1999, 173, 276). Brennan angrily presses the question of "the economic function of the culturalist intellectual" and why "agency is almost never seen in moments of civic participation" (Brennan, 2006, 222–23; cf. Reid & Taylor, 2000).

Pointing toward the public policy realm, Leach argues that typically "the failure of Americans to remember and protect their places" generates more police and prisons to mop up the provincial refugees dislocated by that most exclusionary cosmopolitanism, the corporate-dominated market (Leach, 1999, 181). The American problem posed by Arendt, the "failure of postrevolutionary thought to remember the revolutionary spirit," is linked to our aggravating susceptibility "to the invasion of the public realm by society" (Arendt, 1965, 234, 223; Reid, 1990). The key problem, we argue in chapter 2, is the extent to which popular cultural access to the political legacies of a democratic republic have been marginalized by corporate power and market mythology. David Gross's image of "the past in ruins" and his criticism of Gadamer's appeal to tradition suggest that transformative action leaves behind a happy warrior/Christian soldier mentality bound to conservative republican imagery and technocratic politics (Gross, 1992, 92–106).

Mark Kingwell's brilliant *Harper's* essay connects speed with a transcendental impulse to escape time and mortality (Kingwell, 1998). The American romance with capitalism, the extent of American troubles with place and time, and the religious roots of market mythology (excavated in previous chapters) have structured our vulnerability to speed's problems. Our addiction to postcommunal utopian fantasies may be a "green light" reaction to the inextricable link between place and mortality (cf. Malpas, 1999, 192). Americans must stop trying to substitute mobility for mortality and relearn a politics democratically defending placed communities wherever they are. When foreign policy discussion uses terms such as *blowback* and *the sorrows of empire* we are reminded of a widely unrecognized historical burden. Perhaps our own "truth and reconciliation" process, tasks of memory and mourning, might help get us back on the democratic, republican road. The temporality of speed also obscures the very different temporalities of what Veena Das calls "the work of time" in healing the injuries of violence (Das, 2007, chap. 5). Das highlights that this work of mourning and repair is a labor that goes on beyond the edge of the speakable, slowly and at its own pace, in cycles of reinhabitation of the everyday. Speaking of the healing over decades from the violence of the partition of India and Pakistan, Das speaks of a "descent into the ordinary world but as if in mourning for it. Recovery did not lie in enacting a revenge against the world, but in inhabiting it in a gesture of mourning for it" (Das, 2007, 77).

One of our greatest republican critics of racism and imperialism was Mark Twain, and scholars such as Amy Kaplan have illuminated how his "national identity . . . was forged in an international context of imperial expansion" (Kaplan, 2002, 52). But in the midsummer of 2005 newspapers such as the *Lexington Herald-Leader* were publishing a "travel" piece by Chris Erskine out of the *Los Angeles Times* extolling the "authenticity and charm" of Hannibal, Missouri, on the Mississippi, Twain's hometown, and its "small town innocence and worldly brio" (the latter linked to the river)— part of America's national memory, prospective tourists were assured. As James W. Loewen's survey of "what our historic sites get wrong" states, this is "a Twain without a moral center" (Loewen, 2000, 148). Visitors numbering around 350,000 each year are treated to a domesticated Twain without his laboriously crafted criticisms of racism, classism, and imperialism. Remarkably, a town that had been both a slave market and a stop on the Underground Railroad had written blacks out of Hannibal's history, Loewen concluded. It would seem that Twain's Hannibal has become another American "Hadleyburg." But that brings us back to questions of the dialectic of knowledge and opinion in the politics of place and whether much scholarly discourse has become normatively incapacitated for public interventions of collective remembrance.

Increasing numbers of the U.S. middle class roam our "vast landscape of the temporary" (Leach, 1999, 6) attached to remembering machines that allegedly help normalize the quest for autonomy in a placeless wasteland of corporate palaces and "green zones." But the atomized quest extends from work to "home," a suburban arrangement cracking in the peak-oil era. We speak of strip malls but seldom think of many of our suburbs as setting on reclaimed strip mines. Whether one is living in eastern Kentucky or San Diego, this image might render some insight, although the brutality of mountaintop removal far exceeds the impoverishment of nature-human interaction in suburban sprawl.

The New Activism: Placed Engagement, Scaling Up, Powering Down

A good purchase on the so-called consumer republic is at its weakest point— the point at which it pretends that the profit margin makes obsolete the lifeworld logos. The lie in this metanarrative is its splitting of the cyclicity of life processes into a unilinear historical time that mines the energies and hopes of the reproductive side of life processes—on the false assumption that nature can endlessly replenish itself. As we discussed in chapters 1 and 3, the thin bright line of capital accumulation at the profit margin is falsely painted over the thin green line of ecological balance—substituting a phantasm of plenty for the immanent logic of regeneration and self-maintenance that we call life.[3] In other words, we are all within the Life Round, but our mainstream politics are structured to deny that.

If we ask which people are in a position to see past denial and where the green-wash peels away to reveal the breaking of ecos—it is primarily two sorts of people. First, and least recognized, are those whom Gadgil and Guha call ecosystem people (Gadgil & Guha, 1995). As Vandana Shiva has described, these are people for whom economic livelihood depends on direct subsistence on the land's ecologies (Shiva, 1991). Marginalized from market economies, they depend largely on foraging and subsistence farming and forestry. Second are people whose lives were fairly well contained within the dominant narratives until they became aware of environmental damage in their home, neighborhood, or beloved commons or wilds—thus rupturing the logic of the consumerist dream embedded in the myth of endless economic growth and "progress" (what in North America is called the "American dream"). It is these two sorts of people who have changed environmental politics in the last two decades in the United States. Mainstream environmentalism had been most visibly a largely conservationist, white, male movement to conserve wild areas for recreation and aesthetic and spiritual renewal—drawing much of its energy and sensibility from people in a class position to draw on surplus wealth to free themselves from the space-time of industrial production to savor relatively undamaged natural wilds.

In 2003, when the four New Guinea visitors reached the top of Kayford Mountain, Janet Fout (now Keating) reports that they were "bewildered" (Fout 2003). We also have felt a strange disorientation on passing from Larry Gibson's forests to the sudden, human-made cliff—a bodily sensation of abyss that is a strange mix of physical and what we can only call *ontological disorientation*. As Mary Hufford has said, to look at MTR is to be put "on the brink" of the "unthinkable.... In the presence of an enormous power which threatened to engulf us, we could not speak at first" (Hufford, 2004a). Janet Keating (formerly Fout) says the New Guinea visitors to Kayford Mountain were "bewildered that anyone would systematically destroy the land on such a large scale." In response, Larry says to them, "My mother gave me birth, but these mountains gave me life." His visitors replied: "We have a similar saying: We feed from the breasts of our Mother (Earth)." And the photo of this event in the *Winds of Change* newsletter shows a close circle of Larry and his visitors looking intently at each other against the backdrop of moonscapes to the horizon (Fout 2003).

But what does Larry mean by saying "these" mountains when we can quite plainly see that the mountains are gone? This is what we mean by pluritemporality. It is not enough to say, as strong theories of social constructionism would say, that the mountains are somehow in his head, or in the texts of his speech, but not "there." We believe that Larry is trying to suggest that there are complex and multiple arcs of time that concretize in heterogeneous but integrative ways in *places*—places that are so constitutive of who we are that we cannot let go of them without becoming a different person. Such places are complicated hinges through which the matter and the meanings of history move in nonlinear recursions, and where the past is never simply past. It is the whole point of this book to say that such places are powerful and necessary portals to democracy. This is a nondualistic co-constitution of human and nonhuman—a gift economy of circling interdependencies. This is a way of constituting subjects out of a fabric of being that is not a nameable thing, but a way of turning and returning—a complex kiltering of multiple gyres of finitude. It is a substrate of individual and collective being that is more like the recursive folds of Einsteinian space-times than a thing tidily wrapped in a name. Images of "giving" and "keeping" pervade Larry's speech (B. Taylor, n.d). He calls himself and his networks "Keepers of the Mountains." Human and nonhuman powers of reproduction and regeneration are kiltered together in relationships in which similarity and difference shape-shift into each other in almost topological inversions—like a glove turning inside out. He says that the generativity of "the mountains" is like human generativity. But Larry actively undercuts any notions of reproduction that inscribe dualistic oppositions (human versus nature, voluntary creation versus involuntary repetition). He contrasts "birth"—the originary moment of the appearance of the body—to the unfolding arc of his personal "life," suggesting by contrast the plenitude of life story and the way in which its authorial voice is as much in the ecological surround as "in" him. These are really very profound philosophic and political points he makes in one short sentence.

Larry refuses to leave his mountain in the same way in which Antigone refused to leave her brother's body on the battlefield. There are many different ways to look at Antigone (as the size of the scholarly literature attests). But an insight of Judith Butler is relevant to Kayford Mountain. When Antigone risked her own life by violating the official edict that declared her brother unworthy of burial, Butler says that she is "insisting that her brother is irreducible to any law that would render citizens interchangeable with one another. As she asserts his radical particularity, he comes to stand as a scandal, as the threat of ruination to the universality of the law . . . She stands, Lacan tells us, for 'the ineffaceable character of what is'" (Butler, 2000, 52). The régimes of substitutability with which we are concerned are the global energy markets that decree mountaintop removal an "efficient" way to get coal. (We do not extrapolate these chains of substitutability to the symbolic order in toto as Butler does.) But, with this restriction, her understanding of Antigone is relevant: "Antigone refuses to obey any law that refuses public recognition of her loss, and in this way prefigures the situation that those with publicly ungrievable losses—from AIDS, for instance—know too well. To what sort of living death have they been condemned? (24) . . . If . . . Antigone represents a kind of thinking that counters the symbolic, and, hence, counters life, perhaps it is precisely because the very terms of livability are established by a symbolic that is challenged by her kind of claim. And this claim does not take place outside the symbolic or, indeed, outside the public sphere, but within its terms and as an unanticipated appropriation and perversion of its own mandate (54)."

Larry brilliantly turns the private property regime inside out. His official ability to hold onto Kayford Mountain derives from the rights of private property. But he uses this form of personhood under the law as the pivot from which to inaugurate the rights and logos of the commons. He has declared Kayford Mountain a "world heritage park" (http://www.mountainkeeper.org), making it a planetary commons. By exercising "free-market" rights to choose whether to buy or sell, he has driven the coal companies to a frenzy of escalating offers of hundreds of millions of dollars. He uses the terms of their offer as a public platform from which to speak back in a radically different logic—using notions of value that derive not from quantified market prices, but from the ethical necessity of his sense of reciprocity with the mountains. The mountains made him who he is, and he can do no other than to care for them, to "keep" them—even as they have disappeared all around him over the past fifteen years. This logic is based on a nondualistic hinging of his being with the ecos from which he feels his life to have arisen. By turning market logic inside out, Larry brings the unofficial violence that is the substrate of the property system out into the open, as he suffers multiple acts of direct violence (arson, gunshots, undermining, lethal threats, etc.), while the perpetuators elude the law.

The Third Body of Appalachia/America

The last quarter century has only piled up increasingly urgent evidence for the necessity to re-embed economic production within the cycles of social and ecological reproduction, yet it seems harder and harder to build stable civic webs and democratic political structures to accomplish needed forms of collective conversation and action. Finitude has always been hard for the United States, but recent political changes compound current governmental incompetence in rising to planetary challenges—including the urgent need for attention to the necessary connections between city and country in political struggle.

The re-democratization of agrarian economies is crucial to the needed transitions of the twenty-first century. But political barriers are significant. The New Right's power in the United States came from its ability to join the reactionary politics of working-class and rural moral and religious authoritarianism, with the cronyistic, informal webs of interscalar corporate patronage in what could be called the military-industrial-energy-prison-security complex—which we have called the *third body* of American politics. One way to understand these shocking developments is to note that the social democratic institutions of the New Deal were not so much dismantled as they were privatized in ways that give increasing power to clientalistic politics. This has amounted to a kind of enclosure of processes of ecological and social reproduction that has been integrally related to the U.S. war machine. For instance, in Appalachia, as globalizing corporate interests in agriculture, forestry, and coal increase vertical integration, local and regional markets and ownership have plummeted. Rural communities have become particularly susceptible to interests that promote a model of "development" as the offering of large public subsidies to attract privatized prisons, toxic dumps, and so forth—thereby locking them ever more firmly below the axes of domination where externalities pile up, while wealth, power, and, too often, youth flee. In areas where union militancy, agrarian self-sufficiency, and resilient local cultures once nurtured significant communities of resistance and resilience, we too often see the sorts of civic collapse associated with drugs, police violence, political corruption and fear, and entrenched inequality.

Simon Stylites was a first-century Christian ascetic who spent decades sitting on a very high pole. The political geographies of global economic space are very like Simon Stylites (if differently motivated). On one hand, the loftiness ascribed to it is real. Corporate globalization's highly elaborate circuitry of goods, finances, and people requires and creates real range, timelessness, and mobility of the sort suggested by the term *global reach*. On the other hand, this extraordinarily powerful global economic space rests on increasingly fragile and unstable foundations of violent *emplacement*—symbolic violence of ontological effacement of habitational logics of residents, the various injuries of class with various forms of immiseration under growing global jobs crises, or increasingly direct violence that grows in inverse proportion to the number of jobs that local elites can control.

This creates an unstable political terrain, with new possibilities and new dangers. On one hand, the brutal reconstitution of Appalachian mountains as sectors in global economic space is one of the world's tragic episodes in systematic violence. This violence now reaches gargantuan scale with the speeding up of mountaintop removal. This vast ecological drama is enframed into virtual invisibility by national mediascapes, facilitated by spectacles of faux regulation by government agencies captured by a powerful coal industrial regime despite decades of local and regional resistance. The rationalization of this devastation as the stage for a phantasmal economic development (always heralded but never arriving) has been facilitated by nearby "public" universities that have helped tobacco companies to conceal cancer, funded expensive biotech efforts to deodorize hog mega-factories, and, helped to construct large systems of "viewsheds" to hide industrial forestry and mining from public view—but have done far less to support democratic participation in the coalfields. It is in the semiotic construction and manipulation of viewsheds of its own geographies that the power of King Coal hides itself behind what is called the "corporate veil."

Subjectivization of Nature: The Mountains as a Landscape of Consumption

But there is a parallel process of extraction in the reconstruction of Appalachian landscapes for leisure industries for consumption by mostly urban and suburban consumers. On weekends or vacations, when urban travelers retreat to the mountains for rafting, trekking, shopping for antiques and crafts, family reunions, or contemplative sojourns, there are many macrostructural forces that script this as a "time outside of ordinary time"—a space of leisure and recreation that can only work its magic if it is radically disjunct from the space of work and the spaces of civic responsibility for a collective future.

The same corporate and bureaucratic players that map the mountains as a fungible resource for extraction are intercalated in the "mainstream politics" that veils industrial mega-mining behind crafted "viewsheds" that make the mountains appear a pretty and pristine site of primeval Nature, which is neither coeval with industrial time nor with personal stories. What subjects are allowed by these viewsheds? The passerby who has no material interests, no narrative entanglement in the scene before it. The hinge that binds the viewer to the viewed is an abstract form of appearance that can be consumed with pleasure and without much time by a self abstracted from its everyday material or civic praxis. How many travelers on these roads are provoked to think that it is the coal of these mountains, and their destruction, that is producing over 50 percent of the nation's electricity, or that they as citizens are implicated in the national energy policies that author this?

It is in this context that regional social and economic justice movements tenaciously scale up their actions—labors both political and cultural, as suggested by Ann Pancake's fictional portrayal (Pancake, 2007) of the daughter of a family caught up in these battles in southern West Virginia as she "looks" at Yellowroot, their lost mountain:

> Before when I looked up at that big mountain, I just wasn't able to see it as real. It wasn't like a separateness I felt these days from live mountains. It was just that my mind didn't have any way to hold the dead ones. (106)

> And past where Yellowroot [Mountain] had been, miles of mountains stumps, limping all the way over to what used to be horizon, and what would you call it now? The ass-end of the world. *Moonscape,* that's what many said after seeing it, but I saw right away that this was something different. *Airiness emptying me.* Because moonscape was still something made by God and this was not, this was the moon upside down. (165; emphasis added)

Where Do the Children Play?

Several years ago, a popular song by Cat Stevens asked, "where do the children play?" The key question of the song has, in fact, become a growing public concern. There are at least two important recent studies of American childhood we must put into play in this context. We begin with an image from Richard Louv's study of "nature-deficit disorder," which he contends afflicts not only many children but many families and communities. (In fact, his book documents the extent to which many people were ready to identify the problem in his terms.) Against trends toward the criminalization of natural play, Louv proposes a policy and pedagogical revolution re-naturing childhood health. Our understanding of Louv's key argument is that at the heart of living landscapes of places for existence is our species craving for "the very shapes we now allow to be scraped away" (Louv, 2005, 52). What he calls shapes in the dynamic processes of place, growth, and experience must be understood as the form-rich landscapes needed in the striving of human lives to find and make worlds for flourishing selfhood and creative communities.

Barry Sanders's focus (in *A Is for Ox*) is on the level of orality, language, and story from which he makes a powerful and alarming argument that overreliance on electronic media can seriously disturb the sense of communication as interchange, the connection between literacy and orality. There is taking place a collapse of literacy and a loss of selfhood directly related to several types of rising violence in our electronic age. The current and costly infatuation with horror movies also fits in here.

Sanders reminds his readers that "young people want . . . to feel and to be empowered through their own voices." However, when not helped to generate internalized texts of oral discourse, when encouraged to bypass literacy, youth become "post-illiterates." Quoting Sanders, "society needs to fear ghosts who feel no more real than the shimmering of an image on a computer screen. For them, others are no more real than they are" (Sanders, 1994, 78). Barry Sanders thus provides one answer to Louv's concern for "where will future stewards of nature come from?" (Louv, 2005, 145).

We have to pose a question now. Perhaps these ghosts plugged in to so many technocorporate platforms of globalized space are themselves haunted by remnantial glimpses of lost memories, untold stories, elusive solidarities, and fugitive dreams of action and communion. Are these youth in mourning? Might it be that we have just described their legacies that an adult world is unable to transmit, to share? When the generational hinge secured by place and time weakens, market strategies presage the "cheating culture" recently described by David Callahan (Callahan, 2004). But the problem is not that a theft has occurred but rather that someone is missing. How might the adult world engage this "generation on hold" (Cote & Allaher, 1996) in mourning and renewal?

In *Precarious Life* Judith Butler claims, "without the capacity to mourn, we lose that keener sense of life we need in order to oppose violence" (Butler, 2004, xviii–xix). Margaret Thatcher's market society of atomized humanity is the dystopian rationalization of environmental violence in its ultimate form. If we grant ourselves a capacity to mourn with these children, is there nevertheless a gap between this power and the institutional possibilities for its expression? *What are the political forms that will help us traverse this gap between corporeal vulnerability and social justice, between war and peace?*

Sensibilities of Place and World for Global Justice

We return to the question of why we understand the destruction of place as a ghost-making process for all of us, why it is integral to what George Steiner in *Real Presences* fears may be "our eviction from a central humanity" (qtd. in Steiner, 1989, 49; and also in Sanders, 1994, 49). If we are seeking an ontology for livable communities much like the Reverend Billy, it may well be time to stop shopping and practice the politics of the slowdown. Writer after writer has put a canary into one "coal mine" after another. All the canaries are dead! Yet the cuckoo birds of neoliberalism still squawk, "level playing fields" for "global competition"! What they are really doing is selling tickets to the ultimate horror movie, what we have termed "a phantasm of the Earth as technocratically flattened into total manipulability, usability, accessibility" (Reid & Taylor, 2006, 38).

The hegemonic link between postcommunal professionalism and the transnational corporate state is forged from the logic of fungibility operational to a global labor market. "Humans are reduced to atoms within an infinitely redeployable global mesh of labor markets, appear to themselves and others as spectacles of endless recombinatorial reactivity" (Reid & Taylor, 2006, 29). Here we have the roller rink of global capital and unceasing exploitation as "monster mash" including Yongkang, China, known as the "dismemberment capital" (see Kahn, 2003) and a "free trade prison" near Mexico City (see Bacon, 2005, 223). After this horror movie, people can push their carts in search of "cheap goods" at Wal-Mart.

We have been proposing that instead of retreating to these bargain basements beneath the ecological violence on the upper levels, grassroots struggles for justice cultivate a keener sense of the conditions for global empathy among those displaced from their life-grounds. *So we come back to our central argument: major reclamation projects have to be on the American democratic republican agenda that entails reconfiguring memory and mourning in global regional contexts of action for a more just, democratic, and sustainable world.* Instead of more NAFTA corridors extending the imperial reach of the corporate state, this agenda makes sense when integrated into the new continental politics focused by community preservation and working people's needs recently outlined by Jeff Faux from the Economic Policy Institute (Faux, 2006, 235–53).

Fundamentally, we are seeking that "place within which the political can arise" (Malpas, 1999, 198). Political thinking needs the geography that begins with what we call "the body~place~commons horizon of intellectual responsibility" (Reid, 2005). Our key position on place as it relates to time and political action boils down to (or flames up with) what Merleau-Ponty was getting at when he wrote: "It is through the world first that I am seen or thought" (Merleau-Ponty, 1968, 274). It is through the "durable flesh of the world" that this *takes place*, which is why we speak of critical auspices simultaneously marked by placed sensibility and horizonal imagination in the chiasmic field of co-presence. As Renaud Barbaras puts it, "the becoming-world of sensibility is synonymous with the advent of a sensed world" (Barbaras, 2004 [1991], 155).

What Paul Virilio calls the "gradual dematerialization of the earth's horizon" (Virilio, 1997, 43) is fueled by various sources of epochal change: the earth enveloping our existence recast as world-picture; intellectualizing fantasies of bodiless, placeless existence; the anti-historic time of global media; the academic capitalist market; a postcommunal professionalism. Philip Shabecoff's *Earth Rising*, a study of U.S. environmentalism at the beginning of our new century, is prefaced by a line from the poet Rilke: "Earth, isn't this what you want: rising up Inside us invisibly once more?" To this we would add that a new democratic politics must evoke, among other things, a sacramental sense of world. *And so we once more ask if we do not find that place at the very heart of our existence where we are most radically de-centered—where we re-cognize a world that needs our memories, our grief, and our active care?* Our argument, then, has to be that it is from the places of our "becoming world of sensibility" that a "sacrament of coexistence" (Bugbee, 1961, 158) is possible, enabling our participation with diverse others in the global justice movement.

"Comparative political philosophy," Hwa Yol Jung has written, "is a search and research for what Merleau-Ponty calls the 'lateral universal' that allows interpretation [of] cultural boundaries" (Jung, 1993, 223). In his edited work *Comparative Political Culture in the Age of Globalization*, he describes this as the transversal work of "creating and solidifying the world as the arena in which by first empowering all participants the confluence or transfusion of differences takes place" (Jung, 2002, 15). The political context to this transversal, interpretive process that especially interests us is the World Social Forum that strives for global/local justice alternatives to corporate globalization. The key question we have been pursuing is what ontological configuration of nature, selfhood, and communication is required to empower such groups in their intercultural search for truly critical ecological alternatives to the world as projected by entities such as Exxon, Monsanto, and Archer Daniels Midland (ADM). As we have said before, it is world as an ontological problem that requires particular attention in the American context where the crisis of citizenship, at once practical and intellectual, reflects a constitution of worldlessness produced today by the interplay of economic globalization and cultural subjectivization.

Erwin Straus once observed that in "the psychiatric clinic we discover the breakdown of mutual understanding in its elementary form beyond all historical variations. Psychiatry thus requires insight into the possibility of mutual understanding in its elementary structure, since it underlies all social and historical variants" (Straus, Natanson, & Ey, 1969, 20). Our "primary situation" for Straus gave priority "to the relation with the Allon over the relation with the heteros" (52). Here is one of several formulations: "For you and I do not face each other directly as ego and alter ego. We meet one another in the—common—world. Only because we comport ourselves toward the Allon and because each of us, as a part, has risen up from the common ground, can we enter into communication with one another. In analogy with the Allon we term our partner the heteros, to show, merely by a linguistic relation, that the other fellow, whom we understand, im-parts himself to us as a part of the Allon" (52).

Very importantly for grappling with the postmodern condition, Straus later noted that in the "primary orientation we experience the Allon as 'counter-part'; *invariably it has a physiognomy*" (Straus, Natanson, & Ey, 1969, 66; emphasis added). Discarding the traditional extramundane subject of consciousness, Straus attends to our life-world experience as terrestrial creatures, "a corporeal part of the world, opposing the Allon as a motile being, distinct while belonging to it" (70–71). The norm and pathology of life-world experience is not a strictly subjectivist matter of disorderly behavior but rather a question of flow or disruption in our unfolding sensory relations with a world that is never merely "external." We present Straus as we have in order to underline the *physiognomic* dimensions of the subject's body-world experience at the core of the I-Allon structure of the human condition. Renaud Barbaras's brilliant explication of Merleau-Ponty's ontology calls attention to the significance of Straus's rendering of the "spatio-temporal form of sensibility" (Barbaras, 2004 [1991], 217n). When Merleau-Ponty refers to the nexus of "history and transcendental geology, this very time that is space, this very space that is time," we find ourselves in that durable flesh of the world opening to a "historical landscape and a quasi-geographical inscription of history" (M. Merleau-Ponty, 1968, 227–28). There is nothing logocentric in this chiasmic field of co-presence.

Beyond Flat Ontologies and Virtual Multitudes

This permits our return to Calvin Schrag's notion of transversal communication, and what we have described as its emergent, infrastructural forms of placed temporalization moving beyond and beneath a subject-centered, theory-based universalizing rationality. Schrag's response to the postmodernist philosophers such as Deleuze and Lyotard refigures and resituates "rationality" in the terrain and texture of a "transversal communicative praxis." Following suggestions in Merleau-Ponty, Schrag shows us that the choice is not between trying to rehabilitate domineering vertical universals of a "logocentric epistemology" and resorting to a horizontal pluralism mired in the "doxastic flux of historical becoming" (Schrag, 1992, 168). We would suggest that when political theorists try to "go with this doxastic flux" they are on a treacherous track. They have something to learn from Straus's psychiatric clinic and from what Lefort calls Merleau-Ponty's principle of conservation in becoming (discussed in chapter 5). A politics aspiring to issues linking republican virtue and global justice needs a concept of responsibility that works between particularity and the matrixical, between accrual and care, and that is unafraid of historicity and mortality. This is why we urge reconsideration of the globalizing intellectual in ultra-modernist dress, heralding "mobility as an ontological condition . . . portrayed as the exciting play of an infinite self-fashioning" (Timothy Brennan, 2006, 144).

Hardt and Negri, however, prefer to follow Deleuze and Guattari's idea that the process of capital's globalization must be accelerated because there is only the "non-place of exploitation" requiring the confrontation of "Empire with a counter-Empire." Their claim is that "we must be against in every place" and look forward to the "new barbarians" who, understanding nature to be an "artificial terrain," will "create new posthuman bodies" to "push through Empire to come out the other side" (Hardt & Negri, 2000, 216–18). Earlier we recalled Merleau-Ponty's effort in the 1950s to excavate deeper, more reliable yet still contingently historical levels for Left approaches to politics. Today, the renewal of this project is made urgent by the growing popularity of abstract formulations of the "biopower" of the "non-place of Empire," a new system of "imperial sovereignty" operating under "a single logic of rule," a civil society "progressively withering away," necessitating the quest of a "mobile Multitude" and "nomadic revolutionaries" for a "global citizenship" (Hardt & Negri, 2000). While there is much in Hardt and Negri's analysis with which we agree, we find what they call the "site of ontological constitution" (402) to be at once more rich and terrene and requiring more provincial types of fertilization. There is significant political work to be done this side of an intellectual fixation on the prospect of a nature totally enchained amid powerless places somehow dominated by a system of placeless power.

It is a glaring misuse of Merleau-Ponty to enlist his "flesh of the world" as the "flesh of the multitude . . . an unformed life force," invoking a modernized nature/culture dichotomy (Hardt & Negri, 2004, 192–93). Hardt and Negri then picture a resultant "monstrosity of the flesh . . . an artificial life"—in short, a world in which "we are all monsters," even vampires, yet capable of creating "an alternative society" (193–94). In *Multitude* they also comment on "the capitalist power to put up for sale the metamorphoses of nature, the new eugenics that support the ruling power" (196). But their mode of republican struggle against empire is located "on the plastic and fluid terrain of the new communicative, biological, and mechanical technologies" (Hardt & Negri, 2000, 218). This is exactly contrary to Merleau-Ponty's approach to what they call the site of the ontological constitution. We recall his prescient warning against cybernetic acquiescence in "a sort of absolute artificialism" that is one hazard of their overwrought view of the postmodern "immaterial paradigm of production" (Merleau-Ponty, 1964a, 160; Hardt & Negri, 2004, 142).

Had Hardt and Negri given us a deeper reading of Merleau-Ponty, they would have engaged the machine as "an aspect of our embodiment," as Finn Bowring does in *Science, Seeds, and Cyborgs* (Bowring, 2003, 262). Instead, they write as if everyone has passed over a postmodern divide, as if our transformation into "artificial life" is a fact, as it is only from this monstrous condition that a new and truly democratic society will be born. In their haste to assuage a popular anti-political notion of sovereignty, they have rushed by an understanding of the early modern roots of this misrecognition of machines. It is Bowring who updates Husserl's analysis of this crisis concealed by the neoliberal model of globalization: "By formalizing to enable its detection of the pure and objective boundaries, shapes, magnitudes, properties, and causal relation of a geometrically idealized world, the natural scientific method conceals both the fluid and indeterminate qualities of the 'world of sensibility' in which we permanently dwell and consequently the *act of idealizing* which gives the scientific project its only meaning." Bowring adds: "It is this mechanization of thought and feeling which ultimately makes possible our misrecognition of machines as surrogates, substitutes, or competitors for ourselves" (245).

Enlisting Erwin Straus's account of our upright posture, what he called the I-Allon relationship, Bowring makes clear the stakes of this mechanistic ontology on capitalist auspices. His study, in fact, examines the horrendous variety of ways the global economic machine of the transnational corporations fosters the "social immobilization of the body" and denies "the natural form of the body any organic relationship to personhood" (Bowring, 2003, 265–70). Bowring helps us understand how Hardt and Negri would have social theorists side with "today's genetic and cyborg revolutionaries" who, revamping modern dualisms, pursue a post-humanist agenda that seeks a way out of our constitutive ambiguity, promising a means of understanding the world that no longer has to understand itself (271–77; Bowring draws on Hans Jonas, Merleau-Ponty, and Virilio). As political theory, this entails, as Timothy Bewes has seen, "a willingness to expel all traces of history from the present" (Bewes, 2002, 106). But this deontologization or ontological violence, imagining a multitude in the realm of the virtual, really "inaugurates a new global situation of the impossibility of real political developments" (248–49).

The "virtual powers" of the multitude are said to point in the direction of "global citizenship." Why? Because the virtual and the possible are somehow linked by a "hinge of infinite finitude" (Hardt & Negri, 2000, 361; cf. Bewes,

2002, 254). Little wonder that, as Stuart Corbridge noted in *Antipode*: "*Empire* has been feted as much by libertarians as by intellectuals of the Left" (Corbridge, 2003, 185). Indulging the fantasy of a "counter-Empire, an alternative political organization of global flows and exchange" (Hardt & Negri, 2000, xv) reminds some of us of the least memorable moments of the 1960s when substituting "love" for "politics" seemed easier. As Chantal Mouffe argues, Hardt and Negri give us "another version of the post-political perspective" that poses as common sense today (Mouffe, 2005). She is joined by Samir Amin in detecting a curious convergence with liberal cosmopolitanism (Amin, 2005). Mouffe has little difficulty in establishing the anti-political character of the Hardt and Negri "vision of a globalized smooth space" that promises a global level leap to an absolute democracy of the multitude (Mouffe, 2005, 107–15).

We agree with Mouffe that there is no escaping "the political in its antagonistic dimension" (130). Democratic movements, struggling in shifting domains of power, sovereignty, and hegemony, instead of finding a political bypass in cybernetic connectivity, must not cease starting anew from the latter's lifeworld fundament to our plural condition. The body~place~commons path to this world's agonistic and chiasmic political endeavors points toward the pluriversal hope that comes with building democratic spaces for grappling with corporate globalization in the search for more sustainable forms of life.

In one of his last lectures on the concept of nature, Merleau-Ponty spoke of "the participation of the animal in our perceptive life and the participation of our perceptive life in animality," noting another argument against what he called "philosophical artificialism" (Merleau-Ponty, 1970, 97). His refusal to leave nature in silence connects with the work of Americans such as Loren Eiseley, Paul Shepard, and our contemporary Gary Paul Nabhan. But the main story has been the modern Western intellectual's detachment from living historical experience, and it has many chapters. Shirking the conflictual hermeneutics of the sociohistorical, temporal forms of the body politic, university-based academics today find it safer to wave banners of "multiculturalism" and "global citizenship." As nearby civil society organizations continue their "provincial" struggles, these academics wave their futuristic flags from what might as well be Goodyear blimps of alienated intellectualism. The spectator-theorist leaves students to deal with as best they can the corporate state spectacle operating, as Guy Debord argued, to make history forgotten within culture (Debord, 1994 [1967], 137). In the United States this corporate consumer culture, operative for almost a century, has begat what one of our best social critics described in the 1980s as "minimal selfhood" (Lasch, 1984, 19). Lasch, influenced by Arendt, traced this pattern's emergence from the process by which "a reliable world of durable objects" was replaced "by a world of flickering images that make it harder and harder to distinguish reality from fantasy" (19). Emphasizing the "fading of a durable, common, public world," Lasch observed that for many people there was a weakening "belief in a world that survives its inhabitants" (193).

Ontological Auspices of Social Criticism

While we find Lasch's critical cultural analysis compelling, his appeal to an environmental ethic (1984, 256) is philosophically hampered by undue reliance on Reinhold Niebuhr's castigation of "romantic naturalism" from the standpoint of a certain Christian doctrine of nature as already made or constituted. Lasch no doubt scored points against the counterculture advocates of the 1960s. But when the issues are reframed in light of post-Husserlian postmodern thought, Lasch's resort or appeal to "a core of selfhood not subject to environmental determination" (59) and to Niebuhr's notion of "man's divided nature" (258), founders on perspectives of a tradition radically problematized by the postdualist thinking of Heidegger, Arendt, Dewey, Straus, and, most importantly, Merleau-Ponty.

There is another path to the "site of ontological constitution" other than the one Lasch pursues beginning with his return to the dualistic tradition and faith. The point is not a defense of those labeled by Lasch "the party of Narcissus"; indeed we will take a pass on whether this group confuses practice with technique and advocates a "return to nature" (255–56). Drawing heavily on Niebuhr and Jacques Ellul, Lasch claims this party "glorifies the natural man" and engages in a "primitivistic effort to regain the innocency of nature" as in the Garden of Eden (Niebuhr, qtd. by Lasch, 257). Looking back to this 1984 book it gives us pause that such a powerful account of corporate hegemony and the shrinking of the public sphere seems so caught up in the polemics originating in the 1960s that it gives comparatively little attention to the shift to the Right and a neoliberal globalization agenda. We have been appreciative of Lasch's keen insights during the next ten years, especially into elite attempts to suppress or deflect class issues in U.S. politics (see Lasch, 1995, 92–114; Reid, 2001a, on Lasch, 531–35).

But the 1984 book fixes on the Edenic or pastoralist myth of the American Adam in what has been called "cultural radicalism." It is these same American mythic motifs that linked the cultural mainstream and Reaganism in Garry Wills's brilliant 1987 analysis of the popular overdosing on a presidential mood of "original sinlessness" rationalizing and reinforcing an antiquated

Lockean individualism dedicated to productivism through technological mastery (Wills, 1987, chap. 4). The bourgeois liberal deity of a "free market" mechanism dispensing a natural harmony of interests appropriates an Americanized version of the myth of origins (the "people of plenty" motif) in the ongoing attempt to domesticate and contain democratic struggles. While appreciation of the valuable contributions to social criticism of both Wills and Lasch must acknowledge their undergirding Augustinian influences, this should not deflect attention from the impact of Protestant Christianity in significant formations of U.S. cultural life and politics that help understanding their unfortunate marginalization.

Lasch's critique of corporate consumer culture and its destruction of the forms of public life vital to democratic citizenship clearly reflect Arendt's influence. His sense of the "need to restore the intermediate world of practical activity, which binds man to nature in the capacity of a loving caretaker and cultivator," is one impressive and positive indication. However, his battle with the "party of Narcissus" prompts him to sharply mark off this bond from any "symbiotic union that simply denies the reality of man's separation from nature," which would jeopardize our capacity for transcendence that, in his reliance on Christian tradition, is coupled with a warning about "transcendent pride" (Lasch, 1984, 256). Risking a diversion from our main concern, we pause to point out that Lasch's study might have gained philosophic depth from greater attention to Hannah Arendt's political theory, to the theology of Paul Tillich, brought to Union Seminary from Nazi Germany by Niebuhr, and to Gibson Winter, the University of Chicago social ethicist influenced by Heidegger.

The U.S. corporate state—tending to impose from Iraq to Ecuador its dualist horizon of a capitalist individualism and technological world-picture—operates primarily to institutionalize and to reify cultural and political life. This dualistic structuring of policy and discourse deploys interdependent orientations of subjectivism and objectivism detected as early as the 1830s by Alexis de Tocqueville. Strengthened, moreover, by various institutional transformations, this dualism persists at the ideologized cultural core of increasing episodes of technobureaucratic disaster such as global warming. (It is no coincidence that President George W. Bush has been preaching "freedom" to Iraq while opposing the Kyoto protocols). Finn Bowring's important study *Science, Seeds, and Cyborgs* (2003, 67–86) documents what is happening in biotechnology where the U.S. sector of the "global economic machine of the multinationals" by and large sets the pace. Bowring provides penetrating insights into the ways corporate-dominated research is, to use Habermas's apt terminology, advancing the "instrumentalization of prepersonal life," thus raising momentous questions for "the ethical self-understanding of the species" (Habermas, 2003, 71). We could not agree more with these critical social theorists as to the urgency these issues pose for public debate and democratic common sense (see 105–15). In the United States, however, the leading role of our corporations, government agencies, and universities may also entail the limited reach of this emerging debate. In 1970 Gibson Winter scored the role of religious institutions in reinforcing American privatization as a way of shielding people from confrontation with the "struggle between exploitation and participation" and a widespread addiction to the "fruits of domination" (Winter, 1970, 142–43).

In what is very likely his most important contribution to democratic theory, Lasch wisely utilized Arendt's concept of action (as distinguished from behavior) as he made the case that the public sphere, not "community," was the lodestar for a democratic politics (Lasch, 1991, 120–67). Nevertheless, in recent years we have seen even more alarming political forms operating to derail or even co-opt the anti-progressive populist tradition that Lasch so thoughtfully examined and promoted. He might have considered Arendt's "What Is Freedom?" with its brilliant historical insights into the contributions of the Christian tradition to a subjectivistic construction of "freedom" that has become part and parcel of the modern "world-alienation" highlighted in her magnum opus (Arendt, 1977 [1961], 143–71). In the essay (150), as in the book *The Human Condition* (1958), Arendt is particularly concerned that "the entire modern age has separated freedom and politics."

"Courage is indispensable," Arendt's essay argues, "because in politics not life but the world is at stake" (Arendt, 1977 [1961], 56). Some church-going Americans are hard put to understand the link between trends toward an anti-life society of unlimited risk, including the relegation downward of infant health as a public agenda concern (Bowring, 2003, 227–57), and the denigration of political action and public discourse that allows "care for the world." We need a politics that nurtures both fading and distorted public concerns with the extent to which neoliberal globalization operates (for example, as directed by Rupert Murdoch) as the most recent battle in capitalism's war on an uncommodified, experiential world opening to the sacred. Tocqueville's misgivings about the future of Practical America in Nature's Nation are being instituted in the transnational corporate state's consumer culture of atomized worldlessness marked by what Lauren Berlant calls "its subjugation of embodied forms of public life" (Berlant, 1997, 179). While Berlant's study is not offered as a "redemptive text," she does provide a critical phenomenology of the American citizen's infantilization in a world of public intimacy choreographed by an increasingly global corporate media.

Re-opening Nature, Re-opening Ourselves

Gibson Winter, writing after the 1968 election of Richard Nixon, argued that the American religious heritage to a great extent had capitulated to the exploitative will-to-power of the U.S. technological system. "Our civic and confessional heritages are so completely assimilated to the technological system that they no longer furnish distance and self-criticism" (Winter, 1970, 114–22). The symbiotic intertwining of privatism and technological imperialism has been a problem in mainstream Christianity in the United States, granted that its starkest forms today are most evident at the intersection of the Religious Right and the Republican Party of George W. Bush. Well aware of Reinhold Niebuhr's political work opposing such developments, we would nevertheless propose, albeit briefly, that the theologian's bothersome colleague Paul Tillich might have served Lasch better in his reflections on the problems of nature, selfhood, and rationality (Lasch, 1984, 253–59). However persuasive or not our suggestion, we aim at a connection to the post-Husserlian path taken by Merleau-Ponty, the path to which we want to return this discussion.

In the present context, the question we are raising is whether the project of restoring or reconstructing the intermediate world of practical activity has stronger ontological auspices than Lasch was able to see due perhaps partly to Niebuhr's influence. As far as we are aware, Lasch nowhere mentions Tillich, but we do know he was very familiar with Richard Wightman Fox's biography of Niebuhr (Fox, 1985; Lasch, 1986). Lasch's review notes that Fox does offer an account of the relationship of the two theologians. For us, Fox's dismissive treatment of Tillich as a "borderline nature mystic" (Fox, 1985, 160) should not be the last word since much more is at stake than a shallow reading of one thinker. It is curious that a very able American historian apparently would not delve more deeply into this view of Tillich, whom he acknowledges to be "an original thinker of enormous distinction . . . a professional philosopher and systematic theologian . . . out of Niebuhr's league, as Niebuhr well knew" (258). We want to at least suggest the relevance of Tillich's theology and political theory for work at what has been called the *site of ontological constitution*.

As Tillich was being forced by Nazism to leave Germany in 1933, he published a brilliant study depicting that movement as the revolutionary expression of political romanticism. Finally translated into English in 1977, *The*

Socialist Decision makes clear that while liberal and democratic camps join in breaking with political reliance on mythic bonds of origin, the democratic camp departs from the liberal doctrine of natural harmony and undertakes a search for planning that is democratically based and accountable. When the myth of origin is broken and the ambiguity of origin disclosed, political thinking emerges and has to confront the demand of justice—a justice that Tillich calls "the true power of being" (Tillich, 1977). When Tillich argued for the "ontological unity of justice, power, and love" (Tillich, 1960 [1954], 67–71) he had in mind a politics that understands that "nonbeing belongs to being, that being could not be the ground of life without nonbeing" (Tillich, 1965 [1952], 170). There is a kindred perspective in Terry Eagleton's recent observation: "The non-being at the heart of us is what disturbs our dreams and flaws our projects. But it is also the price we pay for the chance of a brighter future. It is the way we keep faith with the open-ended nature of humanity, and is thus a source of hope" (Eagleton, 2003, 221).

We need to understand the political challenge when the new technologies treat our bodies as "inert and imperishable objects of human design," when the natural form of the body is denied "any organic relationship to personhood" (Bowring, 2003, 269). The corporate state organizes the technobureaucratic sciences in ways that place the conceptual domestication of nature in institutional settings that prioritize drives to profit and power. There is a systematic shortchanging of social and political ecologies attuned to life-world norms and the generative possibilities for democratic common sense. The political ecology of the democratic movement for fundamental change needs an alternative ontology. It was Tillich's view that "nature is the finite expression of the infinite ground of all things" (Tillich, 1965 [1952], 4). This ontological intersection of theology and political theory is one place for questioning the modern Western attempt to dominate nature by turning it into a machine that may reflect a deep failure to "find a way of living with non-being without being in love with it," as Eagleton puts it (Eagleton, 2003, 213).

"Social constructionist" critique has its accomplishments, but intellectual acquiescence in the ontological demise of nature facilitates technocratic domination as surely as the uncritical adoption of corporate-friendly notions of "intelligence" and "informatics" produced by the professional body-machine complex. Our corrective to this "naturalization of the language paradigm" that too often slides toward the open jaws of late-capitalist spectacle has been a Merleau-Pontyian path back to the "liveliness and self-organizing nature of practical reason" respecting the contexts and local relevances of everyday life and enabling a democratic political life capable of engaging world-historical questions such as catastrophic climate change (O'Neill, 1995, 18, 73). As Carol Bigwood has put it, the trouble with the "poststructuralist's culturally inscribed body is [that it is] disembodied and lacks terrestrial weight and locatedness because, like both empiricist and idealist accounts of the body, it has left out . . . the anonymous noncognitive cleaving of our bodies to others and things, to the general incarnate structure of the world" (Bigwood, 1993, 52, 55). In a world of so much economic and political exploitation and social suffering, is it possible to "rediscover the enveloping earth. . . . in all its power and its depth, as the very ground and horizon of all our knowing," as David Abram has suggested (Abram, 1996, 216–17). Yes, and there is also "world" to rediscover.

Our argument has been that accounting for our placed embodiment and its political ecology opening within both "commons" and "world" leads well beyond the wilderness politics and eco-localism that continue to attract "green" activists. Our approach to questions of the scale of struggle must be unlocked from both these "eco-localist" views and from a one-size-fits-all "globalist" theory or strategy that futurizes a universal agent based on an Enlightenment assumption that freedom requires transcendence of the given. When political sensibilities are best understood as infused with the local *and* cosmic surround, drawing regenerative capacities from a shared earth, new solidarities become apparent in global regional endeavors that make a peaceful world a real possibility. This is why we have said again and again that social and political theory must prioritize the search for the generative forms of public space.

8

Learning from the Global Justice Movement

Democratic Hope

The silencing of nature and the commodification of the body have been intertwined in capitalist modernity. Global capital conjures consumption and consumers on the tombs of the world's places and communities. This is why we have labored to show that critical revisioning of the spatial dimension of democratic social theory significantly depends on recovering and reinstituting place(s) against tendencies to reify global economic production. In previous chapters, we make clear that effective argument against enclosure of the commons requires critique of the enframement of the commons. The "spatial turn" radical theory must make hinges on conceptually accounting for the *displacement* ratified by the philosophical and ideological enframement of the commons.

Identifying the ecological moorings of democratic citizenship relocates the space-times of the nation-state in an unbiased politics of the earth at a time when environmental crisis presses issues of global justice. Theoretic care and imaginative exploration of earthly varieties of body and place rebuild democratic republican portals for the ecological citizenship of global regional and other publics struggling to revive the commons. Social theorists sometimes respond to reified, exclusivist representations of place with intellectualizing moves that sacrifice ecosystemic common ground to professional knowledges that reinforce expert authority at the expense of more democratic auspices. If place is "right at the center of humanity" (Cresswell, 2004, 123), then moving boundaries around to load the dice of inquiry seems less fruitful than exploring its deeper and wider dimensions. Trodding the ontological terrain to the clearing of commons and world makes sense before posting the public realm with warning signs on what is "reactionary" and "progressive." Social theorists, after all, have issues of "mobility" and "fixity" and may need to problematize their own structures of feeling before offering political directions.

An alternative agenda for regenerating public culture as a mode of confronting catastrophic climate change is not possible as post-ecological capitulation to global inequality and its twin of political authoritarianism (see the widely published report of the International Forum on Globalization [IFG], Cavanagh, 2002). The construction of such an agenda is inseparable from the democratic hope for a humanity recentered by increasingly sustainable modes of living between "home" and "world." Social theorists have begun to engage the enlacements of global and local reality that are posing staggering new versions of old questions of justice. This comes at a time when scientific bodies predict a preponderance of climate change impacts for peoples with the most limited resources for response. A social theory relevant for democratic action in a translocal politics plowing new eco-cultural terrain between "home" and "world" is the question. A praxeomorphic theory of democratic action is vital for both materializing the principle of subsidiarity and scaling up participation for political equality and social justice. We agree with the authors of the IFG report that a new policy emphasis on local production and consumption (subsidiarity) has to be combined with a translocal politics capable of "ending corporate-state collusion" (105–50). A deeper understanding of the culture of citizen action, however, should traverse persistent gaps between critique of power structures and their democratic reconstruction.

We live in a world moving toward ecological holocaust, an alarming prospect with many dimensions affecting millions of people. For example, one new study finds that agricultural production in developing countries may fall an average of 16 percent, and if global warming progresses at its current rate, India's agricultural capacity could fall as much as 40 percent (Cline, 2007). The key question with which this book is concerned is, *How are social theorists to dwell in this crisis in ways that enliven and illuminate a politics of possibility?* We suggest that no serious alternative to the post-democratic foreclosure of the political would be likely were that dwelling to be preoccupied either with a program of technological fixes or an abstract radicalism hurling defiance at global capital. A progressivist view of history is not a fit vision for a politics of democratic hope. Social theory that keeps finding something "progressive" in what Marx called "the annihilation of space and time" needs the ground check of alternative understandings of place and time and of regionality and historicity. Social theorists academically housed in the United States peer out to the national population most thoroughly indoctrinated in notions of progress and least inclined to a new existence based on the sensibility of limits our planet surely requires. Had they not been caught with such a weak theory of justice—including what David Harvey called "the postmodern death of justice" (Harvey, 1996, 341–46)—they might not feel so indisposed to contributing to a new national spirit of sacrifice. It is fanciful to speak of U.S. political leadership in any other context than reducing the ecological footprint of an incredibly wasteful society. Those versions of academic cosmopolitanism that ignore tasks of civic professionalism are part of the problem.

We turn once more to Christopher Lasch for the point that hope "does not demand a belief in progress." It does demand, as he put it, "a belief in justice" and—he went on—"implies a deep-seated trust in life" that does not prevent us "from expecting the worst." To whichever global region we look, battles for health, place, and the commons are being waged. To keep oneself aloof from such struggles is to detach one's experience from the planet's most vital social ecology generating democratic hope. Our argument has been that political agency's deep and intimate connections with place should be understood as the site of encounter between earth-ground and world-horizon. Places are socially constructed, but this happens in ecologically dynamic matrices entwined with the ultrahuman in a co-evolutionary process that might be called *cosmogenesis*.

In the ecology of emergent democratic space the status of "world" is a key question. This has never been truer than today when one of the mainstays of U.S. culture of denial is corporate consumerist promotion of allegedly cheap goods shadowed by multiplying numbers of ecological and climate change refugees. As Mike Davis has suggested, in our world of cities without jobs where people often turn to religious practices such as Pentecostalism, the next form of slum-based resistance to global capitalism may not be fundamentalism (Cook, 2006, 37). Already to the south of the United States, politically honed and still highly diverse forms of resistance are taking shape from Ecuador and Bolivia to Brazil and Argentina.

Beneath the political and ideological turmoil, what must not be missed is that people from many diverse places and regions are seeking new ways to integrate nature, human sociability, and the creative arts. Out of a remarkably clear determination to reclaim the commons, they affirm the possibility of building new worlds. Body~place~commons is a radical theory of subjectivity as intersubjectivity. As such, one of its vital messages is that social hope and democratic change inhere in collective agency so understood and acted upon. Earth's future no less depends on finding various ways of letting "the voices of social hope enter our institutions" (Valsania, 2007, 203). When institutional logics are grounded in hearing and responding to these voices, then modes of cultivation emerge *in the ecology of democratic change*.

These are some of the ideas involved in the social theory that went into the University of Kentucky Rockefeller Humanities Fellowship program for 2001–2005 that we co-authored. We wanted to help establish the global regional context of activism (citizen action and public intelligence) in both campus and community contexts. The global regional context of activism and the need for intercultural perspectives already had found expression in the programs of such organizations as Highlander Center and the Community Farm Alliance. So we brought together in various enriching combinations Appalachian activists and Global South scholars in a program that highlighted (a) intercultural discourse and debate focused on questions of scaling up participation for political equality and social justice, (b) community-initiated research with assistance from resident academicians, and (c) field visits to community sites in the mountains of Kentucky, West Virginia, and Tennessee. The project was approached with keen and critical awareness of a history of various types of academic-community partnership. One of the program's main points was not just "community participation" but a newly instituted common search for expansive participation by all involved.

Encountering many obstacles, it stands as one experimental model for exploring new forms of citizen mobilization and solidarity, social hope, and the ecology of democratic change. The transnational dimension of energy industry exploitation of the Appalachian region is well established at a time when the link between chaotic climate change and what Lewis Mumford called "carboniferous capitalism" is becoming undeniable. In a nutshell this is why the political struggle against empire and for a democratic republic connects with the global justice movement that has been building from the history-making efforts of Gandhi, Mandela, and Zapata.

Three Contributions to the Global Justice Movement

If social theory aims to contribute to the struggle against institutionalized suffering, it needs what Ashis Nandy, in his remarkable essay "Towards a Third World Utopia," calls "an inter-civilizational perspective on oppression" (Nandy, 1992, 21). Academics in the United States need to face up to ways in which corporate state technology (whether Boeing or Monsanto or others) has "cannibalized science," to use Nandy's phrase. Refusing to learn from what Nandy calls "defeated cultures" helps perpetuate their professional acquiescence to a "culture of instrumentality" that, we have argued, entails complicity with ecological violence (45). In fact, (again enlisting Nandy) we suggest this Western form of technology as knowledge-power in the United States all too often for the most part promotes hierarchical exploitation and consumer dependency. We are afraid Nandy was right some years ago when he observed that it "is unlikely that the Western experience will deter the third world from investing the modern machine with increasingly greater charisma"—especially if we begin with the machine god of the market (Nandy, 1992, 88; cf. Reid, 2001b). Nevertheless, the fight against neoliberal globalization in India since 1991 offers inspiring lessons, many of which have been conveyed to American audiences by Vandana Shiva and Arundhati Roy. But it has been an uphill struggle and weakly accounted for by most highly academicized forms of social and political theory.

This leads us to turn to much too brief consideration of three contributions from different world regions to the global justice movement and to the theory of alternative globalization within which its practical possibilities make most sense. Let us begin with an overview of why we turn to India, South Africa, and Mexico. From India over a period of many years several intellectuals have formulated a brilliant, multifaceted critique of Western developmentalism that relates to much more than that incredibly complex society's ecological crisis. This critique, understood in connection with what Anil Agarwal called the "environmentalism of the poor" (Guha, 2002; Guha & Martinez-Alier, 1998, see 3–21) may cast new light on the American debate on the "death of environmentalism" occurring on the brink of an era of chaotic climate change. From South Africa we call attention to the Declaration of the Durban Social Forum adopted August 28, 2001. It is one model for evading snares in the political economy of identity politics that a number of U.S. academics and activists have found difficult to traverse. Finally, we must discuss the Zapatista movement that challenged NAFTA being given political birth by Clinton and Salinas in 1993–1994. Zapatismo is an alternative to the vanguardism of the romantic Left's Guevarism. We refer not only to the Chiapas-based movement in Mexican politics and its interpretation by Subcomandante Marcos, but also to an international network of various global regional publics. It offers a model integrating global struggles against neoliberalism (the "fourth world war") and indigenous rights and other forms of cultural difference.

India and an Intercultural Critique of Western Developmentalism

Sir Albert Howard died in 1947, the year India gained its independence from Britain. When Howard worked in Indian agriculture in the early twentieth century, he paid "close attention to the day-to-day performance of the peasant world." He respected and learned from Indian farmers' "great experience in conserving and maintaining" soils highly vulnerable to tropical sun and rainfall. Howard realized "that to impose Western methods on Indian agriculture was a fundamental error and that the only thing to do was to 'improve Indian agriculture on its own lines.'" Louise E. Howard wrote in 1953 that her husband had served a "severe apprenticeship" that he regarded as vital for his development as a scientist (L. E. Howard, 1954, 264–65, 193, 17).

What is instructive for social theorists is Howard's appreciation of the local knowledge and ecological wisdom of third-world farmers and the relevance of this knowledge for the ecological uses of new technologies. Alas, what critical historical studies document are the environmental and social costs of bypassing such an approach. Chapters 5 and 6 of Howard's last book, emphasizing that nature "works on very small margins," makes clear the long-range folly of employing machines to "mine" the land. Howard's "principal warning" was that the "pursuit of quantity at all costs is dangerous in farming" (A. Howard, 2006 [1972], 58–68). Nevertheless, as Gail Omvedt argued from Maharashtra in 1995, the unsustainable development of the next several decades included the "the onslaught of 'green revolution' agriculture." Wrapped in the mantle of both "modern science" and "simple state discrimination," this approach simultaneously displaced or "eroded the position of women" and rendered farmers "dependent on external inputs" (Omvedt, 1995, 44–49).

From the "green revolution" of a few decades ago to the "gene revolution" of more recent years, Indian intellectuals such as Vandana Shiva (Shiva, 2000a) and Claude Alvares (Alvares, 1992) have made visible key issues of power, knowledge, and value in exposing the long-range ecological problems of quick-fix programs, biopiracy and the recolonization of the commons, and corporate interests in a system of authoritarian control. Transnational corporations and their elites are in a dominant position vis-à-vis both Global South governments and most Western universities. The latter typically operate in a field of power and policy assigning their administrators roles as junior partners in corporate state coalitions. Where universities are involved, the question is whether and how they might assume autonomous responsibility for the health of their regional places and local constituents—as Wendell Berry puts it, "the sustenance of particular places, creatures, human bodies, and human minds" (qtd. in A. Howard, 2006 [1972], xxiii, introduction). For neither Sir Albert Howard nor Berry would this entail neglecting intercultural research and education. To ignore the Global South literature of critical response to corporate globalization is to weaken middle-class professional abilities to unveil the glossy imagery of global corporate media including, for example, corporate-based multicultural affluence, and see what Mike Davis grimly terms our "planet of slums" (M. Davis, 2006). Especially in chapter 4, we have tried to expose the assumptive forms of what passes for social theories rationalizing globalizing subjectivities with such operational blinders.

Several years ago, Rajni Kothari spotlighted the cultural amnesia affiliated with this neoliberal, marketized consciousness. As Kothari understood in 1993, it is in this world of disembodied, displaced yet encapsulated selves that "the poverty of the poor becomes part of the cultural poverty of all" (Kothari, 1993, 86). Recently, Pankaj Mishra has pointed to the accumulating evidence for a new culture of greed in India linked to an exaggerated commitment to global space based on faith in capitalist development (Mishra, 2006). It is also the case that a number of prosperous Indians inside and beyond India are trying to reconnect their wealth and projects of social justice. Nevertheless, the more significant and unsurprising fact is that as entities such as Monsanto, Cargill, Coca Cola, and Wal-Mart move into India, room is made in transnational elite circles for Indian representatives and their companies. What should impress U.S. readers, however, is not corporate multiculturalism but popular Indian uprisings such as the "seed satygraha" opposing Cargill and the growing clarity of these struggles. As Arundhati Roy said at the 2004 World Social Forum in Mumbai and later that year in San Francisco, what matters is the globalization of dissent against this new imperialism, for no "individual nation can stand up to the project of corporate globalization on its own" (Roy, 2004, 90). Vandana Shiva, lodging her arguments in the United States as well as in India, much as Roy has, was one of the first to call globalization "environmental apartheid" and to question "the export of a non-sustainable Western industrial paradigm in the name of development" (Shiva, 2000b, 112–13).

As Ramachandra Guha has pointed out, eighty years ago Gandhi raised the key question of the "global unsustainability of the Western model of economic development" (Guha, 2006, 231). As a matter of fact, in the last few decades Indian scholars, intellectuals, and activists have penned what is altogether a vital contribution to the critique of developmentalism. Gandhi is only one major inspiration for this critique; as Guha has reminded us, Patrick Geddes, a Scottish pioneer of ecological thinking who spent several of his mature years in India, influenced not only the American Lewis Mumford but also the great Indian sociologist Radhakamal Mukerjee. Guha has documented the importance of Mukerjee's ecological approach to social science and his ideas such as "regional balance" (36–46).

What we think of as the Indian critique of Western developmentalism by such thinkers as Claude Alvares, Rajni Kothari, Ashis Nandy, and Vandana Shiva is inseparable from India's rich dialogues and debates in the field that Mukerjee christened "social ecology." In fact, Guha's critique of at least one type of Western conservationism and his work with Madhav Gadgil on "behalf of the 'ecosystem people,' rather than the omnivores" may be understood as a powerful alternative to the mainstream U.S. model of "development" (Guha, 2006, chaps. 5 and 8). Those of us trying to build stronger roads to sustainability in and from the United States have much to learn from the Indian critique of developmentalism. The significance of this critique has been highlighted by scholars such as Fred Dallmayr (1996, chap. 7; 1998, chap. 9) and Frederique Apffel-Marglin and Stephen Marglin (1990), but it may be even more relevant today. We might also bear in mind Nandy's point that Gandhi's "spirited search for the other culture of Britain, and of the West, was an essential part of his theory of salvation for India" (Nandy, 1988 [1983], 49). And that is one reason our historical perspective makes mention of the collaborations of Howard and Geddes. We turn to another collaborative venture that has never gotten in the U.S. academy the attention it deserves.

What we want to do in this short space is to recall the powerful statement signed by twenty-six individuals at the fourteenth meeting of the World Order Models Project in Poona (now Pune), India, July 2–10, 1978. It stands as the Poona Indictment of the Perversion of Science and Technology fostering a neocolonial system of exploitation, hegemony, and repression continually obscured by mainstream imagery of war against Communism and against Terrorism so adored by the political Right. The statement from Poona pointed to both specific and forthcoming ecological disasters ranging from overfishing the oceans with mechanized trawlers to neglecting renewable energy resources. "Humanity must regain its sanity," the thinkers at Poona contended, "by reasserting the nature of scientific inquiry as the pursuit of truth, leading to technologies which liberate the many rather than facilitate control by the few" (Morehouse, 1979, 415). We return the focus to two of the remarkable group of intellectuals signing the Poona statement.

What Rajni Kothari and Ashis Nandy have helped us to understand is the link between the problem of large-scale violence and a developmentalism bound to universal otherhood, productivism, speed, and an evolutionist doctrine of anti-historic time. In their view, modern Western religion and science have converged in a homocentric worldview and a "climate of arrogance and exploitation, the ethic of survival of the fittest, and a basically dualistic view" of nature and culture. As Kothari contended in 1974, the outcome of this drive to both dominate and be delivered from nature will be an ecological crisis bringing nemesis on humanity and undermining our survival (Kothari, 1974, 43). Nandy writes that the "violence of our age is based not so much on religious fanaticism or tribal blood feuds, as on secular, objective, dispassionate pursuit of personal and collective interests" (Nandy, 2004, 278). If Nandy is right, the critique of technocratic managerialism may lead to a perspective beyond "developmental terrorism" (320–23).

Now that an earth fit for human habitation is dying, it is past time for a social theory rooted in the ecological niches of the planetary ruins of global capitalism and a suffering humanity. In previous pages we have not only linked the logic of fungibility to addictive aspects of "prosperity"; we have also worked to reveal the enabling power of limits in logics of particularity. As Christopher Lasch argued before his untimely death, "In the twenty-first century, equality implies a recognition of limits, both moral and material, that finds little support in the progressive tradition" (Lasch, 1991, 532). This brings us back to Ashis Nandy, who is saying that our idea of prosperity is the problem. This form of prosperity is implicated in both the planet's drift toward ecological catastrophe and in shifting millions from poverty to destitution, a distinction he emphasizes. The same "developmental regime" that keeps making a mockery of promises to banish poverty—even after dropping the project to fix on "security"—also helps operate a structure of denial where official violence is concerned. Need we recall the continuities between the viewsheds concealing destruction in the Appalachian Mountains and global corporate media dramatizations of a few children or youth plucked from the planet's urban slums, sometimes by wealthy celebrities who keep alive ostentatious versions of the "American dream"?

South Africa and the Identity Traps of Unofficial Global Apartheid

Naomi Klein, trying to convey to her readers what had happened to Nelson Mandela's egalitarian vision for a post-apartheid South Africa, quotes what Trevor Ngwane (a former ANC municipal council member) told her in 2001: "Apartheid based on race has been replaced with apartheid based on class" (Klein, 2002a, 108). Klein drew upon South African economist Patrick Bond's work (Bond, 2003). Several studies developed this view in following years.

For example, a January 2003 article by Ashwin Desai puts it succinctly: "The transition to democracy led by the African National Congress was trumped by the transition to neo-liberalism. The new ruling elite and the beneficiaries of the old apartheid regime had already made common cause after the ANC came to power in 1994. Now [in highly protected meetings such as the World Economic Forum in Durban, June 2002] they [have been] cementing their alliance with the corporate raiders in the advanced capitalist world" (Desai, 2003, 16).

In her 2004 article, sociologist Zine Magubane offers a more charitable but still largely complementary view emphasizing the "burdens of history" or the "socioeconomic structures the ANC inherited." She notes the discovery of gold in 1886 and the strong role of the *Minerals Energy Complex* in the South African economy. The MEC's financial influence and favored investment policies point to the underdeveloped state of basic-needs industries, a major problem area for the ANC. In other words, Magubane illuminates the field of power within which the neoliberal turn was made, a structure with some of its roots in the apartheid state before 1994 (Magubane, 2004). Magubane, Desai, and others have suggested that the 1990s transition to democracy involved a significant *corporatist* factor: the institutionalization of certain relations between big unions, big business, and the state. Desai observes that this helps us understand the growing gap or gulf between unionized and better-skilled workers and the masses of marginalized South Africans. He states that the 1996 census indicated that the poorest 40 percent of the population earned less than 3 percent of the national income. The richest 10 percent received over 50 percent of that income. Desai's treatment of the VW (Volkswagen) strike (100–104) and his commentary on the Wentworth strike at Engen, the South African affiliate of Exxon, provide a detailed view of the corporatist system and the role of big unions in sustaining the corporatist system and the ANC elite. While Magubane does not want to foreclose the possibility of the ANC as a vehicle or funnel of change, she finds hope in Desai's observation: "The neoliberal transition has squeezed and spewed out the poor but galvanized them at the same time" (qtd. in Desai, 2003, 18).

Desai is referring to the rise of the new community movements based in families as fighting units that are outside the corporatist structures and suffering high degrees of unemployment, which explains why they are so concerned with keeping water and electricity services (Desai, 2002). The program of groups such as the Soweto Electricity Crisis Committee seems clear enough. The ANC has various forms of power to both quell and allay these civil society protests. It has the monopoly on official violence, it has patronage (e.g., that can be used to co-opt promising opposition leaders), and it has racial nationalism as a way of depoliticizing economic inequality. As political scientist Michael MacDonald, writing about the political economy of identity politics, puts it, "Under apartheid, racial nationalism mobilized opposition; under democracy, racial nationalism suffocates it" (MacDonald, 2004, 653).

Desai, however, suggests that sometimes old identities and myths can be recast and made into effective forms of political opposition. His book (Desai, 2002) discusses how Diwali, the Hindu festival of lights, was rethought and politicized in a program of "lights for all," thus helping foster solidarity in the civic association movement. Fighting evictions and electricity cutoffs, the Chatsworth community activists held a Festival of (No) Lights in which they cast the local city council as a satanic villain pushing them into darkness.

This interest in the merger of politics and culture is central for Desai's title theme, which comes from the indignant reply of one Indian South African to a local ANC official's charge of seeking special treatment: "We are not Indians, we are the poors." For Desai "the poors" is an elastic, nonracial identity for the swelling ranks of the dispossessed. In his 2003 article his interest in new forms of solidarity is evident in the account of the South African Municipal Workers Union strike against privatization of services. His point is that the specter of both job losses and increased service charges outlined "a fertile ground for a linkup between community movements and the organized working class" (Desai, 2003, 24). One constant refrain in many of the protest rallies is summed up by the banner proclaiming, "Water comes from God, it is needed for life."

It would be foolish for us to seek to intervene in this fascinating debate and the brilliant contributions of people such as Bond, Magubane, and Desai. Rather, our much more modest intention is to call attention to what perhaps has been one of the most inspiring documents in the struggle over corporate globalization. We refer to the *Durban Social Forum Declaration* with its remarkable blend of local, national, and global regional concerns "as we confront our common lot not as separate races, but as 'the poors'" (Desai, 2002, see appendix, 150–53). Short as it is, this moving declaration goes so far as to speak of merging struggles between the Global South and the North and bears out Desai's statement that the community movement "has a world-historical sense of itself but focuses on combat with local enemies and thrives on small victories" (149). We would also note his view that the ideological roots of the movement are in "ideas of neighborliness, dignity, and life."

Some of the ideas may seem simple, but they resonate across the planet—in such issues as landlessness and access to water. At the 2001 World Conference against Racism, the dissidents broke with the power elites by rejecting a narrow definition of racism or of rights. Refusing to perform in a conference drama called the South African miracle, they insisted on projecting alternatives through the Indy Media Centre while listening to critics of corporate globalization such as seventy-seven-year-old Dennis Brutus, a veteran intellectual of the anti-apartheid struggle. Undergirding this movement, Desai finally concluded, is *a capacity to sense collective joy and misery that may well be the key pre-theoretical basis for democratic politics itself.* Desai's book helps us understand that what is called the *global justice movement* is fundamentally a struggle for basic and universal rights by an emerging global network of engaged neighborhoods. Ultimately there must be a transformation of power structures that depend on small groups of leaders and reinforce elite prerogatives.

Zapatismo and the Academy of Broken Mirrors

The struggle for democracy in Mexico made at least two great advances during the presidency of Lazaro Cardenas from 1934 to 1940. One was the nationalization of Mexican oil (including the Rockefeller-owned Standard Oil), which the media and many leaders in the United States greeted with outrage and castigation. One of the great stories of anti-imperial resistance is that of the 1940 meeting of President Cárdenas and Nelson Rockefeller. It is said Cárdenas insisted: "We must retain ownership even if the oil has to stay in the ground. Better that than for the people to lose their dignity" (Colby & Dennett, 1996, 94). The second was agrarian reform or a program of redistribution either to individual ownership or, for about half the rural population by 1940, to *ejidos* (communal farms). Sifting the discordant historical perspectives of Carlos Fuentes and Enrique Krauze from the Cárdenas presidency to that of Salinas and the passage of NAFTA in the 1990s lays bare a few fundamental points. Even Krauze admits "the *ejido* had brought about an authentic revolution in the ownership of land" (Krauze, 1997, 483) that helped earn Cárdenas for the remaining thirty years of his life widespread popular regard as "the moral conscience of the Revolution" (480). Krauze, however, contends that the *ejido* and its credit system was prone not only to bad economic results but also to statist/paternalist abuses of political control by the PRI (Institutional Revolutionary Party). Unsurprisingly, Krauze closes with an equivocal account of the privatization "reforms" of Salinas including his attack on Article 27 so close to the heart of Cárdenas's agrarian vision. This is coupled with a biased, unsympathetic view of the Zapatista rebellion in Chiapas, interestingly contrasting with that of Fuentes and others.

Yet Carlos Fuentes (Fuentes, 1996, 86–127), admitting there was no public debate on NAFTA in Mexico, still essentially supports it from a reformist perspective while engaging Subcomandante Marcos in a sympathetic exchange of letters. Fuentes, deeming the Zapatista uprising the "first post-Communist revolution," thus aggravating other prominent Mexican intellectuals, insisted on democracy in Chiapas and in Mexico overall as an intertwined question. But his historical insights deserve attention if not his tendency to an adulatory view of Lázaro Cárdenas and his presidency from 1934 to 1940. Fuentes makes a crucial point in commenting that after the first Cárdenas "his successors stressed development for development's sake, growth directed by the government and its party, with the happy association of a capitalist class born with and from the revolutionary changes taking place" (74).

In fact, the Mexican government and the Rockefeller Foundation forged an agreement in 1943 that led to the initiation of the Green Revolution in that decade. Joseph Cotter's recent study (Cotter, 2003) documents the overall failure of that program to reduce hunger and malnutrition, its environmental costs, and the agricultural dependency imposed on Mexico, which helps explain how disastrous NAFTA has been for rural Mexicans. Largely ignoring the heterogeneous knowledge of Mexican farmers while reducing them to a clientele dependent on professional experts or *agronomos*, the petrochemical industry and corporate state bureaucracies are an all-too-familiar story (321–34). It is exactly the unsustainable approach in India scored by Vandana Shiva and Gail Omvedt. As Omvedt has put it, the key question is whether there can be an ecological movement away "from a centralized global economy moving materials at prodigious rates around the world and piling up mountains of material waste, much of it poisonous and destructive" (Omvedt, 1995, 44). In Shiva's language, the issue is stopping the corporate hijacking of the global food supply by finding political ways to advance the "movements for the recovery of biodiversity and intellectual commons" crucial for democratizing the food system (Shiva, 2000a, 117–23). Cotter's valuable study details the complexities of Mexico's agrarian politics, but what in our context must be highlighted is his very last point. As he put it, with "political empowerment the *campesinos*' wisdom may not be lost or stolen in a maelstrom of neoliberal-induced technological and socioeconomic change" (Cotter, 2003, 334).

This is an apt description of NAFTA, which, in Jeff Faux's analysis, sharply reduced Mexico's ability to supply the basic food needs of its population by simultaneously "opening up Mexico to subsidized U.S. food imports while withdrawing supports for small Mexican farmers" (Faux, 2006, 133). There is not space for us to record the full impact of NAFTA that Faux's study offers. For example, he notes that while Mexico has gained several billionaires in recent years, for most Mexicans "the basic cost of living" has increased, with the poorest households experiencing an increased poverty rate between 1994 and 2000. NAFTA's official promise included bolstering the Mexican economy, creating jobs, and lifting wages stemming the tide of migration. Very little of this information circulates in what passes for political culture in mainstream America. This situation helps explain the strength of reactionary nationalist frames and appeals by the Right in U.S. politics. Some U.S. academics behave as if power has evaporated or at least become too complex to be made accountable in political conflict. Indeed, it seems that questions of power and accountability have disappeared from some academic "migration studies." One important exception is anthropologist Ann Kingsolver's *NAFTA Stories*, a cross-border comparative ethnography that raises several questions including questions about "the integrity of local communities" and the "true costs of relying on fossil fuels" in a global transportation system (Kingsolver, 2001, see 199–209). However, the failure of many scholars in the social sciences and humanities to even get close to a new critical theory of power is glaring.

Political economists holding onto their brains, such as Jeff Faux, know exactly what the global investor class is doing as well as the role of a bipartisan governing class in forging policies such as NAFTA aimed at taking care of these privileged clients largely at the expense of social majorities north and south of the border with Mexico. Remarkably, some in what Lasch would have dubbed the civilized minority of academicians, knowing little about trade policy regimes, warn of "conspiracy theories" while they fall back to sweet phrases about multicultural diversity. What they should know, for example, is that the "gap between productivity and workers' wages is growing" in Canada, Mexico, and the United States (Faux, 2006, 239). They could have noticed that a UNICEF 2000 report on more than twenty OECD countries found Mexico and the United States topping the list with children living in "relative" poverty. They can learn from nonacademic writers such as David Bacon that what is really involved in NAFTA is the construction of a global regional cheap labor market partly aimed at breaking the back of unions in the United States and the Americas. Bacon also makes clear that the agreement has bolstered the cross-border solidarity movement, which, along with migrant labor, has helped revitalize U.S.-based labor unions (Bacon, 2005).

The ongoing studies of Richard D. Vogel focusing on the NAFTA corridors project with its vast economic and ecological implications have to be mentioned (Vogel, 2006). Vogel describes the pauperization of Mexican and Central American working classes and the prospect for most of "short careers of transient servitude" (Vogel, 2007, 10, 21). What Vogel analyzes is exactly what Faux describes as "global class war" while arguing that we must help forge what we would call a *global regional public* advancing a continental economic bill of rights and intercultural programs for democratic development and dialogue. Film writers such as Guillermo Arriaga are exploring the border landscapes for intercultural forms of patriotism in remarkable documents such as "The Three Burials of Melquiades Estrada." Bruce Springsteen's album "The Ghost of Tom Joad"—moving between Youngstown and the Mexican border—provides another example of challenging the cultural-political frames of the transnational corporate state. How then can we explain the hollowness of so much academic talk about migration and multiculturalism in recent years, talk that ironically facilitates the cultural parasitism of corporate globalization?

Perhaps from Chiapas in Mexico's southeast, Subcomandante Marcos has identified what has really happened. "Paradoxically, globalization produces a fragmented world of isolated pieces, a world full of watertight compartments which may at best be linked by fragile economic gangways—*a world of broken mirrors which reflect the useless world unity of the neo-liberal puzzle*" (Hayden, 2002, 281; emphasis added). Mobile professional academics bound to an academic market—a sector integral to the new Global capitalist system—too often simply reflect the cultural fragmentation of this world of broken mirrors even as they imagine a universalized humanity at the end of the neoliberal tunnel. What Marcos aka El Sup has been saying is that this neoliberal agenda will not be stopped with globalized abstractions and the romanticization of violence to which some on the academic Left are inclined. It has been too much for some to swallow, but the Zapatistas embrace, as Tom Hayden has pointed out, "the indigenous, civic society, the Mexican flag, and international Zapatismo" (271). They are fighting to broaden democratic spaces where equality and difference are taken seriously.

Our argument throughout this book is that because the globalization of exploitation takes various forms with differential impacts, this should not be an alibi for emphasizing diversity at the expense of equality. Living an academic life alienated or isolated from the struggles of one's own neighborhood while romanticizing vanguardist heroes of revolutionary fantasy is untenable. The Zapatistas declare: "Our fight is for the homeland, and the bad government dreams with the flag and the language of foreigners" (Vodovnik, 2004, 661). *U.S.-based social theorists would best link the struggles for a democratic republic at home with the movement for global justice by charting the transnational corporate state's historically specific disloyalties to places, peoples, and planet.* Addressing a Basque group in 2003, El Sup's denunciation of a "revolutionary vanguard" role for the EZLN is as clear as possible. He also comments: "We don't grieve when we recognize that our ideas and proposals don't have an eternal horizon" (586–87). In fact, his role in the presidential election lost by Andres Manuel Lopez Obrador has been criticized by Carlos Monsivais, whom he sometimes has regarded as a "mentor."

In his remarkable interview with the NACLA Report on the Americas (Godoy-Anativia, 2007, 7), Monsivais comments: "In Oaxaca, neoliberalism is anything but an abstraction. It is the economic system that forces massive migration to the United States, that provokes massive dropout rates at the primary school level, and that has led to a decline in life expectancy." While he is as clear as Marcos that we are living in a time of pillage, Monsivais goes on to contend that "the left will never become involved in a project of armed struggle," and that guerrilla groups in his country are "not linked to social movements." And yet he sees in Mexico the emergence and growth of a democratic left that is much more real and smarter (exactly what is also needed in the United States). Another insight by Monsivais that finds a parallel in U.S. politics is his comment on the "myth of polarization" that helped swing the 2006 election in Mexico. In U.S. presidential politics for 2008, any tendencies toward serious debates on trade policy and corporate domination of the "global economy" have elicited horrific mainstream images of "populism," sometimes with reaffirmation of "consensus" and "bipartisanship." The Global Investor Class never reaches total elite harmony, but its existence is what is concealed by such images. When Monsivais refers to the real "rift between those who through diverse means take a stand against inequality and those who consider it unfortunate but inevitable," he could be discussing the United States as well as Mexico (Godoy-Anativia, 2007, 9–11). When academic discourse legitimates negative imagery of "polarization" that ignores what Mosivais calls "this cage of savage capitalism," it reinforces the unreality industry concealing ongoing pillage. Universities need, not the *omnivorous* agenda of transnational elites, but a body~place~commons agenda grounded first in their own ecosystems.

Food Politics and Democracy Back to Earth

The Indian critique of Western developmentalism makes clear that popular U.S. corporate state notions of growth and prosperity hasten global encounters with ecological catastrophe. The first half of 2008 brought unmistakable evidence of a world food crisis that attained, at best, modest significance in U.S. politics. Nevertheless, what is beginning to register in social theory and political ecology is the importance of transitioning to more locally based food systems. La Via Campesina, the international advocacy group for small- and medium-scale sustainable agriculture, has coined the term *food sovereignty* and called for the reconstruction of national food economics (with less priority given to international trade). It is part of what Vandana Shiva has called the "global movement for food democracy" (Shiva, 2000a, 122). Navdanya, the Indian movement based on community seed banks that she launched, works to recover biodiversity and the knowledge commons.

These emerging movements, displaying remarkable courage in struggles with U.S.-based corporate powers such as Monsanto, Cargill, and Coca Cola, deserve more attention from public interest scientists, lawyers, and social theorists. From India a number of studies and reports by Vandana Shiva have highlighted the socioeconomic costs of genetically engineered seeds. The higher costs of corporate, hybrid seeds have resulted in financial ruin and even suicide among cotton farmers in states such as Andhra Pradesh. And in the Punjab, where years ago petrochemical-based, industrial agriculture was hailed as a "green revolution," the ecological problems include major evidence of a pesticide-cancer link.

BBC News reported in April 2008 a UN commission of over four hundred scientists calling for a fundamental rethinking of agro-ecological programs, with new attention to small-scale farmers and areas with the greatest needs. Such commissions might be said to be catching up with the movements and struggles of and from which we have been writing. This path is clear enough in Leigh Brownhill's recent study of Kenyan women's struggle against export-oriented plantation agriculture and for reforestation and a subsistence-oriented farming system. Wangari Maathai's Green Belt Movement, begun in 1977, has shown how environmental restoration and food security are intertwined in agricultural practices, rooted in traditions of the gendered commons, that move toward "indigenous biodiverse and mixed farming systems" (Brownhill, 2007, 34–37).

In late September 2008, voters in Ecuador approved a new constitution recognizing the rights of nature. The Amazonian region of this Andean country has been the scene of momentous struggle between Big Oil (e.g., Texaco-Chevron) and indigenous groups comprising about half of the ethnically mixed population. As Eduardo Galeano has noted, the "revindication of nature is part of a process of recuperating ... ancient traditions" of the commons (Galeano, 2008). Members of the indigenous coalition known as

Ecuarunari have voted to support the new constitution, although they find both it and the Rafael Correa government to be problematic in various areas. While the new constitution was approved in spite of opposition by conservatives and the Catholic hierarchy, the struggle over mining policy and its legal context will continue.

There is a very interesting intersection between this struggle and one in Pennsylvania, where townships have reasserted the constitutional right to control their environments rather than acquiesce to a legal process that for more than a century usually puts corporate power ahead of community rights. Earlier in this book we pointed to the Pennsylvania-based Community Environmental Legal Defense Fund (CELDF) working with U.S. community struggles to protect local ecosystems and democratic self-governance. Recovering or recentering community legal authority to make decisions about sludging, factory farms, and massive water withdrawals is a growing concern across the United States. When the Constitutional Assembly in Ecuador met with CELDF directors Tom Linzey and Mari Margil, their discussion of constitutional strategies reflected the translocal and global justice dimensions of democratic republican struggles we have emphasized (Margil, 2008).

Whether the focus is on Ecuador, India, Kenya, or Mexico, the search for the food security of more sustainable programs is an important challenge for social theorists and political ecologists. Raymond Williams was prophetic when in he wrote in 1973 that "work on the land will have to become more rather than less important and central." The "capitalist mode of progressive agriculture" and an "insane overconfidence in the specialized powers of metropolitan industrialism" had most significantly constituted identity traps among some "metropolitan socialist intellectuals" (Williams, 1989, 83–89). Creative thinking for healing the country/city divide would require democratic acts of recovery at once humble and radical.

Re-placing Intellectuals in Globalization Politics

As Rustom Bharucha has noted from Kolkata, this is "a time when communities are increasingly marked and divided" (Bharucha, 2003, 14–15). Living in Indian society subject to outbursts of communalist violence, Bharucha refuses indulgence in paeans to "multiculturalism" to which some U.S. academics are not only prone but likely to consider the epitome of political critique. Given the crude or brutal nationalism of the Right in the United States, it may not be surprising that the larger field of power is often occluded. Quoting Bharucha again, "Without exposing the economic hegemony of globalization, it becomes disingenuous to accept its 'emancipatory results' in the cultural sphere" (32). Instead of behaving much like academic stereotypes of the U.S. Right by demonizing the national, it would make more sense to join Bharucha in seeking an interculturalism that works against the cultural logic of multinational capitalism and its assault on the "ecological bases of world cultures" (see 37, 55–56). On the other hand, a "privileged global intelligentsia" committed to "virtual struggle," (188) cynically aloof from its own cultural and political ecology, and resigned to the status of sutured subjects leavened only by fantasies of "revolutionary subjectivity" may not make for healthy participation in intercultural search or democratic political struggle.

It is time the intellectuals let go of abstractions such as the "multitude" and listened more to people at the grass roots of resistance to global capital not ready to surrender their places in that earthly topology of time and history we would re-illuminate as *world*. It is in terms of this ecological ontology that we understand Erwin Straus's insistence that "man thinks, not the brain" and his pursuit of psychiatric sense in the norm and pathology of I-World relations (Straus, 1963; Straus, Natanson, & Ey, 1969). It seems possible, even desirable, to hear what psychiatrist Straus is saying rephrased in the language of philosopher Jeff Malpas, who has argued that "the structure of subjectivity is given in and through the structure of place," rather than the other way around (Malpas, 1999, 35). Self and world require places, or as Malpas puts it, "our relation to place is both intricate and inevitable" (177). Grasping this, poet-ecologist Gary Snyder once wrote that "the world is places" (Snyder, 1990, 25). The political sense of this for us and for social theorists must be that apart from the body~place~commons nexus all concepts of right and justice devolve into liberal individualist abstractions. But in a global capitalist economy where typically places are ground up to feed the commodification machinery operating on a planet transformed into sheer global economic space, consequences abound for the texture and shape of life-world experience.

Hwa Yol Jung points to the challenge of "empowering *lateral universals* as the intercultural configuration of truth for a "cosmopolitics" simultaneously based on and advancing "a cross-cultural intertwinement or chiasm in which one culture can no longer be the 'negative mirror' of another" (Dallmayr, 1999, 287). This brings to mind a key facet of the global justice movement's attempt to forge a transnational critique of corporate globalization and the global inequalities it has both taken advantage of and aggravated. That sensibility grounded in the body~place~commons articulates a generative matrix of space-time schema building from a sort of "prepolitical suffrage"

(Reid, 1977, 119–26). Some might see this as one level of cultural infrastructure for the "global New Deal" emerging as a North American theme of political discourse and debate. But this theme of U.S. political rhetoric is a perilous one unless carefully and critically theorized. A new reform liberal version of the liberal-democratic politics of pity is not what we have in mind. Body~place~commons is only the pre-political life-ground of universal human rights that needs—indeed, requires—renewed politicization in public space to be effective. The key question is whether such rights are to be "experienced as political capacities" (Ranciere, as presented by Hallward, 2006, 122). If our formulation of a pre-political dimension amends Zizek's, we do so to bolster his contention that the issue is a "right to universality as such—the right of a political agent to assert its radical non-coincidence with itself (in its particular identity), to posit itself . . . 'as an agent of universality of the social itself'" (Žižek, 2005, 131).

American political scientist Cass Sunstein, calling attention to Franklin D. Roosevelt's 1944 State of the Union Address confronting the human need for economic security, has underlined the timeliness of a "second Bill of Rights" (Sunstein, 2004). Sunstein's detailed, compelling case picks up (without a reference) Georges Gurvitch's 1946 argument for a bill of social rights. Such a program, Gurvitch argued, would take into account people as workers and consumers as well as citizens, but in terms of a concept of economic democracy highlighting their participatory role or political agency rather than one of "passive beneficiaries" (Gurvitch, 1946, 10–11, 33, 62, 66). Jenkins and Cox have called attention to the "recent creation of the US Human Rights Network, a membership group that already includes more than 150 mostly community-based organizations." We agree with them that "social justice at home" should gain from reinvigorating a "human rights culture" in the United States (Jenkins & Cox, 2005, 28–29). But we would add that the insular tendencies of American values are more likely to be overcome when such a subculture is part of a transnational movement for socioecological change. In other words, what we seek in the long run is "a shift from the discourse of rights to the practices of horizontal power" based on new forms of knowledge, education, and "modes of social rule" (Aronowitz, 2006, 148).

In our formulation "body~place~commons" is a wedge bursting the bifurcated frames of liberal-democratic politics on capitalist auspices opening to a world animated by plural forms of healing and care. This conception of "social rights" (which in fact is getting some attention today) links with our contention that what is at stake is "the recovery and renewal within a broader grassroots globalization movement of body, place, and a world-in-common"

(Reid & Taylor, 2000, 451). It is a difficult, uphill process reinstituting theory and practice recovering the commons in placed, embodied engagement with the dualisms that operate at multiple levels of hegemonic power to rationalize our ecological exploitation and destruction. Many of these groups are struggling to work creatively with and beyond "the tensions submerged in this dualism's hegemonic power," which typically privileges spatial calculations over place values (453). "Orientalism," then, is another structural tension manifested in a concretely historical dialectic of space and place that as a transnational formation is susceptible to democratic change on the basis of those "lateral relationships [with] the echoes one awakens in the other" (Merleau-Ponty, 1964b, 139; cf. Jung, 1993b, 5).

As Malpas notes: "The grasp of a sense of place is not just important to a grasp of self, nor even to a grasp of the inter-subjective realm of others, but also to a grasp of the world itself" (Malpas, 1999, 189). Writing a few months before his death, Merleau-Ponty urged scientists to return "to the site, the soil of the sensible and opened world such as it is in our life and for our body" (Merleau-Ponty, 1964a, 160). We know now that we live in a world beset by a global ecological crisis of many dimensions. We know too that many of our so-called environmental scientists think that technological solutions are at hand. Some are beginning to reconsider the outer limits of political change in America posed by the corporate state system. For those of us not given to fantasizing solutions without transformative political change, the social theoretic exploration of "lateral universals" vital for intercultural configurations of truth is a much worthier democratic agency project than a politically detached and apparently endless subversion of codes.

For a long time, American political thought has been hampered by "a liberal ideal of subjectivity unable to come to terms with the social otherness vital to the life-world's horizon of cultural objects" and the need for a "sense of the interhuman world as an irreducible primary phenomenon" (Reid, 1977, 117, 122). Today's movement for political change, exemplified by the Zapatistas in Chiapas, Mexico, takes both place and world seriously and works slowly and deliberately (too slowly for intellectuals dreaming of an empire's apocalyptic transformation by the multitude) on the basis of respect for "the concrete locations of contemporary life" (Malpas, 1999, 197). What we hope to have illuminated is how Merleau-Ponty's path to and from the site of ontological constitution takes us to "that place within which the political can arise" (198). It is from these peopled places and regions around our world-in-common that the political tasks of empowering lateral universals for more sustainable ways of life must be undertaken. What Merleau-Ponty helps the political theorist understand is that while the landscapes worked are varied, each is "but a segment of the durable flesh of the world, is qua visible, pregnant with many other visions besides my own" (Merleau-Ponty, 1968, 123).

"Their landscapes interweave" is the crucial observation Merleau-Ponty is making (1968: 142). Describing the axes, depth, and dimensions of the flesh of the world is his way of accounting for how our aesthesiological bodies live "along the contours of the sensible things" (52). When speech "metamorphoses the structures of the visible world," the cultural enchantment of linguistic idealities need not create amnesia for the sonorous beings that collaborated to give voice to "the things, the waves, and the forests" (155). Humanity has yet to inaugurate a politics that truly honors this achievement. We think that body~place~commons is organic for the geomorphology of democratic space supporting such a politics. Historical legacies of democratic republican politics provide suggestive versions of the ecologics various groups seek today. These portals for local and global democracy, justice, and sustainability deserve the most serious attention. Our aim has been to strengthen a social theory and a politics understanding humanity's challenge of catastrophic climate change in these terms. How are we to weave and reweave democratic spaces for seeking a tapestry of global justice and a more sustainable world?

Notes

Introduction

1. Larry Gibson has information about his efforts to save Kayford Mountain at http://www.mountainkeeper.org, accessed March 30, 2009.

2. The organization Ohio Valley Environmental Coalition (OVEC) is based in southern West Virginia and has been at the forefront of lobbying efforts and lawsuits to stop mountaintop removal (MTR). For more on OVEC's many activities, see www.ohvec.org. Other grassroots organizations fighting MTR are Coal River Mountain Watch at http://www.crmw.net/ and Kentuckians for the Commonwealth at http://www.kftc.org. Appalachian Voices maintains an informative Web site at http://www.ilovemountains.org. There are excellent films about MTR, including *Black Diamonds* by Catherine Pancake, http://www.blackdiamondsmovie.com; *Mountaintop Removal* by Haw River Films, http://www.hawriverfilms.com/id11.html; and *Mountain Mourning* by Christians for the Mountains, http://www.christiansforthemountains.org. All URLs accessed March 30, 2009.

3. On the global justice movement, see Aronowitz & Gautney, 2003; Cavanagh, 2002; George, 2004; Holland et al., 2007; Kingsnorth, 2003; Schroyer & Golodik, 2006.

4. We follow Kelso and Engstrøm, who propose the tilde or "squiggle" (~) as the "symbolic punctuation for reconciled complementary pairs"—signifying nondualistic reconciliation of human/nature, mind/body (Kelso & Engstøm, 2006).

5. O'Neill and Eagleton make similar points from perspectives other than the postmodernist approach of Chow (Chow, 2006; Eagleton, 2003; O'Neill, 1995).

6. Bauman, Curtis, and Dallmayr have good discussions of enclaving and neoliberalism (Bauman, 1998; Curtis, 1999; F. Dallmayr, 2005).

7. See Timothy Luke's analysis of the critique of rationalization in social theory (Luke, 1990) for more on this history.

8. Bollier, Linebaugh, McMurtry, and Nonini have gathered important recent discussions of the commons (Bollier, 2003; Linebaugh, 2008; McMurtry, 1998; Nonini, 2007).

9. We get the phrase "connect the dots" from Joan Robinett, a grassroots activist from eastern Kentucky, who uses it to describe both the importance of linking various social and environmental movements and to understand the multicausal connections between what seem to be separate activist issues. For more detailed discussion, see Faltraco, Isla, & Taylor, forthcoming.

10. Important recent books explore connections between democracy, knowledge, and the ecological challenge (Beck, 1997; Cataldi & Hamrick, 2007; Dobson & Eckersley, 2006; Fischer, 2000; Gibson-Graham, 2006; Latour, 2004).

11. Viroli gives an excellent overview of the key ideas and values of democratic republicanism (Viroli, 1999). Literatures on the history of republicanism are vast. In chapter 2, we explore the history of American republicanism and point toward key literatures.

12. For critique of Hardt and Negri (2000, 2004), see Balakrishnan, 2003; Passavant & Dean, 2003; see especially the articles by Aronowitz (2003) and Brennan (2003) in *Debating Empire*.

Chapter 1: Space-Times of the Nation-State and the Effacement of the Body~Place~Commons

1. "Natality" is Hannah Arendt's term for the creativity of human action in public life as the power to always "begin anew" (Arendt, 1958). We expand it to include the emergent phase of all aspects of self, other, and thing creation—the phase of beginning anew (see also Curtis, 1999; Young-Bruehl, 2006:58–59). As we develop in following chapters, we are suggesting analogies between nature and human life that do not fit within Arendt's thinking. She strongly separated public creativity from nature—which she saw as the realm of necessity—and work and householding—which she saw as the realm so bound to necessity that it threatened the creative action of public life. Feminist theorists have productively criticized and unsettled this strong dualism in her thinking (Dietz, 1991, 1994; Honig, 1995). Our extension of "natality" and our greening of her notion of "plurality" (see the introduction and chapter 6) are also attempts to contribute to these efforts to go beyond what is problematic in her public/private, human/nature dualisms, while keeping what is positive.

2. Portals onto growing literatures on the commons can be found in Bollier and McMurtry (Bollier, 2003; McMurtry, 1998, 1999) and the new journal *International Journal of the Commons*.

3. We take the language of "round" from Mary Hufford's important notion of the "seasonal round"—the rhythms of subsistence, market activities, and talk in human

engagement with the forest commons (Hufford, 1997). She has also developed the "Tending the Commons" Web site—a remarkable Internet archive of images and folklore from the civic and forest commons in central Appalachia. The Web site is part of the Library of Congress archives at http://memory.loc.gov/ammem/collections/tending/index.html, accessed March 30, 2009.

4. We should note that Wolin has a more narrow understanding of the role of republicanism in American history than we do. What he describes as the "first body" of the people is the political culture of strong participation in the early decades of the country that most scholars would call republicanism. But, he sees this as existing in fleeting, short historical periods that he calls "demotic moments" in his most recent book (S. S. Wolin, 2008). We explore the relevant historical literatures on republicanism in American history in more detail in chapter 2.

5. In Macpherson's classical exposition, he describes the liberal notion of subjectivity as "possessive individualism" that understands persons as "having" skills and qualities that are like property which can be deployed in aggressive competition with others to achieve advantage (Macpherson, 1969 [1962]).

6. This sentence was written on a day in which the Federal Reserve and the Treasury Department under President Bush are requesting a $700 billion "bail-out" for the Wall Street financial sector.

7. For discussion of the contemporary relevance idea of the republican notion of "competency," see chapter 3 and page 88 of Lasch's *The Revolt of the Elites and the Betrayal of Democracy* (1995).

8. Tsing has a superb discussion of how global capitalism *needs to create frontiers out of the commons it is enclosing* in chapter 1 of her ethnography of forestry politics in Indonesia (Tsing, 2005).

9. In her preface to the second edition of *Patriarchy and Accumulation on a World Scale,* Maria Mies calls this SITA (subsistence is the answer) and summarizes her debate with her critics.

10. For a critical view of the imperialist misuse of the idea of the commons by "development professionals" from the global north, see Goldman (1998a).

11. Rogers provides an astonishing look at the geographies of garbage (2005).

12. Let us pause to note that we have now moved into very difficult questions about the relationships between state, kinship, sexuality, and gender that are beyond the scope of what we can address in this book. As we have said, Western ideologies tend to reduce the complex practices of human and ecological reproduction into mystified and enclosed "family" and "nature" that are hyper-separated from "state" and "economy." This false separation ignores (a) relationships of co-constitution and (b) the different processes that have been (falsely) lumped together into images of "family" and "nature." Povinelli argues that the self-founding subject of the emerging liberal society of the seventeenth century "was born with an *agitated detachment* from any and all forms of social attachment, including the subject's attachment to its own foundation" (Povinelli, 2006, 194), but that this is "phantasmagorical.... The

very conceptual form of state citizenship . . . is based on birth from a human body or a territorial body and thus is inflected by the governing metaphors of flesh—race, gender, and sexuality" (97). In addition, we would emphasize "place" and "civic and ecological commons" as crucial matrices from which the autological subject and the liberal state are fantastical abstractions. We think that further investigation might show more connections here than are now visible (given how autological mystifications distort our scholarly epistemologies). For instance, perhaps the apparent battle by the state to control the family can be understood also as a war against the trans-household neighborliness of the civic commons and the trans-household bonds of extended kinship groups. Complex struggle between states, church authorities, and extended kinship groups over rules of inheritance at the advent of the early modern period affected class formation and property accumulation (211–14). But these struggles over state control of the codes for private property might link with struggles to control the commons in ways that we have not adequately yet considered (cf. Federici, 2004). Finally, the autological reduction of sexuality, kinship, reproduction, and gift economies to the private sphere of the "family" makes it hard to disentangle these dimensions analytically. For instance, metaphors of sexual violence pervade much imagery of collective identity—often as abstracted images of male control over the bodies of women within the group, against Otherized sexual aggression from other groups (cf. Das, 2007, chap. 2). There is a great deal of displacement, projection, and abstraction in this sort of imagery, so it is hard to disentangle how they relate to the political ecology of concrete eco-class relationships.

13. Regarding history of African Americans in Appalachia, which is hidden by stereotypes of the region as "white," see Lewis (1987) and Turner and Cabbell (1985).

14. Analysis of the hillbilly icon can be helpful in understanding how inequality and cultural violence are mystified in the United States, because it can help to refract the false self purifications of white dominance. To say this, however, is not to say that the sufferings of oppressed whites are equal to, or the same as, African Americans and other ethnic minorities. Nor is it to suggest that residents of Appalachians are less racist, or that one should embrace hillbilly stereotypes as necessarily liberatory because they unsettle the cultural mystifications of white power and status (Hartigan 2005b). Smith (2005) is correct that Appalachian studies has too often evaded questions of race and racism in Appalachia, as if the region, because of its sufferings, is somehow ethically exempt from general U.S. problems on race. However, cultural stereotyping of the region provides one useful entrée, among others, into understanding distinctive intersections of race, ethnicity, gender, and class in national imagination that have provided the cultural matter to legitimate historical formations of power and status in the United States.

Chapter 2: Reclaiming the Democratic Republic

1. For a good introduction to Green For All and Van Jones, see Kate Sheppard's recent article (Sheppard, 2008) in the *American Prospect* (www.prospect.org; ac-

cessed March 30, 2009). For a thoughtful discussion of how Appalachian citizen action groups such as Save Our Cumberland Mountains (SOCM) and Kentuckians for the Commonwealth (KFTC) have avoided one-issue and localist traps, see Stephen L. Fisher, "The Grass Roots Speak Back" (1999, 203–10). The constructive role of Highlander Research and Education Center is important in this context.

2. Two very readable reports from the climate change front are Elizabeth Kolbert's remarkable book (Kolbert, 2006) and Matthew Gilbert's very disturbing article in the *Nation* (Gilbert, 2007).

3. See the following two Web sites of the Program on Corporations, Law & Democracy (http://www.poclad.org; accessed March 30, 2009) and the Community Environmental Legal Defense Fund (http://www.celdf.org;. accessed March 30, 2009) and Ted Nace's remarkable study (Nace, 2005).

4. For discussion of these class, ethnic, gender, and ideological shifts in North American environmentalism, see Jim Schwab's book (Schwab, 1994). For a recent call for a new politics, "a new democracy," that is pursued by a "new environmental politics" with a broader agenda that recognizes that the United States' "gaping social and economic inequality poses a grave threat to democracy" see Speth (2008, chap. 11).

5. One of the best examples by an outstanding historian is Gordon Wood, who organizes his influential but controversial study in terms of this tripartite framework (Wood, 1992).

Chapter 3: De-toggling "Consumer Republic" Dreamworlds

1. We use *political terrain* in the sense that Perusek uses it to refer to an often tacit "definition of the limits of the possible" (Perusek, 2006, 86), which establishes the "background conditions" to politics in political contestation and collective action across the full range of public actors—including citizen action, civic organizations, policy communities, government, business, etc. As he uses it, *terrain* refers to a "meso-level" between the lived world of political actors and deep political and economic structures. It has to do with the way in which in certain historical periods, political actors feel that they have a delimited range of action, given their positions of power and voice and their understanding of what the world is like. *Political terrain* functions like a stage setting. "Political actors make history upon a stage received from the past . . . but they inflect this stage with crucial interpretations that set or stretch the limits of political expression in a new period" (86). This combination of power structures and actors' interpretations generates a background sense of political "scene"—or that historically specific political terrain across which contestation takes place and that can change suddenly: "it is as if the actors in a play, often through the unintended consequences of their words and deeds, manage to dismantle the theater and rebuild it, or part of it, in a different image" (Perusek, 2006).

2. To describe this national political terrain we use analytic terms that overlap in meaning but are not identical—such as *mainstream, national symbolic,* and *political terrain.* Reid (2001a) develops the idea of mainstream politics to refer to systems of

inclusion and exclusion in national politics. The mainstream is both actual and imagined. It is actual in the sense that it provides the political space for real contestations among political actors in which they mobilize very unequal powers, resources, and authority. But it is imaginary in that the dominant players create the appearance that the mainstream is the normal and the broadly accepted. As we discussed in chapter 2, the boundaries of this normalized American mainstream are strongly shaped by the technological world-picture and by subject/object dualisms and do not encompass much of the experience, history, interests, thinking, and practices of most citizens. Berlant's notion of the "National Symbolic" is similar but is more concerned with cultural and psychological dimensions. She describes it as "an archive of hieroglyphic images . . . [and suggests] that the collective possession of these official texts—the flag, Uncle Sam, Mount Rushmore, the Pledge of Allegiance, perhaps now even JFK and Dr. Martin Luther King—creates a national 'public' that constantly renounces political knowledge where it exceeds intimate mythic national codes" (Berlant 1997, 103). The boundaries of national politics arise in the co-constitution of national subjects and national publics. Both *mainstream* and *national symbolic* overlap with Perusek's (2006) notion of *political terrain* discussed in note 1. But political terrain is a more dramaturgical idea, suggesting the limits on what political actors can imagine or strategize as possible collective action because of the sedimented stories from past failures and successes in political struggle.

3. Feminist literatures are large, multidisciplinary, and diverse about the ambiguities of the public/private divide. For portals to these literatures, see Burns, Schlozman, & Verba, 2001; N. Fraser, 1993; J. W. Scott & Keats, 2004; P. J. Thompson, 1998.

4. We try to put his notion to positive use in this work, but we should pause first to note the danger, which in Heidegger's case can be seen in his explicit political involvement with Nazism in the 1930s. Cf. Richard Wolin (1993) and Tom Rockmore and Joseph Margolis (1992).

5. Plumwood has an excellent discussion of this meta-level synergism among multiple dualisms, which she calls a "web" of dualisms (Plumwood, 1993).

6. This ad appeared March 27, 2008, in the *Lexington Herald-Leader*.

7. The "we" of this ad is a remarkable collation of contradictions. The ad brings the contingencies of the "everyday" together with the terrible risk and powerlessness of dependency on the corporate collective subjects who really own the energy infrastructure and (through the campaign finance and lobbying systems of the third body politic) much of the governmental policy, planning, and regulation systems regarding energy. This is part of what Ortner describes as the "hidden life of class" (2006, 78–79). Shifts in everyday practices of parenting and juggling risk are crucially related with changing patterns of class reproduction as neoliberalism proliferates risk in ways that differ by class. "The upper classes have elaborate institutional means of preserving money and status" to pass on to their children (98). But, for other classes, practices of parenting become ways to try to secure the children's future by passing on "the means—economic, education, and psychological—with which to

(try to) reproduce their status" (98). We would argue that this ad collates together diverse, class-based anxieties about links between parenting, work, risk, and economic security—in such a way to remove it from collective questions about care for the environmental commons or public control over energy infrastructure.

8. This ad has appeared in several newspapers over the fall of 2007—including the *Washington Post* and *New York Times*. We first saw it in Kentucky's *Lexington Herald-Leader* on August 2 2007.

Chapter 4: Regenerating Public Culture

1. For a contrasting approach to Dewey, see John J. McDermott (McDermott, 1976) and James Campbell's brilliant response to Niebuhr and C. Wright Mills (Campbell, 1995, chapter 6).

2. Cf. Michael Sandel, "The Political Theory of the Procedural Republic" (1988), and Reid's examination of the liberalism/communitarianism debate (Reid, 1990).

3. See, for example, David F. Noble's (1977) and Joseph Rouse's (1987) analyses. What we find disturbing in Diggins's critique of Dewey in this area is that it exaggerates Dewey's limitations and fails to underline his strengths in such a way as to reinforce the evasion of what Habermas has called "today's problem of transposing technical knowledge into practical consciousness" in our dominant ideologies of professionalism. For a more balanced approach to this issue and to Dewey, see chapters 4 and 5 of Jurgen Habermas's *Toward a Rational Society* (1970).

4. See John P. Diggins's 1993 review (118–20). Westbrook emphasizes the indirect influence of Dewey on the New Left, the early SDS in particular (Westbrook, 1991, 549). For a fuller view, see James Miller (1987). Westbrook's concluding pages indicate Dewey's continuing impact on radical democratic theory, e.g., in recent works by Benjamin Barber and William Sullivan.

5. The debate between Coffin and Liebman, moderated by Robert Goralski, was published under the title *Civil Disobedience: Aid or Hindrance to Justice?* by the American Enterprise Institute (Coffin & Liebman, 1972).

6. Reid has been making this argument for over thirty years. See his 1973 *Politics and Society* article, especially 211–25, and his 1974 discussion "The Berkeley School Critique of the American Political Tradition" at 124–38 and 144–45 in "Toward a Post-Modern Theory of American Political Science and Culture" in Reid (1973) and Reid and Yanarella (1974).

7. Of Dewey's many works, those given special consideration here are *The Public and Its Problems* (1991 [1927]), *Individualism Old and New* 1962a [1930]), and *Art as Experience* (1934). Many years ago, Reid was alerted to the political significance of Dewey's *Art as Experience* by Henry David Aiken's "American Pragmatism Reconsidered: John Dewey" (1962). As Richard Rorty has commented, in Dewey's "ideal society, culture is no longer dominated by the ideal of objective cognition but by that of aesthetic enhancement" (1979, 13). For a critique of professionalism as a "quasi-

religion" that partly draws on Dewey, see Bruce Wilshire's *The Moral Collapse of the University,* a book that should be much more familiar to academicians than it seems to be (1990).

8. See Livingston's *Pragmatism and the Political Economy of Cultural Revolution, 1850–1940,* especially 275–79 (1994). Unfortunately, there is no time here to comment on the important debates between Livingston, Casey Blake, and others.

Chapter 5: Merleau-Ponty and the Flesh of the Political

1. Substantial relevance for this argument will be found in the "Statement of the International Peoples' Tribunal on Human Rights and the Environment: Sustainable Development in the Context of Globalization" (Tribunal, 1998); see especially 121–22, "The Right to Environment."

Chapter 6: Participatory Reason and Democratic Professionalism

1. Taylor-Ide and Taylor have a discussion of the "blueprint" approach to development (Taylor-Ide & Taylor, 2002, 51–52, 61).

2. There is a large literature on how government units are influenced by industries they are mandated to regulate. (For recent historical reviews of this literature relating to environmental governance, see Davidson & Frickel, 2004; Weber, 1999.) This process is variously understood according to the following terms: "capture" of government by industry that reorients the regulatory apparatus to serve corporate interests (Kaufman, 2006 [1960]; McConnell, 1970); networks of power that deflect resources toward government units serving corporate interests (Culhane, 1981); internal organizational patterns of "bureaucratic slippage" away from public mandates; entrenched structures of domination by elite networks that creates wider and many layered fields of power that encompass government functioning (Domhoff, 2008; Roelofs, 2008); interweaving of structures of corporate power into nation-state structures to form a "corporate-state" (Corwin, 1964; Hartmann, 2002; Nace, 2005).

3. For a good discussion of this governmental and scholarly fragmentation as well as efforts in the "movement for the habitability of the earth" to "connect-the-dots," see chapter 7 of Orr's book (Orr, 2004).

4. For instance, see the interesting efforts toward "flat" epistemologies of Marston, Jones, and Woodward in their article "Human Geography without Scale" (Marston, Jones, & Woodward, 2005) and the ensuing debate about their article in volumes 31 and 32 of the *Transactions of the Institute of British Geographers.*

5. His label *premodern* is problematic because he does not engage the diversity beyond the confines of Western modernity. What he actually seems to be talking about is European experience as conveyed in classical texts.

6. For discussion of similar dynamics of what Mary Hufford calls "clashing epistemologies" in community/government relations in Appalachia, see Hufford (2001) and McNeil (2007).

7. There are large literatures grappling with these problems of methodological distortion in most disciplines. Solutions proposed have included the following: methodological pluralism in order to get at multiple dimensions of complex realities by training through multiple methods; inter- or transdisciplinarity to encourage collaboration that brings together multiple expertise and perspectives; reflexivity in order to understand the limits of one's own understanding and therefore to imagine what aspects of the world one might not grasp. In addition, some argue for experiences of immersion in "the field" that are as much as possible not scripted by professional or methodological protocols, so that one can make oneself open to the causal and spatiotemporal pluralities of the Real and to the embodied, placed, interdependent play of particularity of being and beings in historically sedimented worlds.

Chapter 7: Translocal Politics, Ecological Hermeneutics, Democratic Struggles

1. "From the Mountains to the Maquiladoras: A TIRN Educational Video" (1993) is available from Highlander Research and Education Center (see http://www.highlandercenter.org/r-b-videos.asp). Susan Williams, lead person for Highlander's Across Races and Nations project, worked for both Save Our Cumberland Mountains (SOCM) and TIRN, now the Tennessee Economic Renewal Network (P.O. Box 6779, Knoxville, TN 37914). Susan was a University of Kentucky Rockefeller Fellow (2004) working with Betsy Taylor, Herbert Reid, and Wolfgang Natter. During her fellowship she began a manual on corporate globalization for grassroots activists. Co-authored by Williams and Kristi Disney, the completed manual, *Grassroots Action for Global Change: Resources for Community-Based Organizers in Appalachia,* is available from the Highlander bookstore (http://www.highlandercenter.org/r-global-change.asp). Anne Lewis, longtime Appalshop filmmaker, has devoted several years to the issues under discussion. Her outstanding documentary *Morristown: In the Air and Sun* (2007) is available from http://www.appalshop.org and from Highlander at the above electronic address. (All URLs accessed March 30, 2009.)

2. For a brilliant critique of ways in which popular approaches to "culture" and "heritage" in Appalachian scholarship and journalism displace regional forms of "agency to shape human and political being in the 21st century," see Mary Hufford's work in progress, "Carnival Time in the Kingdom of Coal" (2006).

3. See our discussion in the beginning of chapter 2 of poet-essayist-farmer Wendell Berry on this (Berry, 1990, 1992, 1996 [1977]).

Bibliography

Abram, David
  1988 Merleau-Ponty and the voice of the earth. Environmental Ethics 10(2; Summer): 101–20.
  1996 The spell of the sensuous: Perception and language in a more-than-human world. New York: Pantheon Books.
Adamson, Joni, Mei Mei Evans, and Rachel Stein, eds.
  2002 The environmental justice reader: Politics, poetics, and pedagogy. Tucson: University of Arizona Press.
Adorno, Theodor W.
  1983 Against epistemology: A metacritique: Studies in Husserl and the phenomenological antinomies. Cambridge, Mass.: MIT Press.
  1997 Negative dialectics. New York: Continuum.
Agrawal, Arun
  1999 Mayhem in Arunachal. *In* Down to Earth 7 (11): 31 October.
Agyeman, Julian
  2005 Sustainable communities and the challenge of environmental justice. New York: New York University Press.
Agyeman, Julian, Robert D. Bullard, and Bob Evans
  2003 Just sustainabilities: Development in an unequal world. Cambridge, Mass.: MIT Press.
Aiken, Henry David
  1962 American pragmatism reconsidered: III. John Dewey. Commentary 34 (October): 334–44.
Alexander, Gregory S.
  1997 Commodity and propriety: Competing visions of property in American legal thought, 1776–1970. Chicago: University of Chicago Press.

Alexander, Thomas M.
　1987 John Dewey's theory of art, experience and nature: The horizons of feeling. Albany: State University of New York Press.
　1995 John Dewey and the roots of democratic imagination. *In* Recovering pragmatism's voice. L. Langsdorf and A. R. Smith, eds. Pp. 131–54. Albany: State University of New York Press.
　2002 The aesthetics of reality: The development of Dewey's ecological theory of experience. *In* Dewey's logical theory: New studies and interpretations. F.T. Burke, D.M. Hester, and R.B. Talisse, eds. Nashville: Vanderbilt University Press.

Allende, Isabel
　1989 Writing as an act of hope. *In* Paths of resistance: The art and craft of the political novel. W. Zinsser, ed. Pp. 41–63. Boston: Houghton Mifflin.

Alvares, Claude
　1992 Science, development and violence: The revolt against modernity. Delhi: Oxford University Press.

Amin, Samir
　2005 *Empire* and *Multitude*. Monthly Review 57(6): 1–12.

Ansley, Fran
　1999 Putting the pieces together: Tennessee women find the global economy in their backyards. *In* Women working the NAFTA food chain: Women, food, and globalization. D. Brandt, ed. Pp. 141–60. Toronto: Second Story Press.

Apffel-Marglin, Frederique
　2006 The potential of fair trade for bio-cultural regeneration of marginalized groups in the south: The case of the Oro Verde Coffee Cooperative in Peru. Conference on "Culture matters: Understanding development from the perspective of marginalized communities." New Delhi, India, October 13–15, 2006. Sponsored by Deshkal Society along with Sanskriti Foundation, Indira Gandhi National Centre for the Arts, Asian Development Research Institute, and Bhasha Research Centre.

Apffel-Marglin, Frederique, and Stephen A. Marglin
　1990 Dominating knowledge: Development, culture and resistance. Oxford: Clarendon Press.

Arendt, Hannah
　1958 The human condition. Chicago: University of Chicago Press.
　1965 On revolution. New York: Viking Press.
　1977 [1961] Between past and future: Eight exercises in political thought. New York: Penguin Books.

Aronowitz, Stanley
　2003 The new world order. *In* Debating Empire. G. Balakrishnan, ed. Pp. 19–28. London: Verso.
　2006 Left turn: Forging a new political future. Boulder, Colo.: Paradigm.

Aronowitz, Stanley, and Heather Gautney, eds.
　2003 Implicating empire. New York: Basic Books.

Bacon, David
: 2005 Children of NAFTA: Labor wars on the U.S./Mexico border. Berkeley: University of California Press.

Bady, Dianne
: 2008 Family cemeteries another victim of mountain massacre mining. *In* Winds of Change: Newsletter of the Ohio Valley Environmental Coalition (September): 13.

Bakhtin, M. M.
: 1981 [1930s] The dialogic imagination: Four essays. C. Emerson and M. Holquist, trans. Austin: University of Texas Press.

Balakrishnan, Gopal, ed.
: 2003 Debating empire. London: Verso.

Ball, Terence
: 1995 The myth of Adam and American identity. *In* Reappraising political theory: Revisionist studies in the history of political thought. T. Ball, ed. Oxford: Oxford University Press.

Barbaras, Renaud
: 2004 [1991] The being of the phenomenon: Merleau-Ponty's ontology. T. Toadvine and L. Lawlor, trans. Bloomington: Indiana University Press.
: 2005 A phenomenology of life. *In* The Cambridge companion to Merleau-Ponty. T. Carman and M. B. Hansen, eds. Pp. 206–30. Cambridge: Cambridge University Press.

Barry, John
: 2006 Resistance is fertile: From environmental to sustainability citizenship. *In* Environmental citizenship. A. Dobson and D. Bell, eds. Pp. 21–48. Cambridge, Mass.: MIT Press.

Batteau, Allen
: 1990 The invention of Appalachia. Tucson: University of Arizona Press.

Bauman, Zygmunt
: 1997 Postmodernity and its discontents. New York: New York University Press.
: 1998 Globalization: The human consequences. New York: Columbia University Press.
: 1999 In search of politics. Stanford: Stanford University Press.
: 2004 Wasted lives: Modernity and its outcasts. Cambridge, U.K.: Polity Press.

Beatty, Jack
: 2007 Age of betrayal: The triumph of money in America, 1865–1900. New York: Alfred A. Knopf.

Beck, Ulrich
: 1997 The reinvention of politics: Rethinking modernity in the global social order. Cambridge, Mass.: Blackwell.

Berger, John
: 2007 Hold everything dear: Dispatches on survival and resistance. New York: Pantheon Books.

Berlant, Lauren Gail
    1997 The queen of America goes to Washington city: Essays on sex and citizenship. Durham, N.C.: Duke University Press.

Berry, Wendell
    1982 The wheel. San Francisco: North Point Press.
    1990 What are people for? San Francisco: North Point Press.
    1992 Sex, economy, freedom and community. New York: Pantheon Books.
    1995 Another turn of the crank. Washington, D.C.: Counterpoint.
    1996 [1977] The unsettling of America: Culture and agriculture. San Francisco: Sierra Club Books.
    2003 Citizenship papers. Washington, D.C.: Shoemaker and Hoard.

Bewes, Timothy
    2002 Reification, or the anxiety of late capitalism. New York: Verso.

Bharucha, Rustom
    2003 The politics of cultural practice: Thinking through theatre in an age of globalization. Delhi: Oxford University Press.

Bigwood, Carol
    1993 Earth muse: Feminism, nature, and art. Philadelphia: Temple University Press.

Billings, Dwight B., Gurney Norman, and Katherine Ledford
    1999 Confronting Appalachian stereotypes: Backtalk from an American region. Lexington: University Press of Kentucky.

Bloch, Ruth
    1987 The gendered meanings of virtue in revolutionary America. Signs: Journal of Women in Culture and Society 13(1): 37–58.

Boggs, Carl
    1996 Uncivil wars: Anti-politics in a Hobbesian world. New Political Science 35 (Spring): 7–19.
    2000 The end of politics: Corporate power and the decline of the public sphere. New York: Guilford Press.

Boggs, Grace Lee
    2000 School violence: A question of place. Monthly Review 52: 18–20.

Bollier, David
    2003 Silent theft: The private plunder of our Commonwealth. New York: Routledge.

Bond, Patrick
    2003 Against global apartheid: South Africa meets the World Bank, IMF, and international finance. London: Zed Books.

Borges, Jorge Luis
    1972 Remorse for any death. *In* Borges: Selected poems, 1923–1967. N. T. DiGiovanni, ed. Pp. 14–15. New York: Dell.

Bowers, C.A.
    2003 The case against John Dewey as an environmental and eco-justice philosopher. Environmental Ethics 25(1): 25–42.
Bowring, Finn
    2003 Science, seeds and cyborgs: Biotechnology and the appropriation of life. London: Verso.
Boyte, Harry C.
    1989 CommonWealth: a return to citizen politics. New York: Free Press.
Brander Rasmussen, Birgit, ed.
    2001 The making and unmaking of whiteness. Durham, N.C.: Duke University Press.
Brennan, Teresa
    2000 Exhausting modernity: Grounds for a new economy. London: Routledge.
Brennan, Timothy
    2003 The Italian ideology. In Debating empire. G. Balakrishnan, ed. Pp. 97–120. London: Verso.
    2006 Wars of position: The cultural politics of left and right. New York: Columbia University Press.
Brinkley, Alan
    1995 The end of reform: New Deal liberalism in recession and war. New York: Alfred A. Knopf.
    1998 Liberalism and its discontents. Cambridge, Mass.: Harvard University Press.
Brown, Beverly A.
    1995 In timber country: Working people's stories of environmental conflict and urban flight. Philadelphia: Temple University Press.
Brownhill, Leigh
    2007 Gendered struggles for the commons: Food sovereignty, tree-planting and climate change. Women and Environments, issue 74/75: 34–37.
Buck-Morss, Susan
    1991 The dialectics of seeing: Walter Benjamin and the Arcades Project. Cambridge, Mass.: MIT Press.
Buell, Frederick
    2003 From apocalypse to way of life: Environmental crisis in the American century. New York: Routledge.
Bugbee, H. G., Jr.
    1961 The inward morning. New York: Collier Books.
Burns, Nancy, Kay Lehman Schlozman, and Sidney Verba
    2001 The private roots of public action: Gender, equality, and political participation. Cambridge, Mass.: Harvard University Press.
Butler, Judith
    2000 Antigone's claim: Kinship between life and death. New York: Columbia University Press.
    2004 Precarious life: The powers of mourning and violence. London: Verso.

Calhoun, Craig
   2002 The class consciousness of frequent travelers: Towards a critique of actually existing cosmopolitanism. *In* Conceiving cosmopolitanism. S. Vertovec and R. Cohen, eds. Pp. 86–109. New York: Oxford University Press.
Callahan, David
   2004 The cheating culture: Why more Americans are doing wrong to get ahead. Orlando, Fla.: Harcourt.
Campbell, James
   1995 Understanding John Dewey: Nature and cooperative intelligence. Chicago: Open Court.
Casey, Edward S.
   1993 Getting back into place: Toward a renewed understanding of the place-world. Bloomington: Indiana University Press.
   1997 The fate of place: A philosophical history. Berkeley: University of California Press.
   2001 Body, self, and landscape: A geophilosophical inquiry into the place-world. *In* Textures of place: Exploring humanist geographies. P. C. Adams, S. Hoelscher, and K. E. Till, eds. Pp. 403–25. Minneapolis: University of Minnesota Press.
   2002 Representing place: Landscape painting and maps. Minneapolis: University of Minnesota Press.
Castells, Manuel
   1996 The rise of the network society. 3 vols. Oxford, UK: Blackwell.
Castells, Manuel, and Martin Ince
   2003 Conversations with Manuel Castells. Malden, Mass.: Polity Press.
Cataldi, Suzanne L., and William S. Hamrick, eds.
   2007 Merleau-Ponty and environmental philosophy: Dwelling on the landscapes of thought. Albany: State University of New York Press.
Cavanagh, John, ed.
   2002 Alternatives to economic globalization: A better world is possible. San Francisco: Berrett-Koehler.
Chow, Rey
   2006 The age of the world target: Self-referentiality in war, theory, and comparative work. Durham, N.C.: Duke University Press.
Chung, Kimberly, Robert J. Kirkby, and Jo Ann Beckwith
   2005 Civic agriculture: Does public space require public ownership? Culture and Agriculture 27(2): 99–108.
Cline, William R.
   2007 Global warming and agriculture: End-of-century estimates by country. Washington, D.C.: Peterson Institute for International Economics.
Cobb, Edith McKeever
   1969 [1959] The ecology of imagination in childhood. *In* The subversive science: Essays toward an ecology of man. P. Shepard and D. McKinley, eds. Pp. 537–48. Boston: Houghton Mifflin.

1977 The ecology of imagination in childhood. London: Routledge and Kegan Paul.

Coffin, William Sloane, and Morris Liebman
1972 Civil disobedience: Aid or hindrance to justice? Washington D.C.: American Enterprise Institute. (Debate between Sloane and Liebman, moderated by Robert Goralski)

Cohen, Lizabeth
2003 A consumer's republic: The politics of mass consumption in postwar America. New York: Alfred A. Knopf.

Colby, Gerard, and Charlotte Dennett
1996 Thy will be done: The conquest of the Amazon: Nelson Rockefeller and evangelism in the age of oil. New York: HarperCollins.

Connolly, William E.
2008 Capitalism and Christianity, American style. Durham, N.C.: Duke University Press.

Cook, Brian
2006 The new slum dwellers. In These Times: 36–37. (Interview with Mike Davis)

Corbridge, Stuart
2003 Countering empire. Antipode 35(1): 184–90.

Corwin, Edward S.
1964 American constitutional history. New York: Harper and Row.

Cote, James, and Anton Allaher
1996 Generation on hold: Coming of age in the late twentieth century. New York: New York University Press.

Cotter, Joseph
2003 Troubled harvest: Agronomy and revolution in Mexico, 1880–2002. Westport, Conn.: Praeger.

Cresswell, Tim
2004 Place: A short introduction. Malden, Mass.: Blackwell.

Cromwell, David
2001 Reclaiming the common. Ecologist 31(5): 44.

Culhane, P. J.
1981 Public lands politics: Interest group influence on the Forest Service and the Bureau of Land Management. Baltimore: Johns Hopkins University Press.

Curtis, Kimberley
1999 Our sense of the real: Aesthetic experience and Arendtian politics. Ithaca, N.Y.: Cornell University Press.

Dallmayr, Fred
1993 Postmetaphysics and democracy. Political Theory 21(1): 101–27.
1996 Beyond Orientalism: Essays on cross-cultural encounter. Albany: State University of New York Press.
1998 Alternative visions: Paths in the global village. Lanham, Md.: Rowman and Littlefield.

2005 Small wonder: Global power and its discontents. Lanham, Md.: Rowman and Littlefield.
Dallmayr, Fred R.
   1999 Border crossings: Toward a comparative political theory. Lanham, Md.: Lexington Books.
Daly, Herman E.
   1996 Beyond growth: The economics of sustainable development. Boston: Beacon Press.
Das, Veena
   2003 Social sciences and the publics. *In* Introduction to the Oxford Indian companion to sociology and social anthropology. V. Das, ed. Pp. 1–29. Delhi: Oxford University Press.
   2007 Life and words: Violence and the descent into the ordinary. Berkeley: University of California Press.
Davidson, Debra J., and Scott Frickel
   2004 Understanding environmental governance: A critical review. Organization and Environment 17(4): 471–92.
Davis, Christopher O.
   2000 Death in abeyance: Illness and therapy among the Tabwa of Central Africa. London: Edinburgh University Press.
Davis, Mike
   2006 Planet of slums. London: Verso.
Dean, Jodi
   2006 Zizek's politics. New York: Routledge.
Debord, Guy
   1994 [1967] The society of the spectacle. D. Nicholson-Smith, trans. New York: Zone Books.
Delgado, Richard, and Jean Stefancic, eds.
   1997 Critical white studies: Looking behind the mirror. Philadelphia: Temple University Press.
d'Errico, Peter
   1926 Corporate personality and human commodification. Rethinking Marxism 9 (2; Summer): 99–113.
Desai, Ashwin
   2002 We are the poors: Community struggles in post-apartheid South Africa. New York: Monthly Review Press.
   2003 Neoliberalism and resistance in South Africa. Monthly Review 54(8): 16–28.
Dewey, John
   1926 The historic background of corporate legal personality. Uale Law Journal 35(6): 655–73.
   1929 [1925] Experience and nature. La Salle, Ill.: Open Court.
   1934 Art as experience. New York: Minton, Balch.

1962a [1930] Individualism Old and New. New York: Capricorn Books.
1962b [1938] Time and individuality. *In* Time and its mysteries. H. Shapley, ed. Pp. 141–59. New York: Collier Books.
1991 [1927] The public and its problems. Athens, Ohio: Swallow Press.
1993a [1935] Liberty and social control. *In* The political writings. Debra Morris and Ian Shapiro, eds. Pp. 158–60. Indianapolis: Hackett.
1993b [1939] Creative democracy—The task before us. *In* The political writings. Debra Morris and Ian Shapiro, eds. Pp. 240–45. Indianapolis: Hackett.

Dietz, Mary G.
1991 Hannah Arendt and feminist politics. *In* Feminist interpretations and political theory. M. L. Shanley and C. Pateman, eds. Pp. 232–52. University Park, Pa.: Pennsylvania State University Press.
1994 'The slow boring of hard boards: Methodical thinking and the work of politics. American Political Science Review 88(4): 873–85.

Diggins, John P.
1979 The socialization of authority and the dilemmas of American liberalism. Social Research 46(3; Autumn): 454–86.
1982 Where does authority come from. Partisan Review 49: 374–84.
1993 Philosophy without foundations, politics without illusions. Reviews in American History 21: 116–20.
1994 The promise of pragmatism: Modernism and the crisis of knowledge and authority. Chicago: University of Chicago Press.

Dobson, Andrew, and Robyn Eckersley
2006 Political theory and the ecological challenge. Cambridge: Cambridge University Press.

Domhoff, G. William
2009 The power elite and their challengers: The role of nonprofits in American social conflict. American Behavioral Scientist 52(7; March): 955–73.

Dryzek, J. S.
2000 Deliberative democracy and beyond. Oxford: Oxford University Press.

Eagleton, Terry
2003 After theory. London: Allen Lane.

Eckersley, Robyn
2000 Deliberative democracy, representation and risk. *In* Deliberative innovation. M. Saward, ed. London: Routledge.
2004 The green state: Rethinking democracy and sovereignty. Cambridge, Mass.: MIT Press.

Ecologist
1998 The globalocal commons. Special section in Whole Earth, Fall. (Written by the staff of the journal *Ecologist*)

Edwards, Michael, and John Gaventa
2001 Global citizen action. Boulder, Colo.: Lynne Rienner.

Ehrenreich, Barbara, and Arlie Russell Hochschild
  2003 Global woman: Nannies, maids, and sex workers in the new economy. New York: Metropolitan Books.
Evernden, Neil
  1985 The natural alien. Toronto: University of Toronto Press.
  1992 The social creation of nature. Baltimore: Johns Hopkins University Press.
Faltraco, Lynne, Ana Isla, and Betsy Taylor
  Forthcoming. Social theory, Appalachian studies, and the challenge of global regions: The UK Rockefeller Fellowship Project, 2001–2005. *In* Academics and activists: Confronting ecological and community crisis in Appalachia. S. McSpirit, L. Faltraco, and C. Bailey, eds. Lexington: University Press of Kentucky.
Faux, Jeff
  2006 The global class war. New York: John Wiley.
Federici, Sylvia
  2004 Caliban and the witch: Women, the body and primitive accumulation. Brooklyn: Autonomedia.
Ferguson, Thomas
  1989 Industrial conflict and the coming of the New Deal: The triumph of multinational liberalism in America. *In* The rise and fall of the New Deal order, 1930–1980. S. Fraser and G. Gerstle, eds. Pp. 3–31. Princeton, N.J.: Princeton University Press.
Fink, Leon
  2003 The Maya of Morganton: Work and community in the Nuevo New South. Chapel Hill: University of North Carolina Press.
Fischer, Frank
  2000 Citizens, experts, and the environment: The politics of local knowledge. Durham, N.C.: Duke University Press.
Fisher, Stephen L.
  1999 The grass roots speak back. *In* Confronting Appalachian stereotypes: Backtalk from an American region. D. B. Billings, G. Norman, and K. Ledford, eds. Lexington: University Press of Kentucky.
Fisher, Stephen L., ed.
  1993 Fighting back in Appalachia: Traditions and resistance and change. Philadelphia: Temple University Press.
Foner, Eric
  1998 The story of American freedom. New York: W.W. Norton.
  2002 Who owns history? Rethinking the past in a changing world. New York: Hill and Wang.
Fout, Janet (now Keating)
  2003 Just say NO to mountaintop removal/Valley fills in Papua, New Guinea. Winds of Change (Newsletter of the Ohio Valley Environmental Coalition): 21.

Fox, Richard Wightman
　1985 Reinhold Niebuhr: A biography. New York: Pantheon Books.
Frank, Thomas
　2008 The wrecking crew: How conservatives rule. New York: Metropolitan Books.
Frankenberg, Ruth
　1993 White women, race matters: The social construction of whiteness. Minneapolis: University of Minnesota Press.
　1997 Displacing whiteness: Essays in social and cultural criticism. Durham, N.C.: Duke University Press.
Fraser, Nancy
　1993 Rethinking the public sphere: A contribution to the critique of actually existing democracy. *In* Habermas and the public sphere. C. Calhoun, ed. Pp. 109–42. Cambridge, Mass.: MIT Press.
Fraser, Steve, and Gary Gerstle
　2005 The neglect of the American elite. Chronicle of Higher Education: B13–B14.
Fuentes, Carlos
　1996 A new time for Mexico. M. G. Castaneda and C. Fuentes, trans. New York: Farrar, Straus and Giroux.
Gadgil, Madhav, and Ramachandra Guha
　1993 This fissured land: An ecological history of India. Berkeley: University of California Press.
　1995 Ecology and equity: The use and abuse of nature in contemporary India. Delhi: Penguin Books.
Gailey, Christine Ward
　1987 Kinship to kingship: Gender hierarchy and state formation in the Tongan Islands. Austin: University of Texas Press.
Galbraith, John Kenneth
　1998 [1958] The affluent society. Boston: Houghton Mifflin.
Galeano, Eduardo
　2008 Nature is not mute. Progressive, April 22: 19.
Garson, G. D.
　1973–1974 Citizenship as ideology. Maxwell Review 10 (1; Winter): 25–38.
Gaventa, John
　1993 The powerful, the powerless, and the experts: Knowledge struggles in an information age. *In* Voices of change: Participatory research in the United States and Canada. P. Park, ed. Westport, Conn.: Bergin and Garvey.
George, Susan
　2004 Another world is possible, if. . . . London: Verso.
Gibson-Graham, J. K.
　2006 A postcapitalist politics. Minneapolis: University of Minnesota Press.

Gilbert, Matthew
  2007 Farewell, sweet ice. Nation, April 19: 26, 28.
Gill, Stephen
  1995 Globalisation, market civilisation, and disciplinary neoliberalism. Millenium: Journal of International Studies 24(3): 399–423.
  2002 Constitutionalizing inequality and the clash of globalizations. International Studies Review 4(2): 47–65.
Ginger, Ray
  1965 [1958] Altgeld's America: The Lincoln ideal versus changing realities. Chicago: Quadrangle Paperbacks.
Giri, Ananta
  2002 Conversations and transformations: Toward a new ethics of self and society. Lanham, Md.: Lexington Books.
  2004 Reflections and mobilizations: Dialogues with movements and voluntary organizations. New Delhi: Sage.
Giroux, Henry A.
  2006 Beyond the spectacle of terrorism: Global uncertainty and the challenge of the new media. Boulder, Colo.: Paradigm Press.
Godoy-Anativia, Marcial
  2007 We are living in a time of pillage: A 40th anniversary conversation with Carlos Monsivais. NACLA Report on the Americas 40(1): 6–11.
Goldman, Michael
  1998a Inventing the commons: Theories and practices of the commons' professional. In Privatizing nature: Political struggles for the global commons. M. Goldman, ed. Pp. 20–53. New Brunswick, N.J.: Rutgers University Press.
Goldman, Michael, ed.
  1998b Privatizing nature: Political struggles for the global commons. New Brunswick, N.J.: Rutgers University Press.
Goodenough, Elizabeth
  2000 Secret spaces of childhood. Michigan Quarterly Review 39(2): 179–433.
Goodin, R. E.
  1996 Enfranchising the earth, and its alternatives. Political Studies 44(5): 835–49.
Goodwyn, Lawrence
  1976 Democratic promise: The Populist moment in America. New York: Oxford University Press.
Gottlieb, Robert
  1993 Forcing the spring: The transformation of the American environmental movement. Washington, D.C.: Island Press.
  2001 Environmentalism unbound: Exploring new pathways for change. Cambridge, Mass.: MIT Press.
Grene, Marjorie Glicksman
  1995 A philosophical testament. Chicago: Open Court.

Grewal, Inderpal, and Caren Kaplan, eds.
　1994 Scattered hegemonies: Postmodernity and transnational feminist practices. Minneapolis: University of Minnesota Press.
Gross, B.
　1982 Friendly fascism. Boston: South End Press.
Gross, David
　1992 The past in ruins: Tradition and the critique of modernity. Amherst: University of Massachusetts Press.
Guha, Ramachandra
　1990 The unquiet woods: Ecological change and peasant resistance in the Himalaya. Berkeley: University of California Press.
　2000 The unquiet woods: Ecological change and peasant resistance in the Himalaya. Berkeley: University of California Press.
　2002 Anil Agarwal and the environmentalism of the poor. Capitalism, Nature, Socialism 13(3): 147–55.
　2006 How much should a person consume? Environmentalism in India and the United States. Berkeley: University of California Press.
Guha, Ramachandra, and J. Martinez-Alier
　1998 Varieties of environmentalism: Essays north and south. Delhi: Oxford University Press.
Gurvitch, Georges
　1946 The bill of social rights. New York: International Universities Press.
Habermas, Jurgen
　1970 Toward a rational society. Boston: Beacon Press.
　2003 The future of human nature. H. Beister and W. Rehg, trans. Cambridge, U.K.: Polity Press.
Hallward, Peter
　2006 Staging equality: On Ranciere's theatrocracy. New Left Review 37: 109–29.
Hanson, Russell L.
　1985 The democratic imagination in America: Conservations with our past. Princeton, N.J.: Princeton University Press.
Hardt, Michael, and Antonio Negri
　2000 Empire. Cambridge, Mass.: Harvard University Press.
　2004 Multitude: War and democracy in the age of empire. New York: Penguin Press.
Hartigan, John
　1992 Reading trash: Deliverance and the poetics of white trash. Visual Anthropology Review 8(2): 8–15.
　2005a Odd tribes: Toward a cultural analysis of white people. Durham, N.C.: Duke University Press.
　2005b Whiteness and Appalachian studies: What's the connection? Journal of Appalachian Studies 10(1/2): 58–72.

Hartmann, Thom
 2002 Unequal protection: The rise of corporate dominance and the theft of human rights. Emamaus, Pa.: Rodale Press.
Hartz, Louis
 1955 The liberal tradition in America. New York: Harcourt, Brace and World.
Harvey, David
 1990 The condition of postmodernity: An enquiry into the origins of cultural change. Oxford, U.K.: Blackwell.
 1996 Justice, nature, and the geography of difference. Cambridge, Mass.: Blackwell.
 2000 Spaces of hope. Berkeley: University of California Press.
 2001 Spaces of capital: Towards a critical geography. New York: Routledge.
 2005 The new imperialism. New York: Oxford University Press.
Hayden, Tom, ed.
 2002 The Zapatista reader. New York: Thunder's Mouth Press/Nation Books.
Hayes, Samuel P.
 2007 Wars in the woods: The rise of ecological forestry in America. Pittsburgh: University of Pittsburgh Press.
Herbert, Eugenia W.
 1993 Iron, gender and power: Rituals of transformation in African societies. Bloomington: Indiana University Press.
Hertsgaard, Mark
 2003 The eagle's shadow. New York: Picador.
Hertz, Noreena
 2002 The silent takeover: Global capitalism and the death of democracy. London: Arrow Books.
Hirschmann, Nancy J., and Christine Di Stefano, eds.
 1996 Revisioning the political: Feminist reconstructions of traditional concepts in Western political theory. Boulder, Colo.: Westview Press.
Hochschild, Arlie Russell
 2000 Global care chains and emotional surplus value. *In* Global capitalism. W. Hutton and A. Giddens, eds. New York: W. W. Norton.
 2003 The commercialization of intimate life: Notes from home and work. Berkeley: University of California Press.
Holland, Dorothy, et al.
 2007 Local democracy under siege: Activism, public interests, and private politics. New York: New York University Press.
Honig, Bonnie, ed.
 1995 Feminist interpretations of Hannah Arendt. University Park: Pennsylvania State University Press.
hooks, bell
 2000 Feminist theory: From margin to center. Cambridge, Mass.: South End Press.

Horkheimer, Max
  1974 [1947] Eclipse of reason. New York: Seabury Press.
Howard, Albert
  2006 [1972] The soil and health: A study of organic agriculture. Lexington: University Press of Kentucky.
Howard, Louise E.
  1954 Sir Albert Howard in India. Emmaus, Pa.: Rodale Press.
Hufford, Mary
  1997 American ginseng and the idea of the commons. Folklife Center News 19(1/2): 3-18.
  2000 Building the commons: Folklore, citizen science, and the ecological imagination. Indian Folklife 1(3): 15-16.
  2001 Stalking the forest coeval: Fieldwork at the site of clashing social imaginaries. Practicing Anthropology 23(2): 29-32.
  2002 Interrupting the monologue: Folklore, ethnography, and critical regionalism. Journal of Appalachian Studies 81(1): 62-78.
  2004a Gleanings from the mending wall: Stream buffer zones as cultural commons. Dee Public Lecture, Utah State University, Logan.
  2004b Waging democracy in the Kingdom of Coal: OVEC and the movement for social and environmental justice in Central Appalachia, 2002-2003. Philadelphia: Center for Folklore and Ethnography, University of Pennsylvania.
Husserl, Edmund
  1970 The crisis of European sciences and transcendental phenomenology. D. Carr, trans. Evanston, Ill.: Northwestern University Press.
International Peoples' Tribunal
  1998 Statement of the International Peoples' Tribunal on Human Rights and the Environment: Sustainable development in the context of globalization. Alternatives 23: 109-46.
Jardine, Alice
  1986 Gynesis: Configurations of woman and modernity. Ithaca, N.Y.: Cornell University Press.
Jay, Martin
  1989 In the empire of the gaze. In Postmodernism: ICA documents. L. Appignanesi, ed. Pp. 49-74. London: Free Association Books.
Jenkins, Alan, and Larry Cox
  2005 Bringing human rights home. Nation, June 27: 27-29.
Johnson, Chalmers A.
  2004 The sorrows of empire: Militarism, secrecy, and the end of the Republic. New York: Metropolitan Books.
Jonas, Hans
  1966 The phenomenon of life: Toward a philosophical biology. New York,: Harper and Row.

Jung, Hwa Yol
- 1993 Confucianism as political philosophy: A post-modern perspective. Human Studies 16(1/2): 213–30.
- 1999 Postmodernity, Eurocentrism, and the future of political philosophy. *In* Border crossings: Toward a comparative political theory. F. R. Dallmayr, ed. Lanham, Md.: Lexington Books.
- 2002 Comparative political culture in the age of globalization. Lanham, Md.: Lexington Books.

Kahn, Joseph
- 2003 China's workers risk limbs in export drive. New York Times, April 7.

Kahn, Peter H., Jr.
- 1999 The human relationship with nature. Cambridge, Mass.: MIT Press.

Kahn, Peter H., Jr., and Stephen R. Kellert
- 2002 Children and nature. Cambridge, Mass.: MIT Press.

Kaplan, Amy
- 2002 The anarchy of empire in the making of U.S. culture. Cambridge, Mass.: Harvard University Press.

Karliner, Joshua
- 1997 The corporate planet: Ecology and politics in an age of globalization. San Francisco: Sierra Club Books.

Karp, Ivan
- 1979 The politics of war: The story of two wars which altered forever the political life of the American Republic (1890–1920). New York: Harper Colophon Books.

Kasson, John
- 1977 Civilizing the machine: Technology and republican values in America, 1776–1900. New York: Penguin Books.

Katz, Cindy
- 2001 On the grounds of globalization: A topography for feminist political engagement. Signs 26(4): 1213–34.

Katznelson, Ira
- 1989 Was the Great Society a lost opportunity? *In* The rise and fall of the New Deal order, 1930–1980. S. Fraser and G. Gerstle, eds. Pp. 185–211. Princeton, N.J.: Princeton University Press.

Kaufman-Osborn, Timothy V.
- 1991 Politics/sense/experience: A pragmatic inquiry into the promise of democracy. Ithaca, N.Y.: Cornell University Press.

Kaufman, Herbert
- 2006 [1960] The forest ranger: A study in administrative behavior. Washington, D.C.: Resources for the Future. (Originally published by Johns Hopkins University Press)

Kazin, Michael
- 1998 The Populist persuasion: An American history. Ithaca, N.Y.: Cornell University Press.

Kelso, J. A. Scott, and David A. Engstøm
> 2006 The complementary nature. Cambridge, Mass.: MIT Press.

Kemmis, Daniel
> 1990 Community and the politics of place. Norman: University of Oklahoma Press.

Kingsnorth, Paul
> 2003 One no, many yeses. London: Free Press.

Kingsolver, Ann E.
> 2001 NAFTA stories: Fears and hopes in Mexico and the United States. Boulder, Colo.: Lynne Rienner.

Kingwell, Mark
> 1998 Fast forward: Our high speed chase to nowhere. Harper's, May: 37–48.

Klein, Naomi
> 2001 Reclaiming the commons. New Left Review 9: 81–89.
> 2002a Fences and windows. New York: Picador USA.
> 2002b No logo. New York: Picador USA.

Kolbert, Elizabeth
> 2006 Field notes from a catastrophe. New York: Bloomsbury.

Kothari, Rajni
> 1974 Footsteps into the future. New York: Free Press.
> 1993 Poverty: Human consciousness and the amnesia of development. London: Zed Books.

Krauze, Enrique
> 1997 Mexico: Biography of power. H. Heifetz, trans. New York: HarperCollins.

Kunstler, James Howard
> 2005 The long emergency. New York: Atlantic Monthly Press.

Kuzminski, Adrian
> 2008 Fixing the system: A history of populism, ancient and modern. New York: Continuum.

Langer, Monika.
> 1990 Merleau-Ponty and deep ecology. *In* Ontology and alterity in Merleau-Ponty. G. A. Johnson and M. B. Smith, eds. Evanston, Ill.: Northwestern University Press.

Lasch, Christopher
> 1980–1981 Response: History in America. Salmagundi 50–51: 188–91.
> 1984 The minimal self: Psychic survival in troubled times. New York: W. W. Norton.
> 1986 Review of *Reinhold Niebuhr: A biography* by Richard Fox. *In* These Times, March 26–April 1: 13.
> 1991 The true and only heaven: Progress and its critics. New York: W. W. Norton.
> 1995 The revolt of the elites and the betrayal of democracy. New York: W. W. Norton.

Latour, Bruno
　2004 Politics of nature: How to bring the sciences into democracy Cambridge, Mass.: Harvard University Press.
Lazarus, Neil
　1991 Doubting the new world order: Marxism, realism, and the claims of postmodernist social theory. differences: A Journal of Feminist Cultural Studies 3(3): 94–138.
Leach, William
　1999 Country of exiles: The destruction of place in American life. New York: Free Press.
Lefort, Claude
　1988 Democracy and political theory. D. Macey, trans. Minneapolis: University of Minnesota Press.
　2005 Thinking politics. In The Cambridge companion to Merleau-Ponty. T. Carman and M. B. Hansen, eds. Pp. 352–79. Cambridge: Cambridge University Press.
Lewis, Ronald L.
　1987 Black coal miners in America: Race, class, and community conflict, 1780–1980. Lexington: University Press of Kentucky.
Lind, Michael
　1995 The next American nation. New York: Free Press.
Linebaugh, Peter
　2008 The Magna Carta manifesto: Liberties and commons for all. Berkeley: University of California Press.
Lingis, Alphonso
　1968 Introduction to Maurice Merleau-Ponty's *The Visible and the Invisible*. Evanston, Ill.: Northwestern University Press.
Livingston, James
　1994 Pragmatism and the political economy of cultural revolution, 1850–1940. Chapel Hill: University of North Carolina Press.
　2001 Pragmatism, feminism, and democracy: Rethinking the politics of American history. New York: Routledge.
Loewen, James W.
　2000 Lies across America: What our historic sites get wrong. New York: Touchstone.
Louv, Richard
　2005 Last child in the woods. Chapel Hill, N.C.: Algonquin Books of Chapel Hill.
Luke, Timothy W.
　1990 Social theory and modernity: Critique, dissent, and revolution London: Sage.
　1999 Capitalism, democracy, and ecology: Departing from Marx. Urbana: University of Illinois Press.

MacDonald, Michael
  2004 The political economy of identity politics. South Atlantic Quarterly 103(4): 629–56.
Macpherson, C. B.
  1969 [1962] The political theory of possessive individualism, Hobbes to Locke. Oxford: Oxford University Press.
Madison, Gary Brent
  1990 Flesh as Otherness. *In* Ontology and alterity in Merleau-Ponty. G. Johnson and M. B. Smith, eds. Pp. 27–34. Evanston, Ill.: Northwestern University Press.
  1997 Merleau-Ponty and Derrida: La differEnce. *In* Ecart and Differance: Merleau-Ponty and Derrida on seeing and writing. M.C. Dillon, ed. Pp. 94–111. Atlantic Highlands, N.J.: Humanities Press.
Magubane, Zine
  2004 The revolution betrayed? Globalization, neoliberalism, and the post-apartheid state. South Atlantic Quarterly 103(4): 657–71.
Mallin, Samuel B.
  1979 Merleau-Ponty's philosophy. New Haven, Conn.: Yale University Press.
Malpas, J. E.
  1999 Place and experience: A philosophical topography. Cambridge: Cambridge University Press.
Marcos, Subcomandante
  2002 Our word is our weapon: Selected writings. New York: Seven Stories Press.
Margil, Mari
  2008 Legal Defense Fund assists Ecuador to write new constitution. Susquehanna 10: 1, 6.
Margolis, Joseph
  1998 Dewey in dialogue with continental philosophy. *In* Reading Dewey. L. Hickman, ed. Pp. 231–56. Bloomington: Indiana University Press.
Marston, Sallie A., John Paul Jones III, and Keith Woodward
  2005 Human geography without scale. Transactions of the Institute of British Geographers 30: 416–32.
Marx, Leo
  1964 The machine in the garden. New York: Oxford University Press.
Matanovic, Milenko
  2002 Art and community: Turning the sword. Yes: A Journal of Positive Futures 22 (Summer): 13–15.
McCarthy, Susan
  2004 Becoming a tiger: How baby animals learn to live in the wild. New York: Harper.
McConnell, Grant
  1970 Private power and American democracy. New York: Random House.

McDermott, John J.
　1976 The culture of experience. New York: New York University Press.
McMurtry, John
　1998 Unequal freedoms: The global market as an ethical system. West Hartford, Conn.: Kumarian Press.
　1999 The cancer stage of capitalism. London: Pluto Press.
McNeil, Bryan
　2007 Mountaintop removal, bureaucracy, and the spaces of disaster. *In* Unnatural disasters. Annual meetings of the Society for the Anthropology of North America, University of New Orleans, New Orleans, April 19–21.
Mead, Margaret
　1977 Introduction. *In* The ecology of imagination in childhood. E. M. Cobb, ed. London: Routledge and Kegan Paul.
Mensch, James Richard
　2001 Postfoundational phenomenology: Husserlian reflections on presence and embodiment. University Park: Pennsylvania State University Press.
Merleau-Ponty, Maurice
　1962 Phenomenology of perception. C. Smith, trans. London: Routledge and Kegan Paul.
　1964a The primacy of perception. Evanston, Ill.: Northwestern University Press.
　1964b Signs. R.C. McCleary, trans. Evanston, Ill.: Northwestern University Press.
　1968 The visible and the invisible. A. Lingis, trans. Evanston, Ill.: Northwestern University Press.
　1970 Themes from the lectures at the College de France, 1952–1960. J. O'Neill, trans. Evanston, Ill.: Northwestern University Press.
　2003 Nature: Course notes from the College de France. R. Vallier, trans. Evanston, Ill.: Northwestern University Press.
Mertes, Tom, ed.
　2004 A movement of movements: Is another world really possible? London: Verso.
Michaels, Walter Benn
　2004 The shape of the signifier: 1967 to the end of history. Princeton, N.J.: Princeton University Press.
Mies, Maria
　1998 [1986] Patriarchy and accumulation on a world scale: Women in the international division of labour. London: Zed Books.
Mies, Maria, and Veronika Bennholdt-Thomsen
　1999 The subsistence perspective: Beyond the globalized economy. P. Camiller, M. Mies, and G. Weih, trans. London: Zed Books.
Miller, James
　1987 "Democracy is in the streets": From Port Huron to the siege of Chicago. New York: Simon and Schuster.

Mishra, Pankaj
  2006 Gaining power, losing values. New York Times, November 22.
Mitchell, Lawrence E.
  2002 American corporations: The new sovereigns. Chronicle of Higher Education: B13–B14.
Mitscherlich, Alexander, and Margarete Mitscherlich
  1975 The inability to mourn: Principles of collective behavior. New York: Grove Press.
Morehouse, Ward, ed.
  1979 Science, technology and the social order. New Brunswick, N.J.: Transaction Books.
Morrow, Raymond
  2006 Foreword to Critical theory, globalization, and higher education: Political economy and the cul-de-sac of postmodernist cultural turn. *In* The university, state, and market: The political economy of globalization in the Americas. R. A. Rhoads and C. A. Torres, eds. Stanford: Stanford University Press.
Morton, Adam David
  2007 Unravelling Gramsci: Hegemony and passive revolution in the global political economy. London: Pluto Press.
Mouffe, Chantal
  2005 On the political. London: Routledge.
Mudimbe, V. Y.
  1988 The invention of Africa: Gnosis, philosophy, and the order of knowledge. Bloomington: Indiana University Press.
Murray, Michael
  1985 Hermeneutics of the world. *In* Hermeneutics and deconstruction. H. J. Silverman and D. Ihde, eds. Pp. 91–105. Selected studies in phenomenology and existential phenomenology. Albany: State University of New York Press.
Nabhan, Gary Paul, and Stephen Trimble
  1994 The geography of childhood. Boston: Beacon Press.
Nace, Ted
  2005 Gangs of America: The rise of corporate power and the disabling of democracy. San Francisco: Berrett-Koehler.
Nancy, Jean-Luc
  2007 The creation of the world or globalization. F. Raffoul and D. Pettigrew, trans. Albany: State University of New York Press.
Nandy, Ashis
  1988 [1983] The intimate enemy: Loss and recovery of self under colonialism. Delhi: Oxford University Press.
  1992 Traditions, tyranny and utopias. Delhi: Oxford University Press.
  2004 Bonfire of creeds: The essential Ashis Nandy. Delhi: Oxford University Press.

Nelson, Dana D.
- 1998 National manhood: Capitalist citizenship and the imagined fraternity of white men. Durham, N.C.: Duke University Press.
- 2006 Cooper and the tragedy of the commons. *In* What democracy looks like: A new critical realism for a post-Seattle world. A. S. Lang and C. Tichi, eds. Pp. 161–72. New Brunswick, N.J.: Rutgers University Press.
- 2008 Bad for democracy: How the presidency undermines the power of the people Durham, N.C.: Duke University Press.

Noble, David F.
- 1977 America by design: Science, technology, and the rise of corporate capitalism. New York: Alfred A. Knopf.

Nonini, Donald M., ed.
- 2007 The global idea of "the commons." New York: Berghahn Books.

Omvedt, Gail
- 1995 Women and sustainable agriculture. New Political Science 17(1): 43–59.

O'Neill, John
- 1970 Perception, expression, history: The social phenomenology of Maurice Merleau-Ponty. Evanston, Ill.: Northwestern University Press.
- 1974 Making sense together. New York: Harper Torchbooks.
- 1995 The poverty of postmodernism. London: Routledge.

Orr, David W.
- 2004 The last refuge: Patriotism, politics, and the environment in an age of terror. Washington, D.C.: Island Press.

Ortner, Sherry B.
- 2006 Anthropology and social theory: Culture, power, and the acting subject. Durham, N.C.: Duke University Press.

Pancake, Ann
- 2007 Strange as this weather has been. Emeryville, Calif.: Shoemaker and Hoard.

Parker, Richard D.
- 1994 "Here, the people rule": A constitutional populist manifesto. Cambridge, Mass.: Harvard University Press.

Passavant, Paul, and Jodi Dean, eds.
- 2003 The empire's new clothes. New York: Routledge.

Pateman, Carole
- 2002 The fraternal social contract. *In* The masculinity studies reader. R. Adams and D. Savran, eds. Pp. 119–34. London: Blackwell.

Perelman, Michael
- 2000 The invention of capitalism: Classical political economy and the secret history of primitive accumulation. Durham, N.C.: Duke University Press.

Perusek, Glenn
- 2006 Shifting terrain: Essays on politics, history and society. Bern: Peter Lang.

Plumwood, Val
    1993 Feminism and the mastery of nature. London: Routledge.
    2006 Feminism. *In* Political theory and the ecological challenge. A. Dobson and R. Eckersley, eds. Cambridge: Cambridge University Press.
Polanyi, Karl
    1957 [1944] The great transformation. Boston: Beacon Books.
Pollack, Norman
    1962 The Populist response to industrial America: Midwestern Populist thought. Cambridge, Mass.: Harvard University Press.
    1967 The Populist mind. Indianapolis: Bobbs-Merrill.
Porter, C.
    1985 Seeing and believing: The plight of the participant observer in Emerson, James, Adams, and Faulkner. Middletown, Conn.: Wesleyan University Press.
Povinelli, Elizabeth A.
    2006 The empire of love: Toward a theory of intimacy, genealogy, and carnality. Durham, N.C.: Duke University Press.
Reid, Herbert G.
    1973 American social science in the politics of time and the crisis of technocorporate society. Politics and society 3 (Winter): 201–43.
    1974 Toward a post-modern theory of American political science and culture. Cultural Hermeneutics 2: 91–166.
    1977 Critical phenomenology and the dialectical foundations of social change. Dialectical Anthropology 2:107–30.
    1990 American liberalism, authority, and the corporate state: A critical interpretation. Annual Review of Political Science 3: 134–59.
    1996 Global adjustments, throwaway regions, Appalachian studies: Resituating the Kentucky cycle on the postmodern frontier. Journal of Appalachian Studies 2(2): 235–63.
    2001a Democratic theory and the public sphere project: Rethinking knowledge, authority, and identity. New Political Science 23(4): 517–36.
    2001b The resurgence of the market machine-god and the obsolescence of liberal democracy: On academic capitalism as unsustainable professionalism. Rethinking Marxism 13(1): 27–44.
    2005 Appalachia and the "sacrament of coexistence": Beyond post-colonial trauma and regional identity traps. Journal of Appalachian Studies 11 (1/2; Spring/Fall): 164–81.
    2006 On critical regionalism, social ecology, and post-development theory: The case of Appalachian USA marginalization. *In* Culture matters: Understanding development from the perspectives of margins. New Delhi: Deshkal Society along with Sanskriti Foundation, Indira Gandhi National Centre for the Arts, Asian Development Research Institute, and Bhasha Research Centre.

Reid, Herbert G., and Betsy Taylor
  2000 Embodying ecological citizenship: Rethinking the politics of grass-roots globalization in the United States. Alternatives: Social Transformation and Humane Governance 25(4): 439–66.
  2002 Appalachia as a global region: Toward critical regionalism and civic professionalism. Journal of Appalachian Studies 8(2): 6–28.
  2003 John Dewey's aesthetic ecology of public intelligence and the grounding of civic environmentalism. Special issue, "Art, nature and social critique," Ethics and Environment 8(1): 74–92.
  2006 Globalization, democracy, and the aesthetic ecology of emergent publics for a sustainable world: Working from John Dewey. Asian Journal of Social Science 34(1): 22–46.
Rich, Adrienne
  1986 Your native land, your life. New York: W.W. Norton.
Ricoeur, Paul
  1966 Freedom and nature: The voluntary and the involuntary. E.V. Kohak, trans. Evanston, Ill.: Northwestern University Press.
  1970 Freud and philosophy: An essay on interpretation. D. Savage, trans. New Haven, Conn.: Yale University Press.
Robinson, William I.
  2004 A theory of global capitalism: Production, class, and state in a transnational world. Baltimore: Johns Hopkins University Press.
Rockmore, Tom, and Joseph Margolis, eds.
  1992 The Heidegger case: On philosophy and politics. Philadelphia: Temple University Press.
Roediger, David R.
  2003 Colored white: Transcending the racial past. Berkeley: University of California Press.
Roelofs, Joan
  2009 Networks and democracy: It ain't necessarily so. American Behavioral Scientist 52(7): 990–1005.
Rogers, Heather
  2005 Gone tomorrow: The hidden life of garbage. New York: New Press.
Rogin, Michael P.
  1987 "Ronald Reagan" the movie, and other episodes in political demonology. Berkeley: University of California Press.
Rorty, Richard
  1979 Philosophy and the mirror of nature. Princeton, N.J.: Princeton University Press.
Rouse, Joseph
  1987 Knowledge and power: Towards a political philosophy of science. Ithaca, N.Y.: Cornell University Press.

Rowe, Jonathan
　2001 The hidden commons. Yes! A Journal of Positive Futures, Summer: 12–17.
Roy, Arundhati
　2004 Public power in the age of empire. New York: Seven Stories Press.
Ruskin, John
　1985 Unto this last, and other writings. New York: Penguin Books.
Sanbonmatsu, John
　2004 The postmodern prince: Critical theory, left strategy, and the making of a new political subject. New York: Monthly Review Press.
Sanday, Peggy Reeves
　1981 Female power and male dominance: On the origins of sexual inequality. Cambridge: Cambridge University Press.
Sandel, Michael J.
　1988 The political theory of the procedural republic. *In* The power of public ideas. R. B. Reich, ed. Pp. 109–22. Cambridge, Mass.: Ballinger.
Sanders, Barry
　1994 A is for ox: The collapse of literacy and the rise of violence in an electronic age. New York: Vintage Books.
Saward, Michael
　2006 Representation. *In* Political theory and the ecological challenge. A. Dobson and R. Eckersley, eds. Cambridge: Cambridge University Press.
Saxton, Alexander
　1990 The rise and fall of the White Republic: Class politics and mass culture in nineteenth-century America. New York: Verso.
Schaar, J. H.
　1981 Legitimacy in the modern state. New Brunswick, N.J.: Transaction Books.
Schrag, Calvin O.
　1992 The resources of rationality: A response to the postmodern challenge. Bloomington: Indiana University Press.
　2002 Hermeneutical circles, rhetorical triangles, and transversal diagonals. *In* Comparative political culture in the age of globalization: An introductory anthology. H. Y. Jung, ed. Pp. 381–95. Lanham, Md.: Lexington Books.
Schrecker, Ellen, ed.
　2004 Cold War triumphalism: The misuse of history after the fall of communism. New York: New Press.
Schroyer, Trent, and Thomas Golodik, eds.
　2006 Creating a sustainable world: Past experiences/future struggles. New York: Apex Press.
Schwab, Jim
　1994 Deeper shades of green: The rise of blue-collar and minority environmentalism in America. San Francisco: Sierra Club Books.

Scott, James C.
    1998 Seeing like a state: How certain schemes to improve the human condition have failed. New Haven, Conn.: Yale University Press.

Scott, Joan W., and Debra Keats, eds.
    2004 Going public: Feminism and the shifting boundaries of the private sphere. Urbana: University of Illinois Press.

Sellers, Christopher
    1999 Body, place and the state: The makings of an "environmentalist" imaginary in the post-World War II U.S. Radical History Review 74: 31–64.

Sennett, Richard
    1981 Authority. New York: Vintage Books.

Shabecoff, Philip
    2000 Earth rising: American environmentalism in the 21st century. Washington, D.C.: Island Press.

Shankman, Andrew
    2004 Crucible of American democracy: The struggle to fuse egalitarianism and capitalism in Jeffersonian Pennsylvania. Lawrence: University Press of Kansas.

Sheppard, Kate
    2008 The green gap. American Prospect, April 24: 18–21.

Shiva, Vandana
    1991 Ecology and the politics of survival: Conflicts over natural resources in India. New Delhi: Sage.
    2000a Stolen harvest: The hijacking of the global food supply. Cambridge, Mass.: South End Press.
    2000b The world on the edge. *In* Global Capitalism. W. Hutton and A. Giddens, eds. Pp. 112–29. New York: New Press.

Shutkin, William A.
    2000 The land that could be: Environmentalism and democracy in the twenty-first century. Cambridge, Mass.: MIT Press.

Silverblatt, Irene
    1987 Moon, sun, and witches: Gender ideologies and class in Inca and colonial Peru. Princeton, N.J.: Princeton University Press.

Sirianni, Carmen, and Lewis Friedland
    2001 Civic innovation in America: Community empowerment, public policy, and the movement for civic renewal. Berkeley: University of California Press.

Sklair, Leslie
    1991 Sociology of the global system. Baltimore: Johns Hopkins University Press.

Sklar, Holly
    2006 The "Dream" is shrinking. Mountain Eagle, March 1: 4.

Slotkin, Richard
    1996 [1973] Regeneration through violence: The mythology of the American frontier, 1600–1860. New York: HarperCollins.

Smith, Barbara Ellen
    2005 De-gradations of whiteness: Appalacia and the complexities of race. Journal of Appalachian Studies 10(1/2): 38–47.
Snyder, Gary
    1990 The practice of the wild. New York: North Point Press.
Speth, James Gustave
    2004 Red sky at morning: America and the crisis of the global environment. New Haven, Conn.: Yale University Press.
    2008 The bridge at the edge of the world: Capitalism, the environment, and crossing from crisis to sustainability. New Haven, Conn.: Yale University Press.
Steinberg, Michael
    2005 The fiction of a thinkable world: Body, meaning, and the culture of capitalism. New York: Monthly Review Press.
Steinberg, Ted
    2002 Down to Earth: Nature's role in American history. New York: Oxford University Press.
Steinbock, Anthony J.
    1995 Home and beyond: Generative phenomenology after Husserl. Evanston, Ill.: Northwestern University Press.
Steiner, George
    1989 Real presences: Is there anything in what we say? London: Faber and Faber.
Stewart, Kathleen
    2007 Ordinary affects. Durham, N.C.: Duke University Press.
Stivers, Camilla
    2009 The ontology of public space: Grounding governance in social reality. American Behavioral Scientist 52(7): 1095–1108.
Strathern, Marilyn
    2004 Commons and borderlands: Working papers on interdisciplinarity. Oxon, U.K.: Sean Kingston.
Straus, Erwin W.
    1963 The primary world of senses: A vindication of sensory experience. New York: Free Press of Glencoe.
Straus, Erwin W., Maurice Alexander Natanson, and Henri Ey
    1969 Psychiatry and philosophy. Berlin: Springer.
Stuhr, John J.
    1998 Dewey's social and political philosophy. *In* Reading Dewey. L. Hickman, ed. Pp. 82–99. Bloomington: Indiana University Press.
    2002 Power/inquiry: The logic of pragmatism. *In* Dewey's logical theory: New studies and interpretations. F. T. Burke, D. M. Hester, and R. B. Talisse, eds. Pp. 275–85. Nashville: Vanderbilt University Press.
Sullivan, William M.
    1995 Work and integrity. New York: HarperCollins.

Sunstein, Cass R.
  2004 The second Bill of Rights: FDR's unfinished revolution and why we need it more than ever. New York: Basic Books.
Taylor, Betsy
  1992 The taxidermy of bioluminescence: Tracking neighboring practices in Appalachian coal-mining communities. Anthropological Quarterly 65(3): 117–27.
  2002 Public folklore, nation-building, and regional others: Comparing Appalachian USA and North-East India. Indian Folklore Research Journal 1(2): 1–27.
  2006 Neighboring. *In* Encyclopedia of Appalachia. J. Haskell and R. Abramson, eds. Pp. 877–79. Folklore Section. Johnson City: East Tennessee State University.
  2009a Grounds for democratic hope in Arunachal Pradesh: Emerging civic geographies and the reinvention of gender and tribal identities. *In* Beyond counterinsurgency: Breaking the impasse in Northeast India. S. Baruah, ed. P. 308–28. New Delhi: Oxford University Press.
  2009b "Place" as pre-political grounds of democracy: An Appalachian case study in class conflict, forest politics and civic networks. American Behavioral Scientist 52(6): 826–45.
  N.d. Ecological poetics, public space and the body. (Unpublished manuscript)
Taylor, Betsy, and Sam R. Cook
  2001 Introduction to special issue, Academics, activism, and place-based education in the Appalachian coal belt. Betsy Taylor and Sam R. Cook, eds. Practicing Anthropology 23(2): 2–4.
Taylor, Betsy, and Herbert G. Reid
  2000 Recovering place-based knowledge and cosmogenic agency in struggles for a sustainable world. Indian Folklife 1(3; October): 10–11.
Taylor, Charles
  1990 Modes of civil society. Public Culture 3(1): 95–118.
Taylor-Ide, Daniel, and Carl E. Taylor
  2002 Just and lasting change: When communities own their futures. Baltimore: Johns Hopkins University Press.
Theobald, Paul
  1997 Teaching the commons: Place, pride, and the renewal of community. Boulder, Colo.: Westview Press.
Thiele, Leslie Paul
  1995 Timely meditations: Martin Heidegger and postmodern politics. Princeton, N.J.: Princeton University Press.
Thompson, Michael J.
  2007 The politics of inequality: A political history of the idea of economic inequality in America. New York: Columbia University Press.
Thompson, Patricia J.
  1998 Reclaiming Hermes: Guardian of the public sphere. Philosophy in the contemporary world 4(4): 44–56.

Tillich, Paul
    1960 [1954] Love, power, and justice. New York: Oxford University Press.
    1965 [1952] The courage to be. New Haven, Conn.: Yale University Press.
    1977 The Socialist decision. New York: Harper and Row.
Tocqueville, Alexis de
    1956 Democracy in America. New York: New American Library.
Trachtenberg, Alan
    1982 The incorporation of America: Culture and society in the gilded age. New York: Hill and Wang.
Tsing, Anna
    2005 Friction: An ethnography of global connection. Princeton, N.J.: Princeton University Press.
Turner, William H., and Edward J. Cabbell, eds.
    1985 Blacks in Appalachia. Lexington: University Press of Kentucky.
Valsania, Maurizio
    2007 Social hope and prophetic intellectuals in a "hopeless world." *In* Toward a new socialism. A. Anton and R. Schmitt, eds. Pp. 183–207. Lanham, Md.: Lexington Books.
Virilio, Paul
    1997 Open sky. London: Verso.
    2005 Negative horizon: An essay in dromoscopy. M. Degener, trans. London: Continuum.
Viroli, Maurizio
    1999 Republicanism. New York: Hill and Wang.
Vodovnik, Ziga, ed.
    2004 Ya Basta! Ten years of the Zapatista uprising. Oakland, Calif.: AK Press.
Vogel, Richard D.
    2006 The NAFTA corridors: Offshoring U.S. transportation jobs to Mexico. Monthly Review 57(9): 16–29.
    2007 Transient servitude: The U.S. Guest Worker Program for exploiting Mexican and Central American workers. Monthly Review 58(8): 1–22.
Wallerstein, Immanuel Maurice
    1983 Historical capitalism. London: Verso.
Waring, Marilyn
    1999 Counting for nothing: What men value and what women are worth. Toronto: University of Toronto Press.
Warner, Michael
    1990 The letters of the Republic: Publication and the public sphere in eighteenth-century America. Cambridge, Mass.: Harvard University Press.
Weber, Edward P.
    1999 The question of accountability in historical perspective: From Jackson to contemporary grassroots ecosystem management. Administration and Society 31(4): 451–94.

Weinbaum, Eve S.
   2004 To move a mountain: Fighting the global economy in Appalachia. New York: New Press.

Weir, Allison
   2005 The global universal caregiver: Imagining women's liberation in the new millennium. Constellations 12(3): 308–30.

Westbrook, Robert B.
   1991 John Dewey and American democracy. Ithaca, N.Y.: Cornell University Press.
   2005 Democratic hope: Pragmatism and the politics of truth. Ithaca, N.Y.: Cornell University Press.

White, Stephen K.
   1990 Heidegger and the difficulties of a postmodern ethics and politics. Political Theory 18(1): 80–103.

Wiley, Norbert
   1994 The politics of identity in American history. *In* Social theory and the politics of identity. C. Calhoun, ed. Cambridge, Mass.: Blackwell.

Williams, Raymond
   1966 [1958] Culture and society, 1780–1950. New York: Harper and Row.
   1973 Base and superstructure in Marxist cultural theory. New Left Review 82: 3–16.
   1977 Marxism and literature. Oxford: Oxford University Press
   1989 What I came to say. London: Hutchinson Radius.

Wills, Garry
   1987 Reagan's America: Innocents at home. Garden City, N.Y.: Doubleday.

Wilshire, Bruce
   1990 The moral collapse of the university: Professionalism, purity, and alienation. Albany: State University of New York Press.
   1991 [1982] Role playing and identity: The limits of theatre as metaphor. Bloomington: Indiana University Press.
   1999 Wild hunger: The primal roots of modern addiction. Lanham, Md.: Rowman and Littlefield.

Winter, Gibson
   1970 Being free: Reflections on America's cultural revolution. New York: Macmillan.

Wolfe, Alan
   1977 The limits of legitimacy: Political contradictions of contemporary capitalism. New York: Free Press.

Wolin, Richard, ed.
   1993 The Heidegger controversy. Cambridge, Mass.: MIT Press.

Wolin, Sheldon S.
   1981 The people's two bodies. Democracy 1: 9–24.

2001 Tocqueville between two worlds: The making of a political and theoretical life. Princeton, N.J.: Princeton University Press.
2008 Democracy incorporated: Managed democracy and the specter of inverted totalitarianism. Princeton, N.J.: Princeton University Press.

Wood, Gordon S.
1992 The radicalism of the American Revolution. New York: Alfred A. Knopf.

Young-Bruehl, Elizabeth
2006 Why Arendt matters. New Haven, Conn.: Yale University Press.

Žižek, Slavoj
1999 The ticklish subject: The absent centre of political ontology. London: Verso.
2005 Against human rights. New Left Review 34: 115–31.

Index

Appalachia: African Americans in, 45, 240n13; civic and forest commons, 33, 160–61, 238–39n3; environmental, social justice movements, 1–3, 54, 113–14, 218, 186–87; history of corporate state in, 49–50, 186, 196–201, 223; national construction of "Appalachia" as Other, 43–46, 49, 198; race, whiteness, racism, 4, 240n14. *See also* justice organizations, Appalachian

Arendt, Hannah: feminist critiques of, 238n1; modernity's problem with authority, 87, 179; "natality," 83, 137; "plurality," 13; "political integration of technical power", 129; post-dualism, 209; public space, collapse of, 26, 194; questions "life as the highest good," 191, 211; on republicanism, 55; on "terror," 183; "world," 8, 169, 190, 208; world-alienation, 211

Bauman, Zygmunt: critique of liberalism, 95; critique of multiculturalism, 75; enclaving, 237n6; "liquid modernity," discontinuity, forgetting, 191; neoliberalism, insecurity, 78; on republicanism, 74–75, 78

Berlant Lauren: disembodiment, depoliticization, 211; "infantile citizenship," 90; "national symbolic," 242n2

Berry, Wendell: on commonwealth, 51–52; critique of "global economy," 52; critique of "wilderness," 52; ecological limits and human well-being, 51–52, 117; on place, 220–21; poem "Elegy," 185; public intellectual, 53, 130; reopening everday, 192; on republicanism, 55; "unsettling of America," 39, 45

Bharucha, Rustom, call for "interculturalism," 232–33

biodiversity: as human and non-human worlding, 9; links with local knowledges, 43, 231, 227; in politics, 130, 174, 181

body: consumerism and disembodiment, 41, 69, 72, 77, 194–95, 200, 203; embodiment as praxical, interactive, and intercorporeal, 5, 10, 80, 90–93, 114–16, 133–40, 152–54; local knowledges as embodied, placed, of commons, 4, 19, 32, 143

body~place~commons: definition, 4–7, 10, 39; as generative, integrative matrices, 19, 91, 157, 167; heterogenous space-times of, 90, 104, 170; insecurity, risk, neoliberalism, 11, 78, 93, 95; not presocial, prepolitical, or outside of history, 136, 143–46, 183; political dimensions of, 154, 157, 189, 204, 208, 214, 217, 233–34; politics of reinhabitation, livability, 54–55, 74, 78–79, 83–84, 114, 142, 145, 187, 194; politics of the local, 2, 153; solidarity as emergent from body~place~commons, 203, 235–36

Bowring, Finn: biotechnology, personhood, 213; corporatized research, ethical choices, 210–11; embodiment, machines, global economic space, 207

Brennan, Teresa, psychology of global capitalism, 114, 152

Brennan, Timothy, critique of "globalizing intellectual," 66–67, 193, 204–5

Bugbee, Henry, "sacrament of coexistence," 78, 204

Calhoun, Craig: academic cosmopolitanism, inattention to economic globalization, 66–67, 187–88; solidarity, identity, "location in the world," 187, 193

capitalism: axes of domination, 42; denial of limits and mortality, 53, 70, 194–98; disaster capitalism, 68; feminist materialist theory of domination (race, class, gender, empire) in, 39–44; hypertrophy of commodity over care chains, 25, 43; recreation industries, landscapes of consumption, 200–201

care: care of the world as political, 153; generativity, 134–37, 185–86, 202; intertwining of human and nonhuman generativity, 51, 197; loss of generativity, 105, 191; of the world, 58, 169, 190

care chains: corporate power and the enclosure of reproductive labor, 88–94; definition, 24; ecological, feminist, political economic theory of, 22–27; neighborliness, civic commons and state formation, 43–44, 90, 124, 239–40n12; neoliberalism, class, parenting and risk management, 242–43n7. See also Life Round

Casey, Edward: place, landscape, self, 138, 183; space/place dualism, 84

childhood: childhood poverty in Mexico and U.S., 228; child's need for nature, world-building play, 134–35, 142, 152, 201–2 (see also Cobb, Edith, and place, body, world-building play of children; Louv, Richard, "nature-deficit disorder"; Merleau-Ponty, Maurice; Sanders, Barry, and electronic media, youth, voice, post-illiteracy); class and childhood, 242–43n7; commodification of childhood, 2; ecological citizenship for future generations, 135; violence, children's loss of selfhood, body~place~commons, 201–2; Walter Benjamin's interest in childhood play, 191

chronotope, definition, 79

citizenship: corporate attack on citizenship, 94; ecological, 6, 84–87, 108, 134–47, 189, 215–16; infantile citizenship, 90–94, 212

class. See eco-class

class, global investor, 59, 66, 70, 77, 142, 221, 227, 230; global investor class (in Mexico), 228

climate change: denial of, 53; fueled by corporate consumerism, 59, 87, 97, 153 210, 216; inadequacy of conservation environmentalism, 51, 57, 64, 76, 218–19; literature on, 241n2; social justice concerns, call for social theory to engage, 3, 132, 169, 214, 216, 236

Cobb, Edith, and place, body, world-building play of children, 134, 142, 152

commodity chains: imperialist spatialities of, 80; Wallerstein on, 22. See also care chains; eco-class

commons: complex space-times of, 4–5, 10, 22–24, 180–81; definition, 12, 22; diffuses risk, resilience, 37; feminist materialist theory of, 20, 22–23, 197; hidden in plain sight, 20, 32–33; laws of, 20, 32, 198; literary analysis of, 21–22, 31–35; not outside history or society, 19, 21–22; scholarship on, 238n2, 238n8; solidarity, as basis for, 40–41, 198, 203; traditional, de facto, 40–41, 231

commons, civic: as basis of cultural world-making, 32–33, 150; as check on crony capitalism, 34, 90, 93; commonwealth accumulation, 51, 52, 189; creative commons in subsistence economies, 11, 43; definition, 25; loss of communities of resistance, 12, 199

commons, ecological: civic commons necessary for protection of, 108, 135; definition, 25; forest commons, 20, 32, 160, 199, 239–40n3; genetic, seed commons, 221, 227, 231; land communalization, privatization, 226; water commons, privatization, 142, 224–25, 232

commons, under capitalism: "disappearing" of, 19–22, 40, 87; enclosure, 41; misuse by "development professionals," 239n10; objectified as mere resource, 22, 82, 145; primitive accumulation ongoing, systemic, 31, 39–48, 80, 95; violence, 198–200

Connolly, William E.: "eco-egalitarian capi-

INDEX · 281

talism," 55; possibility of "fascistic capitalism" in U.S., 56
Cooper, James Fenimore, discussion of *The Pioneers*, 21–22, 31–35
corporate power: attack on Congress by, 93, 102–7; corporate personhood, Dewey on, 122; corporate personhood, legal history, 48–49, 189, 241n3; corporate voice as monological, veiled, "in drag," 52, 93–94, 106–7, 164, 200; enclosure and privatization of care by corporations, 88–95, 198–99; expands in crevices between local, state, federal government, 47; green-wash, 56; "inner boss," neoliberal deference, dependency, and fear, 11, 34–35, 92–96, 216
corporate state: chronotopes of, 46, 70; corporate capture of government agencies, planning, 49, 68, 105, 159, 163, 200, 244n2; crisis of legitimacy in, 97, 107; definition, 54
corporate state, transnational: delocalization of experience, 189, 192–93, 203, 221, 229–30; dualist horizons of subjectivization/objectivization, 70–72, 132; and global inequality, 65; imperialist tendencies of, 55–56
cosmogenesis, 150–54, 157–58, 217
culture: art and democracy, 126, 200–201, 217; as civic labor, 76, 113, 115–16, 186; defined as kiltering of body~place~commons, 39, 135; political art and mourning, 186, 200–201, 203

Das, Veena: nation-states and scholarly epistemologies, 20; sexual violence, gender, national identity, 240n12; violence, mourning, reinhabitation of ordinary world, 194
democracy: body~place~commons as portals for, 13, 145, 157, 181, 197, 215, 236; fascist tendencies in U.S., 56, 111; liberal reduction to "interests" or "opinions," 141; multiculturalism and the reification of difference, 141, 153, 192; neighborliness, civic commons and, 225; neighborly communities (Dewey) 124; plurality, fluency, complex space-times of, 13, 176, 184
Dewey, John: civic professionalism, 72; discussion of Art as Experience, overcoming dualism, rebuilding public space, aesthetic ecology of daily life, 110–17, 243n7; Lippman-Dewey debate, 121–22; "local as ultimate universal," 153; Niebuhr-Dewey debate, 119–20; on republicanism, 55; selfhood, "creative democracy," public intelligence, 126–31
Diggins, John P.: on Dewey on science, 242n3; liberal-realist critique of Dewey, 118–20, 124, 242n4
dualisms: dualist horizons of subjectivization and objectification, 70–71, 78, 87, 116, 121, 166, 180, 193, 207; non-dualism, hinge, reversibility, 80, 133, 139–40, 157, 171, 237n4; overcoming, 4, 108–9, 155, 165; subject/object, 173, 177; "toggle switches," 80, 85, 156, 165; web of hegemonic dualisms, 44, 85, 103, 165, 242n5

eco-class: definition, 26; feminist ecological economics, class as social relations of reproduction and production, 22–27, 39–44 (*see also* care chains; commodity chains); labor, organizational challenges of, 189, 199; Life Round, capitalist domination (class, gender, race, empire) as mystification of, 42; neoliberalism and domination of care chains, 90, 185–201; regions peripheralized and Otherized, 43–46, 50, 180, 199; resource wars, 53; ruling elites, 68; unequal ecological costs, globalization, class domination, 66–67, 77–78, 199, 225
energy systems: Big Oil advertising campaign against government energy policy, 87–94, 98–107; fossil fuel regimes, 47, 51–52, 64–65, 87, 93, 107, 195; industrialized agriculture and fossil fuel, 227–28; King Coal, 11, 164, 186, 200; sustainable, decentralized systems, 52
environmentalism, civic: examples of, 109, 112, 117, 148, 149, 181; Gottlieb on "environmentalism of daily life," 110–11; Shabecoff on care for place, 149; Shutkin on, 110, 148–50
environmentalism, in U.S.: critique of Deep Ecology, 135, 142–46, 168; memory and mourning in, 187, 190–91; race, class, and gender in, 57–58 148, 150, 196, 241n4; religious green movements, 65; technocratic managerialism and blindness to embodied,

INDEX

local knowledge, 56, 143, 145; "wilderness" and "conservation" critiqued, 51–52, 57, 196, 214

Faux, Jeff, effects of NAFTA on inequality in Mexico, 203, 227–29
finitude: call for a politics of limits, 4, 52, 117, 140, 181, 187, 197, 217, 223; capitalism's flight from, 40–42; participatory reason and acceptance of, 184; valued in Puritan notions of commonwealth, 40; Western philosophy's fear of, 169
Fischer, Frank: "counterexpertise" of activists, 175; experts as "specialized citizens," partnering in participatory research, 113, 163, 181; participatory inquiry, 109–10, 238n10
flesh: critique of Hardt and Negri's misuse of Merleau-Ponty's idea, 206–9; democratic theory and the durable "flesh of the world," 138–42; intercorporeal, non-dualistic, hinge between self/other, body/world, human/non-human, 133, 139, 203, 205; key concept of Merleau-Ponty's thought, 133; undoes Western dualisms, 155, 157, 236
food systems: biodiversity and indigenous, local knowledge, 231; corporate power in, 52, 199, 220; food democracy, 157, 231; food sovereignty, 52, 231; globalized agriculture, critique of, 53, 158; relocalizing, 181, 231. *See also* Green Revolution, critique of
frontier, myth of: infinite space, wilderness without place or history, 40, 154; reified "nature," Western myths of first discovery, 86; used by global capital to enclose commons, 239n8
fungibility, logics of: consumerism as grid of fashion, 101; definition, 172–74; elementalization is key hegemonic mechanism, distorted by theories of "essentialization," "representation," 172–74; interlocking rationalisms (market, bureaucracy, technocracy) as toolkit for neoliberal globalization, 41, 67, 73, 145, 147, 156–58, 174, 223; liberal rationalities as, 30, 150; particularity as opposite of fungibility, 171, 197; space-based universalizing rationalities, 9, 151, 160, 177; technological world picture, 68, 70–71, 104; universal otherhood, 41, 86, 101, 135, 222; violence of, 223

gender: abstract liberal citizen as male and white, 30, 84; causal interactions between state and kinship, 44, 84, 94, 158, 239–40n12, 242n7; gender domination through dualization, mystification, exploitation of the Life Round, 26–27, 44, 85; patriarchy, state, class formation, 27; race, class, imperialism and gender, 166
Gibson-Graham, J. K.: economic "being-in-common," 182; naturalization of the economy, 82
Giri, Ananta: links among dominations (gender, race, ethnicity, caste), 166; nation-state affects scholarly epistemologies, 20; overcoming dualisms of concrete/universal, 167
global economic space, 9, 153, 158, 233. *See also* market machine god; neoliberal globalization
global justice movement: as alternative globalization movement, 2, 75, 147, 190; as defense of commons, multi-issue, 2, 40, 44, 79, 148; definitions, 2, 237n3; lessons from, 215; linkages between American and global justice movements, 55, 78, 186; place-based but transveralizing solidarities, 2, 138, 153, 186, 203, 226, 233, 245n1; solidarity within, 3, 75; undoing reified oppositions between global and local/NIMBYism, 82, 84, 126, 149–50, 204, 214. *See also* justice organizations
Green Revolution, critique of, 53, 157–58, 220; in India, 231; in Mexico, 227

Hardt, Michael, and Antonio Negri, critique of: empire without center or place, 74, 206; inattention to ecology of global economy, 74; misuse of Merleau-Ponty's notion of "flesh of the world," 206–9; "nomadic revolutionaries," 16, 117, 238n12; scholarly critiques of, 238n12
Heidegger, Martin: dwelling, 83, 242n4; hammers, the ready-to-hand, 6; place, region, 192; post-dualism, 209; skipping over, 85; truth as alethia, 183; world-picture, 192
hope: academe lacking, 3; as emergent from body~place~commons, 154, 217; at grassroots level, 3–4, 130; hope, place, story, 151; political, democratic, 116, 215, 218

INDEX · 283

Hufford, Mary: civic and forest commons, 33, 43–44, 239n3; "clashing epistemologies" of government/community, 244n6; on depoliticizing, culturalist approaches in Appalachian Studies, 245n2; King Coal's monological voice, 164; mountaintop removal, ontological disorientation, 196; mourning, corporate power, destruction of place, 186; nation/region monologue, 46; "seasonal round," 238–39n3; "spectacular forest of innumerable rotations," 159–60

identity politics: in Appalachian social movements and studies 153–54, 240n14, 240–41n1, 245n2; argument for interculturalism, not multiculturalism (Bharucha), 221, 233; critique of multiculturalism, 193, 221, 229, 232
illth, definition, 5. See also Ruskin, John
India: Indian critique of Western developmentalism, 220, 222–23; North East, 156; partition, violence, mourning, 194
inequality: antithetical to democracy, 35, 58–59; increasing in Mexico, 227; increasing under neoliberalism, 5, 95, 135, 141–42, 199, 223; intersections Indian developmental state, precapitalist and neoliberal inequalities, 158; oligarchy, 66, 56

jobs crisis, global, 116, 217
justice: climate justice, 186; intergenerational claims of future generations,135
justice organizations, American: Alternatives for Community and Environment, 148; Center for Health, Environment and Justice (founder, Lois Gibbs), 57; Community Environmental Legal Defense Fund, 54, 232, 241n3; Community Farm Alliance, 78, 130, 181, 218; Genetic Engineering Action Network, 130; Kentuckians for the Commonwealth, 78; Program on Corporations, Law & Democracy, 54, 241n3
justice organizations, Appalachian: Appalachian Alliance, 114; Coal Summit 2002, 130; Highlander Center, 186, 218; Keeper of the Mountains (founder, Larry Gibson), 1–3, 196, 198, 237n1; Ohio Valley Environmental Coalition, 51, 78, 186, 241n1; Save Our Cumberland Mountains, 51, 186, 241n1; Tennessee Economic Renewal Network, 186
justice organizations, environmental: Green for All, 51, 240n1; People of Colour Environmental Leadership Summit (1991), "Principles of Environmental Justice," 148
justice organizations, global: Durban Social Forum Declaration, 225; Green Belt Movement (founder, Wangari Maathai), 231; Peoples Global Action, 78; Poona Indictment of the Perversion of Science and Technology (1978), 222; World Social Forum, 3, 76, 78, 124–25, 186, 204, 221

Kayford Mountain, West Virginia, 1–4,196–98, 237n1
kiltering: definition, 90–91; of diverse knowledges of body~place~commons, 167; of heterogeneous space-times, 23, 197, 206; learned nonhuman and human behavior, 24; unkiltering, 81
Klein, Naomi: "brand-bombing," 125–26; centrality of commons to 21st century politics, 40–41; on globalization in South Africa, 223
knowledge: as emergent from body~place~commons, 132, 147, 151–52; field sciences as place-based, able to link with local knowledges, 161, 170; integrative, transdisciplinary, place-based, 149, 175, 177, 181, 183, 215; local knowledge, 43, 56, 113, 155–56, 160, 220; local knowledge as emergent from body~place~commons, 32, 109, 128, 143
knowledge, fragmentation of: Archimedean Fix, Cartesion dualism, 73–74, 78, 124, 166, 178; corporatization of universities, 181, 200; grassroots critique of expert knowledges, 174; in modernity, 163, 176; modernity as decontextualizing, 157–58; overspecialization, 105, 109, 158, 177; science as disembedded from body~place~commons, 57, 145; specialization and loss of democracy, 14, 189, 238n10
knowledge, local: definition, 184; ignored by experts, 227; participatory action research, 110; pro-science, place-based local knowledges, 161, 176

Kothari, Rajni, critique of Western developmentalism, 221–23

Lasch, Christopher: contradictions in U.S. democracy, 95, 209; minimal selfhood, 208, 210–11; populism and citizenship, 60–61, 77

Latour, Bruno: against dualism nature/society, subject/object, 9; democracy, knowledge, ecological challenge, 238n10; pluriverse, 167; social constitution of science, 174

Lefort, Claude: fiction of "diversity-in-itself," 141, 153; on Merleau-Ponty's "principle of conservation in becoming," 140, 205

liberal-democratic polity: dangers of technocratic managerialism, 56, 104; interest group pluralism, critique of, 63, 105, 119, 141; proceduralism, critique of, 121; vulnerability to corporate power, 54–56, 59, 66, 76, 106, 154

liberalism: atomized individual in, 29, 71; contradictions of, 59–60, 76, 86, 95, 119; covert domination within (race, gender, class, empire), 30, 62, 68; difficulties with collective, intersubjective, given, 29, 30, 83–86; disembodiment and abstract citizenship of, 79, 84, 233, 235; negative liberties in, 29, 75, 87; problems engaging inequality, 58, 84

liberalism, reform: contradictions of, 96; politics of the civilized minority (Lasch), 77, 125

Life Round: as articulation of ecological and social reproduction, 23, 26; building solidarities around, 130, 148, 187–89; domination by mystification of, 41, 45, 90, 195; effacement of, 50, 158, 180

Linebaugh, Peter: enclosure of commons inherent in capitalism, 31, 40; legal rights to, traditions of, commons, 32, 51, 238n8; rights to commons in Magna Carta, 20

Livingston, James, critique of: culturalist, subjectivist misinterpretation of Dewey, 121–24; misuse of Gramsci and Raymond Williams neo-Gramscian approach, 122–23

Louv, Richard, "nature-deficit disorder," 201–2

Luke, Timothy W.: "alternative modernities," 178; contemporary grassroots activism as "populist social ecology," 65–66; elite classes and late-nineteenth-century populism, 77; social theoretic critique of rationalization, 238n7

mainstream: borrows specious political legitimacy from commons, 19, 80; construction of "right" and "left" in, 96, 230; definition, 80, 241n2; effaces the commons, 19, 53; elite, corporate control of, 86, 123; limits to, 66; marginalizes grassroots politics, 54

Malpas, J. E.: place and the political, 203; place linked with death, 194; subjectivity constituted in place, 152, 192, 233, 235

Marcos, Subcomandante: concreteness of political, 124; exchange with Carlos Fuentes, 227; neoliberalism as "world of broken mirrors," 229; WTO as "death train," 191; Zapatista voice within global publics, 219

market machine god: definition, 40; dream of individual upward mobility, 46, 223; fetishization of market, 38, 66, 69, 72–73, 83–86, 104, 158, 207; illusory promise of security, 4, 223; naturalization of economy, 82, 97; shatters chronotopes of body~place~commons, 40, 58, 71, 80, 85–86, 90, 94, 103; splitting of economy and polity, 38, 54, 81; veils oppression (race, empire, class), 195

Merleau-Ponty, Maurice: chiasmic field of co-presence, 139–40, 203, 205; human development and the grounds of ecological citizenship, 134–35; intercorporeality, subjectivity as intersubjectivity, 135–40; lateral universals, transversal politics, 83, 116, 122, 138–42, 150–54; on ontological silencing of nature, 137; post-dualist, ecological philosophy, 83, 115, 132–34, 155

Mexico: land reform, contestation over globalized agriculture, 226, 230; NAFTA, inequality, damage to rural economy, 227; Zapatista critique of neoliberal trade, 2, 226, 230, 235

modernity: contradictions of self-founding, 6, 84, 179; as flight from the given, 6, 170; modern doubt as serious play, unsettling "law of identity," 178

moonscapes: ecological annhilation, 11, 196, 201; googling for, 1–3; violence of subject/object dualism, 180

mountaintop removal (MTR): devastation from, 1–2, 237n2; mourning, 10, 195–98
mourning: death, suffering, aging, burial, 51, 140, 194, 197, 202; interplay mortality, natality in the Life Round, 22–24; Leon Fink on migrant workers and, 185–86
multiculturalism. *See under* democracy

Nace, Ted: corporate personhood, 48–49; corporate state, 244n2; expansion, contestation of corporate power, 54, 71, 189, 241n3; U.S. anti-corporate politics 1770s–1870s, 47–48
Nancy, Jean-Luc: politics of reclaiming world against "general equivalence," 191; world, place, 182
Nandy, Ashis, critique of Western developmentalism, 218–19, 222–23
natality, reinterpretation of Arendt's notion, 22–24, 83, 137, 238n1
nation-state, chronotopes of: economic modernization splits linear, cyclic time, 46, 102; effacement of rural, 39, 46, 198, 232; render the commons invisible, 20, 81–87
nation-state, necessary for democratic, alternative globalization, 14
nature: nature-deficit disorder, 201; rights of, 231
nature, in American political culture: constructed as mechanistic Other, mere resource, background, 21, 53, 82; subjectivization of Nature, 200
Nelson, Dana D.: on the commons in James Fenimore Cooper's *The Pioneers*, 21–22, 31–35; "presidentialism," 93; U.S. public space coded white and male, 30, 41
neoliberal globalization: critique of "free trade," 65, 67, 147; culture of greed, 221; enclaving, depoliticization, 7, 153, 189, 200–201, 204, 221, 237n6; enclaving, subjectivization, worldlessness, 11, 81, 140, 142, 152; fraying middle-class lifeways, 50, 95; increasing inequality, 221; NAFTA, 186, 203, 227–28; place management, inequality, mobile capital, regional growth coalitions, 162, 164, 198–200, 224; speed, mobility, 194, 206; undoing global/local reification in theories of, 165; WTO, 69, 76, 186, 191

O'Neill, John: climate change, 214; instituted consciousness between violence and utopia, 154; non-dualistic co-being of subjective~objective, "time's body," 133, 152, 154; "prepolitical suffrage" of embodied, lived being, 135
Ortner, Sherry B.: parenting and "hidden life of class," 242n7; social theory inadequate on economic class, 141
Other, social construction of: association with death and reproduction, 42–46; in capitalist domination, 49, 62, 86, 166; neoliberalism and trends in Othering, 96

participation: democracy and participatory inquiry, 109, 110, 116, 158; grassroots, 141;
participatory action research, 110
participatory reason: able to track continuities in reality, overcome fragmentated knowledges, 162; definition, 155, 171, 183–84; as emplacing and contextualizing, 157; the "field" and "sciences of—(un)anticipated outcomes" (Davis, Christopher O.), 183
particularity: continuity of creatures, things, persons, 81, 116, 126, 139, 151–52, 162, 165, 170, 180, 197, 205; definition, 170–71; difficult for modernity and postmodernity to grasp, 6; non-dualistic relationship of particular (or concrete) and transversal (or lateral universal), 8, 135–37, 150–53, 156, 167, 171, 204–5, 233
partnership: between community, experts, government, 155–56; community/academic, 184; corporate/governmental/professional/civil society complexes that increase or decrease democracy, 159, 162; critique of top down, "blueprint" development led by experts or government, 157–58, 180, 244n1; multisectoral, multidisciplinary democratic dialogue, 55
place: dialectic of space and place, 84, 130; displacement, 1, 5; loss of, 115–16, 142; place-based logics, 151–52; place management, crony capitalism, neoliberalism, 35, 49, 162; reactionary politics of, 83; sprawl, 195; theories of, 142
Plumwood, Val: capitalist public space coded white and male, 41; Deep Ecology as monologic, 168; "disappearing" of ecological being, 20–21, 41; nature, female put under

"coverture," 94; oppressive dualisms linked in "web," 166, 242n5
plurality: and democracy, 14, 128; greening of Arendt's notion, 13, 238n1; in professions as communities of inquiry, 176, 179, 180
political terrain, definition (Perusek, Glenn), 241n1
populism: farmer/labor & cross racial alliances in, 67; Henry Demarest Lloyd's *Wealth against Commonwealth*, 67, 76; negative stereotypes of, 59–60, 65, 77; Richard D. Parker on academic "anti-populist" sentiment, 125; Timothy Luke's "populist social ecology," 65. *See also* U.S. Political history: 1870s–1890s Populist movements
Povinelli, Elizabeth A.: "autological" self, freedom as social disembedding in liberalism, 84, 86, 239n12; "empire of love," 81; "genealogical society," 165; "intimate event," 86, 90
production chains. *See* eco-class
professionalism, civic: autonomy vs. engagement, 120, 169; call for, 78; defined as tending of body~place~commons, 143, 155, 167, 177–78, 184, 191, 232–33, 245n7; democratic deliberation, methodological pluralism and, 162, 169, 177; as discussed by William Sullivan (in Work and Integrity), Bruce Wilshire (Moral Collapse of the University), 112; examples of, 130; John Dewey on 110–12
professions: corporatization of university, 98; Craig Calhoun on cosmopolitanism, 187; epistemologies shaped by space-times of the nation-state, 20, 155; globalization and left cosmopolitanism, 73–74, 113, 115, 122, 130, 149, 193, 206, 208, 216–17, 221, 229; as intellectual commons, 176; methodological rigidity, professional power, neoliberalism, 159, 178; neoliberalism, professional identity and disciplinary cultures of deference, 66, 169, 179, 188; postcommunal professionalism, 70, 72, 78, 98, 113, 115–16, 149–50, 177, 188, 203; reclaiming, re-placing universities, 116, 132, 188, 208, 218, 230; role in disembodiment, displacement, privatization, 3, 177; technocracy as undermining democracy, 109, 124, 159, 161
progress: linear temporality, 101–3; myth of,

30, 39, 46, 52–53, 69, 94, 196, 217. *See also* finitude
public intelligence: and democratic deliberation, 125; undoes segmentations of modernity, 155, 113. *See also* Dewey, John
public/private divide: feminist literatures on, 242n3; fragmenting of spheres of experience, 11 31, 86; gendering of, 38, 44, 240n12; linked dualisms in, 81; reconnecting home and world, undoing dualisms, 82, 84
publics, global regional, 78, 116, 127, 190, 193, 225, 229; replacing publics in bioregions, 116, 193
public space: coded as white and male, 30; corporate power engulfs, 87, 106, 194; cronyism as hidden fabric of American state, 33, 50; definition, 12, 25; feminist theories of, 84; fragmentation of knowledge, crony capitalism, 163, 175; loss of, 64, 72, 98, 105, 194; market as metaphor for, 41, 79, 92; splitting of spheres, fragmentation of knowledge, loss of democracy, 163–64, 177; splitting spheres, segmentations of modernity, 85, 109, 112, 115, 147, 200
public space, democratic: aesthetic ecology of, 116, 152–55, 187; reclamation of, as political task, 14, 74–79, 109, 147–52, 187, 191, 211; republican metaphors for, 27, 60; theories of green public space, 168; Zapatista reclamation of, 229

race: abstract, liberal citizen covertly marked as male and white, 84; and class, gender, empire, 62, 166, 180; spatial dynamics of, 45; whiteness, 45, 240n13
refugees: climate change, 217; displacement, economic migration, 11, 193, 203, 228; ecological, 53, 188; neoliberalism, displacement (Mexico), 230
regionalism, critical, 114, 127; Appalachian Alliance, 114; bioregionalism, 192; Coal Summit (2002), 130; Genetic Engineering Action Network conderence (2002), 130; social ecology and, Radhakamal Mukerjee, Lewis Mumford, 222
"republic," consumer: chronotopes of, 103; definition, 87; literature on, 97; mystifies and appropriates republicanism, 69, 87, 99, 106–7
republicanism: citizenship as embedded

in body~place~commons, 58, 81, 83, 98; citizenship in, 60; commonwealth as the political body of the commons, 36–37; competency, 38, 61, 65, 94, 239n7; definition, 14; fear of dependence and inequality as defining characteristic, 34–35, 37, 59; fear of politics of deference and pity, 77; hostility to empire, 30, 65, 75, 194; interdependence, 79; love of concrete and particular way of life, 38; non-dualistic understanding of private property and commonwealth, 36, 198; notions of liberty in, 34, 37, 75; permeable boundaries between the civic commons and the state, 28, 35; scholarship on, 14, 238n11
republicanism, conservative: gives grounds for rise of liberal and neoliberal ideologies, 28, 61, 71; ideological legitimation of capitalist technologies, 61–62, 71–72; race and gender heirarchy in, 38
republicanism, democratic, 38, 61; as continuing legacy for global justice movement, 74–75, 96, 141, 193, 236; as continuing legacy in U.S. grassroots activism, 53–59, 82; as green alternative for 21st century, 38, 50; theorists of, 55, 238n11 (*see also* Arendt, Hannah; Berry, Wendell; Dewey, John)
republicanism, producer, 39, 47–48, 60–61, 122; negative stereotypes of, 77
Ricoeur, Paul: consent, 151; hermeneutics of suspicion, 7
rights, human: arising from prepolitical grounds of body~place~commons, 234; second Bill of Rights (Sunstein, Cass), 234
Ruskin, John: notions of "illth" and "wealth," 5, 36; value, as availing "towards life," 5

Sanders, Barry, and electronic media, youth, voice, post-illiteracy, 201–2
scale: bias against the local, 39, 45, 121, 147; local hinged with global, inter-scalar relationships as source power, 49, 153; "militant particularisms" (Harvey, David), 152; subsidiarity, principle of, 216; undoing reified dualisms between local and global, 165
Sennett, Richard: critique of professional autonomy, 112–13; Diggins critique of, 118–19
Shiva, Vandana: food democracy, 157, 227, 231; globalization, fight against, 219, 222; globalization as "environmental apartheid,"

221; Green Revolution, critique of, 220; subsistence economies valued, 196
social theory: anti-dualism in, 7, 155, 191; call for alliances between social theory and field sciences, 167, 170, 181, 183; critique of fragmentation of knowledge, 177; critique of universalizing grids, 9, 238n7; defined as ways to attend and tend to world, 7, 9; possible contributions to global justice movement, 3–6; reclamation of democratic public space as political task, 214; theories of reinhabitation and recentering, 6, 184, 190, 215–16, 229
social theory, critique of: "baroque" (Sanbonmatsu, John) spectator theory, 180, 208; decentering tendencies, flight from the given, 6, 165; detached, endless subversion, 235; disembodying poststructuralist thinking, 214; "flat" theories of knowledge, fear of meta-, 9, 166–67, 205, 244n4; inattention to economic class and inequality, 6, 141; postmodernist, post-political, subjectivizing tendencies, 121, 153; self as negativity, 138, 182, 190
solidarity. *See under* body~place~commons; commons; global justice movement
South Africa: beyond identity politics in alternative globalization struggles, 223–26; community movements against privatization of water, for public services, 224, 226
space: space of flows (Castells, Manuel), 115. *See also* place; space-times
space-times: fluency moving between spatiotemporal frames, 157, 161, 196; folded, not flat ontologies, 167; heterogeneous, 39, 151, 167, 197; politics of the slow down, 132, 194, 202
Speth, James Gustave: ecological crisis, 70, 131; new environmental politics against inequality, 241n4
subjectivity, intersubjectivity: as constituted in body~place~commons, 5, 10, 138, 196; dialogical self and democracy, 117; nondualistic understanding of self/other, self/world, subject/object, 133, 137, 139–40, 205; numbness, 111, 114; unworlding and loss of continuity of self and other, 114–15, 126, 209
subsistence and gift economies, 41, 43, 52, 188, 196–97; creative commons in, 11

sustainable communities, emerging forms of, 97, 156–58

technological world picture. *See under* fungibility, logics of
thin bright line: falsely painted over thin green line of enabling ecological limits, 195; fantasy of endless market expansion, 41, 25, 83, 85; violence, threats, war, 34, 198, 199, 223
thin green line: denial and disguise of, 25, 195; dynamic interplay of life processes, environmental supports and limits, 23, 83, 85
time. *See* space-times
Tsing, Anna: creation of "frontier" in enclosing commons, 239n8; forest commons, 33; "globalization as blob," 165; "spectacular accumulation," 34, 104

U.S. political history: 1770s–1820s republicanism, struggles between conservative and democratic, 27–39, 47–48, 59–61; 1770s–1860s anti-corporate and pro-business ideologies, 47, 71; 1820s–1870s rise of liberal ideologies in complex links with inequalities (class, race, gender) and cronyism, 28–35, 41–46, 61–62; 1870s–1890s Populist movements, 31, 39, 48, 62, 66–67, 75–77; 1870s–1910s rise of the corporate state, 44–50, 58–59, 66–72; c. 1900s–2000s American empire, 44, 46, 62–65, 67–68, 73–75, 194–95; 1930s–1940s reform liberalism, 59, 63; 1980s–2000s rise of notions of "consumer republic," 64, 68, 71, 87–94, 98–107, 126, 195; post–New Deal entrenching of crony capitalism, authoritarianism, reaction, 52, 199–200
U.S. polity, core images of: "first body" of the people (a republic of citizens), 27, 47–48, 105–7, 239n4; "second body" of the U.S. (a political economy), 28–30, 32, 47, 164; "third body" of the U.S. (crony capitalism), 33–34, 47, 49–50, 88–94, 105–7, 164, 198–200

viewsheds, 200, 223. *See also* corporate power: corporate voice as monological, veiled, "in drag,"
Virilio, Paul: "globalized time of generalized interaction," 188, 207; speed, depoliticization, "death of geography," 183, 188, 190, 203
Viroli, Maurizio, on republicanism: liberty as lack of dependency, 34, 37; not communitarian, 38; participatory deliberation about res publica, 37

Warner, Michael, "republicanism as metadiscourse" in Revolutionary-era America, 60–61
world: as basis for solidarity, 116, 235; care for world-in-common, 58, 138, 140, 182; definition, 8, 12, 80, 233; dwelling, 192; flesh of the world, 132, 133, 139 (*see also* Merleau-Ponty, Maurice); as ontological problem, 136, 167; the "ordinary" (Stewart, Kathleen), tensional fields of, 91; self-emergent from embodied, placed worlding, 138 (*see also* Casey, Edward; Merleau-Ponty, Maurice); social theory as tending and attending to, 7; substrate to political subjectivity, 80; world-building, cosmopoetics, 6, 134, 150. *See also* cosmogenesis
world, loss of: neoliberalism as war against world, 9; political economy and disordering of experience, 114; threatens citizenship, 97, 136, 141, 189; unworlding, loss of history, geography, the political, 11, 102–3, 183, 194–95; violence, world loss, 194 (*see also* Das, Veena); Zapatistas on neoliberalism and loss of world, 229

Žižek, Slavoj: globalization as postpolitical, 153; universality and political agency, 153, 234

HERBERT REID is a professor of political science at the University of Kentucky and the editor of *Up the Mainstream: A Critique of Ideology in American Politics and Everyday Life.*

BETSY TAYLOR is a cultural anthropologist and senior research scholar at the Alliance for Social, Political, Ethical, and Cultural Theory at Virginia Polytechnic Institute and State University.

The University of Illinois Press
is a founding member of the
Association of American University Presses.

University of Illinois Press
1325 South Oak Street
Champaign, IL 61820-6903
www.press.uillinois.edu